D0651366

ECHOES OF
THE GREAT WAR

ECHOES OF
THE GREAT WAR

The Diary of the
Reverend Andrew Clark
1914–1919

EDITED WITH AN INTRODUCTION BY
JAMES MUNSON

FOREWORD BY
ASA BRIGGS

Oxford   New York
OXFORD UNIVERSITY PRESS
1985

Oxford University Press, Walton Street, Oxford OX2 6DP
Oxford New York Toronto
Delhi Bombay Calcutta Madras Karachi
Kuala Lumpur Singapore Hong Kong Tokyo
Nairobi Dar es Salaam Cape Town
Melbourne Auckland
and associated companies in
Beirut Berlin Ibadan Nicosia

Oxford is a trade mark of Oxford University Press

British Library Cataloguing in Publication Data
Clark, Andrew
Echoes of the Great War.
1. World War, 1914–1918——England——Great
Leighs (Essex) 2. Great Leighs (Essex)——History
I. Title II. Munson, James
940.3'426752 DA690.G824/
ISBN 0-19-212984-8

Library of Congress Cataloging in Publication Data
Clark, Andrew, Rev.
Echoes of the Great War.
1. World War, 1914–1918——England——Essex. 2. World
War, 1914–1918——Great Britain. 3. Essex——History.
4. Great Britain——History——George V, 1910–1936.
5. Clark, Andrew, Rev. I. Munson, James. II. Title.
D547.8.E87C57 1985 940.3'42 85-5663
ISBN 0-19-212984-8

Printed in Great Britain
at the University Press, Oxford
by David Stanford
Printer to the University

FOREWORD
by Asa Briggs

DIARIES, no matter with what centuries they are concerned, are among the most valuable sources for the historian, and of equal value whether or not they were originally intended for eventual publication. Some are concerned with great events, others with the routines of life. Andrew Clark's war-time Diary, deliberately written to be read, sees 'great events' through the eyes of 'little people'.

The First World War was a war of unprecedented scale and was called 'great' at the time. Yet Clark's vantage point, which he had the imagination to realize was a useful one, was neither that of the battlefield nor of Whitehall but of a village rectory in Essex. Given longer perspectives, the First World War still stands out as the great divide in twentieth-century experience. Just how big a divide it would be was not clear when Andrew Clark began his Diary. Four years later, in March 1918, an anonymous writer observed in a national periodical that what seemed to be 'a stormy welter of waste and woe' would doubtless seem to future historians 'a tortuous stream of cause and effect'.

Clark catches the sense of all this. He is concerned with the immediacies of experience and response and with collecting all kinds of material, even the most trivial and ephemeral, to reveal such immediacies to future generations. The 'Great War' was to be captured for posterity in no fewer than ninety-two exercise books, beginning in August 1914 and continuing beyond the Armistice to the end of 1919, the year of the Peace Treaty. The account, some three million words in length, is so 'voluminous'—to use Clark's own adjective—that James Munson was confronted with a formidable task when he began to make selections. Even so, the flavour is kept.

The 'Great War' still lingers in the 'modern memory'. So many people were affected by it, directly or indirectly, that years later, when a second World War began, the poet Vernon Scannell was to write

> Whenever war is spoken of
> I find
> The war that was called Great invades the mind . . .

Clark shows how the news of war and its ramifications invaded his Essex village of Great Leighs, although he preferred the word 'echoes', which he chose as the title for the Diary.

There are, indeed, echoes of other diarists in Clark's manuscript. He himself had published editions of Anthony à Wood's *Life and Times* and John Aubrey's *Brief Lives*, wonderfully revealing books which still have their connoisseurs. It was through his long connection with the Bodleian Library in Oxford that Clark chose to deposit his War Diary there and where, sixty years later, James Munson discovered it. The connections with bookmanship and with Oxford were both important. Clark had some of the same motivations as the 'Mass-Observers' of the 1930s, but his cultural pedigree was quite different. It was different also from that of his parishioners. He was a Scot living in Essex. Yet there was a link because his father had been a farm labourer and he was the Rector of an agricultural parish.

Andrew Clark arrived in Great Leighs in 1894; he was then thirty-eight years old and had been a priest for ten years. He was to stay in the village until his death in 1922. He has now put his village on the map, and in future it will doubtless be compared with Kilvert's Bredwardine, Flora Thompson's 'Candleford' and Ronald Blythe's 'Akenfield'.

Worcester College, Oxford
February 1985

CONTENTS

ILLUSTRATIONS

INTRODUCTION
by James Munson

On 2 August 1914 as news of Germany's declaration of war against Russia reached England, the Reverend Andrew Clark, Rector of the village of Great Leighs in Essex, began to keep a diary. It was a diary not of himself or his family but of the Great War then beginning and its effects on English life. He described the contrasts between his peaceful village and the battlefields of Europe, between the quiet, slow, ordered life of rural England and the horrors of twentieth-century warfare. Day by day, often hour by hour, he noted down everything he heard or saw or was told that pertained to the war.

He first called his Diary 'Echoes of the 1914 War', but as the years passed he changed the title to 'Echoes of the Great War in an Essex Village'. The volumes mounted: by the end of 1914 there were eight; by the end of 1916, fifty-four; by the time of the ceasefire on 11 November 1918 he was on his eighty-fourth volume and another eight were to follow. Altogether he wrote ninety-two volumes containing over three million words: it is one of the largest and most comprehensive diaries ever kept in English history and one of the most unusual. Andrew Clark always insisted that:

This War Diary is—above all things—a village diary dealing only, of first intention, with matters falling within the personal knowledge of the inmates of the Rectory, and, if with outside places or matters, almost entirely such matters as were brought into the Rectory by correspondence.

The heart of the Diary always remained in the village of Great Leighs. As the months wore on, however, the pace of life quickened and people's horizons broadened: no community could stand aside from the conflict. There were thirteen men from the village in the armed forces when war began; by the end of the war the number had risen to sixty-seven. Nineteen never returned. This widening of the conflict was quickly reflected in the Diary.

Andrew Clark grasped that this was a people's war unlike any in

British history. His Diary reflected this: he transcribed or pasted in letters from men at the front, whether in Flanders, Salonika, or Italy. He gathered information and recorded rumours wherever he went—in railway stations, blacked-out train carriages or village shops. He approached men on the way to the front, officers on leave, shop-keepers, farmers, tradesmen, delivery-boys and clergymen to garner first-hand accounts. Gradually a network was created that included friends, family, and relations. The war also produced a massive increase in printed matter—leaflets, pamphlets, notices, tracts and bulletins—and all these were dutifully inserted and footnoted where necessary.

Because Clark knew shorthand he could quickly write down what he heard. Later he transcribed these 'suites' of notes, as he called them, into the Diary. When he was at home he recorded the day's events as they transpired. He was precise, demanding, and objective, normally excluding all family matters not pertinent to the course of the war. Therefore he omitted noting his own wife's death in 1916. It was not just his reserve: he did not want his War Diary to be deflected from its central concern which was the course of the war and its effect on English life. He did note, however, a few days later that mourning was very difficult to obtain because of the enormous casualties on the Western Front. He followed the successful academic course of his daughter, Mildred, because she was a prime source of firsthand information regarding troops, hospital work, and life in his native Scotland.

The Rector never censored and seldom commented on what he heard. The sole exceptions were occasional outbursts against bishops and politicians, two groups of men for whom he had scant respect. For 1,793 days he kept up the Diary, from the day German troops began marching into Belgium on 2 August 1914 until the peace treaty was signed on 28 June 1919. He missed only eight days through illness: one in 1915 and seven in 1916.

———

Andrew Clark had long been fascinated not just by village life, but by the lives of ordinary people whose individual stories make up the warp and weft of British history. He was, himself, one of the people: he was born on 5 June 1856 in the tiny hamlet of Dollarfield, then just south of the town of Dollar in Clackmannanshire, the son of a farm labourer and the grandson of a farmer. Clark was a bright boy and was fortunate to grow up in Dollar, with its excellent Academy. The school was both a boarding school and a parish school for boys and girls. In addition to Latin, Greek, French, German, English, writing, and arithmetic the boy had a variety of practical courses which encouraged his wide field of interests. In each year he gained the chief honours in his class. In 1871, when he was fifteen, he went on to St Andrews University. In 1875 he came up to Balliol College, Oxford, using the prize money he had gained at St Andrews to pay his way. At the end of his first year he moved to Lincoln College, where a scholarship awaited him.

The young Scotsman fell in love with Oxford and it was a love he would never lose. He took a double-first in Greats in 1879 and returned to St Andrews to act as assistant to Lewis Campbell, Professor of Greek. In 1880, Bishop Christopher Wordsworth of Lincoln, his old college's Visitor, nominated him to the vacant fellowship in his patronage. It came as a complete surprise to Andrew Clark who returned in triumph to Oxford. In 1881 he was appointed tutor. Two years later he was ordained deacon and, in 1884, priest. From now on he combined the two great callings in his life: scholar and priest. His career prospered. He lectured in logic and served as his college's chaplain. He also served as incumbent at two Oxford churches, St Michael's-at-the-North-Gate and, later, All Saints. He proved himself a popular and successful parish priest.

His scholarly interests came increasingly to lie in historical research and he became adept at translating medieval English church records. He soon extended his range to include seventeenth-century history and in 1889 he began bringing out his masterly edition of Anthony à Wood's *Survey of the Antiquities of the City of Oxford*, written between 1661 and 1666. This brought Andrew Clark considerable notice, and was followed by a five-volume edition of Wood's *Life and Times*, based on the papers left by this irascible but amusing diarist. He edited a book on the colleges of Oxford but his real goal was to write a history of the Civil War as it affected Oxford life. He later wrote that he was 'grieved to find how very slight notices of it had been made by people who lived through it'.

In 1886 Clark married Mary Walker Paterson, a daughter of the Provost of St Andrews. She came from a large family and her brothers were successful merchants, farmers and Episcopal clergymen. She was thirty-five and he was thirty when they married and it proved a happy and successful marriage. They took a house in fashionable North Oxford and their first daughter, Mary Alice, was born in 1887. Family tradition says that Andrew Clark's wife did not take to University life, that she was shy and that she could not keep up with the entertaining expected of a rising young don's wife. Then, in 1894, the living of Great Leighs became vacant; Lincoln College held the patronage. Andrew Clark's decision to leave Oxford must have been a hard one, but on Palm Sunday 1894 the new Rector took his first service. It seemed that a new life was beginning for at the end of the year he wrote to an Oxford friend: 'I have found the duties of this most scattered parish so engrossing that I fear further writing or editing on my part is hopeless.'

However Clark soon found that he could combine his duties as parish priest with his work as an historian. He published a history of his old college and a two-volume edition of John Aubrey's *Brief Lives*, based on original manuscripts. He brought out a *Guide* to the Bodleian Library and editions of medieval Registers and diocesan documents. He taught himself Spanish and Italian to add to his German, French, Latin, and Greek and he began studying the Basque language. In 1895 his Alma Mater, St Andrews, awarded him the honorary degree of Doctor of Laws. Perhaps inspired by this he applied for the Professorship of Humanity at St Andrews in 1899 but was unsuccessful. He also made an attempt to return to Oxford which came to nothing.

The Rectory of Great Leighs provided Andrew Clark with a scholar's retreat. His study was cluttered with stacks of documents under examination. Mrs Mary Cope is one of several villagers who remembers him. As Mary Ward, she was a maid at the Rectory from 1903 to 1907 and recalls that the Rector spent most of his time in his study, where 'he was always writing and reading'. The Rectory had two maids and a groom–gardener, and something of a Scottish air about it. In the kitchen there was a girdle kept for scones and cakes, while porridge was standard breakfast fare. He also subscribed to the *Scotsman*. All this gave him a certain feeling of detachment which only heightened the quality of his observations. It was never so strong as to draw him apart from the life of the village or the daily problems of a young housemaid. Mary Cope remembers his great kindness, as well as his home remedies: whenever she was coming down with a cold the Rector would appear at her door with a glass filled with layers of whisky, castor oil, and more whisky. He would stay until it had been drunk and claimed it cured colds.

Andrew Clark described himself as 'one of the old-fashioned people', content to let others get on with their own lives. He had a deep but undemonstrative piety, a great store of common sense, an enquiring mind, a love of natural justice, a dislike of dogmatism and pomposity and a strong identity with the people from whom he had sprung. His most telling attribute was his independence of mind, which he passed on to his second daughter, Mildred, who was born in 1896. He made it his rule, for example, 'while in harness as a clergyman', to attend no political meeting. 'Personally', he went on, 'I have very decided opinions in politics; but, as a beneficed clergyman, I rule politics out of my province. My attitude is not appreciated by the Unionist party managers.' He was as independent in politics as in everything else but his independence was tempered by self-restraint. This proved an invaluable combination in his role as a diarist.

His independence did not suit the diocesan Bishop, J. E. Watts-Ditchfield of Chelmsford, a staunch Evangelical (while Andrew Clark was a moderate High-Churchman), a teetotaller and a man devoted to 'crusades' and 'movements'. Andrew Clark angered many when he argued for a simplified and modernized *Prayer Book* 'easily followed by laymen and adapted to modern conditions'. He angered his Bishop by refusing to attend clerical meetings and 'quiet days'. When his policy of non-cooperation became too much the Bishop called personally to ensure his attendance at a forthcoming 'retreat'. The Rector went but left early.

If Andrew Clark was not popular with his Bishop he was very popular with the villagers of Great Leighs. Clark was a tall and heavy man: Mr Gordon Ward can still remember his ungainly walk as he came down the lanes in his 'wideawake' hat. Mrs Leonard Port remembers his hearty laugh as he shared a joke with her father-in-law who kept one of the two village shops. He often suffered from rheumatism, bronchitis, and 'turns', or fainting spells, and he complained about failing eyesight and diminished hearing. But his frequent ill health did not prevent him from continuing his researches. His popularity in the village only stirred his interest in its history.

This interest was brought to a head during the South African War. The Rector knew that few villagers got daily papers so he posted bulletins of war news on the brick pillar in the wall opposite Sam

Stokes's blacksmith's shop. He regretted not keeping a diary of the war years because he saw at first hand how easily yesterday's stories and rumours were forgotten. In 1903 he began sending historical contributions to the *Essex Review*; by 1918 he had sent in no fewer than seventy-seven articles and fifty-two 'Notes'. His range was enormous: emigration to New England, witchcraft, ship-building, oatmeal-making, boy-bishops and the Black Death. He based his articles on 'Collections' he had made from records and reminiscences of village people. These were sent off to the Bodleian and he warned his old friend, Falconer Madan, Bodley's Librarian: 'I feel very uncomfortable because, as Macbeth saw the murderous dagger before him, handle to his hand, I see a row of other quarto note-books—all wagging Bodley-wards in hope of shelter.' The Bodleian noted that from 1885 to 1913 Andrew Clark's donations came to 282 separate volumes.

From the history of Essex Andrew Clark turned to Great Leighs, and in 1913 he sent off the first complete volume of yet another series which he called 'Collections for Great Leighs Parish'. His aim was to write a 'systematic history of the parish (i.e. from Elizabeth's reign downwards)'. He scoured the village for records and firsthand recollections. One of his greatest sources was the Taylor family who kept the post office and a wheelwright's shop. Young Harry Taylor was his friend and he wrote to him in 1913:

When I came here, twenty years ago, I had much writing to do about Oxford University and its Colleges, about the extraordinary language of the Basques (the tribe between France and Spain), and about monasteries and their records. I would have been much better employed, had I set to, at once, to search out the remarkable history of this most interesting parish.

The parish of Great Leighs which Andrew Clark found so interesting straddled the 'Great Road' that led from Chelmsford in the south to Braintree in the north-east; it is now the A131. Although some villagers could just make out the distant lights of London, the village itself remained quite isolated, largely because in the 1840s the railway had missed it. The population in 1914 was only 614 people, spread over 3,054 acres. Farms made up the village, and narrow lanes with high hedges joined the farms. The village included the hamlet of Fuller Street but most people lived along the Great Road. At the corner of the Great Road and the Boreham Road stood St Anne's Castle, which claimed to be the oldest licensed premises in England; it also claimed that it had originally been a pilgrim's inn but these were boasts which Andrew Clark did not take seriously. Off the Boreham Road and away from the shops and schools were the church, the Rectory and Lyons Hall, home of the Squire, J. H. Tritton. There were two schools (one Council and one Church) and two other public houses, the Dog and Partridge and the Dog and Gun. The village had two shops, a blacksmith's, an undertaker, some new market-gardening supplying vegetables to Covent Garden, and Jesse Wright's timber business which specialized in willow wood. Finally there was the Victoria Arms, formerly a women's ale-house which had lost its licence and become a coffee-shop. Andrew Clark noted that it was, however, 'still frequented by its old clientele of women gossips'.

Agriculture dominated village life. May Thorogood, daughter of the licensee of the Dog and Partridge, remembers as a girl of eleven getting up to draw pints of beer at six in the morning for the harvest workers. They had come with their steam engines from Bishop's Hall farm to thresh the corn. Wages were low and Mary Cope's father got 11s. a week as a horseman. But women could add to the wages by picking stones from the fields (for a penny a bushel) or gleaning the fields after the harvest as Ruth had done in the field belonging to Boaz.

The village had its own constable, PC Cole, although there was little crime other than the occasional tramp to be moved on. Dr Smallwood called regularly and held a surgery in a cottage hired from Jesse Wright. If he was not available people used their own remedies: when Harry Taylor sliced off the end of his thumb, his mother simply stuck it on again and wrapped it with 'lily leaves and brandy'—madonna lily petals steeped in brandy. It healed perfectly. Villagers also had their own peculiar forms of speech. Andrew Clark had always been fascinated by language and noted down what he heard: 'I am got work' meant 'I've got work'; 'I haven't the gemmuck for anything' meant that one did not have the gumption, or capacity. W. H. Dee, the church clerk who figures regularly in the Diary, told the Rector after a snowfall, 'This is the head fall for some years' which meant that it was the heaviest fall for years. A thunderstorm was still a 'tempest'; snails were 'hodemedods'; frogs were 'little Jacobs'; mud was 'slud'; a woodpecker was a 'waffle'; dew was 'dag'; sherry was 'sherry wind' and houses were 'housen', an old survival. If a farm labourer went out early in the morning he would grab a 'dewbi', or 'dew bit', a small snack; and, if he returned wet through, he was 'dreening wet'.

Village life was dominated by the Tritton family which plays a leading part in Andrew Clark's War Diary. J. Herbert Tritton was Lord of the Manor and his seat was Lyons Hall, opposite the church and about three-quarters of a mile down the Boreham Road from the Rectory. 'Ol' Squire Tritton', as the villagers knew him, was seventy when war broke out. He was a partner in Barclays Bank which had once been Barclay, Tritton, Bevan & Co. The Trittons had been at Lyons Hall for just over one hundred years. Mary Cope remembers her father telling her that the family were 'real gentry' and as such deserved, and got, a curtsy.

Gordon Ward remembers that the Trittons were 'very well proportioned'. Their two motor cars, which Gordon's father drove as chauffeur, were equally imposing as they negotiated the narrow lanes. The American-built Overlander was for wet days and the Daimler, for dry. There were five sons and four daughters and Harry Ward taught each of the four girls to drive the Overlander. He, like his son, had a great store of patience; but, as Gordon Ward recalls, 'you wanted patience in those days'.

The Trittons had done much for the village: the sick were taken to hospital in one of their cars; food was distributed; help given when babies arrived; a village pump was built and a clock put on the church tower. J. Herbert Tritton's four daughters were great doers of good works. Elizabeth Tritton, as the eldest daughter, was known as Miss Tritton and she conducted classes in wood-carving and metal-work at the Gordon Youth Club.

The Trittons also dominated church life and with their guests and retainers filled five pews in the parish church. Mary Cope remembers after more than seventy years the rustle Mrs Tritton's silks made as she came up the aisle and the delight of watching Squire Tritton place a gold sovereign in the collection plate: it was, after all, a tenth of her year's wages. To Andrew Clark the Trittons were a mixed blessing. He appreciated the family's generosity to the parish and the church but he found their Evangelical fervour hard to take. To counterbalance the parish church's 'High' services, J. Herbert Tritton erected a corrugated iron building on his property. It was designed as a parish hall and as a home for the village's Nonconformists. Its official name was the Mission Room but villagers soon called it the 'Tin Tabernacle'. As it faced the Boreham Road, Andrew Clark, like Trollope's Vicar of Bullhampton, had to pass it whenever he walked to church.

In addition, every August saw a succession of Sunday afternoon evangelistic services in front of Lyons Hall, where Mr Tritton himself or specially invited preachers thundered away. Estate and house workers were expected to attend and afterwards the gardens were open to the public. Moody and Sankey hymns were sung and perhaps reminded Andrew Clark of the parodies sung to the same tunes in his undergraduate days at St Andrews. Because of the proximity of the services to a large cedar tree, the Rector referred to them as the 'Under-the-Cedar-Tree' meetings. The situation was not helped by the fact that the Trittons' butler, William Redman, was an extreme Anglo-Catholic who became a close and valued friend of the Rector's.

Despite their difficulties, Rector and Squire created a working partnership which benefited the village. If the partnership was not based on deep friendship, it was founded on mutual respect and self-restraint. It remains a credit to both men that it worked so well. Ronald Tritton, J. Herbert Tritton's sole surviving grandson, remembers his grandparents as stiff, formal, and forbidding. But most villagers appear to have got on well with them. Reg Ketley, a farm labourer at Moulsham Hall farm, recalls that J. Herbert Tritton was a 'proper ol' Squire: he kept us up to it and all—a very proper man, but very friendly'.

In the summer of 1914 village life carried on as usual. By the end of July the clover-hay had been harvested and pea-picking for Covent Garden Market helped to supplement villagers' incomes. The Sunday school children had their annual outing to Maldon in Fred Fuller's brakes and Harry Taylor, now a lance-sergeant in the Essex Territorials, went off to his summer camp. The Trittons were in residence and at the Rectory, Andrew Clark's groom–gardener, Charlie Ward, got the pony cart ready to drive Dr Clark to Chelmsford to catch the up-train to Liverpool Street Station. He was once again on his way to Oxford to mark examination scripts. This time he was taking Mildred who was at home, studying for the entrance examinations for St Andrews where she wanted to read medicine. On his return to Great Leighs Clark meant to complete the eighteenth volume of his village 'Collections' and turn to the stack of Buttery Accounts from Jesus College, Oxford. When he got back home, however, the eighteenth volume of notes was put on the shelf and never finished. He turned from researching the past to recording the present.

In March 1915, when he was already on the twelfth volume of his

War Diary, Andrew Clark wrote to his friend, H. H. E. Craster, Sub-Librarian at the Bodleian, that he was keeping 'an extraordinary "War Diary"—but very voluminous'. Three months later he offered it to Bodley's Librarian who noted in pencil at the top of the letter, 'June 25, 1915. Accepted as a very unusual type of work.' In September the first twelve volumes arrived and the remaining volumes were sent off by post, as soon as they were completed. The last notebook was deposited on 23 December 1919.

Since then few people have looked at the Diary. Its length is daunting: ninety-two volumes of exercise books, each tied with a ribbon and measuring eight inches by six and a half, containing no less than three million words. In addition to the War Diary, Andrew Clark also gave the Bodleian a mammoth series entitled 'English Words in War-Time'. In this he collected, indexed, and annotated cuttings to show the war's influence in changing the English language. There were sixty-five volumes. He also compiled volumes of cuttings on war humour, copies of official proclamations, advertisements, official notices, recruiting posters and leaflets and, finally, cuttings about air raids.

There could have been few men better qualified to undertake such wide-ranging tasks. But perhaps not even Clark realized what a unique record he was leaving behind him. Though always rooted in village life, Andrew Clark's War Diary became a record not just of a village but of the individual stories of the men and women who made up the nation. These were the people who were individually and collectively caught up in the greatest war the world had ever seen. Through this Diary we see the war as they saw it; we see British life changing as they saw it change, from day to day, stretching over five long years, and we see it all in stories, adventures, and tragedies told in their own words.

EDITORIAL METHOD

In preparing these selections from the Diary I was anxious to retain as much of its variety and immediacy as I could. The flow of the Diary would have been destroyed if ellipses had been used to indicate every omission. Ellipses are only used, therefore, when quoting material, such as letters, that was copied verbatim or, in most cases, inserted into the Diary itself.

My aim has been to retain that compelling sense of involvement which the Diary evokes. Editorial matter has, therefore, been kept to a minimum. All comments in parentheses come from Andrew Clark's own pen. I have used square brackets to supplement or to correct entries only when necessary, and have added footnotes to provide background information. I have silently corrected obvious slips of the pen and altered idiosyncrasies where they would otherwise have caused confusion. These were normally due to the speed with which Andrew Clark took his notes and the enormity of the task he set himself. Whenever possible I have retained his own presentation and spelling, some of which was peculiar, for example 'ancle' for ankle and 'surprize' for surprise.

As an editor I have been comforted by Andrew Clark's own hope that his Diary would be used: frequently he provides 'Clarkian diagrams' or newspaper cuttings to aid the reader. Quite frequently he addresses the reader with regard to items sewn into the Diary by his daughter, Mary Alice. Thus, in 1916 a circular from the Waifs and Strays Society was included. Beside it Andrew Clark wrote: 'Unfold softly and refold in present creases. Bad paper.'

Letters written by Andrew Clark, not included in the Diary, but printed here, are indicated by an asterisk.

ACKNOWLEDGEMENTS

I first came across Andrew Clark's War Diary while doing research for my Oxford doctorate in the early 1970s. Years later I discussed the Diary with Mr Alan Haydock of the BBC. He shared my enthusiasm and produced three programmes for Radio Four based on the Diary. He encouraged me in my desire to have at least part of the Diary published.

I selected at random the name of a literary agent and wrote to him in London. Mr Donald Copeman replied, not from London but from his home in Felsted, a village only four miles north-west of Great Leighs. He introduced me to his good friend, the Revd A. H. Franklin, MBE, a successor, as it turned out, of Andrew Clark at Great Leighs. He had in his possession the batch of letters from Andrew Clark to William Redman along with some of Redman's own recollections and the eighteenth and final volume of Andrew Clark's Great Leighs 'Collections'.

Mr Franklin put me in touch with Mr Alan Tritton, a great-grandson of J. Herbert Tritton and the present Lord of the Manor. He and his wife, Diana, proved most helpful, lent me photographs and books and introduced me to their cousin, Mr Ronald Tritton. They also secured help for me from Barclays Bank, PLC, for which I am most grateful.

I then contacted the present Rector of Great Leighs, the Revd John Bryant. He has proved a pillar of strength. He showed me round the village, collected numerous photographs and reminiscences, and introduced me to Mr Reg Ketley, Mr Gordon Ward, and Mrs Leonard Port. All these people told me of Andrew Clark and of Great Leighs as it had been in their youth.

The Revd John Bryant also introduced me to Miss Kathleen Taylor, only daughter of the Rector's good friend, Sergeant Harry Taylor. She has loaned me numerous letters, memorabilia, photographs, and her father's memoirs. She also talked to people who remembered Andrew Clark and has proved a most excellent and zealous researcher.

Through the good offices of the Bishop of Tasmania I finally made contact with Andrew Clark's legal heirs, his two grandchildren, Dr Alison Mackenzie of Kettering, in Tasmania and Mr David Oberlin-Harris of Totton in Hampshire. They have provided me with much needed photographs and family history and I am most indebted to both of them for their encouragement and help.

In August 1984, Radio Four broadcast the three programmes based on the Diary. Among those listening were Mrs Mary Cope, then ninety-five years old and Mrs S. R. Saltmarsh (*née* May Thorogood). Both gave me their reminiscences and lent me valuable photographs. Mrs Cope also kindly gave me the letters she had received from her brother, Charlie Ward, when in the Army. Mr Bruce Baillie and Mr Peter Lee of Dollar Academy have helped me in tracing Andrew Clark's boyhood days at Dollar.

I wish to thank Mr D. G. Vaisey, Keeper of Western Manuscripts, and the Bodleian Library for permission to publish extracts from the Diary and from other manuscripts in its possession. Mr D. S. Porter and the staff of Duke Humfrey's Library were always considerate and helpful. Finally I would like to thank Mr Giles Barber, Librarian of the Taylor Institution Library, Oxford, Wing Commander A. M. Moncrieff, DFC, DFM, Mr and Mrs Peter Gray, Mr John Seaton, Mr Alex Kerr, Mrs Dora Woodhams, Mr Rupert Walters, Miss Veronica

Hitchcock, Features Editor of *Radio Times*, and Mr Russell Twisk, Editor of the *Listener*. I am especially grateful to Dr Richard Mullen for his constant encouragement and unfailing help, and to my parents who first introduced me to the uses and pleasures of history.

With the publication of these selections, the work begun by Andrew Clark in August 1914 has been brought, partially at least, to the conclusion he intended. He was a most lovable as well as a most remarkable man and his War Diary will, I hope, stand as much as a tribute to the man who kept it as a memorial to the men and women whose lives and sacrifices he so devotedly recorded.

Oxford
All Souls Day, 1984

TO
THE MEN OF GREAT LEIGHS
WHO GAVE THEIR LIVES
FOR KING AND COUNTRY
IN THE GREAT WAR

THE village of Great Leighs, although it is within thirty-seven miles by road of London, is singularly isolated. It has no resident in the habit of going regularly to London. The work of the village is self-centred, on the farms, in the smithy, the wheelwrights and carpenters. The Great Road, once a coach road and drove-road of importance, has ceased to throb with through traffic. It is quite away from any railway station.

It seemed, therefore, not out of place to put down, from day to day, such echoes of the Great War as reached the Rectory from outside, ignoring (of course) all information directly or indirectly from newspapers, but giving authentic written scraps of genuine village origin.

It had always been a deep regret to me that I had not kept a village record of this sort throughout the Boer War. Several men from Great Leighs, or whose parents lived in Great Leighs, went through that war, and some died in the field. Their letters have contained matters of much interest. The rumours which passed round in the village were peculiar, and their origin difficult to explain. The war had, however, well begun before I thought of such a village record; and when I did think of one, I neglected its commencement, being (like most folks here) under the mistaken idea that the end was not far off.

The actual writing out of the Diary was begun on Wednesday, 19th August [1914]; but, for a day or two, it was irregularly kept, partly because of the inclusion of back matter. I therefore give a table of the earlier days—as they should have been kept. From Monday, August 24th, [it was] continued day by day, regularly.

Official Bulletins: One of the new features of this war's arrangements was the posting at Country Post Offices of Saturday's 'War News'. These bulletins were put up regularly, Sunday by Sunday; but, as a rule, were extremely meagre.

1914

Sunday, 2 August. I took duty for the Reverend W. R. Baker, Vicar of Hagbourne, Berkshire. On my way to the station, about 9 a.m., I looked in at the Oxford Union Society rooms and found the Steward posting on the entrance-door (from Frewin Court) a telegram that Germany had declared war on Russia. I went back to my rooms to tell my daughter, Mildred, the grave news. In Hagbourne Church, instead of the sermon I had intended, I mentioned the grave news and spoke for a little on the impending war, and the sacrifices it would call for. The Churchwarden thanked me for doing this. Several parishioners had sons in the Services and all would count it a kindness to have received such early intimation that the critical moment had come.

Tuesday, 4 August. Went to Barclay & Co., Old Bank, High Street, Oxford, to get money to take us to Great Leighs. Found banks all closed by Government order. I would gladly have stayed in Oxford for a few days, but the lodgings had been let and so returned to Great Leighs. I had to ask a friend in Oxford to cash me a small cheque to pay my way home.

Wednesday, 5 August. At Great Leighs learned from the newspapers that war had been declared on Tuesday.

Saturday, 8 August. Rumours in village, no doubt having origin in letters from soldiers to their friends in this village and district about sailing of a British Expeditionary Force to France. There were various reports in the village that a British Army was to be embarked for the Continent, Ostend, it was believed; and that transports had been in readiness at Southampton for a fortnight.

Sunday, 9 August. J. Herbert Tritton, Esq., Lyons Hall, confirmed report of British Expeditionary Force. He told me that his son's regiment—the Coldstream Guards—was under orders, but that his son, Captain Alan Tritton, did not know on what day, or from what station, or from what port, or to what destination the regiment would go.

Notices given out in Church: of meeting to consider knitting and sewing of garments for soldiers; of intention to use form of service of intercession on Su. 16 Aug. 1914.

Tuesday, 11 August. Meeting in the Mission Room Great Leighs, at 7 p.m. to consider whether and in what way the parishes of Great [and Little] Leighs could help in providing garments for the sailors and soldiers in the field, in hospital and in camp. The Rector who had called the meeting, explained its purpose to a large meeting of women and girls of the parishes and then withdrew.

Sunday, 16 August. By sending especially to the Post Office I got the form of Intercession and it was used in Church this day. Here is the first of the Official Bulletins, to be issued during the War on Sunday mornings. Not only was this posted at the Post Office, as promised; but this copy was sent to me in time to be put up in the Church Porch before 11 a.m. Service.

OFFICIAL WAR NEWS

German plan of invading France seriously delayed by resistance at Liege and intervention of French cavalry. Consequently French have carried out mobilisation and concentration without hindrance. Various minor Belgian and French successes reported. German crews to quit the German vessels 'Goeben' and 'Bresleau' at Constantinople. NO BRITISH CASUALTIES.

Here is the list given me of those in Great Leighs parish who had gone on service, for whom the prayers of the congregation were desired in the course of the official Office of Intercession. It was posted at the Church. List in handwriting of Olive Tritton, fourth daughter of J. Herbert Tritton and compiled by her from the official papers of the County Relief Committee:

Royal Navy
  Ernest Cloughton, HMS *Recruit*
  Robert Batchford, HMS *Lydiard*
  James MacLaren, HMS *Rosario*

Army
  Alan Tritton, Captain, Coldstream Guards
  Ernest Stubbins, Royal Garrison Artillery (private)
  Ernest Suckling, 9th Lancers (private)
  Henry Hull, Essex Regiment (private)

Reservists
  William Stubbins, 21st Lancers (private)
  Joseph Rogers, Essex Regiment (private)

Territorials
  Harry Taylor, 5th Essex Regiment (sergeant)
  Victor Digby, 5th Essex Regiment (private)
  Frederick Love, 5th Essex Regiment (private)
  Charles Cook, 8th Essex Cycling Corps (private)

[The following notice, in the handwriting of J. H. Tritton, was also given to the Rector to be put up if he agreed:]

At 12 o'clock noon each day the Church bell will be rung so that those within hearing may pause and offer a prayer for all who have joined the Colours.

The bell is to be rung by W. R. Redman, butler at Lyons Hall. He is a singularly interesting man, of extreme High Church (St Paul's, Knightsbridge) views but with a really accurate and wide knowledge of most matters ecclesiological and hagiographical.

Tuesday, 18 August. A brigade of Territorials marched through Great Leighs from Chelmsford. It comprised 6,000 men; hearing that the troops were in movement, I closed the Church School at 9.50 a.m. and sent the children in charge of the two mistresses to see the sight. The children had a good place. Two of the regiments were exceedingly footsore. One of the young soldiers explained that the march was an amusement for him, accustomed daily to tramp miles of ground in ordinary farm work, but it was desperate hard for shop-lads and clerks, who for years had never been off pavements, and were in the habit of nothing more than jumping on and off a train.

About 11.30 a.m. a regiment of foot came and halted from the bridge to St Anne's. They were very footsore, dirty and tired and glad to lie down on the grass by the roadside. They bought up all the ginger beer and most of the lemonade at St Anne's and the village shop. The cottagers were delighted to chat with them and brought apples and plums which were much appreciated. Mr John Dean, of St Anne's, put to his horses in his farm waggons and drove relays of the most footsore to their camping ground at Oaklands.

There was much chaff between the villagers and the men at the halt. One of the men had a woman's head tattooed on his arm; and was told that he was taking his girl's photograph with him to the war. Another man told the folk about him that he was going to bring back half the Kaiser's moustache. There was a lively dialogue between a little gamin and a late driblet, limping along:

'Any more coming?' the boy asked.

'Yea, there're a lot of Germans behind.' was the answer.

'Get out. If there were, you wouldn't be going slow like that. You'd be just flying.'

'Bet your life!' the soldier answered and crawled on.

Old Chas. Collins, ex-under-gamekeeper and village patriarch, spent the whole day watching. It took him a long time to get home, because on his way there he stopped every wayfarer, and went into every cottage, to tell his story: 'There's never been a sight like that in Great Leighs.'

I asked the Headmistress [of the Church School] to let some of her girls and boys, in place of their ordinary written exercise, give a description of what they had seen, in their own words. [The Rector also asked the Headmaster of the Council School to do the same: fifteen essays were sent to him. Some were included in the Diary while the rest were deposited in the Parish Chest. The following is by Phyllis Emma Wright:]

Great excitement prevailed this morning by soldiers passing through this village. There were between 7 and 8,000. At 11 different regiments of foot soldiers came marching along. We were allowed to go down to the corner to see the soldiers by the kind permission of Mr With, our master. Near Mrs Ports the order was given for the soldiers to fall out and rest for a few minutes. One of the poor men had to stay behind, his feet were skinned and bleeding. He took his puttees, also his boots and stockings off and rubbed his feet with vaseline and powder. An officer gave him a Red Cross paper for number 7. When that number passed he held up his paper; then they stopped and helped him in. An Officer is easily distinguished from a private. He carries a beautiful sword in a leather case; he also wears [a] different uniform. They had many different kinds of carts, some of them belonged to the army; others had been taken from tradesmen and large firms. They would be paid for the horses and carts which were taken. Some of the soldiers looked happy and some looked

The Revd Andrew Clark (1856–1922), Rector of Great Leighs,
Essex, from 1894 to 1922

Mildred (*standing, left*)
and Mary Alice Clark
with their mother, *c.*1911

An early photograph of Mrs Clark and Mildred
in the family pony-cart

Mildred Clark (*centre*) in her nurse's uniform, VAD Hospital,
Braintree, 1914

tired and miserable. A section of the cycling corps passed here today also. . . It was a beautiful sight which I shall never forget.

Friday, 21 August. Last night Mrs Earl said that in a letter from her daughter, in domestic service in London, she was told that 'five' foreigners had been seized attempting to poison the great reservoir at Chingford, Essex, the most recent and most important source of supply for London. This afternoon she has been told in another letter that 'six' Germans had been shot.

Monday, 24 August. At Little Waltham troops are billeted for the night. Mrs Suckling, a widow had expressed her willingness to have two. She found immediately a big '4' chalked on her door. A house-holder is allowed 2s. a day for each soldier. In return, he has to find them shelter of roof and two meals (breakfast and a weak supper). They sleep on the floor of a room, with their own blankets.

Wednesday, 26 August. Appeal for enrolment of Special Constables in Great Leighs parish, and especially for motors and cyclists, brought by Miss E. M. Tritton on behalf of her father, J. Herbert Tritton.

There will be a meeting in the Mission Room, Mond. August 31 at 8.30 p.m.

6 p.m. Godfrey Gerald Barker has just called to say goodbye. He is waiting for his uniform to join the depot of the 21st Lancers at Tidworth, Wilts. His father, Col. Gerald Edgar Barker, of the 6th Middlesex, left by the 4.18 p.m. train from Braintree. Officers in uniform travel free. He brings several reports: that the Scots Greys is cut to pieces; that a large number of regular troops has gone out in support, practically all the available regulars in the country; that a big naval battle may be expected next week; that in a few weeks, as soon as the harvest is finished, there will be conscription.

Friday, 28 August. Report says that word has been brought from Chelmsford that the British casualties up till now number 10,000. Report current in Braintree—that a Russian force has been brought to Yorkshire and landed there; and that the East Coast trains have been commandeered to transport them rapidly south en route for the French theatre of war.[1]

---

[1] The Rector later tracked down the origin of the famous 'Russian Troop Myth': in August Russian officers arrived in Scottish ports from Archangel to take up staff

Saturday, 29 August. Letter received by afternoon post, 2 p.m.:

August 28, 1914

Dear Dr Clark,

Now that the harvest is over I am arranging to summon a meeting of the men and women of Great and Little Leighs in the barn here on Sunday afternoon, Sept. 6, in order to make clear to them the causes and the justice of the war and the Nation's need for soldiers; and further to make an appeal to the young men to offer themselves. It is especially necessary to get the women, otherwise I would have suggested a joint parish meeting. It will be at 3 o'clock and I trust will have your approval and if possible, your presence. Yours truly,

J. H. Tritton.

It is reported that after a special meeting at Great Waltham under Col. W. Nevill Tufnell, to beat up recruits, only one recruit joined. The Colonel is *the* territorial magnate of this part of the county, but is at present not in highest favour in his own parish.

Sunday, 30 August. Reports from Braintree: twenty-eight men of Courtauld's Braintree crape-works, after a recruiting meeting, volunteered for service. The government is said to allow—per week—to each man 8s. 9d., to his wife 7s. 7d. and 1s. 2d. for each child. The hospital of the Red Cross at Braintree was very much out of pillow cases. Mrs Lave of Gosfield Hall, a very wealthy but most eccentric widow-lady, had lent four, all carefully marked with her name and stringent orders that they should be returned when no longer needed.

On my way to Church for a Christening at 6 p.m., Miss Lucy Tritton, elder daughter of H. L. M. Tritton of the Hole Farm, Great Leighs, met me, jumped off her bicycle and told me that her father had heard from someone in the 'Home' office (she said) that a large Russian force from Archangel had landed in Scotland and was being speeded south by rail to take its place in the theatre of war in Belgium. I mentioned the report of Saturday's evening paper, that a train-load of 200 Russians escaped from Germany into Switzerland and France, had reached England. But Miss Tritton was positive that her information was authentic and correct.

My elder daughter, Mary Alice, attended the evening service at Fairstead, one of the ring of parish churches which lie round Great

---

positions or to purchase munitions. As they were travelling south there were also widespread and secret movements of Territorial troops in sealed trains at night. The two facts merged into one myth.

Leighs. The Rector, Thomas Sadgrove, preached a horrifying sermon, on the horrible scenes of the battlefield and exhorted all the young men to join the army. He had a big Union Jack hung in front of the pulpit, instead of the pulpit-hanging.

Monday, 31 August. The morning postman reported a great scare at Chelmsford on Sunday. An Ichabod telegram had been received there (founded on the reports with which *The Times* Sunday issue had been hoaxed, as I judged) telling that the British army had perished and that France was beaten. The 'wire' was so full of despair that Chelmsford people could not take their tea. Happily, a little later, an official contradiction restored spirits and brought back appetite to normal conditions.

Meeting to enroll Special Constables: The meeting was held in the Mission Room, Joseph Herbert Tritton in the Chair. There were forty persons present, including all the farmers not too old to serve and others. The Chairman stated briefly that there was great need of the services of Special Constables throughout the country. Sir Richard Pennyfeather, CB of Little Waltham Hall, who, as a distinguished member for many years of the Metropolitan Police Force, was competent beyond others to explain the need for, and duties of and the legal powers of, such Special Constables.

Sir Richard said that Special Constables were urgently needed. The legislation of last month had laid upon the ordinary police an enormous amount of extra duty. A specially onerous, but most important duty, incumbent both on citizens and police, is that of watching 'spies'. There are at least 50,000 aliens (Germans, Austrians and Hungarians) in this country. Of these a large number come regularly, week by week, to the market at Chelmsford and elsewhere. The police have further to keep a register of every alien and to make sure that no alien goes more than five miles from his address, without a permit. Special Constables also are to arrest all persons speaking to the dishonour of this country. The main duty will be to protect all roads and especially the abutments of bridges, telegraph posts and the like. The hired agents of the enemy may try to do damage and if our fleet or army suffer any reverse they are sure to be very much bolder and more active.

[The two names at the top of the list of volunteers were J. H. Tritton and the Revd Andrew Clark.]

Tuesday, 1 September. Village lads are not very pleased at pressure put by the Squire to compel his two footmen to enlist. To use the phrase of one of the lads, the 'idle sons' of the house ought to have set the example of going, though married, with children and something over the age.

Village gossip makes fun of the projected savings of Lyons Hall (Village opinion is always spiteful and disparaging and ungrateful.):

(a) either butter or jam, not both.

(b) no cake at tea—but only one seed-cake (for show) which no one cares for and is not cut.

(c) meat at only one meal a day.

(d) only fruit from Lyons Hall gardens.

(e) no cream; all cream to be made into butter which now sells at a high price.

Wednesday, 2 September. Dr H. G. K. Young of Braintree told Miss Mildred Clark that on Su. 30 Aug., the Russian troops were fed in Colchester; that the Gurkhas were in highest feather at coming to European War. King George was the greatest and wisest of Kings. He first had gone to India to be crowned there and he first had perceived that they were worthy to stand shoulder to shoulder with the British troops in the greatest of wars.

Mrs Albert Taylor, wife of Albert Taylor, postman, son of Henry Taylor, wheelwright, and Sub-Postmaster of Great Leighs—an exceptionally kindly natured, gentle-spoken woman, said (14 Sept. 1914) 'Well, it may be very wrong; but I don't mind saying it, that I should be very glad if the Kaiser were shot.'

At 5 p.m. an aeroplane passed over the Rectory grounds, but very high up. (Aeroplanes have been seen crossing over this parish on several days, but these occurrences have not been noted as I had no definite hours given me.)

At 5.45 p.m. James Turner, farm labourer at Lyons Hall, came for a 'harvest-home'. This is a traditional tip contributed by the parson to each farm towards the jollification which the men hold on their own account on completion of harvest.

Thursday, 3 September. Letter from Oxford from my aunt [Miss Janet Haig Bowie], an invalid:

2 September, 1914

Yesterday 600 men were said to be at the Cowley Barracks, mostly from the [Oxford University] Press . . . The Press men were put on short time and all unmarried men were told that they must enlist. If they did so, their places would be kept for them. If not, they would be discharged and not taken up again. Of course, there was no appeal and so most of them enlisted.

It was said last Friday that 80,000 Russians passed through here. No one was allowed to see them. But for several days, only one passenger train was running, and the railway would not send luggage in advance.

Sunday, 6 September. Another day of intense heat—deep blue sky— only the faintest white clouds; pastures and gardens burnt up by the long drought. Apples, pears and acorns falling prematurely. Mr T. Stoddart, Rector's Churchwarden, tells me that although it is a time of stress and sorrow of war, it is the wish of the parish that the Harvest Festival shall be held next Sunday just as usual in thankfulness for the extraordinary bounty of this year's harvest and unbroken harvest weather.

RECRUITMENT MEETING IN LYONS HALL BARN

The meeting was in Lyons Hall barn, a large lofty barn, sufficiently lighted by big open folding doors, but shady enough and with pleasant through draughts enough to abate the glare and intense heat of a fierce afternoon. The women, as is usual in an Essex village, came in first, the men waiting outside till the women had all come in. Punctually at 3 p.m. J. H. Tritton came in, accompanied by Mrs Tritton, Miss Tritton and other ladies. On the platform were: Major Kenny Herbert, a one-armed Engineer; Sir Richard Pennyfeather, Little Waltham Hall; Major Taylor, brother of the Mayor of Chelmsford; Lord Southwark, formerly MP for Colchester; hon. Charles Strutt [Conservative MP for East Essex, 1895–1905] of Blunt Hall, Witham, brother of Lord Rayleigh; M. E. Hughes-Hughes of Leez Priory (who had bicycled over); Herbert Leslie Melville Tritton, of the Hole Farm; Major William Brown of Bishop's Hall and others.

J. Herbert Tritton, chairman, said:

Fellow parishioners of Great and Little Leighs, you have been accustomed to assemble in this barn on various occasions—social, philanthropic, religious, but never on a more momentous occasion or to hear of a more righteous cause. The invitation, inviting you to attend this meeting, asked you to meet to consider the causes of the war. One cause stands out before all others, and can be expressed in four words: Germany meant to fight. We were bound to our neighbours, the little Kingdom of Belgium ... [and] the great French republic ... I do want to say to the fathers and mothers of these two parishes—do not stand in the way of your son's going to fight for the country. This I can say as one who has given a beloved son to do the same ... Directly the great need is explained, our young men will be willing to offer themselves.

Think of what it would mean if we were to have our country over-run as Belgium is, and the scenes of horror there, of daily occurrence here ... We have justice on our side, and we know it; we have the defence of the country to take on us, and we know it. From the bottom of our hearts we can say: God Save the King and God defend the right.

Major Taylor was invited to speak first, because he was going on as far as Stansted to speak there: He said:

Lord Kitchener asked 500,000 men of whom 100,000 were wanted at once. That first 100,000 is provided and in doing so Essex has done her share. We have gone even further, for nearly 300,000 have now come forward ... But Lord Kitchener, who understands better than any man in this country what the needs are, repeats that the full 500,000 must come forward if we are to succeed in this formidable war ... Lord Kitchener appeals to every man of nineteen to thirty-five to enlist ... but not on the usual conditions. Ordinarily a man enlisted for twelve years: now he enlists only for the period of this war.

Lord Kitchener also asks all old soldiers not over forty-five to rejoin the Colours and if they are Non-Commissioned officers, the period is extended to fifty years ... For every man's wife who is in the army, the War Office will pay a separation allowance of 7s. 7d. a week. In addition a further allowance for each child in the house ... Every married man is able to set aside one-third of his pay to be paid direct ... to his wife ... In this way a weekly pay of 10s. to 11s. is assured in every case.

Further, by agreement with the Government, the Soldiers & Sailors Friendly Association will augment the Government allowance [by] ... a sum which will make up the weekly payment, ... if there is a wife and child, [to] ... 14s.6d. If wife and three or more children, then at least £1 a week.

To every working man who may think of serving his country at this crisis I would say—don't worry about your family in your absence: they will be well looked after ... Supposing a man says, I am prepared to serve but not out of this country. Then I answer—Thanks to the vast number of Territorials who have volunteered for service abroad, at any opportunity of men being wanted to go to the front it will be left to all between nineteen and fifty who now enlist to choose, at their own option, for home defence only and that during their service they are to remain in this country for its defence.

There is one example which moves mothers to make some sacrifice for the sake of the country—the example of Queen Mary and her sons. Queen Mary is as devoted to her sons as any mother can be, and her sons as devoted to their mother as any son can be; but both are serving their country: the Prince of Wales [later King Edward VIII] is drilling with the Grenadier Guards, making himself fit to go to the front; Prince Albert [later King George VI] is attached to a battleship in the North Sea for your protection. If the Queen makes this sacrifice, other mothers may be prepared to do the same. There will be a meeting to enlist recruits at the Council School on Friday (Sept. 11th) at 7.45 p.m.

Major Kenny Herbert (served in the South African War, lost an arm there by a wagon accident):

It is said that the Englishman of today is not like his father, grandfather or great-grandfather, and that the feather of the Englishman today is the white feather . . . For the last twenty years Germany has been spending millions on millions of money, one on the top of another, to provide ships of war, guns, soldiers.

That will go on in the future if you do not volunteer to do your duty to win victory today. You will be conscript soldiers in a Prussian Army. You will be bullied and ill-used by Prussian drill-sergeants. You will be ordered about like dogs by Prussian officers . . . Our own sailors say that under modern conditions it is possible that a German force of 50,000 or 60,000 men might, at any moment, be landed on our shores. These men would not get out alive but after they had been hunted down, their passage would be marked by a wide tract of devastation and misery . . . If you do not come forward you will be doing the very thing which the German Emperor wishes. There is a line in a grand old song which is almost a hymn. It says, 'Britons never shall be slaves.' The Kaiser wants to leave out one word, and read 'Britons shall be slaves'.

Lord Southwark moved a vote of thanks to the speakers:

As President of the Chamber of Commerce he might add one other word. If there is one man whose ability and work have done his country greater service than others, that man's name is J. Herbert Tritton. His advice has been of enormous value for the wise guidance of the financial and commercial interests of this country.

Montague Hughes-Hughes, Esq., seconded:

You, who know me, know I am a man of few words. I may tell you that I have an only son. He has been hard at drill in the Inns of Court Territorials. He has, as I learn this morning, been offered a commission in Lord Kitchener's army, has accepted it and will go wherever he is sent. I am getting an old man; but I have always stuck to the motto: It's dogged that does it. This war has been thrust upon us, and there is no question that we must, and will, see it through.

The Revd Andrew Clark and Major H. L. M. Tritton were asked to speak.

The meeting ended about 4.15 p.m. Mrs Tritton invited many ladies and gentlemen to tea in the shady grounds of Lyons Hall. Among those present were Lady Southwark and Lady Roxburgh who said that all the German army allowed a soldier's wife was 1s.6d. a week.

In the evening there was a report in the village that the Kaiser had asked Russia to grant him terms of peace, that he might be able to give his whole attention to France and Great Britain.

Monday, 7 September. 8.30 p.m. Swearing-In of Special Constables for Great and Little Leighs. The Chair in the Mission Room was taken *pro forma* by J. Herbert Tritton. The Chairman said privately that the officials had asked him to withdraw his name on the ground of his age (seventy). The swearing-in was conducted by Sir Richard Penny-feather, JP.

The first drill was fixed for Monday, September 14th. at 6.30 p.m. Sir Richard suggested that without waiting for further orders the Special Constables should take aliens in hand according to instructions given.

Montague Edward Hughes-Hughes, JP of Leez Priory told me that an old servant of his had written that from her bedroom window she had watched train after train for hours, passing by night to Bristol. There were no lights in the carriages, but by the light of the cigars and cigarettes they were smoking, the black beards of the Russians could be seen.

Tuesday, 8 September. Today I went to the station to see a friend going through and saw several trains pass, full of soldiers. One had posted a big notice in the window: BERLIN FIRST STOP. It is reported today that Albert Wright, one of the strongest young farm-hands in the village, is going to volunteer. Jimmy Lewin, the 'boy' who drives Mann's (the baker's) cart is going to do the same; but, as this rests on his own statement this is not believed. Charles Rayner is also to offer himself but the villagers think he will be rejected because of his weak chest.

Miss Tritton tells me a delightful story of Mrs Bearman, a deafish woman in Fuller Street, one of whose sons (who used to work at Lyons Hall farm) has been called out. The old lady said she 'did not know exactly where her son was, but he was at the front; he was at the front for sure.' In answer to an enquiry whether she did not feel very anxious about him, she said 'Ah, but Miss, I have one great comfort. He sends his wash to me every week.' He is apparently as far off as Warley [eighteen miles away].

Wednesday, 9 September. Mrs Dean offered to put up the officers of the Artillery (who bivouaced in the field opposite on the night of their stay) but they declined with thanks. They always share with their men, so two slept in the Council School, two under the hedge. The men are reported to have been a singularly gentlemanly contingent, small farmers many of them. There were quite two hundred of them.

They told the villagers that their officers were as good as brothers to them. It was quite common for an officer to dismount, and for a weary private to ride for a bit while the officer walked.

Harry Sargeant, son of Thomas Sargeant (head-gardener at Lyons Hall) an employé at the Marconi Works in Chelmsford, told his mother that he wanted to enlist. She took her tape-measurer and told him that his chest measurement would cause his rejection. When he next came home he reported that he had been to the recruiting-office in Chelmsford, where it was found that his chest was 33½ and not the minimum 34. But he had bought a pair of dumb-bells, and in a fortnight was going to offer himself again.

Thursday, 10 September. Luckin Smith, the Chelmsford Provisioners, say that they no longer call the well known thick smoked wurtz, 'German Sausage' but 'Dunmow Sausage'. W. Ketley's son says that in Chelmsford and district there are now 17,000 troops. The men are supposed to have a pound of meat a day and the housekeeper in whose home they are billeted is paid 9d a day for cooking their meals for them. Young Ketley says that, by fault of the butchers, some of the men quartered on him have not had more than 8 oz. apiece of meat, the weight being made up of bones.

Monday, 14 September. At 6.30 p.m. the Special Constables met at the gate of Bishop's Hall for their first drill—twenty-two present. It was decided that, by reason of cows which had been at pasture in Mr

Brown's field, the drill should be in Mr Jack Stephen's field, next to it. The drill was carried out vigorously till light failed (7.15 p.m.). It was undertaken under various unusual difficulties: the surface of the field was very uneven; there was blowing a gale and the drill-instructor's voice was mostly inaudible; the instructor is not a tall man and he stood beyond much taller men than himself so that his demonstrations ('You move this way' 'You wheel that way') were invisible to three-quarters of the company. The right-about movement produced time after time the most ludicrous clumps or dispersed confusions which produced shouts of mirth on the part of the company when they took breath to see the tangle they had got into.

Tuesday, 15 September. 9.30 a.m. Miss Lucy Tritton said that one of Sir John French's staff-officers,[1] invalided home, has expressed a decided opinion that the war will not run into 1915.

My groom-gardener, Charles Ward,[2] bemoans deficiency of stature and of chest-circumference which shuts him out from enlisting and being paid to see Egypt or Malta or Gibraltar or France or Germany. There is a great village feeling against lads who are of age and physique to enlist and who have not done so.

Saturday, 19 September. Mrs Scott of Braintree got a Belgian with wife and child and brought them to the [vacant] cottage. She supplies coffee, bread and butter and other requisites and they make their own breakfast. At noon they come into the house and have their big meal. Their evening meal they make in the cottage, with provisions supplied by Mrs Scott.

Sunday, 20 September. Col. Egerton of Chatham Hall says that the German army is fighting magnificently. The rations of jam served out to our troops are, he says, to avert scurvy: the troops being unable to receive regular supplies of fresh vegetables. The battle that is now in progress will be the very biggest in the history of the world.[3]

[1] Sir John French was Commander-in-Chief of the British Expeditionary Force until December 1915.

[2] Charlie Ward came to the Rectory in 1909, a lad of fifteen. He looked after the pony and drove the trap when required. He was also responsible for the paddock, kitchen garden, orchard, and lawns. For this he got 16s a week. He was devoted to Andrew Clark. Reg Ketley remembers him as a 'regular ol' country boy'. His sister was Mrs Mary Cope.

[3] The first Battle of the Aisne followed the German retreat after their initial push into France had been stopped in the Battle of the Marne. Fighting continued until 28 September and trenches were dug for the first time.

5.30 p.m. Major Wm. Brown, Sergeant of the Great Leighs Special Constables, called in with a circular received from Sir Richard Penny-feather requiring Great and Little Leighs to visit stackyards and hay-ricks from 6 p.m. onwards by constables taking four hours of duty at a time, three days a week. Major Brown proposed 'masterly inactivity' on the ground that it was: unneeded—there being no likelihood of damage in this way, each farmer jealously guarding his own property; impracticable, in so wide a district with places so scattered over a network of roads. It was, he said, likely to have two bad results: to suggest the incendiarism it is intended to prevent; like the cry 'Wolf!' to weary the Special Constables prematurely when in the future real occasion for their services may suddenly arise. The Circular further required the Special Constables of Great and Little Leighs to make a return of all foreigners resident in their parishes. As there is not a single foreigner in Great or Little Leighs this return will not take long to compile.

Thursday, 24 September. Mrs Scott has great difficulty in 'conversation' with her Belgian refugees. She speaks French and German fluently. They speak no English, French or German—only Flemish! The wife was a dressmaker; the daughter is said to be a very sweet, prepossessing child. Joseph Rogers is reported 'missing'.

Friday, 25 September. People in Braintree connected with the Army and medical services express grave apprehension that the new casualty list will be a terrible one, since the fighting has been so fierce, incessant and prolonged.

Saturday, 26 September. 1.30 p.m. at lunch at Lyons Hall: The Coldstreams, having suffered so heavily, are now withdrawn from the front. The Guards are in terrible want of socks. With the constant marching, each man wears out a pair a week. To help the Coldstream Guards some friends of the Regiment are sending 1,000 of each of shirts, socks, tins boracic ointment, packets of peppermints.

Sir Richard Pennyfeather plumes himself that he has caught a spy. An elderly woman with a strong German accent, selling lace at Little Waltham, was arrested by his order. She said that her husband was a doctor, in a small way, at one of the East Coast towns, but by Sir Richard's order she was imprisoned for the night. In the morning her account of herself was confirmed but Sir Richard, still suspicious, has ordered her to be kept under public surveillance. This is probably the lace seller who caused great alarm to the Tufnell household at Langleys, Great Waltham. She made in the neighbourhood most minute enquiry as to the number and character of the rooms in the mansion and as to the age and habits of all its inmates. The Langley people imagined she was a militant suffragette, planning an incendiary outrage.

Monday, 28 September. Gossip through Miss Madge Gold of Chatham Hall. Mr Barclay of Monken Hadley is a Glasgow man. Mrs Barclay says: that Prince Louis of Battenberg is a prisoner in the Tower of London on suspicion of espionage; that there are also shut up as spies Princess Henry of Pless (sister of the Duchess of Westminster), Sir Ernest Cassel, the racing magnate, and Mrs George Cornwallis-West, a Society person.[1]

A convalescent soldier at Braintree has a succinct history of his war experience. 'I was taken up in a railway train to the front; in fifteen minutes from my arrival I was firing in the trenches; just half an hour later I was back in the train, going back wounded. The man next me in the firing line had had two days of it and reported that it had been "just hell".'

Members of the Royal Commission on Ancient Sites and Buildings, paying belated visits of enquiry to outlying farms and houses have met with much suspicion, amounting almost to violence in these parts, in the last fortnight. 'By the life of Pharaoh, Ye are spies!'

On our way back to the Rectory, to a meeting of Church School Managers, my Senior Churchwarden (Thomas Stoddart) wondered whether, in the history of this parish, the Rector and the two Churchwardens had ever drilled together.

Tuesday, 29 September. The farmers in the district are making special

---

[1] Prince Louis, First Sea Lord, was a naturalized British subject who married a granddaughter of Queen Victoria. He would be forced from office in October.

Princess Henry of Pless was born Mary Cornwallis-West. Her husband was the Prince of Anhalt-Cothen-Pless. Ironically, in Germany she was also regarded as a spy because of her strong British patriotism.

Sir Ernest Cassel, KCMG, was a German Jewish financier and philanthropist. A naturalized British subject, he had been a close friend of King Edward VII.

Mrs George Cornwallis-West was the former Mrs Patrick Campbell, the actress. Her husband was the brother of Princess Henry of Pless. Until 1913, Lady Randolph Churchill, mother of Winston Churchill, was married to Cornwallis-West.

efforts to get the land ready for winter-wheat sowing. There is also a shortage of horses, the most powerful farm horses having been taken for Army purposes. The steam plough or scarifier is much in use this year.

In consequence of the invitation to subscribers to view the Braintree Red Cross hospital the idea got abroad that a train of wounded was to arrive. All afternoon the station approaches, the streets from thence to the hospital (Workhouse) and the hospital front were beset by throngs of people. The expectancy of the street-crowd was brought to boiling point by the arrival one by one of the uniformed staff, dashing up on bicycles or even motors. They had come to show visitors over the building and explain the arrangements, not to minister to the wounded in war.

At 11 a.m. at Long's the old white pony dashed wildly up the orchard; the fowls cackled violently; the dogs barked furiously. Miss Edith Caldwell went out to find the big collie, 'Teddy' holding up a half company of Territorials marching from Little Waltham. They asked if they might cross the orchard; Miss Caldwell said certainly and added that they were welcome to pick up the fallen apples. The officer after using wild words at the delay of the men to emerge from the orchard, sent the drill sergeant to hurry them up. When he had got them on the run, every man was munching an apple.

Wednesday, 30 September. The billeting sergeant (at Great Waltham) said that where people would really be inconvenienced by soldiers billeted on them the sergeants had orders to avoid doing so if they could by any means. Where, however, they were treated rudely—'We won't have any of your sort in our house'—they said nothing but marked the house down for five or six.

Thursday, 1 October. Some tiny bits of evening gossip but I was unable to take them in, much less to record them, having had to pack to bed under enfeebling conditions of a feverish cold and sore throat and the maddening pain of toothache, face-ache and aching eyes.

Saturday, 3 October. A villager told me that soldiers from Broomfield had been 'shampooing' all night at Nokes' farm = sham fighting.

Popular belief in the passage of the Russians—Archangel: Scotland ports: English railways: Cardiff and Bristol—continues. The latest explanation of absence of news of them is that their guns went down in the wreck of the 'Oceanic' off the Scotch coast. They cannot get to work till fresh artillery is got for them from Archangel.

Monday, 5 October. 1.45 p.m. I went to ask the officers to tea, supper or breakfast, but they declined on the ground that on those bivouac days they stayed in the field with their men and did not enter houses.

Monday, 12 October. 5 p.m. (till dark 6.15 p.m.) drill of Special Constables in Mr Jack Stevens' field. Prodigal amusement was provided for the company by the evolutions of the Rector, absent from the last drill, who was left to his own devices to discover a new movement begun last Monday's drill. By kindly wrist-pulls from T. Sargeant, by shoves forward or backward by Stanley Jordan (trained in the Essex Yeomanry), by impatience of F. R. Lewin, his front-rank man at the original mustering off, he was pulled, shoved, hustled into unexpected positions. He feels quite capable of suggesting very distinct improvements in the words of command of the drill-manual. With a little rational simplification they would be more easily learnt by recruits for the regular army, and by old and out-of-date special constables. Several of the 'orders' are conspicuously irrational.

On returning home from drill I find a long 'impression' provided for me by Miss Tina Preeston of Clockhouse, Braintree, originating from her brother, a captain in the Royal Horse Artillery, invalided from the front. It is of importance to put on record these opinions of an individual soldier, be they right or be they wrong, because impressions of the war (as they reach us in the village) come from 'official' (and therefore *ordered*) sources or from blatant newspapers.

I start with a frank criticism of the Belgian Army: it is a friendly 'fallacy' to suppose that the Belgian Army has shown either courage or resistance. So soon as it was attacked by the Germans, every Belgian force made tracks to the rear.

The Germans in their attack on Belgian villages had really much provocation. At the first arrival of the Germans the regular Belgian forces made themselves scarce, but when the German troops began to enter the village, Belgian girls of fifteen or sixteen, revolver in hand, rushed out into the street and shot down Germans. When the Germans defended themselves, their action was exaggerated and misrepresented.

Wednesday, 14 October. 3.45 p.m. Mrs Sophia Fitch, wife of Walter

Fitch, agricultural labourer, near Dog and Gun, came to have their application signed for the effects of their son, Dick Fitch, of Second Essex Regt. killed in action. Dick Fitch was a lad of just nineteen and enlisted so recently as a year ago last June. Mrs Fitch has had twelve children; Dick's is the first death in the family.

Jas. Rogers heard a day or two ago that his son, Joseph Rogers, previously reported missing, was now ascertained to be a prisoner in Germany.

Thursday, 15 October. Canon Tancock (or someone with authority) asked Mr Hedgethorn, Schoolmaster of Little Waltham, when the soldiers of the Buckingham regiment came there, to ask them politely not to do any damage in the Drill Hall. When the first soldier came to seek admission, he said in his own schoolmasterly way: 'You are not to come in here unless you promise ME that you won't break anything and that you will leave it quite clean.'

The answer was quite sharp: 'If you don't get out of that door, I will knock you and the door in.' Mr Hedgethorn cleared out, without further remark.

Saturday, 17 October. 11.30 a.m. Notice up at the Police Station, opposite the Post Office that:
(a) no lamps must show in shops;
(b) as few lights as possible may show in the streets;
(c) no lights must shine from windows of upper storeys;
(d) no lobby-lights to be used, unless shaded, so as not to show outside.

1 p.m. the Policeman served a copy of this notice on the Rectory. He says this house is on the line along which hostile airships are expected to travel.

Sunday, 18 October. About 10 a.m. the Church Clerk (Wm. Herbert Dee) called in to say that the Post Office bulletin reported four German destroyers torpedoed off the Dutch coast. The tension of feeling in the village presently shown by the haste with which the lads made to convey the news from one end of this wide and thinly peopled parish to the other. It was just as in Macaulay's *Lay*:

> Some ran east and some ran west,
> Crying 'the day is ours.'

VISIT TO OXFORD: 19–21 October

Monday, 19 October. Left the Rectory at 9.55 a.m. or so; passed the Church at 10.6 a.m. All the way onwards, through Great Leighs and Little Waltham parishes—past peaceful rural operations, cutting hedges, breaking clods, spreading manure. Not a sign that a soldier had ever been in the district. As I waited for the ticket-office to open, I found James Caldwell.[1] He told me that Mr Stoddart had approached some of the farm-lads with an admonition that they ought to enlist. They met him with the counter-threat that they were waiting for the farmers' sons of the district to show them the example.

In the Porter's Lodge at Lincoln College the Porter's wife told me that in College five sets of rooms were unoccupied. Lincoln was very fortunate in having so few rooms empty, more so than, in proportion, many of the larger Colleges.

———

Tuesday, 20 October. Mrs Sargeant, wife of Thomas Sargeant, Lyons Hall gardener, had a delightful story of a German spy at the Boreham end of Great Leighs parish. Harry Brown (a nephew of Lizzie Oddey) saw a man near Nokes's farm drawing plans of the roads. He took no notice above board but went towards the Bedfordshire Yeomanry camp at Terling till he met two of the Yeomanry on horseback. He told them his story. They cantered up; asked the man the way to Terling, noticed his foreign accent and when out of his sight, galloped back to Terling whence two soldiers, on cycles, were sent out. These found the man still taking notes. They had a good look at him; thought him very suspicious; arrested him as a spy; and handed him over to their superior officers. (He was possibly an Ordnance Survey reviser.)

Saturday, 24 October. The Ordnance Survey reviser, having come at an inopportune time, is being treated with great suspicion. He called at Long's and asked Miss Edith Caldwell whether he might look round; he produced a long official document. Rather than read this she called

[1] James Caldwell originally came from Glasgow; he was, in 1914, a senior partner in Sun Chemical Ltd of Finsbury and dealt with electrical engineering and laboratory apparatus. In Scotland he had been in the Glasgow Highlanders and in London he had been a sergeant in the London Scottish. Andrew Clark praised him as 'a man of wide experience, industrial and military; very observant and very just'. He was also church organist of Great Leighs. He was normally referred to as 'major', a title associated with his work in the Church Lads' Brigade.

her father. With Mr Lewis Campen, farmer, Little Waltham, he fared even worse. Mr Campen took the man for a spy and his Ordnance Survey map for a blind and was going to take him into custody when the Little Waltham policeman passed and certified his honesty and official status.

Monday, 26 October. Miss Clarice Flack, daughter of Mr Charles Flack, tenant of 'Fitzandrews' in Great Waltham parish, brought some scraps of news: The Ordnance Survey reviser, within the last few days, had the time of his life. He went into the How Street (a hamlet of Great Waltham) Post Office and asked much information, which the sub-postmaster gave him. Afterwards he wondered whether his enquiring visitor were a spy or not and began to fear he had done wrong. Thereupon he bicycled, in hot haste, to the office at Great Waltham. Reinforced there, he and his supporters searched out the questioner and compelled him to show them his official papers. But that was not all: six Special Constables, one after the other, arrested him in their respective districts of the wide parish of Great Waltham. Finally he went to Langleys to implore protection from Colonel Tufnell, JP.

Tuesday, 27 October. This morning our cook, Lizzie Oddey, a village woman, brought a village report she had heard last night. 'The victory of the English is now quite sure. Lord Rayleigh[1] has been looking at the thing in the sky. He told one of his workmen that if it turned to an eagle, the Germans would win; and, if it turned to a bear, the English would win. It has turned to a bear.'

So far as I can conjecture, this 'dark speech' bears this interpretation. Lord Rayleigh, at Terling Place, has a powerful telescope and has been studying the comet. He may have made some joke about the astrological inference from its position in relation to the constellations *Ursa* and *Aquila*.

Wednesday, 28 October. When the Berkshires were here, bivouacing in the Cole-Farm meadow, across the street from the Church School, two of the schoolgirls (Emma Sargeant and Violet Ward) were

[1] John William Strutt, OM, third Baron Rayleigh, was a noted physicist and mathematician who had left Cambridge University for his home, Terling Place, to carry out private research. J. Herbert Tritton's fourth son, Claude, had married his niece. Through this marriage the Trittons became connected not only with the Strutts but with the Tufnells of Great Waltham.

overheard making a confidential petition to some of them that the soldiers would bombard the school so that they might have a long holiday.

Thursday, 29 October. F. B. Rogers, Music Master and Organist of Felsted School called. He is a Cornishman (Falmouth). Opinion in Cornwall is that espionage has been long continued, shamelessly mean, and dangerously effective. When he was at Falmouth, just after the outbreak of the war, it was found out that a man who had been for twenty years a ship's chandler there, had been all the time a paid agent of Germany. He had two sons, one in the navy, one in the army, sub-agents working under their father. When he was arrested, the police had great difficulty in preventing his being lynched.

He says that it is reported that there really *is* in the Convent at Bocking a young Belgian girl with both hands hacked off.

A state of things verging on sedition and mutiny is reported among the Special Constables of Little Waltham: Sir Richard Pennyfeather, their chief, is a very amicable but fussy, ex-Paymaster of the Metropolitan Police, very full of terrors from spies prowling about to blow up bridges and cut down telegraph poles. He has therefore, sent the Little Waltham Special Constables (grocer, butcher, baker and other comfort-loving citizens) out as patrols, night by night. Unhappy Little Waltham Constables, 'Why should they only toil, who are the roof, the crown of things', while Great Leighs outer-darkness takes its ease in full measure?

Friday, 30 October. 6.45 p.m. In the Church School the Special Constabulary of Great Leighs met for inspection. The roads in Great Leighs are to be patrolled nightly from 9 p.m. to 5 a.m.

Sir Richard Pennyfeather related how the spy hunt at Little Waltham had been fully justified by a recent event. Recently on one wet evening, his patrol had found a man sheltering beside a haystack; they had seized him but discovered no bomb or fire-raisers, and therefore set him adrift. Politeness restrained emotion for the moment. But when Sir Richard had burned himself out and his motor had taken itself off, the pent-up merriment broke forth. It was irresistibly comic that a man in authority should be ignorant of the common tramp and his habit of wet nights, of sleeping rough.

Postcards—patriotic and anti-Kaiser—were largely sold in Braintree—Oct. 1914—three specimens are here preserved. [One postcard read:]

Potsdam, Berlin.
October, 1914.

Mine dear Cousin,

How vos you going along? How you vos? Do not kom to see me for I like not your ships. I vos kom to see you if you move dem ships away. You not be frightened, I kom for your goots!

Vot I kom for? Vot I wanted? I vants der leedle Bank von England for mine Frau. I vants der dockyards. Mein Gott!! Take dem big ships avay and I at once kom. I vants der leedle Isle von Wight and her luffly cows ver I sall hold vun big regatta.

I vant dose leedle places, India, Canadas, Australias, for mine sohns. I haf seven (Hoch der Kron Prinz), and der each vants von ver he can sit in der sun and eat his Leber Wurst and trink his Laager. Deutschlands uber Alles. Top Dog.

Gott in Himmel, you have much more dan is goot for you mine dear cousin. But Ireland I vants not. No! Der Teufel!

Greetings from WILHELM

P.S. Move dem ships away or I get angry and kom not.

Monday, 2 November. I received today the weekly Bulletin—that for the twelfth week of issue. It contains no reference to the sinking of a cruiser in the Straits of Dover, but that adverse item of news was widely known in the village on Sunday morning.[1]

The patrolling of the roads in Great and Little Leighs began this night. This patrolling is absolutely unneeded. There is nothing in Great Leighs that it would benefit an enemy to destroy.

Tuesday, 3 November. 12.45 a.m. left the house to go on patrol. Found a sweetly-bright moon-light, a singularly mild air; and a gentle breeze from South-West. Just at the end of the Terling Road (Fuller Street) I met my fellow-watchman on the beat, Mr Edwin Luckock; put the official armlet on his left forearm, and handed over to him the truncheon. Except the coughing bullocks and the three dogs, not a

---

[1] The rumour referred to the sinking of HMS *Audacious* off the Irish coast on 27 October. The ship had struck a mine laid by a German submarine. The Government only released news of the sinking in November 1918. Andrew Clark noted this on 15 November 1918.

sound was heard, from first to last, except the sighing of the telegraph-wires in the soft breeze.

Mr Luckock [a retired missionary] told me how different it would have been on such a night in Africa. On bright moonlight nights, the natives keep up most of the night, talking and laughing loudly. On moonless nights the houses are closely shut up and there is total silence.

Wednesday, 4 November. 10.15 a.m. visited the temporary hospital in the Union Workhouse, Braintree. The sentry at the gate was a City of London Territorial: it is said that trenches are to be dug from Panfield [about four miles north of Great Leighs] along a line of twenty-eight miles. It is said also that part of these trenches will be left open, till there is no fear of a German descent on the east coast and an advance inland.

All the streets in Braintree were full of men, strolling up and down or standing in groups. Joscelyne's the stationer, has fitted up two shop desks with blotting paper, ink-pots and pens, so that men can address postcards. As a result they have sold some thousands of picture cards and postcards in the few days which have elapsed since the troops arrived. Outside the Wheatsheaf a barrel organ was playing, a great group of Tommies standing about, a few couples of them dancing in the street.

Thursday, 5 November. At choir practice, 8 p.m., breathless report from Little Waltham as to tragic happening at Chelmsford, the night before. At the Marconi Station there, one of the sentries was shot dead. It was presumed that this was done by German agents in a motor. Hasty telephones in all directions to the troops to close outlets from Chelmsford. This brought troops in fiery haste from Broomfield to the ash tree at Waltham. Here they improvised a barricade. For this purpose they borrowed traps and carts from Mr Fred J. Rusk and others. The same was done in all the other exits from Chelmsford. This incident shows the utter inadequacy of the measures taken by the authorities. It would be quite feasible to bar all the roads in this district by setting up at appropriate points strong rough gates and posts like the old toll-gates.

Saturday, 7 November. A son of Colonel R. Egerton's chauffeur, 'Jacky' Wood, a very nice lad, has been at the front as a trumpeter-bugler. He saw the charge of the Gurkhas. At first you could not see them, they had taken cover so well. Suddenly there was 'a perfect yell' as they leapt up and rushed on the enemy. The moment they came on the enemy you could not tell which was enemy and which was Gurkha—and all the time there was yelling and shouting.

When a British cavalry force charges, the younger officers dash off, letting forth the usual hunting yells, and the men yell out any call that comes to their fancy, as they gallop: 'This way to the stalls'—'The three-penny entrance this way'—'Three shies a penny.'

Mrs Wood, the bugler's mother, sums up the situation in a characteristic Essex word—'Jacky says them Germans are chronic.' When a pain is very sharp, it is, with an Essex villager, *chronic*.

Monday, 9 November. 3.30 p.m. Visit from Dr R. P. Smallwood with a big budget of news: There is a government reward of £100 for information which will lead to the discovery of any place from which the hostile aircraft gets supplies which has latterly been sailing to and fro over Scotland.

An officer in one of the hospitals assured Dr. S. that this part of evidence as to German preparedness to invade France and survey-work in anticipation for it is strictly true. A few years ago there was an agitation in France to have very conspicuous notice-boards put up at cross-roads, for the better direction of motor-traffic. The contract was undertaken by a German firm, which brought its own staff of workmen. By accident, since the war began, some of these have been taken down. In every case it is found that behind the board or plate by which the notice-arm was fastened to the wall of the house, a brick or stone was loosened and behind it, a paper put ready with full instructions as to the district, its roads, its houses and its supplies.

The Walthams are still very much exercised at the action of the man who purports to be revising the Ordnance Survey numbers: his conduct is irreconcilable with the usual behaviour of a government employé. He goes about everywhere making notes; he does this alone, and he does this even on Sunday afternoons. Now did ever any one hear of a government job which did not provide pay for at least two men helping each other to do nothing; and did ever anyone know of men in government jobs who failed to take week end holidays every week? The villagers say this wants looking into.

Gossip at Mrs Barker's at Lynderswood this afternoon: Mrs Gale of

Rayne place [said] a nephew of hers—on sick leave from India—a Royal Engineer—was sent for to undertake some special duty at the War Office. His last letter to her says that the Germans are about to put their might and main into an attempt to break through the French line at some weak point. If they succeed in doing so, then there is an end of all hopes of ending the war soon. In that case it will be necessary to pour a ceaseless stream of men into the field. Military men are agreed that cannot be done without conscription.

The Colonel who was recently at the Cunningtons (at Queenborough) told Mrs Gale that the reason why so many officers were picked off by the Germans was because of their silk ties. These officers, to prevent them being conspicuous objects, were forbidden to wear belts in action. But while the men's tunics were buttoned close up under the chin, the tunics of officers had a slight collar opening at the neck, and behind that opening a silk tie. Altho' this tie was khaki-colour, the glistening of the silk stuff was noticeable, even at a distance.

The other day a man was seen tampering with the water works at Braintree. The alarm was given, but the man made off. He escaped, but left behind a brand-new bicycle.

Tuesday, 10 November. [Letter from Mrs J. Herbert Tritton to Mrs Andrew Clark.]

9 November 1914

I am so touched by the kindness of the dear Mothers in the Mothers' Meeting in offering to help with the work for the soldiers in Alan's regiment. His last letter says that the cold is intense at night in the trenches.

I think the most needed things at the moment are mufflers and mittens . . . Poor things, I am afraid they can get very little sleep as the shells are constantly breaking round them at night, but Alan says his men are magnificently brave and cheerful though it is a tremendous strain.

He evidently thinks one side or the other will be done up before long, but he adds, 'I do not think it will be us.'

I had a charming letter . . . from a friend who has one of the wounded Coldstream men in her charge. He says he (Alan) took a Lieutenant with him to fetch a pail of water that the men might wash, and that he is always so thoughtful for them.

He arranged a voluntary service for them on Sunday week, when they had a short time off and the men wound up saying 'Our captain is such a good gentleman and a splendid leader' . . .

Old Mrs Sam Childs had a letter from her son Jack which had come 'through the censor'. She didn't know what that meant but supposed it was to show he was in France.

Wednesday, 11 November. 3.25 p.m. Miss Elizabeth Tritton called: Miss Tritton has just seen an American who has come straight from Berlin. He was allowed to visit one of the camps there in which English are detained. He had full leave to talk to the soldiers privately and to ask if they had any grumble to make. They told him distinctly 'no'. The food was very plain, but good. The officers in charge of the camp were extremely considerate. The only vexation was the very great number of hard and fast rules which had to be observed, but they expected that.

Miss E. M. Tritton and her sister, Nettie, have been at Bermondsey Workhouse helping to care for Belgian refugees there. One or two of them have died there. The report of the death of a woman refugee so moved the poor women in the alleys of Bermondsey that they clubbed their small offerings and sent twelve wreaths for her funeral.

Saturday, 14 November. At 2 p.m. in Rectory Barn first meeting of Boy Scouts—meeting at first in charge of Miss Edith Caldwell and Miss Mildred Clark. Six boys only attended, with promise of others to attend next meeting.

Sunday, 15 November. News circulated in village from the Post Office Bulletin of Lord Roberts' death in France. One of my notebooks in [the] Bodleian contains copies of two notes of his on a point in conjunction with the battle of Waterloo, interesting as showing the extreme courtesy of the old Field Marshal in answering an entire stranger's query.

Tuesday, 17 November. [Letter from Mrs J. Herbert Tritton to Mrs Andrew Clark.]

16 November 1914

We are deeply thankful again for good news of Alan to-day although he is still, of course, in great danger at Ypres. He was eleven days in the front row of trenches within 200 or 300 yards of the Germans. Now he has moved to the second row, but I do not think there is much more rest there as they are shelled apparently night and day still.[1] In his letter this morning he sent his very special remembrances to Dr Clark . . .

Wednesday, 18 November. Word was sent from Chelmsford to Great Leighs that aeroplanes would pass over Great Leighs today. The message was sent to prevent the population from panic. There has been so much talk of invasion by German airships. I have not heard that anyone has seen them.

Thursday, 19 November. The second post came not till 3.45 p.m. later than usual. He brought a set of circulars as to recruiting. There were dozens of them came to Great Leighs and the distributing of them no doubt made him late.

VISIT TO OXFORD: 20–21 November

Friday, 20 November. Reached Oxford at 11.50 a.m. At the OUS [Oxford Union Society] I obtained a list of undergraduate members in residence: early in Michaelmas term 1914: 1,417 of whom 565 are 'freshmen'.[2]

Saturday, 21 November. 9.15 a.m. I bought at 'Boots' shop at Carfax end of Queen Street a bottle of Eau-de-Cologne with an elaborate explanation that it is not from Koln, or anywhere else in Germany, but of purely British make.

I left Oxford at 10.3 a.m. by a very good train: I was very fortunate in my compartment. On my right hand was a stout, clean-shaven, dark-haired Welshman, a commercial traveller. He had just been on a long business round in South-West Wales. There were in the towns there a great many Belgian refugees. These were maintained by weekly voluntary contributions. He was a very intelligent, well-informed man and succeeded in drawing out much information from the soldiers.

[1] The First Battle of Ypres was the last large battle on the Western Front in 1914. The Allied counter-offensive ended the German push to the coast. By November the armies had settled into trenches and the lines established would not vary more than ten miles either way until 1917.
[2] The number of matriculations, which was usually slightly above the number of freshmen undergraduates, in 1914 was 663. In 1913 it had stood at 1,022. By 1917 the number fell to only 188. In 1919 it soared to 2,892.

On my left hand was a sergeant of the South Staffordshire, a strongly built man with extremely clear cut and pleasant features. He told me he was now completing his seventeenth year with the Colours. He had served in Baluchistan and the Punjab. The fanatic savages of the Himalayas, in his opinion, were outdone in savagery by many of the Germans. The Boer War, he said, was 'a picnic' in comparison. In several of the actions he had seen more shells discharged in twenty minutes than he had seen in the whole course of the South-African War. He said that this war is 'not fighting, but murder'.

Opposite me was a very tall young fellow, of the mounted ASC [Army Service Corps] men. He was badly wounded in the left leg. He had written a 'poem' about the war, which he offered to show us but he had so much to say that he never got the length of showing his MS and so has lost the chance of perpetuating his literary effort in this record.

He said it was well known now that the position at Mons had been sold to the Germans by the French General who had been appointed to take post there. He said that all that had been in the papers about German brutality was far short of the truth. In a chateau the British troops found a largish party of Germans who had murdered the inhabitants and then set themselves to drink up everything in the cellar. While they were still drunk a party of British soldiers came up— and took no prisoners. He said the destruction in France and Belgium was inconceivable. On many miles of roads the dreadful slaughter of the war is in evidence.

Our troops had to give up trying to buy things in village shops: the shopkeepers pushed back their money: 'Non—Anglais ver' good. No take money. Non!' In another village, the parents told them of their two daughters—one about sixteen—another eight—who had had both breasts hacked off and bled to death.

The trouble with the Germans is their enormous numbers. All the while our men are thoroughly beating the German force in front of them, another German force, equally strong, is entrenching itself further back. If we had as much as three against four Germans or even one against two, our men would sweep the field.

The ASC man showed me specimens of the bullets of the three armies. The British bullet, which is clean and makes a merciful wound; the French bullet, which has a long copper head and may be poisonous; and the German bullet, which has a disc at the back-end.

When the point penetrates a body the disc causes the bullet to expand, so causing a terrible wound in the flesh.

On his left hand was a young fellow, in what I took to be the uniform of the Oxford Territorials—a subaltern (certainly). He listened with all ears to the talk.

About half-past one, there came down High Street [in Chelmsford] a strong column of men marching, singing lustily: Are we downhearted? No. They were obviously new arrivals and in a mood for a joke, so when they came opposite me I salaamed with a low bow and my cap in hand. At once there was a great roar of laughter and a combined Hurrah, which brought out all the shopkeepers to see what had happened. They were Warwick artillery.

———

Saturday, 21 November. In the course of the afternoon (about 3.30 p.m.) a motor stopped at the Rectory gate bringing an officer enquiring for Mr Lewin 'Special Constable'. Mr Lewin was out with the Scouts. He had come from Braintree to ask about a suspicious motor.

The officer asked how many Boy Scouts there were and was told there were sixteen, and more expected. He said he was very glad, because they had been of great service in many places. When Mr Lewin was told of this, he was very glad because there were people in Great Leighs who were jeering at the movement.

Monday, 23 November. The troops were digging trenches in Mr Hutley's land. He went out and told them to stop. The officer in charge said that of course it was open to him to raise objections. But if he did, the military authorities would order him and his family out of the house and convert the house into a hospital.

Thursday, 26 November. Charles Ward tells an amusing story: Joe Brock's sister's son, a lad called Dawson, got leave for forty-eight hours. When he came to Chelmsford, he was the only soldier in the train. The Chelmsford people thought this was suspicious; pounced on him as a deserter; imprisoned him in the guards' room, and wired to his regiment. Finding that he was on furlough, they came to him at 2 a.m. to tell him he was free. But he, very sensibly, refused to budge till daylight, and insisted on being provided with a meal and a blanket. In the morning he just had time to see his people at Felsted.

10.30 a.m. continuous burst of firing Boreham or Great Baddow direction. Not rifle as I think, but machine-guns. A cock-pheasant generally takes refuge in the Rectory grounds from the Lyons Hall shooting party. This morning he has been very disturbed by the noise and has been uttering shrieks of displeasure from his fir-tree. A fine specimen of the biggest of our woodpeckers, with beautiful red-cap, is more regardless of mere noise. During it all he has been assiduously digging for grubs in the lawn outside my window.

3 p.m. afternoon post brought a letter from Mrs Tritton [to Mildred]:

November 25, 1914

How very kind of you to have sent off the beautiful socks.

To our great joy and delight, as you will hear, Alan walked in on Saturday night late, being given a week's rest. He had been in the trenches up to midnight on Friday and he had to march his men 20 miles ... He goes back next Saturday to relieve the other Officers who are then to have a week ...

Alan is having severe work from the dentist and has so many people to see, relatives of his brother Officers who have been killed and visiting those who are wounded etc.

He is taking out with him 200 Testaments which he wishes to give to them with Lord Roberts's beautiful message written in August lithographed in each copy ...

Saturday, 28 November. Miscellaneous gossip: from F. J. Cooper, Revenue Officer, Felsted. He says the report in the Army is that we are able well to hold our ground but are not yet ready to advance in force. When the first portion of Kitchener's Army is sufficiently trained to take its place in the field, then the advance will begin.

Monday, 30 November. 4.15 p.m. Dr Smallwood called. He was told that the authorities were thoroughly satisfied with the state of affairs at the front. The enemy everywhere along the line was effectively held, and if at any point, by a sudden violent attack the enemy's forces broke through, the breach could speedily be made good, with damage. No advance was in immediate contemplation. The army will rest till its numbers could be decisively increased by fresh troops. The first 50,000 of Kitchener's Army were almost ready for the field. They were men of exceptional value both in physique and intelligence.

VISIT TO OXFORD: 2 to 4 December 1914

Friday, 4 December. Journey back to Great Leighs: I went to the station quite half-an-hour before train-time, in order to have a quiet read of a morning paper. But when I got there I found a troop train empty of men who were crowded into the refreshment room or dotted along the platform. They had 'Glengarrys', as I would call them (but some people wrongly call them 'Balmorals'), i.e. oval folded Highland bonnets. I knew them to be Royal Scottish Fusiliers.

I am not blate [bashful] with my Scots tongue, and so I asked the group in my broadest Doric:

'Whaur get ye those Glengarrys?'

The men were rather astonished and indeed somewhat angry, at hearing 'braid Scots' on a Southern platform—so they replied, somewhat sulkily,

'They were served oot ti us.'

But I was not to be beaten off so readily—and asked again,

'An' whaur micht that be?'

'Jist at Greenock' was the answer.

'Weel,' I continued, 'I hae' na been to Greenock, but I hae' been to Glesca' [Glasgow].'

'That's no far off' one said.

'No?' I went on. 'Fine I ken that. Greenock's just a bit down the watter.'

Finding they had a genuine countryman, they became communicative. While I was talking a pleasant-faced elderly lady, with a very sweet voice came up to the group and asked them where they were going. The sergeant and other men saluted, and the sergeant said in his best English, 'Well ma'am, its rather a secret, but I'll tell ye. We are going to Berlin. But we don't quite know at what junctions we are to change on the way.'

The dame was so highly amused at this that she went off to the railway bookstall and got a great bundle of daily papers and handed them to the men. Her example was contagious. Other waiting passengers handed over their papers and bought others.

———

Friday, 4 December. Dr R. P. Smallwood told me that his nephew, a subaltern in the East Yorkshire reported that the Regiment was recently terribly cut up. They had got to the trenches and ought to have taken cover. A clear command came from a little way in front, ordering them to advance. Supposing it to be one of their own officers, they advanced and were mowed down by machine-guns. It was a German, speaking perfect English.

VISIT TO OXFORD: 7 to 11 December, 1914

Wednesday, 9 December. 9 a.m. at the Divinity School to take *viva voce* Pass Mods. It was plain that very few of the candidates were English. There was a considerable sprinkling of Hindus, and one unmistakable negro, who did not get through. The others were declared by their speech to be Americans.

Of the few veritable English, one was an elderly parson, with very bald head, of Marcon's Hall. The motto 'Respect the aged' helped him through. One of the amusing incidents was the fate of a Rhodes Scholar. He had been professor of Latin in a United States University, and had made interest to obtain a Scholarship to come to Oxford to show the effete Britishers how to study. He was ploughed, failing absolutely in Logic.

Another American had got so into the way of throwing his arms about that he indulged in this gesture at the beginning of every answer. He was a little man, with close-cropped fair hair, and gold-rimmed spectacles, and the effect was extremely ludicrous.

A third began every answer with 'Yes, Sir!' and a statement that he thought the question entirely a fair one, but he was not always prepared with an answer to it. Both these scraped through.

———

[*Saturday, 12 December.*] F. W. Metcalf, Dental Surgeon of Duke St, Chelmsford, motored over (8.15 p.m. and stayed till 9.30 p.m.). Mr Metcalf brought some items of war gossip: Mr Metcalf does dentistry for Belgian convalescents. Other Belgians have told him that over and over again they have passed decapitated bodies of children lying by the roadside. A doctor serving with the London Scottish was attending twenty-five wounded in a barn. He sent for ambulance carts to take them off the field. Before the ambulance came Germans arrived and shot all the twenty-five. Mr Metcalf charges Territorials nothing for extracting teeth; and only cost-price of materials. He has, however, a box into which he asks his free patients to drop something for the Belgian refugees.

Monday, 14 December. This morning I received the Official Bulletin for the eighteenth week of issue: its meagreness shows almost a stoppage of action in the Western theatre of war.

Tuesday, 15 December. 1 a.m. a wet night with wind blowing, but light enough to see. Met Major Wm. Brown outside his house (Bishop's Hall) to begin patrol-duty. Rain and wind at times severe. Both of us soaking wet. Not a living creature seen or heard of.

At Miss Digby's cottage (an elderly sempstress) in the Council School lane, Miss Digby, having seen them [the regiment from Dunmow] coming had a basket of apples ready for them. But an officer thanked her very graciously for her kind offer, but declined because the men were not allowed to accept them on the march. When the sergeant's detachment came along the offer was made again. The sergeant climbed a clothes-pole to see if the officer was at hand, bringing up the rear. Then he took an apple himself and handed one to each man. He asked them 'Have you all got one?' and was answered 'Yes!' when the officer came in sight and the apples disappeared into pockets double-quick.

Wednesday, 16 December. 4 p.m. Miss Madge Gold says the Tufnells of Langleys, Great Waltham, report German bombardment of Scarborough and Hartlepool, but 'our fleet is in attendance'. (It was Mrs Bristowe, a county lady who made use of the delightful phrase 'our fleet . . .'.)

Miss Madge Gold says that in Little Waltham the populace have discovered another 'German fort': 'Cranhams' was owned by Herr —— Wagner, who is now said to be an Austrian. Formerly some called him a Russian, others a Pole. The villagers say that at Cranhams, (a) there is a concrete floor for the emplacement of heavy guns of a fort which would command Chelmsford and the Marconi works there; and (b) there is a store of arms and ammunitions.

Thursday, 17 December. Mr C. Wroot's (the Little Waltham butcher's) man, Jim Ennis (I am not very sure of the spelling) called. He says that in Little Waltham all those who had put down their names for home defence have had warning that they must be ready, at any time, to receive and obey a four days' notice to attend at a place of rendezvous.

Friday, 18 December. 1.45 p.m. W.H. Dee, parish clerk, said the report in Braintree this morning was that a German fleet was on the east coast. The troops in Braintree were marched out in a hurry.

Tuesday, 22 December. 10.20 a.m. PC Coles, on his round, obligingly left me specimens of recruiting hand-bills. These show the obstinacy with which, to save itself the confession of past error, the Government shirks its plain duty of compulsory service. The country lads say, and to my mind say justly, 'If so many men are needed by the country, let the country say all *must* go.'

1.15 p.m. the infant-boy of Fred Cloughton was christened in Great Leighs Church, receiving the baptismal names Eric Charles Mons. The only reason I could discover for the *Mons* was that the child's mother's sister's husband's brother is 'at service on the water!'

Wednesday, 23 December. Told by Frank Metcalf, Dentist, Chelmsford: 'There has been a strain of Hebrew blood in my mother's family. The Semite has come out very visibly in her brother—Jacob. He has a hooked nose, a very black beard, and the general appearance of a villainous German Jew. He has been since the beginning of the war engaged in buying horses for the Government. Recently, he drove up in great style, in a car on which OHMS [was] written conspicuously outside. While he was indoors interviewing a horse-dealer, an old woman pointed to the car and asked the policeman who was standing by "What's up now?" The policeman was a wag, and said—"Why, ma'am! haven't you heard? They have just caught a German spy." The old woman said nothing, but when the foreign-looking supposed "spy" came out she let fly half-a-brick at him. She missed him, but fetched the policeman a fair "crack" on the side of the head.'

Friday, 25 December. 7.5 a.m.: foggy morning—thick white fog. 2.45 p.m.: fog still lying low down.

10.45 a.m. morning post brought letter from my sister-in-law [Mrs May Paterson]:

21 December 1914

My cousin, Mrs Martin-Nicholson ('Birdie'), who is a hospital-nurse, has been nursing the wounded in Belgium and Warsaw, and has returned to London.

In Petrograd she was graciously received by the Dowager Empress, who is a very charming but very slangy old lady.[1] Wilhelm is no favourite of hers. She asked Birdie if she did not consider him vulgar and detestable. Birdie said, 'I quite agree with Your Majesty.' Thereupon she told Birdie a little story about him and finished up by saying, 'He is a silly ass!'

Monday, 28 December. 10.25 a.m. a heavy thunderclap of a big gun fired in Shoeburyness direction. Others, at intervals, later.

11.30 a.m. a day of singular gloom, but no rain as yet.—Vanity of conscientious note-making! Rain began just when I had dried the preceding entry, and closed the notebook!

Wednesday, 30 December. 9.15 a.m. morning post [from J. H. Tritton]:

29 December 1914

The blow has fallen—killed in action Dec. 26th. is the brief official—and only—communication. We shall doubtless hear particulars soon.

We give thanks to God for him and ask prayer for ourselves . . .
[P.S.] Personally I should send to the Headquarters Belgian Relief Association, Aldwych, W.C.

I preserve the brave letter of the father in which he answers my query as to the disposal of our Belgian Relief Fund Collection and intimates his loss.

Notes of things seen and heard in a drive to Chelmsford: At Endway there were six khaki soldiers on cycles trying to get past a drove of heifers. They were yelling—'Get into rank there in front', 'Form fours there' and so on.

---

[1] The Dowager Empress of Russia, Marie Fedorovna, was the widow of Tsar Alexander III. She was a sister of Queen Alexandra, consort of Edward VII.

The parish church of
St Mary the Virgin,
Great Leighs, Essex

The Rectory of Great Leighs where the Diary was written

J. Herbert Tritton, Lord of the Manor and a Director of Barclays Bank

1915

Friday, 1 January. I wired to take the sense of the Tritton family as to a Memorial Service on Sunday 10 Jany.

Saturday, 2 January. Letter from Miss Elizabeth Tritton:

Thank you so very much for your telegram and the kind thought . . . We are *very* anxious that it may be for young Fitch also if you wd. be so kind as to talk it over with his parents . . . wd. Mrs Fitch choose a hymn too? . . .

Our loss is so great—Alan was such a perfect son and brother, as you know, and the blank can never be filled in this life. But we are very proud of him, and we look back on the happiest memories. We have had beautiful letters about him . . . a long one from his Colonel and he did not suffer the least.

Monday, 4 January. At Beckenham, Kent, the Territorials designate the RAMC [Royal Army Medical Corps] as 'Rob-all-my-Comrades corps'.

Arthur Fitch, of this parish, is supposed to have gone down with the *Formidable* [sunk in home waters by a German U-boat on 1 January]. I was too ill to stay up and consequently let my notes slide.

Tuesday, 5 January. Was still in grip of influenza. Got up at 9 a.m., very shivery and shaky. Morning gloomy and bitter, with wet fog. No change for hours.

Widow Stubbins, char-woman at Lyons Hall and at Little Waltham Rectory, has a son invalided from the front. Pte. Willie Stubbins' story is a remarkable one. He was in the 9th Lancers. He was one of the fifty who were left out of 600 of that regiment, effective after the charge at Mons. In the darkness of night, he and a chum lost touch with the regiment and could not judge in what direction to move, and spent the night in a wood.

In the morning they saw a party of Uhlans [German cavalry] coming up towards them. In front was a line of barbed-wire entanglements.

The two Lancers put their horses at this fence, and just cleared it. They wandered for some days but at last found the shattered remnant of their own regiment.

At Ypres Stubbins was wounded and lost consciousness. When he regained consciousness he found that his uniform had been stripped from him. At the hospital they found a uniform for him, but for a much shorter man, so that he is painfully conscious of the shortness of its legs and sleeves.

Arthur Fitch had been nine years in the Navy. Mrs Fitch says he was the kindest of all her family to her.

Wednesday, 6 January. Copies of telegram and letter as to death of Lieut. J. A. Paterson [Andrew Clark's nephew]:

WAR OFFICE, LONDON   8th November

Deeply regret to inform you that Lieut. J. A. Paterson, Bedford Regt. was killed in action 30th. Oct. No further details. Lord Kitchener expresses his sympathy. SECRETARY. WAR OFFICE

BUCKINGHAM PALACE, 12th Novr. 1914.

The King and Queen deeply regret the loss you and the Army have sustained by the death of your son in the service of his country. Their Majesties truly sympathise with you in your sorrow. PRIVATE SECRETARY

Mrs Brownrigg, wife of the Dean of Bocking,[1] Miss Helen Tancock, daughter of the Rector of Little Waltham, and Miss E. M. Tritton, are great advocates of 'the League of Honour' which binds young women not to walk out with Territorials. An enthusiastic advocate of this movement puzzled a group of Belgian lady refugees by speaking to them about 'votre Légion d'Honneur' and the good girls enrolled in it.

Sunday, 10 January. Twelve noon. Memorial Service: in memoriam Captain Alan George Tritton, Coldstream Guards. Private Richard Fitch, Essex Regiment. Private Arthur Fitch, RMLI [Royal Marines Light Infantry], *HMS Formidable.*

Monday, 11 January. 1 p.m. My sergeant, William Brown, called to forbid me going patrol-duty as Special Constable tomorrow.

---

[1] Bocking, once a village, was by 1914 a part of Braintree and the home of Courtauld's works. The Deanery of Bocking is an Ecclesiastical Peculiar and the Dean is in effect vicar of Bocking. The Brownriggs were friends of James Caldwell.

5 p.m. a note from Mrs Arnold, wife of Richard Arnold, tenant of Fulbornes farm: 'I hope for the sake of all your parishioners that you are not *thinking* of going on *constable duty* tonight—get rid of your cold first. If a *'Spy'* happens to come We will all forgive you for remaining in.'

3.10 p.m. PC Cole told me that there are several of the villagers who are terribly alarmed at the Special Constable patrols. At night they hear the sound of measured footsteps pacing along the road past their house, where no passer-by is expected, and they lie and tremble, questioning whether it is tramps or invaders.

Thursday, 14 January. About 3.45 p.m. Miss Lucy Tritton called. She (aet. 19 circ.) has been recruiting in the village, mainly among her grandfather's (J. Herbert Tritton's) dependants. She thinks she has secured:-

Frank Cloughton. His mother says she has done well by the country—this son has gone into the Yeomanry; other two sons are already gone forth from the house, one into the navy, the other into the Metropolitan Police. Village gossip says she added that she had also a daughter in heaven. This is, however, fabricated.

Stanley Willis, Mrs Jennings' man who drove her carrier's cart, has long wished to go and has at last got someone to take his place.

Monday, 18 January. 6 p.m. Meeting of Special Constables at the Church School: The Chairman, Major William Brown mentioned that during the Napoleonic war, there had been a county committee which had drawn up a scheme of routes by which women and children, cattle, horses, vehicles and (as far as possible) supplies might be moved inland, in case of an enemy landing.

Following that precedent an Emergency Committee had, for some weeks, been in session. There was to be a similar committee in every police division of the county to assume the direction of the movement of people and cattle. The Special Constables in each parish would have the duty of directing the column of fugitives along the route chosen.

Major W. Brown, having conveyed in very decided terms, the equally decided opinions of Great Leighs Special Constables as to the absurdity of the patrol duty, Sir Richard Pennyfeather wrote to Major W. B. that Capt. Finch admitted that the night patrol duty might be greatly reduced until further order.

Mr James Caldwell addressed the meeting on the subject of the Volunteer Drill Service: The movement was, to begin with, a purely voluntary one. Every one who joined would have to provide his own uniform, and his own rifle. The intention was that men of over thirty-eight years of age, and under that age if rejected by the medical officers for foreign service, should combine to form a thoroughly trained force for home defence. The members would not be taken abroad. All, from their joining to the end of the war, would be under military law. They would replace Territorials, if these were required elsewhere. Already 1,000,000 men had joined.

Thursday, 21 January. In the afternoon, 3 p.m. onwards, various visitors: Mrs Ernest Collingridge came. Ernest Collingridge has just returned to France after the usual 'seventy-two hours' leave. The following are some bits of his sayings when at home: correspondence of soldiers at the front is strictly censored. When a soldier writes a letter, it is left open to be perused by his lieutenant. The lieutenant then passes it on to the Censor. This supervision is, however, avoidable if any soldier of the writer's acquaintance is coming home on leave. Such a man collects letters from all his friends and is allowed to bring them home unchecked, and post them in England. Letters from home are uncensored and unopened, if there is written across the back 'from the wife of —'.

Many of the Indian troops are fine, tall, well-built men and physically command great respect from the average English soldier; but their tastes have too much of savagery about them to win favour. A Territorial was very proud of a piece of shell which had burst beside him, and of the spike and badge from the helmet of a German whom he had bayoneted just in time to avoid the German's thrust. A Pathan listened gravely, who understood and spoke a little English, while these were being shown and explained to the Terrier's mates. 'Souvenir!' he said scornfully, 'no good. Here right souvenir.' He put his hand into the voluminous folds of the shawl wrapped round his breast and produced a cord on which he had strung the ears of all the Germans he counted himself to have slain. These he was keeping carefully to take back to India to his wife.

Saturday, 23 January. Minor notes arrived at through Boy Scouts meeting: James Carpenter has two brothers at the front, [and] 'counts

44

right long' till he can enlist. He is sixteen plus. He reckons that if the war lasts one and a half years longer, he will be seventeen and a half. More men will be needed, and not probably obtainable unless the age is lowered. His chest is fast expanding, so in a year and a half he thinks he will be past the chest-minimum.

Monday, 25 January. This morning two Great Leighs boys went into Chelmsford to enlist: 'Tom' Taylor, son of George Taylor (a carpenter who works at Lyons Hall); 'Bob' Jiggens. This was a very unruly boy when at the Church School. He is now eighteen, and wanted to enter the Navy. But as his mother would not sign the necessary papers for him he has enlisted.

Tuesday, 26 January. 8.10 a.m. I made bold to send a letter to this effect to the Rt. Hon. the Lord Kitchener:

My Lord,

Soldiers' letters often speak of the difficulty and loss experienced in taking messages and supplies from the second to the front-line trench, across the exposed interval.

I make bold to suggest a simple contrivance which seems capable of minimising these.

Let there be in each trench an ordinary salmon-rod reel, with the ordinary length of line. Let the message be enclosed in a waterproof satchel ... fastened securely to the two lines at their ends. By winding and unwinding the reels in the trenches, this case could be drawn backwards and forwards across the zone of fire ...

The same contrivance might be used at night to convey rations or cartridges ... Bigger reels could be used, with stout cord ...

Yesterday, Mr C. Wroot's man 'Jim', who drove his cart and the tall boy who came for orders, both left to enlist.

One of the sons of C. W. Rayner, tenant of Lowleys farm, says that the soldiers billeted at Little Waltham are at feud with W. G. Hedgethorn, the consequential schoolmaster. They call him 'Crippen', 'that little beggar Crippen'. Some time back, and ever since, he has made a great noise because 'the soldiers have damaged the valuable piano in the school'. They at last got tired of hearing about this piano; went to see it; and found it was a German make. Now they hail him as 'the pro-German', and cheer him as they pass, for 'the great care he takes of the Kaiser's goods'.

Wednesday, 27 January. The great Hedgethorn is distinguishing himself by his zeal and activity. He and the companion of his [Special Constable] beat have a strong rope stretched across the road, so that they stop and question all vehicles. The soldiers at Little Waltham state the language used by the occupants of the arrested vehicles outdoes the furthest effort of the proverbial 'army in Flanders'.

Thursday, 28 January. Last evening PC Cole was sent round the village to stick up posters, at all principal places, that no lights should be visible from houses from 5 p.m. till 7.30 a.m. next day. Last night also under special instructions, the Special Constables then on duty visited all places from which lights were shown and refused to depart till the lights were put out or effectively concealed.

Friday, 29 January. 4.30 p.m. Dr Smallwood called with (as usual) a budget of gossip: At 'the House of Prayer', Pleshey, the Sisters have eighteen Belgian soldiers, convalescents. Dr Smallwood more than suspects that some of the wounds were self-inflicted. The fact that the tips of fingers of the left hand in different cases have all been injured in exactly the same way is certainly very suspicious.

The north-west quarter of Great Leighs now accounts for my Oxford visits in a manner very satisfactory to itself. A young farmer, John Cousins is a Special Constable, and was present at the meeting when Major Brown explained that, in case of invasion, the fugitive column was to find its way through Hertfordshire into Oxfordshire. He went home and told all this to Mrs Cousins. Next day she explained it all to the wives of their farm-hands, adding: 'You see it will be all right. The Rector has just come back from Oxford. No doubt he was sent there by the Government to arrange about quarters for us.'

The parishioners are much exercised as to whether the no-lights order will be so construed as to forbid Evening Service on Sundays. The younger people are much attached to the music of the evening service. If the service were put back to 3 p.m., as it used to be, the members of the choir, owing to distance, could not attend at that hour, and the service would have to be read.

Saturday, 30 January. Three nights ago, at the beginning of the evening watch, outside a village in this neighbourhood, a motor dashed up and was stopped by the soldiers. The driver produced a printed card '—— Vere Esq., Notley Lodge, Notley'. The Special Constables from the village were ten minutes late in arriving at their post. On their arrival the soldiers told them what had happened. The SC's at once said that there was no person of that name in the district, and no house called 'Notley Lodge'. The officer then sent some soldiers on motor-bicycles, with bayonets fixed, to try to overtake 'the spy' who had escaped. But, of course, they found no trace of the car.

Several people in Leighs are most unreasonable about the no-lights order, and will require to be summoned. Mrs Louis Wright, e.g., refuses to darken her windows, on the plea that she is 'not afraid of Zeppelins'.

Sunday, 31 January. 6.30 p.m. James Caldwell, organist, had arranged for a very bright service [for Evensong]. I note this in order to enter a Great Leighs definition of the organ-blower: 'He is the boy who puts the wind into Mr Caldwell on Sundays.'

Monday, 1 February. 8.45 a.m. morning post brought me a formal acknowledgement of my letter to the War Office:

30 January 1915

Sir,

With reference to your communication of the 26th. inst. I am directed to acquaint you that the matter has been considered and it is not desired to take any further action in regard to your proposal.

I am, however, to thank you for bringing your proposal to notice . . .

PC Cole called to say that the lights-out order was withdrawn.

Tuesday, 2 February. The supposed spy: I have been able today to get the details as to this story. The post where the man was stopped was between Braintree and (Black) Notley. Two circumstances are very suspicious: (a) that the trenches, which have been in construction for some time, are at Notley; (b) that the man should have a printed card with a surname '*Vere*' and a house-address 'Notley Lodge' which are both false.

Saturday, 6 February. James Carpenter, one of the Boy Scout 'leaders' is enormously fond of his connection with a Braintree workshop in which ball-bearings are made for gun-wheels. He asked another 'leader' to saw some branches for him, and was told he might do 'his dirty work' for himself. 'Look here' was his retort, 'you've just got to do it. *I've* been doing Government work all day.'

Sunday, 14 February. Some odd matter is turning up in connection with men who have been called up in consequence of the way in which the form issued by the Parliamentary Recruiting Committee[1] has been filled up: at Terling, in a row of six cottages, the only person who could write was the wife of one of the labourers. Her husband wanted to go, and so she wrote 'willing' in the best hand she could. Her five neighbours came to her, and asked her to fill up their return. She did so mechanically, using her own return as a fair-copy. The result was that they were all returned as 'willing'. When the call came five unwilling and 'strong-language-using' men found themselves constrained to go with the one willing man.

Monday, 15 February. Miss Madge Gold was at the Alhambra [cinema] about a fortnight ago. There was flashed on the screen the legend 'The Hero of Mons', whereupon a little thin man appeared on the stage, his chest gleaming with medals—the Victoria Cross, the Légion d'Honneur and others. He made a modest speech saying 'I have only done my duty.' Since then he has been sent to prison as an imposter. He bought his V.C. for 30s.; his Legion d'Honneur for 25s., and a third medal for 5s.

(Mrs Gold, widow of —— Gold, had two children—Geoffrey Gold, in the Flying Corps, and Madge Gold. Her second husband is Col. Egerton.) The members of the [flying] corps have got for themselves such a bad name that strong disciplinarians from the other branches of the army-service are put at the head of the Corps. The members of the Corps are no longer allowed to wear their badges in the restaurants.

On the Saturday Geoffrey Gold's fellow-airmen (the Dare-devils they style themselves) came up to a farewell dinner before he left for France. Gordon Bell, the airman, was at the supper. He is one of the first 100 who learned flying. Only some six of them are alive now. He was at Mons, and was for ten days and ten nights in the air, almost without rest. At the end of this time he came down in a wood, smashing his aeroplane to such an extent that not one spar of it was left

[1] The Parliamentary Recruiting Committee was an all-party committee which sought to organize voluntary recruitment. It distributed forms to every household in the country. The aim was to compile a National Register of men 'willing to enlist'. These men would then be 'attested' by the nearest Recruiting Officer as required.

attached to another, and breaking his own ancle and wrist. While he lay there a pompous colonel came up, and called out 'Hullo! had an accident?' G.B. had a bad stutter, and said 'N-n-no. It is r-r-really a hobb-b-by of mine to come down like th-th-this.' The Col. was very wrathful, and said he was not accustomed to being spoken to like that by a subaltern. 'What's your name and number?' 'H-h-hadn't you b-b-better l-l-look for the number in the b-b-back of the car.' At that moment stretcher-bearers came up and cut short the confab.

6.30 p.m. meeting of Special Constables in the Church School: Major Brown reported that the Emergency Committee for the Chelmsford Petty Sessional Division had repeated meetings and the result of its deliberations as regards flight of residents into Hertfordshire had been printed. He gave each Special Constable a copy of these printed directions.

It had been proposed that this paper should be distributed to every cottage. Mr Brown had vigorously opposed this, as likely to cause needless uneasiness and alarm; he knew very well that if even 3,000 or 4,000 Germans landed on our coast, there would be 'a most awful fright' and wild scenes of panic. The Special Constables would have their work cut out for them to keep people in reason.

Tuesday, 2 March. From Mrs Richard Arnold a conundrum: How is it that the Kaiser got his trousers burnt? Because he tried to sit on the Kitchener.

Mrs Vickers (Waltham House, Great Waltham) has sent out a great many parcels to the troops at the front. Each contained—a pair socks, a cake soap, a tin of boracil vaseline, a small tin of Keating's insecticide powder (this is specially commended by the recipients), a tin into which two bars of chocolate have been crushed; boot laces, a handkerchief, an aniline pencil, and a sheet of paper with edges shaped so as to be folded over it for an envelope. In some few also a small Testament. The acknowledgements which have come back have been on partly printed cards, obviously supplied by the army officials. The *men's* writing is usually very unartificial and artless. The addresses are, in every case, in the same hand—no doubt a corporal or a sergeant, of rather better education, set on this job.

Saturday, 6 March. Joseph Nicholls who is reported killed had been for some time in the Northamptonshire Regiment. Mrs Nicholls, of

Little Leighs, cannot read. On receiving a letter from the War Office, she knew something was wrong and took it to Little Leighs Rectory. It was the official tidings of the death.

Sunday, 7 March. James Caldwell told me that in Chelmsford there are great complaints about the heartless carelessness of the military doctors. One called to see a soldier who was very ill and said, 'Oh— you just get up and go on parade, and you'll be all right.' The man was suffering from very acute pneumonia and was dead in two hours.

James Caldwell dwells on the certainty that the war will be hard, prolonged and costly. From what he knows of Germany, he doesn't for a moment believe that Germany can be 'starved' out. The Germans are both foreseeing and methodical. Our way is very different: we do not provide for the future, and then when the sky falls in on us we try to pick ourselves out of the mess.

James Caldwell also says that if in the train you venture to suggest that before we bring the war to an end, we must count on a hard, prolonged and costly struggle, not without some very heavy defeats, you are pounced upon as a pro-German. The English newspapers are much to blame, for producing a false impression that everything is going well, whereas we are doing no more than holding our own against a German screen, behind which the German staff is maturing its plans and massing its men and guns.

Mr Caldwell's daughters assure us that if their father were offered a commission in any battalion going into France, he would accept it at once.

VISITS TO OXFORD: 10–13 and 15–19 March

I was in Oxford taking part in Pass Moderations. I was very harassed by miscellaneous duties and found little time, and had less reserve-strength, for taking or making notes. So I confine myself to setting down only what I distinctly recollect:

Thursday, 11 March. 8 a.m. at breakfast an elderly 'traveller' whom I had not met before—Mr Lazenby by name—told me about the troops at Northampton and Bedford. At Northampton they had Tommies enlisted from the Welsh mining districts and these were rough enough. But they were nothing to the men from the north of Scotland at Bedford. Many of them were 'just terrible'. A lot of them were fisherfolk from Peterhead and these smelt as if they had never washed. It was just awful for the poor people in whose cottages they were billeted.

Friday, 19 March. Concluded *viva voce*—and the end of my term as Pass Moderator.

Saturday, 20 March. Returned to Great Leighs: In the underground carriages between Liverpool Street and Praed Street was this recruiting poster—attempting to be 'funny'—'England *v.* Germany. Sign on at once for the grand international final. Every man counts.' It is characteristic of the minuteness with which matters in England, in spite of the supposed interruption of communication owing to the war, and characteristic also of the inability of the German mind to appreciate English 'humour'—that this should have been reported in Germany and gravely commented on by German newspapers. Witness this cutting from *Daily Express*, London, Tuesd. 23 March:

The popular recruiting poster asking for 'players' for the 'International' is taken quite literally by the *Vossische Zeitung* of Berlin, which declares that 'the English are now bidding for recruits by the offer of special spring sporting facilities in Germany.'

———

My younger daughter's notes of things seen and heard in a visit to St Andrews [to sit her entrance examination], Dundee, Newport-on-Tay and Cupar, Fife between Wedn. 10 March and Tuesd. 23 March. From King's Cross to St Andrews: one sailor, standing on the platform with all his belongings wrapped in a blue-check handkerchief, watched with envious eyes an officer who was being shown into a first-class compartment and was having his suitcase and pillow arranged for him by a guard and a porter.

A Leven (Fife) lady—an officer's wife—received a letter from her husband of this nature:

Blotted out (Presumably Place and Date)
p. 1: Dearest Wife, All the rest blotted out.
p. 2: All blotted out.
p. 3: All blotted out.
p. 4: All blotted out except subscription, Your devoted Tom.

Enclosed in their note: 'Madam, Your husband is quite well but is much too communicative. Censor.'

The Highland Light Infantry in Dundee have, as a mascot, a big collie-dog. He wears a little blue coat, with these words—'I am serving my country. Why are not you?' The other day, he was found serving his country by rolling about, in the gutter, with a dirty little mongrel.

Mrs Ella Paterson (widow of my brother-in-law, James Paterson) has an Aunt 'Leo' —— who lives with a Miss White. Miss White's brother 'Freddy' White is in the trenches. On one occasion, when he was in charge, there were a lot of German dead scattered about between the British and the German trenches. He succeeded in telling the German officer in command that his men would not fire on the Germans if they came out and buried their dead. This was agreed to, and then came out a party of Germans for this purpose.

After the dead had been removed, about twenty of the Germans, with their officers, came across and offered to surrender. Freddy White said he could not take them. He had promised that he would let them go back to the trenches, unmolested. Next day, however, they walked over again and gave themselves up. Most of them were German waiters in London.

Journey from Scotland: At Newcastle an ASC man was saying goodbye to his wife and two children (a girl of about three and a boy of about two). He stood on the platform by the door of his compartment until the whistle sounded. Then he stepped on board the train, and drew the door to. A howl, a loud long howl, went up from both children who had, up to that moment, thought they were going with their father. He thrust a penny into the girl's hands 'to buy bulls eyes'. But that was no comfort. It was not bulls eyes she wanted, but 'daddy'. When the train steamed off, the passengers could still hear the piteous wail of the forsaken babes.

Thursday, 25 March. This afternoon it is reported that there are many fresh soldiers in Chelmsford and in Bocking. The War Office is now favouring the quartering of soldiers in long rows of wooden huts, in preference to billeting. One extension set of huts is going up at Chelmsford.

Friday, 26 March. It is said that four village lads are going to offer themselves for service just after Easter.

4.30 p.m. Miss Madge Gold called—too often mentioned to require further introduction. As usual, she brought a budget of vivacious views of the war, from a local point of view.

Her brother, Geoffrey Gold, had written, narrating his experience at Neuve Chapelle. He was one of the 'flying-men' who took turns to circle over the German trenches and Headquarters. He dropped a lot of bombs. He was particularly interested in two fat old Germans, who lost their heads, and ran about blindly, like persons demented finally crashing into each other full tilt. His letter doesn't say whether these two old fogies were hurt or not.

The day after the battle the British airmen seem to have 'gone mad' and four of them wrecked their machines. Geoffrey, after getting to land, failed to stop his machine and went full 'butt' into a haystack.

At Brighton one of the officers who called on her grandfather told Madge Gold that the Prince of Wales was 'a perfect nuisance' in the trenches; he did not know fear; the men in the trenches were never happy when he was there, fearing some accident to him through his recklessness. He is splendid as a despatch-rider because he goes right ahead through everything.

Wednesday, 31 March. In London the young officers of Kitchener's army are, many of them, objects of public derision, by reason of their silly 'swank'. They get their commission; purchase the most expensive of motor cars, coloured khaki; and then show themselves off by racing in it up and down Hyde Park. Some of the Royal Naval Reserve are even more manifestly ridiculous, for they, having obtained their commission, immediately get a car, painted dark blue with enormous letters RN printed in red on all the panels.

Thursday, 1 April. I was told this afternoon that at the Great Waltham meeting yesterday evening, Capt. Norman stated that the troops at the front had been on short rations because [of] the dockers' strike at Liverpool.

Saturday, 3 April. Geoffrey Gold appears in *The Times* as appointed 'Assistant Equipment Officer'. Col. Egerton says he has no idea of what this office is. Geoffrey's sister, Madge Gold, said it would not interest me further than just to note it in my war-record, as (accordingly) I have done.

Sunday, 4 April (Easter Sunday). 1 p.m. Leslie H. M. Tritton told me the expectation in army circles is that before long there will be a combined forward movement, of all allied forces, on every front. Mr

Redman said he had given Mrs Tritton notice that in about three weeks' time he would leave for ambulance work at the front. The Duchess of Bedford had promised him a post.

6.30 p.m. Mr W. Redman[1] had placed on our altar, for this occasion only, a super-frontal which he has just completed for some great London church. The super-frontal was a strip of beautiful white silk brocade—with magnificently stitched letters of gold, running from end to end: 'Laudamus Te, Benedicimus Te, Glorificamus Te'. The clerk (W. H. Dee) was greatly relieved when Mr Redman assured him that nothing heathenish nor Romanist lurked beneath the strange motto—but only the words of the Post-Communion service [the Gloria]—'We Praise Thee, We Bless Thee, We Glorify Thee'.

Personally I much prefer English. But that preference Mr Redman looks upon as part of the results of the deplorable neglect of my education in 'Church' matters.

Monday, 5 April. 12.15 p.m. Mr Jas. Caldwell told me the small arms factories are not able to turn out the rifles needed at sufficient rate. Nor can the cloth factories supply stuff for uniforms. The War Office aims at three million men, but has not as yet equipment for them. If things go on as at present there will be no resort to conscription in any form.

Tuesday, 6 April. We heard yesterday that my daughter, Mildred Clark, has passed at St Andrews both in the Medical Preliminary and in the Arts and Science Preliminary.

Wednesday, 7 April. 3.45 p.m. An officer called to ask my opinion as to what might be expected in the way of further recruits from this parish. I told him frankly that all men likely to go had gone, and that any eligible man left would not go unless compelled. I used the local saying, 'If they want us they can take us.' He told me that this [is] what he was told everywhere.

4.30 p.m. Miss Lucy Tritton, daughter of Major Leslie Tritton, is going on 21 April to St Albans Cottage Hospital to learn nursing. The most repellent feature of the service, she thinks, is the stiff collar she must wear.

[1] W. R. Redman was a self-taught expert at needlework. In 1911 he had made a frontal for Great Leighs altar from Mrs Clark's wedding dress of velvet, white silk, and cloth of gold.

Sunday, 11 April. 11 a.m. Edward ('Teddy') Bearman, Essex Regiment, was in his khaki at church. In khaki he is a fine, tall, wiry soldier-like fellow.

12.20 p.m. Mrs Ernest Taylor told me another nephew was in Canada at the outbreak of the war; but returned at once to enlist. He has been till now at a station in Kent, but his regiment is now under orders to march from Kent to Colchester—I wonder whether they will follow the route of the Kent Royalists in 1649?

Monday, 12 April. Miss Mildred Dobson, Warden of University Hall, St Andrews (the hall of residence for women students) wrote asking Mildred to come into residence at once and to apply for the Carnegie Trust fee-grant for this Summer Session.

12 noon. Miss Madge Gold called: her brother has been taken off from actual flying duty and placed for a month as 'equipment officer' in the shop. His nerves have been shaken not only by flying, but by the fact that a German machine dropped a bomb on the British aerodrome, about four miles back from Bethuny and blew to pieces two men just beside him. This is a German success which has apparently not been recorded. It is to be feared there are many such.

Tuesday, 13 April. Story from the trenches—from Major Edward Deacon out in France with the Essex Yeomanry—per Major H. L. M. Tritton: in the trenches a German looked up and called across the interval, 'Are you Varvicks?' Answer 'Yes!' 'I've a widow [*sic*] and two childs in Birmingham' he then said, and had for answer, 'If you don't put that dashed head of yours out of sight you'll have a widow and two orphans in Birmingham.'

Miss Lucy Tritton says that our signal code people on the East Coast got hold of the German code, and sailed up the coast one night recently, showing it from time to time. They got answers seven times; Miss Lucy Tritton says that since the war began, eight of her 'best boys' have been killed in action. When the war is over there will be no old friend for her to dance with.

Friday, 16 April. There have been a great many troops moving about lately, and I hear they are sending many thousands to France every night. This accounts for the boom in recruiting, since they have now room to train more men. All the same, I should not be surprised to see some form of conscription passed by Parliament presently. For, although they may not be required, we must have them ready in case of necessity. I think things are favourable for us at present, but we have a very hard three or four months before us, if the war is to be ended this year.

Mrs Vickers' daughter Maude was at Waltham House at lunch today and told two war-stories: Her husband is a Special Constable. Order had been issued that immediately in receipt of news of a German landing, all households were to pour out their cellar-contents, to prevent Germans getting mad drunk and committing atrocities. There was great lamentation at the prospect of destruction of good wine and the order was revoked.

This story she has at first hand, from the RAMC man who says it happened to himself. He was taking wounded back from the front, and had placed in his ambulance one wounded Indian and three wounded Germans. When he opened the ambulance door, on arrival at the hospital, he was confronted by the grinning face of the Indian who was very proud of three corpses of Germans killed *en route*.

A lady visiting Mrs Vickers, told [how] at Cheltenham ladies had got up huts for the soldiers in which tea and coffee were served and also suppers. The ladies took turns in waiting at supper. After a few days the lady in chief charge asked a group of the soldiers whether they had any complaint. They hummed and hawed, and required some pressure to make them speak out what was in their minds. They had two requests: (a) We want spittoons; (b) We would like our own girls to wait on us, and not any of them toffs.

Sunday, 18 April. Mr Stoddart told me that Mr Caldwell, drill instructor of the Special Constables, had persuaded him not to attend the drill tomorrow. He is elderly and finds it difficult to make out the commands. Being deeply conscious that, from physical failings, I myself hinder the drill, I made the same request. I am at times very deaf and do not hear the command distinctly enough to make it out. Being crippled with rheumatism, I cannot step out as the men thirty years younger than myself do. I judged from Mr Caldwell's readiness to grant my request that he was not sorry to drill the company with me not in it. But three at least of the company will miss the joy of shoving me into my place.

Tuesday, 20 April. 12.10 a.m. in continuation of my patrol: Many lights were seen after midnight in the windows of cottages and houses.

Both elderly people and children seem to have got into the unnatural, hysterical condition of dread of the dark.

Very evil reports reach me of the immorality of young women in Chelmsford, Halstead and Terling, where soldiers have been quartered. The leading women at the Mothers' Meeting this afternoon affirmed that the illegitimacy of this year in all these three places will be shocking beyond not only record, but belief.

Saturday, 24 April. Morning post (8.30 a.m.) brought the voluminous circulars of the National Church League with their fantastic suggestion that a poor country parson, eight miles from a railway station should journey to London, and pay hotel expenses there, in order to hear speeches—by clerics and laymen—some of whom he never heard of, and others whom, by report, he is not prepared to like.

We have had staying with us this week-end Mrs Stephenson-Suringar, formerly lecturer for the County Education Committee in domestic subjects. Some years ago she married a young Dutchman, Johann Suringar. By Dutch custom she prefixed her name to his name. Mrs S.-S. has a story of a North Country Territorial in the trenches. He was very puzzled by the Germans opposite calling out 'Gott mit uns.' Then came the delivery of woollies from a working party at home and he, with the others, got a pair of mittens. Next time he heard 'Gott mit uns' he shouted back 'Well, you needn't be so proud about it. We've got mittens too.'

While she was back in England Mr Suringar was in Holland, winding up his affairs. He looked a German, and in business talked German. Supposing him to be a German, quite a number of Germans on their way to and from England bragged how easy it was to circumvent English passport rules. In their pride at their cleverness, they explained to him the different ways in which passport restrictions might be laughed at. When he next wrote to Mrs S. he sat down and wrote all the details he had been told. One was as regards the photos in passports. These the Germans took off and substituted their own. This is now impossible because, as Mr Suringar suggested, the photo is stamped, and not merely the passport.

Mr Jas. Caldwell came in and spent part of the evening: There is an abundance of men of experience in this country but excluded by the War Office because a year or two over the peace regulation age. Commissions are given freely to lads from school who are idle, pleasure-seeking, dissolute and set their men a bad example. In the trenches they are hysterical, observe no precautions and get shot.

Tuesday, 27 April. W. Redman has again been disappointed of getting into the RAMC, on account, apparently, of being over the age limit. He is now canvassing to get employment in one of the hospitals in France. This is decidedly one of the instances which one comes across of the very best men for particular work being thrust away.

Thursday, 29 April. Much comment had been caused by the action of Col. W. N. Tufnell, the largest landowner by far in the district, whose mansion 'Langleys' is one of the stateliest houses in the county. He has been, since the beginning of the war, very active in going round to recruiting meetings. Now, it is said, he has refused to take anyone in, on the plea that, although water is laid on, drinking water has to be carried to the house from a spring in the park. He has also refused leave to all his tenants to accept billeted men, on the plea that there is chicken-pox in Great Waltham. Langleys, it is said, is to be closed up and the Tufnells are going off to Cornwall tomorrow. The troops are said, in the village, to be commenting in very severe terms on this proceeding.

Friday, 30 April. 2 p.m. J. Herbert Tritton told me that he returns to his town house on Wedn. 5 May. He thinks that his two footmen will then enlist, and that his butler, Wm. Redman, will obtain duty at an ambulance centre. Mr Redman's first wish had been to go out as servant to one of the Army Chaplains, but the Chaplains are not allowed servants.

Saturday, 1 May. 7.40 a.m. at the gate into the meadow by the spring I had a conversation with Wm. Milton, foreman of Lyons Hall farm. He does not approve of the profusion of recruiting posters which on their present visit the squire's daughters have put up on all tree-trunks, gate posts, barn walls next the road on Lyons Hall estate. 'Enticing more men away from the land, when too many have gone already. If the government want more men let them take idlers, not workmen. Unless the war is over before August, and some of the men come back, there will not be enough men to get in the harvest.'
  I hear from workmen's women-folk that much indignation is felt among farm-hands at being badgered to enlist. Three of Mr Tritton's

men are said to be leaving today. They complain bitterly that their master's daughters and grand-daughters come pestering them when they were at work in the fields; and that they brought a sergeant who ordered them as if he were a lord and they were his slaves. Their constant sentence is 'We will go, when we like, or when we are ordered.' Conscription, being just, would be welcome.

Sunday, 2 May. Mrs Phillips (wife of the cowman) and Constance Stoddart the dairymaid had been at the end of last week, hoeing turnips [at Lyons Hall farm]. Phillips, I heard, was very indignant and vowed that if his wife was to work in the fields, he would stay at home. Other workmen have asserted the same of themselves. Today's post brought me a letter from my younger daughter:

30 April 1915

My dear father,

I have collected quite a budget of military news for you this week . . . During the vacation a Miss Jacobs has been staying in the Hall. She works in the Natural History Museum in Edinburgh . . . She was telling me that many of the prisoners brought to Edinburgh express their surprise at finding it still standing. In Germany it is said that the town is now a heap of ashes after successful bomb-raids. On a spy taken early in the war was found drawn up the arrangements to be put into effect after the Germans entered Edinburgh. One thing was that certain of the leading citizens were to be kept as hostages. A list of their names was added and the amount each could be forced to pay . . . The Highland Cycling Brigade received orders last week to go to the Dardanelles, but to their huge disappointment the order was cancelled. The same thing happened to a battalion of—I think—Black Watch stationed at Kirkcaldy. The Colonel wrote to Lord Kitchener saying how disappointed the men were as they were so keen to go to France, and asked if for this reason it could not somehow be arranged. His reply was: 'Dear Colonel—I hope you will be all as keen next Christmas. Kitchener.'!

Miss Wing, a Norfolk girl, was travelling in . . . the beginning of the year. In her carriage was an untidy, ill-shaven, dirty looking Tommy. At one station a highly-polished little Terrier got in and at once turned on the Tommy for his untidy appearance. Such people, he said, gave the British Army a bad name . . . Then he proceeded to describe at great length the manœuvres his regiment was engaged in. He thought it a great pity when he learnt that the Tommy never had such manœuvres; they taught you, he said, what actual war-fare was like and fitted you up for the trenches. 'When do you expect to go to France' he asked sneeringly. The ill-kempt Tommy slowly stretched himself. 'This is the third time I have been sent home wounded' he answered. 'I am going now to the depot for fresh clothes and leave to-night to rejoin my mates.' The Terrier collapsed completely! . . .

I am also enclosing my account. I see that they have to be paid before the 7th of May. This I hope is the last time I shall ever have to ask for money. Best love to you both . . .

Monday, 3 May. In this morning's paper the sinking of the *Recruit* was noted. Serving in this ship was Ernest Cloughton, son of Fred Cloughton, shepherd on Lyons Hall farm. This afternoon his father received a telegram (official) informing him that his son was among the drowned.

Thursday, 6 May. Reports from the village represent it in a very depressed state of mind: (a) the sinking of the *Recruit* just off Clacton-on-Sea, a place well known to many villagers here, in which Ernest Cloughton was drowned increases the feeling of insecurity and dissatisfaction that aircraft and submarines are left unchecked; (b) Lloyd George is believed to be planning to rob farmers of profits obtained by increase of price of wheat and to tax labourers' wages; (c) indignation is felt at the supineness of the authorities in not *taking* the loafers of military age; (d) another man has left Lyons Hall farm.

I am told that most (my informant said 'all') of the farm-hands on Lyons Hall farms are to present to the farm-steward (Thomas Stoddart) a demand for an increase of wages; and, if this be not granted, are going to give notice to quit.

I am told that 'the foreman at "The Warren"' in Little Leighs parish is all that is offensive—an offensive Radical, an offensive 'Chapelite', an offensive 'Brotherhood', and that he comes into Great Leighs and makes very offensive speeches saying that the authorities are sending out our poor lads to certain slaughter, and that the Germans are winning all along the line, and will win thoroughly.[1]

Saturday, 8 May. 4.30 p.m. a major and a captain called to enquire about treasonable talk reported by me.

Mr Richard Arnold, following the example of other farmers in this parish and district, has granted his labourers an increase of wages.

Sunday, 9 May. The resentment of farm-labourers at being badgered

---

[1] The 'Brotherhood Movement' was a working-man's organization among various Nonconformist denominations. By 1914 it had a definite 'radical' overtone to its politics.

to enlist is shown by the fact that every recruiting poster from the Rectory to Lyons Hall has been torn down; torn into shreds; and cast away.

Monday, 10 May. 9.40 a.m. Thomas Oddey, father of the Rectory cook, reports that on Saturday an aircraft (he is an old labourer and styled it 'one of them high things') passed over Boreham. It was so high that rifle shots failed to reach it. The officers at Boreham believe that its object was the tall Marconi poles at Chelmsford, where there is an important wireless station.

I finished today the transcript of the deed (1555) by which Richard Rich of Leez founded a chantry, obit and doles in Felsted.[1]

Tuesday, 11 May. 6.30 a.m. Fred Sutton came to sweep my study chimney, as he has done for many successive years. He is efficient and very tidy. He charged 3s. even though coming from so far [Braintree]. He is in distress about his son, under age, who has gone to enlist.

4.30 p.m. Mothers' Meeting tea: Mrs Bearman is in distress about her son by her former marriage—A. Wylds—She had intimation that his arm was shattered by a shell, that he was in hospital, that an operation would be necessary and has not since heard.

Wednesday, 12 May. 4.15 p.m. F. J. Cooper, Revenue Officer, called. His landlord has written from France that the Essex Yeomanry has gone through heavy fighting. Collingridge was the only married man in his troop, and during the action his comrades compelled him to be the man who was left, a little to the rear, in charge of their transport waggon.

James Caldwell said he had just come from London and has seen there personally an invalided officer of the Canadians. This officer told him that the report about the 'crucifying' of Canadians was true. He had himself seen one of his men who was nailed by bayonets on to wooden boards. Of 2,000 men, only 220 in his division were now fully fit for duty owing to the poisoned gas.

Mr Caldwell said that there were this afternoon great tumults in the East End of London. The people are stung to fury partly by the

[1] Sir Richard Rich (?1496–1567) was Speaker of the House of Commons and a virulent Protestant. He is now remembered for his perjury against Sir Thomas More. He also founded Felsted School. Andrew Clark carried on his local historical work and contributed twenty-five articles and notes to the *Essex Review* during the war.

Lusitania murders[1] but still more by the torture of the Canadians. Everywhere they have been attacking Germans and German shops. One result of the Lusitanian and Canadian sufferings has been a tremendous rush of recruits.

Thursday, 13 May. Morning's post (8.45 a.m.) brought me only a recruiting march notice of 2/5th Btn. Essex Regiment [calling for Dr Clark's assistance in advertising the march]. I spent a long time writing postcards to schools, shops, public-houses, post office and individuals. I wrote to Lt. Col. F. Taylor my frank opinion that men would not enlist, unless conscription ensured 'the slackers' would be made to enlist with them. I am sure the village mind is quite made up on that point.

Friday, 14 May. Received by morning's post [from Miss E. H. Tritton]:

Thank you very much for your letter. I am writing at once to Claude[2] at Rouen about Pte. A. Wylds but the answer takes a little time as he is so fearfully busy. I know how glad he will be to find out all he can. I will call and get the posters next time I am near.

Saturday, 15 May. In the early morning it was bitterly cold. I awoke twice shivering. I dreamt also of Canadian camps buried in snow.

1 p.m. a car passed with an officer and a lady; soon afterwards the band passed, silent and walking disorderly. Close after them the rest of the detachment walking very unsoldierly. One officer was mounted. I took off my hat, which he did not acknowledge. His men had had more manners than he. It was a very poor show. I was told by a spectator not ill-disposed to recruiting that the speeches were 'very poor stuff'.

Mrs Bearman heard about her son today. A letter from the War Office said he was dangerously wounded. The Chaplain at Rouen hospital said he had been very ill for three days and asked that his mother might be told.

Sunday, 16 May. Miscellaneous talk before service: W. Redman is going abroad next week; the two footmen are already gone. J. Herbert

---

1 The Cunard liner, *Lusitania*, was sunk by the Germans in the Irish Sea on 7 May: 1,195 passengers went down with the ship.

2 Claude Tritton had returned from British East Africa at the start of the war and had joined the Army Service Corps.

Tritton told me that Great Leighs did not look well in the Recruiting Lists. There were still thirty-six men of military age in Great and Little Leighs who had not offered themselves. About thirty-six had volunteered for service.

Tuesday, 18 May. Morning's post brought a letter from Margaret S. Lilley, Stroud Green, London, the young widow of Tom G. Lilley, sometime poultry farmer of Cole Farm:

Here it has been so turbulent. Rioting was going on quite near here. It is a mercy that they have interned the Germans at last. It ought to have been done long ago. It is a pity that our folk descended to lawlessness, but it was the only way our people could show their feelings in the matter. We have a great camp of German prisoners of war (soldiers) not far from here. Could you believe that some people were actually canvassing for *cakes* for them!

7.50 p.m. Miss E. M. Tritton called: She says the Essex Yeomanry have suffered terribly in a recent action. They took a first line of trenches, and were sent forward to a second, which they took but were not able to hold. In falling back they were mowed down. Col. Deacon is killed.

Wednesday, 19 May. The village is much agitated about the heavy loss reported in the Essex Yeomanry, and anxiously waits for details. Practically everyone has relatives or intimate acquaintances in that regiment.

Albert Wright did not know whether his brother, Herbert, was with the Essex Yeomanry at the fatal action.

Thursday, 20 May. House shakes at frequent short intervals by single discharge of a great gun southwards—e.g. 9.30 a.m., 9.40, 9.45. I noted these as I was writing these jottings and sketching out my sermons.

There is a bitter feeling in the village that details of the charge of the Essex Yeomanry are being officially held back, because they would show that the men were thrown away by the incompetence of the superior officers. The War Office, it is hinted, may hope that this will not be so obvious if other events have come between.

Friday, 21 May. Received by this morning's post—8.45 a.m.—a note from Miss E. M. Tritton enclosing a slip from her brother [Lt. Claude Tritton]:

My dear Diddy,

I had 2 hours yesterday afternoon and spent them in a long and finally successful search for Wylds in No: 9 General Hospital. Strangely enough he had just recovered from an operation and though he was feeling rotten he was quite cheery and able to talk. I talked to the sister and gathered that he had had a shrapnel bullet extracted from his arm but that it didn't heal properly and was rather septic. So they had to open it up again. She says that there's no apparent reason why he should lose his arm or not get all right again and he will in all probability be sent home.

Saturday, 22 May. [Letter from Mildred Clark.]

20 May 1915

My dear Father,

I am sending a few more (Latin) sentences. Many thanks for correcting them. I will attend to the corrections. But would you mind not giving me such shocks again: I opened one envelope and found therein 'as I write this the bullets are whizzing over my head' and then I realised it must be a prose.

Miss Thistlethwaite . . . tells me that it was quite a common thing for the townspeople [of Dingwall] to rush down to the station when they heard spies were being taken through; . . . they used to see not one or two but twelve or fourteen at one time—Men who had been posing as fishermen . . . they were arrested and sent south under a strong guard in a train where were also some wild, west-Highlanders. One of these when passing down the corridor, looked in at the prisoners carriage and became so enraged at the sight of the Germans that he rammed his fist through the carriage window, cutting one of the spies rather badly about the face. He was placed under arrest, but was fearfully proud of himself for he said, 'If I haven't been to the front I have at least wounded one German.'

Chelmsford was reported to have been very noisy and very unpleasant for traffic this morning; great number of Tommies, four-abreast, with recruiting ribbons, were parading Duke Street and High Street, singing 'Will You Join the Army?'

Much doubt prevails concerning Col. Edward Deacon's fate. In spite of the positive assertions by a trooper that he saw him fall dead at the second trench, other reports continue to affirm 'wounded and missing'.

Sunday, 23 May. Joseph Smith says he has notice from the War Office that his barns are to be ready on shortest notice, for occupation by troops, and that all his transport (horses and carts) may be called upon for military service. He says that many farmers have received the same notice. Mr Thomas Stoddart says the soldiers who spoke to him used a very high figure as regards number of men who might be collected in Essex—a 'quarter' of a million.

Connie Stoddart says that one hundred of the Oxon. and Bucks. Reserve at Little Waltham were yesterday picked out to go to the front to fill up the gaps. They were 'downhearted' without doubt.

Mrs W. Suckling had a letter from her prisoner-son this morning. He had been wounded in the thigh, though this was not reported. He begs her to continue sending food. He is half-starved and become very thin.

Monday, 24 May. Mrs George Wright had a letter from her son's depot officer. Her son Herbert ('Hubby') Wright had been searched for everywhere, since the late disastrous action, and was still missing. The officers feared he was killed.

Mrs Louis Wright, Great Road, had a letter from her husband, Louis Percy Wright. He is without a wound. He is one of his company who is so escaped. It breaks the men's hearts to see so many empty saddles.

Godfrey Barker recently wrote to the gardener at Lynderswood. He had been up to within near sound of the guns, and then double-twisted his ancle and was sent back. Now he is back and is in the trenches. He is very well but the continuous noise makes him sometimes feel a longing to be back in the grounds at Lynderswood looking after the chickens.

The village is very much amused at a reported address of Mr Edwin Luckock, in Chapel on Sunday evening: he, so it is said, 'wished with all his heart that the Kaiser had been dead when he was born'.

Thursday, 27 May. 9.30 a.m. report in village that bombs were dropped last night on Southend. Albert Wright and George Taylor believe they heard the explosions. PC Cole saw the flashes.

4.30 p.m. Mrs George Taylor tells about the bombs. It was at 11.15 p.m. George Taylor had gone to bed. Mrs T. was in another room with an invalid sister (Annie) from Maldon. They both heard the explosions and went out. There were a great many of the bombs. They went off with a sound 'pop', very like the crack of fireworks at the Crystal Palace. The Taylors thought they were at Chelmsford.

Monday, 31 May. 11.30 p.m. Went on patrol. 11.45 p.m. a bright light flashed up for a little at the south end of Chatham Green, apparently on the Great Road, like a powerful acetylene lamp, suddenly uncovered and held at an angle. It was answered at once by a similar light at quite the other end of Great Leighs. Possibly by the military at Little Waltham and Braintree.

Tuesday, 1 June. 2.30 p.m. heard from Post Office that the postman said that Germans had been over London last night and that Paddington Station was burnt. On this account I reported to CO, Oxon. and Bucks. Light Infantry, Little Waltham, the lights we saw last night.

Wednesday, 2 June. Mrs James Collins, Endway, had a letter from her daughter, Minnie (who is in a situation near Paddington), 'The Zeppelin went over Whitechapel: we heard nothing of it. The papers are not allowed to say anything about it.'

Friday, 4 June. 4 p.m. Nettie Tritton called. She has five days' leave from her charge of the Belgian refugees at Earls Court. She wanted me to put up again in the Church porch a list of those men of this parish who were serving. I said, for myself, No! It had been so painful removing the names of those who were killed that I could not force myself to do it again. I gave her free leave, if she liked, to put up such notices for herself.

4.30 p.m. Kate Paterson, of Glasgow, came on a very short visit. She was a professional nurse, but had retired. In April she was appealed to act as matron of a private hospital at Lingfield, Surrey. There was a young Canadian, who just escaped being gassed. The poison stream passed just above his mouth and nostrils, but injured his eyes. His business was to crawl out and listen for movements in the enemy-trenches. It was very risky work. He gives a very bad report of mismanagement. Other wounded confirmed the report that at Neuve Chapelle our own guns shelled our own men. There had been some very bad 'generalship'.

The wounded all agree that the danger of pestilence is very great. Everywhere in Flanders you see feet and hands, legs and arms, of imperfectly buried bodies sticking out of the soil. The authorities are doing their best to scatter lime over all such places, but the supply is far short of the need.

Saturday, 5 June. 8.45 a.m. morning's post brought me a number of circulars: from the Bishop of Chelmsford, enclosing a letter from the two English primates with orders to read it [a Pastoral Letter calling for continued prayer along with war work] on Sunday, June 6th. The *Star* (evening newspaper of Wedn. 2 June 1915) commented on this arch-episcopal utterance with force and humour: 'Gas and Gaiters'.

Kate Paterson says the wounded spoke to each other in immense condemnation of the incompetence of several generals, and of the young officers—ignorant boys—who have replaced those who have fallen. The men do not relish going out to the awful noise again, but say 'As we must go, we will put a good face on it.'

Louis Wright's own story has come home. He was not in the Essex Yeomanry charge nor in the trench. He had been sent back in charge of the Colonel's horse. So here is good material to judge of the reliability of stories from the battlefield.

Sunday, 6 June. At the evening service I substituted the reading of the Bishop's and Archbishops' letters for the sermon, and to make further room for them took only one of the three Evening Psalms and shortened both lessons. Even so, the service was too long. Various of the congregation asked afterwards what *I* would do on July 11th.[1] One shrewd fellow said he didn't know whether bishops were able to write any better sense, but he did think they might write *shorter* letters.

Monday, 7 June. I received this morning the Official Bulletin for the 43rd week of issue; this bulletin is most meagre. It has no reference to the Essex air raid of this week, nor to the South East Coast air raid of this week. It has not a word to say about the disastrous repulse of every British division at the Dardanelles on June 4th. This is, I suppose, the 'tremendous victory' promised there by Winston Churchill.[2]

It is arranged that a women's meeting should be held at the Mission Room to arrange about sewing jute-bags for sand-bag work.

Tuesday, 8 June. At Great Leighs Post Office today, the wife of an

---

[1] Sunday 11 July was the day assigned by the Bishop of Chelmsford for special services, inter-denominational if possible, 'to arouse the conscience and to stir up the hearts of all to offer everything at this time for the Service of the Country'.

[2] The Dardanelles campaign, designed to eliminate Turkey from the war and to establish a third, Balkan front, had begun with British shelling of Turkish gun emplacements on 19 February. The first Allied landings on the Gallipoli peninsula took place on 25 April.

Essex Yeoman was making enquiry for her husband. She had been told by the authorities that he could not be traced. In one of his letters he said he was friends with a labourer (Wright by name) from Great Leighs. This must be Herbert G. Wright, son of George Wright, who is 'missing'.

Thursday, 10 June. James Caldwell was summoned on the jury at Chelmsford Assizes on Monday, and kept dancing attendance on M. and Tuesd. He was complaining to one of the authorities. This gentleman saw his Special Constable's badge, laid his finger-point on it, and said, 'That exempts you.' 'Surely not' Mr Caldwell added, 'I have seen several cases in which that plea has been rejected.' 'In other counties possibly' was the reply. 'But Essex is *in the danger zone* and, therefore, its Special Constables are exempt.'[1]

Friday, 11 June. W. Redman has left the service of Lyons Hall and 4, Lowndes Sq. S.W. The family were going to have no male indoor servants. He is going into service with a lady (Mrs —?— Pinkerton) who has a town house in Hyde Park Street. He has not been able to carry out his desire for ambulance work in France.

Saturday, 12 June. There is a general feeling that the soldiers met casually on the roads are much more depressed than were the troops in these parts. Report from the VAD [Voluntary Aid Detachment] hospital at Braintree that the Territorial patients are 'making themselves as ill as they can' because they don't want to be sent out of it.

Monday, 14 June. 11.15 p.m. started to go on patrol duty as Special Constable; 11.30 p.m. met F. R. Lewin, the companion of my patrol. I put down here two items of Mr F. R. L.'s conversation: Farmers think the impending danger is that when the crops are dry and ripe, enemy aircraft may drop, broadcast, incendiary bombs, which could cause widespread destruction.

—— Andrews, who works in Walter Willis's smithy at Dragon End,

---

[1] Few counties were more affected by the war than Essex. Thousands of troops were kept there because of the fear of a German invasion; others were *en route* for London where they would depart for the front. Near Great Leighs were two major centres of war industries: Braintree had Lake & Elliot, Courtaulds and Crittalls; Chelmsford had Cromptons, Hoffmanns and the Marconi Works. London's northern anti-aircraft defences were located in the county. Essex also had its share of Belgian refugees, prisoner-of-war camps, hospitals, and convalescent homes.

was for some time in the Dragon tap-room, very facetious about Great Leighs Special Constables—'they were no good: they never came round: they were afraid to be let out in the dark'. So various pairs of them have been beguiling the tedium of their patrol by playing little games on Andrews. There is a sheet of blackened sheet-iron and a piece of chalk kept in the smithy shed on which customers write down their special orders. Andrews cannot read. One morning he found a brief, business-like order, as he thought, written on this sheet. He waited till his master would be up, and took it in to him. Walter Willis put on his spectacles and read: '5.30 a.m. Andrews not yet at his work. He is always late.'

Another night, they took a stout string and tied it to the handle of his front door, took it right round the end of the house, and tied it to the handle of the back-door, so that each door might be opened about an inch, but neither of them enough to see out. Then Andrews came down to go to his work, and shouted at the lads who (as he thought) were holding the door against him. At last, he had to knock through the wall to his neighbour in the next cottage, to come downstairs and release him.

Wednesday, 16 June. [Letter from Andrew Clark to Falconer Madan.]*[1]

16 June, 1915

My dear Librarian,

May I, counting on your known indulgence, venture, in the slang terms in which I have been involved, to 'put you up against' two 'tall propositions.'

An Essex village war-diary. Often in the course of the South African war, I deeply regretted that I had not begun noting the oddities of village report and opinions that I came across. When the war began I resolved that I would not be guilty of that error. I have, therefore, from day to day, put down in writing what I have heard, or received, about the war, so far as it has affected this village . . . The first set of these (Aug.–Dec. 1914) now awaits only indexing.

Would the Bodleian care to have the 8 vols. They are sufficiently paged and supplied with contents; and shall be indexed so as to cause no trouble . . . They will be sent on approval, to be withdrawn if not acceptable.

They are quite frank in expression of opinion. If they are accepted, they ought to be reserved in some way. There is nothing in them which any graduate need be excluded from . . .

[1] An asterisk is used throughout to indicate material not included in the Diary but added by the editor. For the origin of this material, see pp. xxi–xxii above.

Thursday, 17 June. 8.40 a.m. this morning's post [brought a letter from Mildred]:

10 June 1915

My dear father,
. . . I heard an amusing farewell outside the post-office to-day: 'Good-bye Jock. I'll maybe see you knocking about across the water'—'Aw, weel we'll meet anyhow in Berlin.'! . . . Dora Ramsay is nursing in a Military Hospital. She says that the more she sees of the British Tommy the more she admires him. He is always cheerful no matter what he is suffering, grateful for the least thing done for him and so considerate of his nurses . . .

On Saturday last . . . it was widely reported in Dundee that the Crystal Palace had been destroyed by bombs. Travellers from London were surprised to hear it and said it was unfortunately untrue . . .

Dr Ryle says from my class-exam. papers I ought to get a first-rank . . . We are serenaded about twice a week now. The men sing abominably and as I hear them coming up the drive and don't want ten minutes of pantomime songs under my windows I must put out the light.

Friday, 18 June. With a big effort today I got abreast once more of making cuttings for my *English Words in War Time* series, and pasting them into their proper places. The series now passes its 50th volume: but most of them have yet to be indexed.

Saturday, 19 June. 6.40 p.m. James Caldwell called: He has no confidence that the Government will produce munitions in adequate amount, at least for two months yet. What is needed is plant. It's disgraceful the manner in which for ten months the Government have kept the nation in ignorance, and have persisted in stating that 'everything is going on all right' when it was not. Even with what is now being done, munitions will not be forthcoming in sufficient quantity, unless the war continues much longer than is supposed.

Mr Caldwell is very disappointed with the course of the war. We were told that when the better weather came, the great push would be made. The great push has not been made, although we are now at mid-summer and we are doing no more than just 'holding' the Germans.

Lord Kitchener is probably the man really to blame for the policy of too great silence. The result is not good. Not only are wild rumours readily believed as to failures in the field; but people are beginning to discredit the official reports of successes.

Tuesday, 22 June. This morning hay-carting of all sorts is in full swing. Crop being very light, ground very dry the cut hay and clover are ready at once. Two industries fast becoming extinct in Essex were visible this morning: (a) wooden hurdle making for temporary sheep-fencing. 'Alix' Alefounder has quite a stack of these, beautifully made; (b) thatching—'Joe' Brock is thatching at the cottages in Cole-hill field. In the big glebe field Richard Arnold's men are carting clover-hay.

Sunday, 27 June. Mrs Deacon last week found a wounded soldier, who said that, just before he was knocked over, he had seen Col. Deacon, disabled, but not by a very severe wound. The chances of his being a wounded prisoner are therefore more hopeful.

9.15 p.m. another instance of the painful uncertainty in which people are as to their relatives' fate in the war. A brother-in-law of Mrs H. J. Hicks, Supply Stores, Great Leighs, was reported 'killed' in one of the early battles. Six weeks later he was reported 'prisoner'. This was at Xmas. Since then not a word has been heard of him.

Monday, 28 June. It is characteristic of the village mind that it is too feeble to accept a simple fact. It must add legendary details. Thus, in the case of Herbert G. Wright, of the Essex Yeomanry, reported 'missing' at the time of the 'charge' of that battalion: village reports have been (a) that he was blown to pieces by a great shell, without his comrades seeing it; (b) that he was buried in the trench by the blowing in of its edge. On Saturday there ran a confident report along the Great Road that his father, George Wright, had had a letter telling how his son had been wounded, had crawled three miles to ambulance, and died there. Only a lie; no letter of any kind received.

Tuesday, 29 June. Pea-picking is the great money-making industry of the year in this village. Many villagers count on it to make this year's rent. I was told this week that one woman was bragging that she, with her children helping, had made 14s. a day. The work begins fairly early in the morning, but leaves off not later than 3 p.m., so that the sacks may go by waggon to Chelmsford and reach Covent Garden market (by goods train) for the early morning sale next day.

11.30 p.m. Was joined [on Special Constable patrol] by the companion of my watch, Mr Fred R. Lewin who told me: Fred Carpenter, son of Mrs Carpenter, housekeeper at Little Leighs Rectory, is now back on leave after his wounds. Mr Lewin told me a number of Fred Carpenter's *dicta*: (a) there is no end to the Germans. You shoot them down by the thousand, but more thousands seem to spring out of the earth; (b) if they had had the spirit of a louse they would have driven us into the sea. But they are too faint-hearted to press home an attack. Two Englishmen are always able to hold ten Germans; (c) the French are no great fighters. They do not do well except when they have troops of ours beside them. Then they are ashamed to hold back and show off. The Belgians are better fighters; (d) after all that has been said about the entrenchments of the Germans we shall, when the time comes, break through them easily enough. We shall drive the Germans out of France and across the Rhine. Further we shall not be able to go. We shall have to stop then and let the Russians act, and do their bit; (e) the casualty lists do not return half the men who are killed. It will be a year or two after the war before anything like a full list is made out; (f) it is very painful when you see a comrade knocked over to be unable to help, but it is so. The wounded know this and do the best they can; (g) the men in the fighting-line have been so impressed by what they have learnt about German cruelty to prisoners that, if they find themselves cut off, they turn their weapons on themselves; (h) the Germans have practically stopped taking prisoners. They butcher the wounded; (i) the men in the ranks say that no British prisoners will come back from Germany. They will be butchered.

Wednesday, 30 June. I was told today that W. Redman had been (yesterday) in Great Leighs saying goodbye. He gets £5 a year more in his new place and there is only one lady in the family.

Fred Carpenter says that the men at the front are convinced that the prisoners-of-war do not receive the parcels sent out to them. The Germans embezzle these and compel the prisoners to write saying they have received them, and to ask for more. Even in our own fighting line men do not receive one half of the things sent out to them. Parcels are systematically stolen, either in this country or during transit.

Fred Carpenter says the belief at the front is that the war will last over Xmas 1915, and even over Xmas 1916. The guess competition most in favour is—in what way Germany can be made to pay Great Britain and Canada for the expenses of the war. France, Belgium, Italy, Russia will obtain provinces in Europe. South Africa, Australia, New Zealand will have something in the way of German colonies. But there will not be enough German money to go round and Great Britain and Canada will have nothing.

Monday, 5 July. Mr James Caldwell said that at Bocking he had been told a message had been sent officially to Mrs Deacon telling her that her husband, missing since 13 May, was a prisoner.

Major Brown said that this gave hope that some of the privates of the Essex Yeomanry (missing since then) including Herbert Wright, might also be prisoners. On the other hand, he had been told by a man who was present that [as] he had seen some of the Yeomanry 'blown to smithereens', he could not tell who they were, but they could never be identified.

Wednesday, 7 July. 8.45 a.m. this morning's post brought me a letter from my daughter [Mildred]:

4 July, 1915

. . . I heard a lively story about a Scotch regiment to-day. They were burying the dead after an engagement and had begun to shovel earth on a German, when the man recovered consciousness and cried out 'Me no deaded, me no deaded.' 'Agh' cries the Scotie, 'Shovel some earth on him, Geordie. Them Germans is such liars that one can't believe a word they say!'

Saturday, 10 July. Chelmsford householders complain of damage done by officers quartered on them; e.g. by tearing carpets by unnecessary roughness and of sulky, or even uncivil, looks and language when it was suggested that more care might be taken. Inexcusable damage was also done by such negligence as leaving the escape-pipe in a bathroom closed and the supply tap running, so that the water overflowed and brought down the ceiling in the room below.

The Rectory ground hay was this afternoon got in stack, not much injured by having lain for two days in the wet, but a pitifully small stack.

Sunday, 11 July. 9.45 a.m. Miss Constance L. Stoddart told me that her father (Thomas Stoddart, Churchwarden) had arranged to take the Sunday school children to Maldon on Thursd. this week, in brakes, leaving Great Leighs Church at 8.30 a.m. They would take their own dinners, as they do to school. Tea would be provided at Maldon.

Tuesday, 13 July. Afternoon's post (2.15 p.m.) brought a letter from my daughter [Mildred] written at Newport, Fife:

11 July, 1915

More spies! One was caught on Tuesday taking photographs of the Tay Bridge. There is a mania for them, for a few weeks ago the Bishop's daughter was going in for a French oral exam and asked the three Ramsays if she could go with them for an afternoon to speak French. As it was a lovely afternoon they went to Arbroath intending to walk along the cliffs. They got into the train at West Ferry station, into a carriage where one man was sitting and jabbered French all the way. They got out at Arbroath and had only gone a few steps from the station when they were arrested by two policemen, who said their fellow-traveller had reported to the police that four suspicious-looking foreigners were in the town. Fortunately Miss Robertson had one of the Bishop's cards with her, and they were allowed to go on the cliffs.

Thursday, 15 July. 9 p.m. Barometer (rising) at 29.5½. The Sunday school children's brakes passed on way from Maldon to the Great Road. They were in highest spirits, singing and cheering and setting all the dogs barking. They had had a delightful day, no thunder and only a few drops of rain.

Saturday, 17 July. Yesterday Louis Wright got home from France on forty-eight hours' leave. His children were out pea-picking and had to be fetched from the field.

Friday, 6 August. 2.30 p.m. reached Great Leighs thoroughly tired out. [Dr Clark had been in Oxford from 20 July to 6 August marking Oxford Local Examinations.]

Saturday, 7 August. Learned that the 1/5th Essex had sailed, it is supposed for Dardanelles. With them went Sergeant Harry Taylor and Edward Bearman.

Tuesday, 10 August. I heard today that two more Great Leighs lads had enlisted. Harry Jiggins, who looks after her pony for Mrs Richard Arnold and Len Cook who works for Mr —— Witney, Chadwick's. This Cook is the third brother who has enlisted. The eldest brother enlisted first and is most indignant that his younger brother has gone to the front, while he is still in England.

Wednesday, 11 August. 8.45 a.m. morning's post brought a letter from Little Waltham evincing the perturbation of the villagers in the prospect of filling up the National Register forms, under threat of £5 penalty for false entries.

7 p.m. Mr James Caldwell called about the accommodation of the Industrial School's Chelmsford Church Lads Brigade: they must be housed in some barn or other building. Would I therefore allow the use of the Rectory barn?

Thursday, 12 August. 12.30 p.m. Miss E. M. Tritton called with the National Registration papers for this house. She says the cottagers are much interested in the Register. Last night Mr Caldwell told me that in his part of the parish the women were terribly afraid that the Register was the beginning of a plan to take away their men-folk. In his case, the villagers would tell him their real thoughts; in Miss Tritton's case they would say just what they thought she would like them to say.

Saturday, 14 August. I was told today that Len Cook had been accepted for RHA [Royal Horse Artillery]; Harry Jiggins had been rejected.

The [Industrial School] boys at the Rectory barn were just mad with delight of the big field and the keen air. Four of them had an hour's 'punishment-drill,' i.e. standing solemnly at attention in a row—for dancing on the top of the big manure-heap and setting loose pent-up odours, pungent but not pleasant.

Sunday, 15 August. The 'Cadets' were not successful with their camp cooking. The tea for breakfast was badly infused; the bacon not properly fried. The stew (beef, suet dumplings, cabbage, carrots) promised so badly that they brought the pot down to the Rectory kitchen. In the afternoon, some of them told me that, when it went back, it was delightful.

Tuesday, 17 August. By a great effort I have now (7 p.m.) overtaken arrears of my *War Diary*, by inserting at end of volume xii the more important circulars which had accumulated during my absence in Oxford [20 July–6 August].

About 9.45 p.m. an airship passed over Great Leighs. The buzz of it was distinctly heard at the Rectory. It came from Braintree way and (to judge by the sound) made a half circle over here, and then went toward Chelmsford. Just after it had passed, there was a tremendous report, as of the 'one bang' of a single big gun—loud as thunder but far more sudden and limited. It shook all windows in house, and caused a bath leaning against a wall to clatter down on floor.

Wednesday, 18 August. 8.30 a.m. the Boy Scouts are out for physical drill and short march, singing as they go.

Miscellaneous military notes as told me by Mildred Clark, this morning: At Dundee each recruit has about ten people (men, women and children) standing outside the compartment, to make a weeping farewell. On Mond. 9 Aug., as the 11.45 a.m. train was steaming off out of Dundee station, a mill-girl, obviously sweetheart of one of the recruits cried out from the platform 'Oh Jimmy! don't go.' Out of the window of the next compartment a head was promptly put out, with the shout 'Shall we throw him out of the window to you, Miss?'

One of the reasons why recruiting is slow in Dundee is the belief which the Dundee women have got that permanently wounded men are to receive only 1s. a week as pension. One of the women said to Miss Alice Paterson the other day 'It isn't likely that I'm going to let my sons go to the front to get a leg or arm off and then come back to me with only a shilling a week.'

At 12.45 p.m. I had a request to help provide underclothing for a girl who is going to hospital in London. Mrs Harry Lewin has certainly a big family (as families now reckon bigness) of young children:

Dr Sir
Mrs Lewin would be glad if you could please kindly lend her a little help as she has to take on[e] of her little girls to london hospital for an operation of her foot and she needs several little articles of clothing to take her comfortably clothed and if you could Please send her a small trifle she would be very grateful as she has so many little ones to look to for clothes . . .

Yours truly
Mrs H. Lewin

4 p.m. Miss Edith Caldwell's notes of last night's Zeppelin raid: At Chelmsford five bombs were dropped, of which three did not explode, and no person was hurt there. One went through a house, but did not explode. The Zeppelins passed on toward London and are reported to have done much damage at Stratford, Leyton, Ilford and Blackheath. The report in the village is that the bomb at Chelmsford went through the roof, through a room in which a child was sleeping, and buried itself in the ground-floor.

The villagers here have a story that while the Irish troops (London Irish) were at Braintree two of them one evening stopped a young fellow coming out of Braintree. One of them held the man; while the other went through his pockets, and relieved him of 30s. Next day the man went and lodged his complaint. The troops were paraded so that he might point out his assailants. He was not able to identify them.

Thursday, 19 August. The baker's man told Mrs Everett that the Zeppelin was hovering uncertain in its direction, over Great Waltham. A big motor which had been in waiting suddenly showed very bright headlights, and took the road towards Chelmsford. The Zeppelin followed and when well on its way, the motor put out its lights and disappeared.

Reports as to air raid of Tuesd. 17 Aug. 1915: (a) Leytonstone station has been laid flat, and forty-nine people killed. This news is prohibited because it is within six miles of London and it is not wished that the Germans should know how nearly they had reached the capital; (b) at Chelmsford the bomb burned the pillows of the child's bed, but the child had slipt low down into the bed and was unhurt.

Friday, 20 August. 11.30 p.m. met the colleague of my patrol (Mr F. R. Lewin). He was in great glee. At Endway, on his way to meet me, he had held up a motor car, as having too bright headlights. The driver was Major Wm. Brown, 'Sergeant' of us Great Leighs Special Constables. Major Brown explained that he had put on small lights and drove slowly as far as the end of Little Waltham. Then being 'on his own dunghill' he lit his big lamp, to allow him to travel fast.

Having met Mr Lewin, we went toward Endway. Just there we held up a bicyclist, to see if he had the commanded red-light at the tail of his bicycle. He had not, but he was Mr Ernest Taylor, one of our most esteemed colleagues as Special Constable.

Mr Lewin says there is a strong village report that a motor, with bright headlights, flashed along the Great Road guiding the Zeppelins on Monday night. It is difficult to believe that these reports, coming independently from different sources, and dovetailing in with each other, are groundless. A heavy censure rests on the authorities who refused to set up barrier-gates.

Saturday, 21 August. A sign of the extension of motor traffic is that F. G. Hicks, Baker, Little Waltham, has a grand new delivery motor van. An instructor is with Ames (Mr Hicks' man) teaching him how to drive. Ames' unassisted performances are looked forward to with terror by the villagers. His recklessness, when in charge of an ordinary baker's horse-cart, does not inspire confidence as to his control of a motor.

At the Boy Scout camp today Mr Leonard Hayward, in charge of the [Essex Industrial School, Chelmsford] Boy Scouts, was disturbed by Major Brown's cows just across the fence. He got out of his tent barefooted to shoo them from that corner. First of all he stepped into a bed of nettles. Next, in reaching in the dark to find a stone to throw at the cows, he put his hand into a tin in which the boys had been collecting wasps. Next he set one foot on a fly paper and steadying himself to pull it off set the other on it.

Wednesday, 25 August. Mrs Tritton had a number of wounded soldiers to tea. I counted sixty-one men. I had a talk with some: [One man] is in the Westminsters (16th London). He went through all the Boer War. This war is a much bigger thing, but it is much better organised. There is no fear of disease over there—now. Burial arrangements are almost perfect. The Germans don't bury their dead. They pile them up as a screen in front of their trenches. At night our lads creep out and bury as many Germans as they can. It is a risky business because if the Germans hear, or fancy they hear a movement, they turn their flash-lights on and fire. The water supply in all cases is good. The hospital arrangements are almost perfect. The grumbles among the men are all about small matters.

I was surprised at the extreme lowness in which men spoke to each other as well as to myself. I asked the retired medical man in charge, whether this was a subdued tone they had got into owing to having been long in hospital. He said possibly it was part cause, but the main cause was the trenches, in which any voice louder than a whisper brought a hail of shrapnel on them.

There was some talk about the German army. All agreed that they were splendid fighters, especially the Prussians. Many of the men had picked up a good deal of French. So far as simple sentences went they could understand French spoken and could speak French themselves. All were loud in praise of the extreme kindness they received from the French peasantry everywhere.

Several of them were very sore about recruiting not being brisker. A common suggestion was that now our forces had gone some way ahead, and left behind them battlefields and towns and villages over which the tide of war has flowed and ebbed, this country should run cheap railway and motor excursions for some weeks. If our men at home could only see what has happened in France and Flanders there would be recruits galore.

One of them was rather proud of a speech he had made at a recruiting meeting, since his coming back wounded: a lawdy-da gent. in fine tailored clothes, got up and said he hoped Englishmen in the meeting would do their duty by enlisting at once. So I got up at the back of the hall and shouted to him, 'You big hulking lazy lout, why don't you enlist yourself?'

Monday, 30 August. 3.30 p.m. Marjorie Tritton, youngest daughter of Major H. L. M. Tritton called asking for 6*d*. novels. I answered that all I had were going out this week or next to the Dardanelles, for 'A' Company, 5th Essex Territorials, where is my friend Sergeant Harry Taylor.

5.15 p.m., in spite of many interruptions I have today made good progress with touching up the first volume of my War Diary (1914) = 2 Aug. to 7 Sept. 1914, in hopes of sending it and some of the volumes next to it to the Bodleian next week.

Wednesday, 1 September. F. J. Cooper's sister is on a short visit to Felsted. Miss Cooper was a nurse in the hospital at East Leeds. One of the soldiers is a young fellow of the Bedfordshire Regt. He is dying slowly, of a bullet wound in the head, which has partly affected his speech so that he can only drawl out his words. When he is asked what it was like at the front he smiles and drawls out that it was 'glorious fun while it lasted'.

The 5th Essex have taken out with them to the Dardanelles a battalion joke: Percy Ridley is a major in the battalion, but has been refused leave to go out with them because of 'a beastly knee', result of an accident, which may go out of joint at any sudden strain. He speaks in a haw-haw tone, easily imitated, and always provocative of mirth. When riding with the battalion he was pensively rubbing his beastly knee, sniffed the air, turned round in the saddle, and called out in his peculiar voice, 'I smell a fox. Whot! Whot!' It is the ambition of every man in the battalion to startle his mates into hilarity, by an unexpected 'replica' of the exclamation.

Thursday, 2 September. Mrs J. Herbert Tritton gives an amusing account of the social divisions which trouble her daughters in the work among the women munition-workers. There are two classes of these women, and they have very opposite ideas of what is fitting. The girls of the student class think smoking a necessity of life, but view with unutterable horror any person who is drunk or verging on drunkenness. The girls of the factory-working class think tipsiness is an ordinary incident in the day's course, but if a girl smokes, she is thought to be simply 'terrible'. So strong is their feeling that the factories have to provide two canteens, one for each class. The factory-girls have also a snobbish conceit that the 'loidies' despise them, and will not be friendly with them. Hence they resent any friendly advances.

A little after noon today Col. Gerald E. Barker, Mrs Barker and their son, Lieut. Godfrey G. Barker, motored from Gillingham to their home, Lynderswood, near Braintree. They wired to various friends to come to Lynderswood. I give here various bits of their talk: Godfrey Barker (who is a great big fellow): If you are behind one of our own guns, you can see the shell as it leaves the muzzle and follow its flight a long way over the trees. But you cannot see a shell coming from the enemy. You can only hear the whizz. Then, if a trench is handy, you drop into it without ceremony. If there is no trench you plop flat, face down on the ground and if you want to be funny, tickle the ribs of the man nearest you.

The universal belief in the army is that very shortly they will send out a 'feeler' but there will be no real move till next spring. Kitchener and the Allied Army leaders, it is thought, will just keep the Germans hard held for some months, gradually weakening. Then there will be a concerted move from Russia, the Dardanelles, Italy, France and Flanders, and, from the day it begins, the war will not last longer than six months.

In the army it is thought that, recently, things at the Dardanelles have been progressing just speedily. A little while ago, the situation was almost hopeless.

A naval officer told Jas. Caldwell yesterday that our navy is making use of captured German submarines. Two gunboats trail a hawser between them. When they feel that a submarine is entangled they wait perfectly stationary, till twenty-four hours have passed. Then they breech the vessel, or raise it to the surface. The vessel is then made ready for a British crew and taken into our service. By order of the Admiralty the strictest silence is observed. The Germans cannot tell whether the submarines they have sent out have got to foreign waters, to work there, or whether they have come to grief.

This agrees with what my daughter heard in St Andrews from one of the women who came with the excursion to that town. Her husband was an undertaker. He was taken off navvy work and put on with other men to the task of opening captured submarines, removing the bodies, and burying them. The vessels are then thoroughly disinfected; repainted and put in commission with a British crew.

Friday, 3 September. This morning's post (8.45 a.m.) brought a formal receipt [for 5s.] for sending *Overseas Daily Mail* for a year to Sergt. Harry Taylor.

Lady Locock, 'Oaklands', says she is a heartbroken wife! The National Register forms are being tabulated by her husband and he knows the 'official' age of every woman in Braintree district, but will not tell her even one.

Mr Mitchell is manager of the Marconi Works at Chelmsford: says he is certain there are three houses in Chelmsford in communication with the enemy's agents outside that town, partly by means of wireless, partly by flashing signals. They send their wireless when Marconi Works are busy sending messages so that their electrical discharges pass unperceived.

Sunday, 5 September. 10.45 a.m. James Caldwell told me that a nephew of the Dean of Bocking is commander of *HMS King George V.* He says that British captures have enormously reduced the number of German submarines. Since the *Lusitania*, the boats which take them are not so solicitous as they were before, to save the crews. When they find a submarine entangled in wire hawsers, they finish their own arrangements quietly before attempting to pick it up.

Wasps have been very troublesome today everywhere. I had to kill three in church during Communion-Service. At lunch I had to kill several, which pestered me. Afterwards, several invited slaughter in my study.

Wednesday, 8 September. Mrs Brownrigg, Bocking Deanery, says that last week when the Courtaulds paid the wages of their employés in Bocking, each man received 2s.6d. over his wages, each woman 2s. The firm explained that, owing to the war, they were making larger profits. This augmentation would be paid weekly, in future, till further notice.

Thursday, 9 September. 12.30 p.m. windows shaken by concussion of a big gun at Shoeburyness. I have been very busy today paging (where incomplete) and packing up vol. i–vii of my *War Diary* (1914), vol. i–iv and vol. vii–xiv of my *War Diary* (1915) and vol. xxxviii of my *English Words in War Time*. These twenty quarto MSS volumes were sent off this afternoon.

Friday, 10 September. 2 p.m. Major William Brown, Sergeant of Great Leighs Special Constables, came with a type-written order from Capt. J. A. Unett, Chief Constable for Essex, requiring all church services to be over before dusk unless the windows were effectually darkened.

6.30 p.m. the Reverend Reginald Fawkes [Mrs J. H. Tritton's brother-in-law] called: this week a cousin of his (in military command) told him that there is a general impression in Army circles that there will be presently a big move on the western front. But that front is said to be trenched and mined like a fortress.

Saturday, 11 September. This week was, I understand, the week for counting parcels at Great Leighs Post Office. This week's number beats former records but it had the help of parcels sent by villagers to their friends in camp, of the two parcels which are sent (each close on 11 lb.) from this village every week, to Joseph Rogers and Ernest Suckling, prisoners-of-war, and also of my *War Diary*.

Sunday, 12 September. I gave out in Church this morning the order that there must be no evening service. Consequently this Sunday would be the last for the present. Next Sunday, instead of Evening Service, service in afternoon at 3 p.m. It is very great grief to me to have to leave off the evening service. I shall try to find out whether Mr Tritton would curtain his Mission Room windows, a much smaller building and grant me the use of that.

8.15 p.m. a heavy white mist on the meadows by the church. Stars shining brightly. No moon. In the dim light, even with all but a few lamps put out, the church windows showed so conspicuously that the wisdom of the 'lights-out' order was incontrovertible.

Monday, 13 September. Went to lunch (1.30 p.m.) at Lyons Hall—as usual, everyone most kind, conversations bright, and makes one wish that the family were resident, instead of visitant. Mr Tritton told me that he had sent for Mr Barnard of Chelmsford to take measurements in the Mission Room as to possibilities (by green blinds) of effectually darkening that building. I may have the Mission Room every Sunday evening at 6.30 p.m. for services. I may also have it for an occasional week-day lecture by myself or anyone whom I may bring to lecture.

The Budget will be no pleasant reading for any of us. The government must, by taxation, provide for payment of interest on its borrowings. It may double, or treble, income tax.

Tuesday, 14 September. Various items of village gossip: Some time ago Major H. Leslie M. Tritton of the Essex Yeomanry pressed his groom (—— Sayres) to join the Yeomanry. He did so, but now says he is sorry he did not take a month's notice. Stanley Jordan (Chauffeur) a fortnight ago, cheerfully chose the month's notice. He had served in the Yeomanry, and is reported to be of opinion that 'no one will force him to serve again, when he doesn't want to.'

Thursday, 16 September. There is a canteen at Woolwich arsenal, which is open continuously. In this canteen certain ladies supply free tea, coffee, cocoa, bread and butter, three times a day. It is served, and the work is done by voluntary helpers. Marjorie Tritton, younger daughter of Major Leslie Tritton, is to be one. She is to serve from 10 or 11 a.m. to 3 p.m.—brew tea, cut bread and butter, serve and wash up.

Mr James Caldwell gave us the other party's view of the Woolwich canteen. The men hate it, but have to use it, since it is the only refreshment place allowed within the arsenal. They do not want their tea free. They hate being served by young ladies, whom they are shy of, but would like a motherly working woman.

He says also that the men report that the women who are going into the munitions works are no use. They have never handled a tool and can do nothing. They crack up in a week, and then things are at a stay until a fresh batch is got, equally useless.

Saturday, 18 September. 11 a.m. Old Mrs Walter Cloughton called. Her daughter, Caroline, brought a report that 'Red' Bearman had been wounded at the Dardanelles a fortnight to three weeks ago.

5.30 p.m. Mr Richard Arnold's men finished harvest today. 'Bill' Collins came, as their envoy, to ask 'largesse'—(damage to me 2s. 6d.)

Monday, 20 September. In Great Leighs yesterday there was a sensational report that —— Seabrook, of Little Waltham, had been arrested as a German spy in connection with the recent air raid. On that occasion he showed a brilliant light which guided the Zeppelin. On former occasions he has been in the habit of flashing signals at night to enemy aircraft.

Seabrook was driver of a contractor's car in Chelmsford; bought —— farm, built himself a small rough-cast house there and planted fruit trees. He is a very hard-working, respectable man; but somewhat intolerant in his expressions of extreme anti-church and Socialist opinions. His political violence caused heated resentment at the last contest in this division. He and Mr A. Riley of Alsteds, Great Leighs, are the twin pillars of Little Waltham Chapel. The sole foundation for the report is probably only his having been summoned for refusal to darken his lights. He is quite of that obstinate type. (12 noon Mr T. Stoddart called. He said the report had got attached to the wrong man. It arose from Mr —— Seabrook, of a big house in Broomfield, now under repair, having left the district.)

Private A. Wylds is now in hospital at Cardiff. He was shot through the shoulder. When he got to the base hospital, the surgeons looked at the wound. He was put under chloroform, and, as he was becoming unconscious, he heard one 'gentleman' say 'that arm is no good; we will have to take it off.' But another gentleman, whom he did not see, said 'he has done his little bit: let us do our best we can for the poor lad, and try and save the arm.'

He thinks the wound was kept open for weeks by putting cloths into it. Now the arm hangs quite stiff and the doctors tell him he will be discharged, as unfit for further service.

He has been at Cardiff for some time. There the wounded are very well attended to. The nurses are lady nurses and most kind. When he does come back among civilians he hopes he will get a job, and will always be pleased to think that he has done his bit, and not been like so many young fellows at home, walking about and doing nothing.

Tuesday, 21 September. 11.30 p.m. met Mr Lewin in lane. He says that the report is that —— Seabrook of Broomfield has been arrested and taken away, in custody. Suspicion attached to him because he and his motor were about all the time on each of the three raids. His car, when examined, proved to have a wireless installation.

Braintree industries have begun to be disorganised by the rush to munitions works. —— Williams, fishmonger, has closed shop and gone as a munitions worker. Four of the Hope Laundry women left their work this morning to go 'munitioning'.

Most of the women in this parish and in the district are potato-lifting today, and have been for some days.

4.30 p.m. J. Herbert Tritton told me that: it was quite certain in France and Flanders, along our whole front, for every German soldier there were five British; (ii) that we had an enormous cavalry force, which was intended to be used when the time came; (iii) that in London everybody expected the big movement to begin about the end of this week.[1]

Monday, 27 September. W. Ketley at the Railway Stables in Chelmsford receives and packs and sends off the vegetables and fruit contributed in Chelmsford district for the Fleet. Last week two tons (nearly) were sent.

Yesterday I heard a long story about —— Seabrook of Broomfield. When the Zeppelin dropped bombs on Maldon, Seabrook was there with his car. When it passed over Witham and Broomfield on its way to London, Seabrook was there. On both occasions of its visiting Chelmsford, Seabrook was there. The report was that he was held up on occasion of the second air raid on Chelmsford, and his motor car was found to have a wireless-installation in it. Whereupon he was arrested. This evening there is a report in the village, purporting to have come from a 'military man in London' that —— Seabrook has been court-martialled and shot.—Such reports, however, about detection and shooting of spies and secret agents—have been common. Confirmation of any of them is lacking.

Tuesday, 28 September. 7 p.m. I gave a lecture on the course of the war during the last twelvemonths. In spite of the torrents of rain, there was a big attendance, quite filling the Mission Room:

[1] The rumours were fairly accurate: on Saturday, 25 September, there would be a British assault at Loos and French assaults on the German lines in Champagne and at Vimy Ridge. By 14 October British casualties would stand at 60,000 while French losses would exceed 150,000 men.

I suppose the first feeling in thinking over the war is a feeling of disappointment, of sorrowful disappointment. It seems such a long time to look back upon; we are aware of enormous efforts which have been made in the country; we know about the terrible losses which have been sustained abroad and yet so little seems to have been accomplished. The enemy's lines face our lines and the allies far beyond the enemy's own frontier; the enemy's forces have advanced a long way into Russia. On the one frontier, things are no further on than they were a year ago. On the Eastern battle-line, they seem much worse. So, as I said, there is a feeling of disappointment and discouragement.

That feeling is, I think we must admit, quite natural; but it is not well-founded.

The war has lasted for one year, one month, and twenty-four days. Now that is not a long time as wars go. Our last South African war lasted three years and three months. Our Ashantee War lasted a year and two months. The Crimean War ran two full years. The war which we call the Peninsular War lasted from July 1808 to Apr. 1814—getting on for six years.

Then, again, we have to remember that this war is, in the full sense of the word, world-wide. It has not been confined to one continent only but has spread over every continent and every ocean [including] the North Sea [with] more subtle and more difficult tasks [such as] the floating-mines. For these there was at first no provision. They were against a solemn agreement entered into by Germany with the nations. Secondly there were the submarines. Germany, with its talent for destruction, had gone thoroughly into the construction of these. These did much damage. Then our seamen were put on their mettle and have waged successful war against this new peril. A third, newer and stranger source of danger remained, the Zeppelin. When these giant air-ships were first spoken of—in Sept. 1914—our newspapers made fun of them. But with heedfulness and preparedness, that danger also is melting away.

We must say that in the course of this year—1915—there have been great doings—great successes. But what about our land warfare? Here, also, let us remember that there are other continents than Europe. There is Africa. A year and a month ago Germany held a very strong position in Africa. On the east of Africa Germany had a vast territory called German East Africa. In South-West Africa Germany had two colonies—Togoland and Kamerun. Egypt: here again, Germany thought it had a grand chance to make the Nile run red to the sea with British blood. So you see, we have, in this last year, had to fight out each corner of the great continent of Africa. On one corner a carefully planned invasion has been hurled back. On two other corners the allies have taken three great enemy lands. On the fourth corner, victory is coming our way.

I am not an authority upon sweeping up a room. I have often, when the process began and I have been anxious to finish a piece of writing, been wishful to sit through it. But I have been promptly ejected. I understand, however, that in sweeping up a room, you begin at the corners and get all the dust of the rest of the room to the fire-place. Then little remains to do. That is what we have done in this war. Germany has been swept out of the four corners of the world. There remains the sweeping into the fire—the driving the Germans back into Germany.

Here we come, therefore, to what we have thought most of during the past year—our army in Flanders and France. What is to be our judgement on that? Germany had everything prepared for the fiercest of assaults. France had to draw its troops from long distances from Paris. British troops were few. The heart of France lay open to a sudden thrust. That thrust was made and failed; the tide of battle was swept back across the Marne, and across the Aisne. Beyond that we have not yet made good our advance.

Why? because the Germans brought up immense reserves. [But] the fiercest attempts of Germany against our lines with over-powering superiority in guns, with terrible, unexpected, forbidden weapons, of poison gas and liquid fire, have been shattered. And our men, and with them Belgians and French, have held fast.

We are not only to think of the battle front, but of what has been going on behind it. Could anyone have said that a great new army could be sent into the field in less than a year? Yet that has been done.

One other matter remains—a name of grievous meaning and memory for many in Essex—The Dardanelles—what can we say about that? It was, every authority admits, a very tempting opportunity, to bring Constantinople to reason, to let Bulgaria know that the allies were not to be trifled with, to get through from Russia her vast stores of wheat and oil-fuel, to pass into Russia munitions from Europe and the United States.

Grievous bad generalship and bad management have been shown. But the gallantry of our troops has got a firm hold of this biggest of natural forces; the Turks have been severely checked at every attempt to regain the ground; we hope that soon here also—the word will be victory.

Thursday, 30 September. This evening the Dean of Bocking told Mr Jas. Caldwell that he had heard from an official at the War Office that 570 officers had been killed or wounded in the last few days' fighting. The full extent of the losses would not be published at once, but sections of it from day to day. The loss in officers had been out of all proportion heavier than in men.

Friday, 1 October. James Caldwell explains the disproportionate loss among officers in this way: The young subalterns have not had time to be properly trained in field work. They know their squad-drill thoroughly, but have no idea how to manage their men in open formations. So from ignorance of how to act, in order to save their men (as they think) they make themselves far too conspicuous. If only they had with them a good sergeant-major from the Regulars, it would be another story.

It was known in Little Leighs, by telegram on Wedn. evening (29 Sept.) that 'Willie' Hughes-Hughes, son of M. E. Hughes-Hughes, of Leez Priory, had been killed. He was a captain.

Saturday, 2 October. 5.45 p.m. Jas. Caldwell called. He is a member of the 'Services Club', the club-room being what was recently the German Athenaeum. Members are all in the services now, or have recently been. A number of young officers, on their two or three days' leave in London, get rooms there. From them Mr Caldwell hears much about the war. They are now very cheerful; say there are all the men that are wanted, and all the munitions; and that the present advance will, by sure stages, be pressed through.

Thursday, 7 October. This morning (8.30 a.m.) a considerable body of troops and transport (foot-soldiers, waggons) came this way across Gubbions Green. Before 10 a.m. another great column (guns, much infantry, Red Cross waggons) came this way. All along the line of march the cottagers came out offering the men apples. When they got to Lyons Hall, the officers told the cottagers 'Don't give these companies apples. Keep some for the men in the rear. The ones in front are always well supplied, but rear men come off very badly.'

Yesterday evening Thomas Stoddart brought back a story from Braintree market that Germans had landed at Yarmouth, but that the boats from which they had disembarked had been captured. Others had brought back the same report, and it was rife in the village this morning. Origin of report as yet unknown.

Friday, 8 October. This morning's post brought me a letter from Kincardine, Kincardine O'Neil, NB:

6 October, 1915

My dear Sir,
Thank you so much for your kind letter. It is indeed kind of you to remember me ... I so often think of you and Great Leighs; I spent many

happy days there. And now I am in your country—how delightful it all is . . . We have ten soldiers in the village and I generally manage to see them every day. It is sad to see them, poor fellows, but they seem quite happy. One has lost both his eyes; the others, legs, arms, etc. They are well looked after here, and strange enough, one of them came from Chelmsford. He has been a schoolmaster some where close to Chelmsford. I have forgotten the name of the place. He was gassed . . . We shall be returning South . . . With all kind thoughts and thanks,

Most respectfully yours,
William R. Redman

8 October, 1915*

Dear Mr Redman,

I send herewith the long delayed volume.[1] I shall be glad to hear from you, when you have leisure and opportunity, any corrections or suggestions you may have to make . . .

I have two other petitions to make, which I will put in the forefront of this letter.

Can you get for me, from any of the gamekeepers or shepherds you meet, a sprig of *sphagnum moss*. I do not recognise any moss I know by that name. As a boy I used, in fishing, to traverse long stretches of moorland, but, of course, took more notice of flowering plants than of mosses.

The second request is that, if you have opportunity, you would find for me name, village, and regiment of the wounded Schoolmaster from Chelmsford district. The actual fact would go nicely into my local notes.

I do not know your part of the country, but Mrs Clark does. My own home is near Stirling; my hills are the Ochils. I often think of them, but do not now hope to see them again. Mrs Clark is in the grip of an incurable malady, which at times causes great pain. When not in pain she is very active.

My younger daughter has gone to the winter session at St Andrews University. She did extremely well there in the Summer Session.

I shall always be glad to hear from you . . .

Dr Smallwood called this afternoon: He had today a soldier who said his name was Windows, and that he had a pain. What could you expect—said the doctor—did you ever hear of a window without panes. He was surprized that the man did not seem to enjoy the joke. The doctors of Essex have presented the Red Cross Society with a fully-equipped motor-ambulance.

Saturday, 9 October. 5 p.m. report brought to the Rectory that J.

[1] This was Dr Clark's collection *Lincoln Diocese Documents, 1450–1544.*

Herbert Tritton had given notice to Ernest Taylor, his estate carpenter. He is 'fit for munition work'. It will be an unhappy parish when all the good men are driven out of it.

Monday, 11 October. This morning's post brought a letter from my daughter, Mildred, dated 9 October, 1915: 'I travelled up last night with three soldiers . . . Quite a boy was hobbling painfully along the platform on two sticks. I said what a pathetic sight it was. "Indeed it is, Miss" said one of the Tommies, "he went a route-march in a new pair of boots and can't walk for blistered heels" so he told me!!!'

7 p.m. in Church School—monthly meeting of Special Constables. Major Brown said that at Chelmsford they had got together a number of extra-Special-Constables, for the purpose of warning the inhabitants that Zeppelins were on hand. These 'extra-specials' are to have long poles, with pads on the end, to reach up to rap upon upper-storey windows. Major Brown justly says that this is utter folly, because the first action of every sleeper so aroused will be to light gas or candle, and every street will be alight in a moment.

Wednesday, 13 October. 9.20 p.m. a Zeppelin scare in the Great Road part of the village. A Zeppelin was reported to have just flown from over the Rectory. It was heard but not seen. It quenched the lights in all the cottages and brought the inhabitants out to stop bicyclists and make them turn their lamps low to prevent their lights (adapting Otterbourne ballad)[1]

> let any flying mortal ken
> that a stragglin' town lies here.

In all probability it was one of our own aeroplanes from Chelmsford.

Thursday, 14 October. Police-Constable Cole said today that the report was that the Zeppelins were supposed to be making for Buckingham Palace. It is said in Chelmsford that from the beginning of the War the King and Queen have not regularly spent the night at Buckingham Palace, but slipt off to one of their London friends. The roof of the Palace is now protected by sand-bags.

---

[1] *The Battle of Otterbourne* is one of the earliest English ballads. It is based on an attack on Otterburn Castle in Northumberland in 1388 by Scottish raiders returning to Scotland.

Another village opinion: Those Zeppelins don't know their business. Why don't they drop their bombs on Parliament—when the MPs are there? A lot of them could be spared.

Sunday, 17 October. Mr C. Wroot, butcher, Little Waltham, is positive that on Wedn. evening a Zeppelin passed directly over *his* house. But when he went his rounds on Thursd. and Frid. he found, within a radius of three and a half miles, every house claimed that the Zeppelin passed over *it*.

Monday, 18 October. Mr F. J. Lowden (manager of Downing & Co., Wine Merchants, Braintree) called at 11 a.m. He had 'Sherwood Foresters' billeted on him and has had letters from them at the front. The opinion among the soldiers is that only enough troops will be left in the trenches to contain the Germans and that the bulk of our forces will be transferred to another theatre of war. Our line is now so strongly entrenched that it will be as hard for the Germans to pierce through it and get to Calais as it will be for us to pierce through to Berlin.

11 p.m. went on Special Constable patrol. It is a brilliant moonlight, so distinct that I laid my notebook on the rail of the gate into the Weir pasture and wrote notes in it. My presence at the corner there seemed to disturb for a moment a pheasant roosting in one of the trees. It moved on its perch, shook the withering leaves, and gave forth a low call of alarm.

11.30 p.m. was joined by Mr James Caldwell. He told me that the Argyll and Sutherland Highlanders had found two of their men crucified, nailed to a tree. Since then they have naturally been in a fury, and it has been bayonet not quarter for Germans. Their wrath is well known among the other regiments who amuse themselves by inventing grim stories to set it forth.

Thursday, 21 October. The Chelmsford recruiting officers are wearying for Lord Derby to have done with his futile six weeks' attempt to bolster up volunteer recruiting. They go down to Hoffmann's Works at leaving-off hours and take stock of the hundreds of strong bodied young men who have sought jobs there to avoid enlisting. These men they long to swoop down upon.[1]

---

[1] The Earl of Derby, Secretary of State for War, was put in charge of a final attempt to increase voluntary enlistment and avoid conscription. Canvassers were appointed

About 11 a.m. yesterday the Great Road was filled from end to end with foot-soldiers. In the afternoon officers went to all the larger cottages and asked if they would make tea. The men paid 1*d*. a cup for tea and 1*d*. for bread and butter. This tea-providing went on from about noon to 5 p.m.

This afternoon a good many of the men were limping along, crippled with rheumatism from last night's damp. The villagers took them in; gave them tea; and sent them on.

Sunday, 24 October. I hear from Little Waltham that the Seabrook story is a fiction. —— Seabrook has left because he has let, or sold, his house.

Mr Jas. Caldwell also told me that opposite our lines in France, German soldiers have shown a disposition to come and give themselves up, even when no attack is intended on them. They seem in places to be without officers, reason unknown.

Monday, 25 October. 5 p.m. Major Wm. Brown called. He had been asked to find someone who would canvass for recruiting under Lord Derby's scheme. I said frankly that I would not—because (a) it would do no good, lads' 'backs had been set up' by being pestered by women canvassers, and by their friends being dismissed by employers; (b) it is quite contrary to my own opinions which are (i) that enough men have been taken off field work, leaving idle youths loafing about town; and (ii) that, at the beginning of the war, Government ought to have adopted some equable form of compulsory service. Mr Brown said that, in this district, there were more lads of military age who had not enlisted, than in most districts. He said also that more and more lads and young men are seeking shelter in munition work.

Friday, 29 October. 4.30 p.m. Dr R. P. Smallwood called. He says the officers [of the Oxon. and Bucks. Light Infantry] are at present investigating an occurrence at Great Baddow. One of the men was on sentry-go there at night and was shot through the left forearm. He said an enemy had done this. The officers suspected that he had done it himself. It is reported all over the country that men are inflicting

---

and were given access to the Parliamentary Recruiting Committee's *National Register*. Men in certain 'starred' occupations such as munitions work or mining, were excluded from the canvass.

wounds on themselves, from weak-minded desire of breaking the monotony of camp-life by having an exciting story to tell.

Tuesday, 2 November. 11 p.m. stopped my writing and got ready to go on Special Constable patrol. Stars, large and small, superbly bright. Orion and the Plough both very distinct. Other groups so resplendent that I bitterly regret having been so long indoors that I forget my boy's knowledge of their names, and of the names of the 'bright particular stars' in them.

Thursday, 4 November. As regards my hair-cutting a bit of village humour falls to be made note of. On Su. afternoon, 24 Oct., the Old Testament lesson was Daniel IV, in which is mention of Nebuchadnezzar's 'hair grows like eagles' feathers'. One censorious dame opined that the Rector must have dressed up to look like Nebuchadnezzar, his hair was so long and wild. Now, the criticism, but not the critic, is changed—'the rector has surely been in jail: he has all the look of a newly discharged convict, with the prison-cut.'

Mrs John Cousins, of Gate House farm, says her husband is mad to go out to the war; thinks it his duty. But she says there are two duties to be attended to first—his farm and five children.

Wednesday, 10 November. Harry Taylor, sergeant, is at home for this week. My wife thinks he looks ever so much older than when he went out [to the Dardanelles] several months ago. She has the same impressions of others who have been out and have been home on leave. He is anxious to get well and to be again on service.

Thursday, 11 November. Major W. Brown called. He told me it was the oddest of all things to see the ambition of men nowadays to be in uniform. When he himself as a young man joined the Yeomanry, his chapel relatives looked upon him as a reprobate, who had done something desperately wicked. The other day at Chelmsford he saw one of these people, 'a Pharisee and the son of a Pharisee', in VTC [Voluntary Training Corps] uniform, marching about as if slaughter was his honourable trade.

Miss Madge Gold said this afternoon that Little Waltham men of the 1/5 Essex Terrl., home on sick leave from the Dardanelles, say that the worst thing is the women snipers of the Turks, who are so carefully disguised and keep so still that they can hardly be discovered. When an aeroplane goes overhead, they keep still, but they cannot restrain their curiosity, and look up and the whites of their eyes betray them. One, who was shot, had about fifty identification disks, her arm loaded with watch bracelets, and four English soldier's postcards.

Saturday, 13 November. Mr James Caldwell called this evening. He said Lake & Elliot's new machinery was now in perfect operations and a great many young women were employed, making at least £1 a week. Many of them were of quite superior social class. He had talked with a foreman, who said the women-workers were doing splendidly. Lads were often selfishly thoughtless, and larked about. The women worked thoughtfully and steadily.

Mr Caldwell says that about a fortnight remains for Lord Derby's recruiting effort. Its success, in spite of open threats and pressure by employers amounting to compulsion, is doubtful. Its failure would give general satisfaction.

'Wybie' (schoolboy name of George S. Wiseman), a married man with children, has been dismissed by the Prudential Assurance Company, for which he has been a traveller for some years. The firm will employ no man of military age. Yet we have 'voluntary service'.

Wednesday, 17 November. 4.30 p.m. Dr R. P. Smallwood called: He brought me a slip with some notes of soldiers' talk. They have a variety of songs, which they sing among themselves to hymn tunes. It is very difficult to get the words of any, as they do not like letting outsiders know about them. He has however got the first verse of this parody of *Hymns Ancient & Modern* no. 331 (We are but little children meek)

> We are but little soldiers meek
> Who only earn eight bob a week
> The more we work the more we may
> It makes no difference to our pay.

The almost in-universal use is *na pooh*—apparently borrowed from French *il n'y a plus*—which applies to anything which is ended or non-existent. Of an acquaintance reported killed in action, a soldier will say 'Poor Bill's reported this morning to be na pooh', or 'I see he's gone na pooh.'

Sunday, 21 November. Miss Fowler, from Tettenhall, has a story of a Tettenhall seaman. He wrote home, describing the terrors of the sea,

when an enemy ship was firing on his ship, and a submarine popped up
to direct a torpedo at it. He then remembered a sermon of the vicar's
which told him 'when in trouble, to look up.' He looked up, and there,
hovering overhead, was a Zeppelin making ready to drop bombs.

Monday, 22 November. Miss E. Vaughan, of Rayne,[1] called: she is
under-housekeeper for the VAD hospital at Braintree: The operations
have been done with local anaethestics, and these have been very
successful. The men don't mind pain, and would rather have it than be
chloroformed or drugged. They occasionally ask Dr Young to extract
troublesome teeth, but won't have anything. An Irishman who
required to have a shot-wound re-opened refused any drug—but, if he
could have had it, would have liked 'a good sup of whisky'.

Essex people use the expression 'to make a hand of' in the sense 'to
kill'. This is an example: 'I do hope that poor fellow won't make a
hand of it', i.e. commit suicide. An old woman came to Miss Vaughan
the other day with a theological difficulty. The German airmen went
very near heaven, did they not? Miss Vaughan admitted that they
certainly flew very high in the sky. 'Well, then' the old woman went on,
'I wonder why, when God has them up there near heaven he doesn't
make a hand of them.'

Tuesday, 23 November. Mrs Fowke told an excellent story about
'war-widows' at Tettenhall. One came to the clergyman and begged
for money from the parish funds to provide her with mournings for her
husband who had been killed. He handed over the application to the
Ladies Committee. They were doubtful of the propriety and knew very
well that she had shewed the man no great affection. However as she
wept and wailed, they gave way. Shortly afterwards the husband
turned up on leave. The clergyman went to call, and she told him
'When I saw Bill come in at that door I was that angry with him that I
could have knocked him down.'

Saturday, 27 November. 3 p.m. J. Herbert Tritton called. He told me:

[1] Miss Eliza Vaughan, a local government rate collector, lived in the nearby village
of Rayne, then a separate village west of Braintree. Through her interest in Essex
history, her many contacts with local people and her work in the hospital, she would
become one of the Rector's most important sources. He affectionately referred to her
as 'Miss Eliza Vaughan, the suffragette of Rayne'.

that very shortly a great push is expected to be made along the whole France–Flanders front; Germany is feeling the pinch acutely, and that in the winter the masses of Germany will at last know what the war has meant; that the extension of German effort into the S.E. campaign is wholly in our favour; that for every shell fired by the Germans against our lines we are able to fire three; that many of the German shells do not explode, showing that there is insufficient supply of suitable material or skilled workmanship; the Banks in London are feeling the absence of their clerks and have had great recourse to women clerks. Barclay & Co., in their different branches, now employ about 250 and will by and by employ 500 more. At their head office in Lombard Street a whole floor is now set apart for them. They are now able to use the adding machines. Formerly, to work these required, at every line, a strong pull of a handle, beyond a woman's strength. Now the motive power is supplied by an electric current.

Monday, 29 November. I was told, on reliable authority, that the chief reason why more people in Great Leighs had not come forward as Special Constables was that they had been canvassed to do so by a lady. County men resent female canvassing. The same is true as to army recruiting.

4.30 p.m. Dr R. P. Smallwood called, with various war gossip: operations on the Western front seem suspended for six months. His cousin's letter arrived the other day—'I suppose you may think that I ought to have wonderful things to tell you about our doings. But this is how it stands. Once in six months we have a big battle and then I am so horribly frightened that I can't remember anything . . . Then for six months nothing takes place and I am bored to death.'

Tuesday, 30 November. Letter from 31, Hyde Park Gardens [from William R. Redman]:

29 November 1915

My Dear Sir,
    I am leaving Mrs Pickering on the first of January as she says she cannot keep men while the war is on and men wanted so badly for other things. So I must look out for something else to do. London is very dark and dreary now, not like London of two years ago. When will this dreadful war finish? It is too dreadful to think of. I sometimes think it will soon be over. The loss of life has been too terrible to think of . . .

30 November 1915*

Dear Mr Redman,

St Andrews day, day of my patron saint personally and by country, has brought me . . . your very kind letter, and the *sphagnum moss* which recalls the hills that I never hope to see again. So far as I can judge I must often have passed clumps of it on 'Maudie Moss,' an extensive moor high up in the hills, which we boys crossed several times each summer on our more distant fishing days or when we went to top of Ben Cleuch, the highest Ochil summit, with a view over half Scotland . . .

I am extremely sorry to hear that you are again unsettled. I personally think that everyone who can possibly do so should hold on as before. I do not think the war will continue long into next year. In my poor judgement it would not have continued so long as it has but for the incompetence of so many of our generals . . . Medical men and officers back from the Dardanelles speak very strongly about this. Two of the soldiers' sayings they bring back set it out—

(i) The Turks are stubborn fighters, but we could have beaten them off the field, except for the help they had from their allies the British fleet and the British War Office.

(ii) Turkish snipers are rewarded with sums rising from 2s.6d. for a private to 10s. for a colonel, but if a sniper wounds a general he is promptly shot for depriving the Turks of a valuable help supplied by the British War Office.

Certain victory, in some cases, seems to have been turned into murderous defeat by the navy shelling our troops when they were driving the Turks from place to place at the point of the bayonet . . .

Mrs Clark's illness gradually develops. We hope you will, as you have opportunity, let us know of your welfare . . .

Wednesday, 1 December. [Letter from Andrew Clark to Sergeant Harry Taylor.]*

1 December, 1915

My dear Harry,

I enclose your leaf, which will always show that you have been right up against the Turks.[1] . . .

Mr Arnold's men are ploughing the glebe field on west side of Weir pasture. When I looked out yesterday morning, I thought at first glance that there had been snow in the night. It was an immense flight of sea-gulls—bigger than any I have hitherto seen here—feeding in the new ploughed land.[2]

[1] The leaf was really two leaves from a book of Turkish Army regulations which Sergeant Taylor had picked up at Gallipoli and given to the Rector for identification. Dr Clark had sent it to a friend in Oxford who read Turkish.

[2] The enormous bombardments along the Western Front caused a great displacement of coastal bird life in Belgium and France. Many birds sought refuge in England.

Both Monday night and last night were very rough nights of wind and rain. On both nights I was on patrol duty—but as I have had a sharp bronchitis I cut outdoor watching short and left the guarding of the lanes to mud and wintry weather and pitch-darkness. My deputies were quite efficient. The peace of the parish and the safety of the nation have not suffered . . .

Friday, 3 December. [Letter from Andrew Clark to William R. Redman.]*

3 December, 1915

Dear Mr Redman,

You will be pleased to know about the use I have made of the sphagnum packet.

There is a very nice Red Cross hospital in Braintree, in a wing of the Workhouse which has been granted for that purpose. It has had its full number of twenty-five patients, but, at present, has sixteen only. It has been very successful, having a very skilful surgeon, Dr Young of Braintree, and a good many patients have left, cured. The cases have been all shot-wounds (rifle or shrapnel) in the limbs, face, neck . . .

I sent part of the moss to an old friend, part I preserved to be sent to Oxford [in the Diary], with my clippings from *The Scotsman* about its use as a surgical dressing. The bulk I sent to Dr Young, on the chance that he might care to see it. He is delighted with it; has often wished to see it, on account of what he has read about it in medical journals. He will keep it carefully, because it seems admirable for dressing of particular wounds, and when he gets a suitable case will try it . . .

Mrs. Clark yesterday and to-day has been in much pain . . .

Sunday, 5 December. The military authorities had asked that no more sand-bags should be sent, but Mrs Batchford's grandson at the front said more were needed, and she had more respect for his opinion than for the War Office. Miss Annette Tritton has lengthened her list on the Church door, of men in service: Leonard Cook, Essex Yeomanry; Thomas Sargeant, Royal Flying Corps; Harry Sargeant, Rifle Brigade.

4 p.m. bugles blowing at Terling. Major Brown's bullocks were being let out from the yard to drink. The bugler stirred the soul of one bullock to emulation, and it proceeded to proclaim to the world that it could, with the musical instrument nature had given it, bellow louder and longer than any instrument of brass.

Monday, 6 December. 7 p.m. monthly meeting of Special Constables. On my way to it, I had to wade ancle-deep, in a muddy river, from the

Rectory gate to the School gate. Major W. Brown said that much against his will he had had to undertake the recruiting duty for Lord Derby's Committee. It was 'the most unpleasant job he ever took on, to recruit your neighbours' sons, your neighbours' men, your own men; but no one else would touch it.' Not a single married man had expressed willingness to serve. Five unmarried men had assented. The Committee wired to him asking him to collect the lot and motor them over to Chelmsford. Now it was arranged that the Recruiting Officer and the Doctor [Dr Smallwood] will attend in Great Leighs. No one hates conscription more, but he would like to see conscription for the purpose of roping in some of those who refuse to serve. There are several such in Great Leighs.

The general impression of the meeting seemed to be that Lord Derby's scheme would prove a failure, and that the Government would be compelled to resort to the Militia ballot, or other form of compulsory service.[1]

Today I made good progress with various portions of my writing. I finished the two papers on Enclosure of Common, with special reference to Great Leighs, and they have gone to the *Essex Review*. I have all but finished *Barnstone Notes 1641–1649*, and hope to send them tomorrow to *Essex Review*. I have also brought up to date and inserted in their places clippings for *English Words in Wartime* and for the 1915 advertisement bundles which have been in arrears for some time.

Thursday, 9 December. At the Council School last night, 6.30 p.m., only *four* are said to have turned up. Albert Wright, son of Geo. Wright, and brother of Herbert G. Wright, was one. Albert Wright is horseman at Bishop's Hall, and a very reliable member of Great Leighs choir.

I have this morning at first hand, what I believe to be a perfectly true story about the care taken by army doctors. Friday was a very terrible evening of cold and wet. Mr Hagger, manager of the Rayleigh Arms at Terling, saw a private fall, like a trunk, just outside that house. He had him carried in. The man appeared to be dead. A message was sent to the army-doctor but he positively refused to turn out. The Rayleigh

---

[1] Conscription would finally be adopted in January 1916 but the Act would apply only to unmarried men between the ages of eighteen and forty-one. In May 1916 a second Act would include married men. In neither Act was Ireland included.

Arms people did the best they could. The man a day or two later said that he was feeling very unwell and did not attend to parade. The officer sent such an imperative message that he went: was awarded four days CB (confinement to barracks) and on his way back, collapsed, heart trouble. When his billet was discovered, four comrades were found to take him to it in a hand-cart. The army-doctor called next day and said that, except for the prompt treatment he had had in the Rayleigh Arms the man would have died. All these things are perfectly well known in the district, and, of course, immensely help recruiting!

Today I have been feeling far from well, though not as ill as yesterday.

Friday, 10 December. I am told that two lads (Charlie Rayner, son of the tenant at Lowleys); and Fred Mansfield (brother of the foreman at Rochesters) and one Little Leighs lad (Jim Lewin, drives bread-cart for Fred Mann, baker) have gone into Chelmsford today to enlist.

Saturday, 11 December. There has been a great turn-up in the village yesterday and today. Some of the farmers certainly had notice to send all their men to be medically inspected as for service.

6.30 p.m. Mr Caldwell called: Mr Joseph Smith's men at Long's Farm were told by their master that he could advise them neither one way nor the other. They could discuss the matter among themselves, or take Mr Caldwell's advice. They came in a body to Mr Caldwell. He advised them to go. If they were called out, their master would be able to say whether they could be spared or not. If they did not put down their names now, it was doubtful whether, if they were called upon, there would be any possibility of appeal. Similar advice seems to have been given by most farmers, and the consequence has been a great rush of men to the recruiting offices. This is not voluntary recruiting, but compulsion in a dishonest form. The officer who attended at the council school on Wedn. evening this week said that, if men hung back, they would be hauled out with a rope round their neck. This is voluntary enlistment!

Albert Wright was passed on Wednesday. He is head horseman for Major Wm. Brown. Major Brown said he could not be spared, unless the farm was to be stopped.

Sunday, 12 December. Of the Great Leighs men: Jim Turner has not passed the doctor; Charlie Rayner and Fred Mansfield have passed.

Monday, 13 December. Bill Duke (choirman) and George Ketley (who both work at Lyons Hall) were sent back as medically unfit from recruiting offices. Recruiting in Great Leighs has been much better of late. Report in village that Reggie Ward has frozen feet. He has been out only about three weeks.

Tuesday, 14 December. At the Mothers' Meeting this afternoon it was reported that A. Wyld is under order to go to France in New Year week. He pointed out that his right arm is still withered and that he would not be able to shoot. The army doctor's brutal answer was 'Well, if you can't shoot, you can stop a bullet.' The men feel the going out the second time much more than they did the first time, because they know what it means.

Saturday, 18 December. Chas. H. Ward, my man, says that, after the battle of Loos, the *Daily Mirror* published a picture of a girl, found in the pocket of a wounded soldier, who had lost his memory, and whose identification disc had been lost, in the hope that his relations might see it. The lad's father (who is Chas. Ward's uncle) recognised the picture to be that of his daughter, which his son had taken with him. He wrote to the *Daily Mirror* and the lad was traced to Notley Hospital, where he still lies, having never recovered his memory.

Friday, 24 December. Miss Taylor says that her brother, Sergt. Harry Taylor, is to be married at Norwich on 28 or 29 December. He is very anxious to have one of his brothers present. My daughters have volunteered to take the letters round that day, and clear the boxes, to set Albert Taylor free.

Saturday, 25 December. 11 a.m. much larger congregation than could have been expected. Choir of men only, women absent: singing of psalms and canticles very bad. 12.20 p.m., towards end of service sun broke through and candle-light became superfluous.

2.30 p.m. the cock-pheasant is very gravely feeding in the shelter of the laurel bushes which shield him from direct impact of wind and rain. Afternoon so dark that even by big study window, I can hardly see to write. The mildness of the season is shown by the return of big house-flies on the study window-panes.

Sunday, 26 December. Edward Bearman of Fuller Street has had Christmas week and was in Church this morning.

The 'Derby armlet' was in evidence today. It is a band of dark khaki cloth, about four inches wide, with a red crown on it. Arthur Thos. Stoddart had it on in Church. I passed, on my way back from morning service, a lad, bicycling with it. It is for men who have been 'attested' for service.

Monday, 27 December. Various St Andrews' notes told me today by my daughter: Miss Thomson is another woman student at St Andrews. Her brother is in the 137th Brigade. The brigade has seen circular letters distributed broadcast in England by a man who is trying to raise money to build a 'chapel-of-ease' for the brigade near their Headquarters, just behind the lines. They are considerably annoyed at this, because it threatens to upset their deep-laid plans of building a cinema. They are approaching the necessary amount but they are afraid that if 'that fool' gets in first with his 'tin tabernacle' they will be forbidden to erect their cinema.

Tuesday, 28 December. 12.15 a.m. I have not been in so violent a wind since I stood on the brae-head by my grandfather's house at Lower Mains, Dollar, Clackmannanshire, on the night when the first Tay Bridge was blown down.[1]

The corporal of the Great Leighs Special Constables (Mr James Caldwell) who was due to take me out has not come, having judged wisely that the 'great shoulders of the hurricane' are sufficient guard against invasion by air or sea tonight.

The officers of the soldiers now quartered in Braintree are referred to in very contemptuous terms by passers-by—'miserable little bounders', 'disreputable looking beasts', and so on.

Fragment of a theological discussion heard in Bishop's Hall farm-yard, between two of the hands: Albert Wright (who has been 'converted') 'There is nothing my God cannot do.' His 'unconverted' mate—'Yes, there is. He can't make an uphill without making a downhill.'

Wednesday, 29 December. 8.15 a.m. my daughters brought the letters for the morning post. Sergeant Harry Taylor came home to the Post

---

[1] The first Tay Bridge collapsed on the last Sunday of 1879. The disaster, in which ninety people were killed, is now best remembered in William McGonagall's immortal poem, 'The Tay Bridge Disaster'.

Office last night. This morning he left, to be married at Norwich, and was accompanied by his sister (Minnie Taylor) and his brother (Albert Taylor—our morning postman). The old father thought it was too far for 'the young ladies' to go the whole round, so he took his staff and went the Little Leighs portion.

This morning's post brought a postcard from Ernest Suckling, wounded and taken prisoner in the battle of Mons, to whom the villagers send out almost weekly parcels of comforts and food:

2 November 1915

Dear Madam just a P.C. to let you know I am quite Well and was very pleaced with the food you Sent out to me I am so Glad to Say that some One thinks of me. And I whish you all a happy Christmas. & a Prosper New Year. From Yours Truly . . .

Thursday, 30 December. 8.15 a.m. my two daughters brought round the morning-post. Sergt. Harry Taylor having served a year beyond his time has got leave of absence for a month.

Jim Ketley, Railway Stables, Chelmsford, has packed between twenty and thirty tons of vegetables for the fleet since 6 July. There are other depots in Chelmsford. Chelmsford has sent in the second largest supplies of any town, being outstripped only by Glasgow. So Jim Ketley says.

Friday, 31 December. 2.45 a.m. a loud concerto of cats, just outside. I have heard no caterwauling equal to it since I was a boy at Dollar. The wind is, and has been, blowing a gale from S.W.

4 p.m. Dr Smallwood called. He says one of the jests of the district is connected with maiden ladies of the name Green, members of the banking family long established at Colchester. They live near the Marconi works at Chelmsford which are believed to be a special object of Zeppelin raids. When they retire to rest each night they hang on their bed head a greatcoat and a small bag. In the bag are their jewels, a little money, some hairpins and other toilet requisites. So that they are prepared for flight to some place of safety in case of bomb dropping.

December, 1915.

In 1915 the Income Tax officials distributed their demand notes by hand-messenger. This charge of 2s., for profit of authorship is made on a small royalty [£1.7s.0d.] from the University Press, Oxford, in respect of my edition of John Aubrey's *Brief Lives*, and is therefore of the nature of a government fine for doing some work for English letters.[1]

[1] The rate at which the Rector's work for English letters was fined was 9d. in the pound as his earned income was under £2,000.

1916

Saturday, 1 January. 12.5 a.m. my daughters, who had sat up to welcome in the New Year, came to wish me a Happy New Year.

Mr Jas. Caldwell called—very bright and informative: It is now quite certain that compulsory military service will be adopted. The *Daily News* and the *Star*, owned by the same people, are futilely raging against it. They represent the labour party, the members of which are not in the least concerned that the young men of the country should be exposed to the perils of war, but are terribly afraid that after the war their own power for mischief should be annulled.

It is positively disgraceful to see the crowds of men of twenty-five or so who sit all day in cafés in London, sipping coffee, smoking cigarettes and playing dominoes. Mr Caldwell took refuge from a shower this week one day in 'The Mecca' Cheapside: found it full of such men—and not an armlet to be seen among them, though he slipped round the room looking for them.

One of the first compulsory acts will be to bring under necessity of going where they are sent battalions embodied 'for home service only'. Such battalions have been forbidden for some time to accept any fresh members.

Monday, 3 January. At the end of the [Special Constables'] meeting there was desultory conversation: Lighting-up orders are issued to take effect from Sat. 10 Jan.—(i) lights on vehicles are required to be shown after half an hour after sunset. (ii) all vehicles—including bicycles, perambulators must show red rear-light and headlight. This headlight is not to be clearly seen—but is to be shaded by whitewash or tissue paper. Special danger is occasioned by the use of flash-lights. They are now common, every Tommy, every agricultural young labourer, every schoolboy has one. They are sold for 1s. each, the manufacturers reckoning on their profit out of the refills. The men and boys are continually flashing these lights, on the road-way, on the foot-paths, on the ditches, so that people driving carriage or motor or riding bicycle are hopelessly confused and in constant danger.

In the course of some talk as to the probable duration of the war (i) Major Brown said there was no prospect of it ending for a long time yet, since Germany would have to be utterly crushed before she would accept the terms likely to be imposed; (ii) Major Caldwell said he heard in military circles in London that the official date for the end of the war was Sept. 1917.

Tuesday, 4 January. I forgot to enter: Mr Caldwell says that in spite of their raving against compulsory service, the *Daily News* and the *Star* have doubled their circulation at the cost of the *Daily Mail* and the *Evening News* since the attack of these latter against Lord Kitchener. In railway compartments, if a *Daily Mail* or an *Evening News* is brought in, the company seize it, tear it in fragments and throw it out at the window.

Another note of Major Caldwell's: feeling in London is very strong in condemnation of the Government Press censorship. The Government is treating the people of Great Britain as if they were incompetent children. Events are forbidden to be published which are days old in the columns of every Continental newspaper. Solemn pretence of official secrecy is made of matters which are published, in full details, in every German newspaper.

Friday, 7 January. The village gossips are much exercised over the Government's exhortations to practise economy, addressed to a village like this where no one has ever done anything else and where there is no increase of money received, since no one has war-work, and appeals to invest money in the war-funds, where no one has any reserve either to give or to invest. They have an instance in point, if extravagance is sinful (as the Government says) why did Mr Asquith not check it in the case of his daughter's marriage.[1] If the national funds are in such need as the Government says, why doesn't Mr Asquith sacrifice a tenth of his large income, and other members of the Government likewise, to the national need?

Saturday, 15 January. A report is current in these parts that one of the

[1] Asquith's elder daughter, Violet, had married his private secretary, Maurice Bonham-Carter, in November 1915 at St Margaret's, Westminster. The wedding was a great Society event and was much criticized at the time.

Kaiser's sons is a prisoner in the Tower and has been for some time.

5.30 p.m. Miss Edith Caldwell called. She brought the envelope [stamped 'opened by Censor'] of a letter (undated but one day this week) from my daughter Mildred: Major Caldwell says this is the first instance he has seen of a letter being opened by the censor, posted in this country to a home address. Possibly some fleet-movement is in design, or execution, to account for this new departure. (Two of his own letters have been censored, but they came from USA.)

Tuesday, 18 January. Our sister-in-law, Mrs May (*née* Cole) Paterson, widow of Thos. Arnold Paterson, grain merchant, Liverpool, left this morning after a short visit. Her brother, Godfrey Cole, is a merchant's clerk in Liverpool; Godfrey's sister-in-law, 'Birdie' Gripper, is a trained nurse. She was at Brussels, nursing Belgian wounded, when the Germans took the city. They kept her there to nurse the German wounded. In this hospital there were 1,000 German soldiers. She was the only woman and the only English person. Wherever she was, even on hospital duty, a sentry with fixed bayonet was stationed beside her. One day the *Kommandant* sent for her. She was taken, under charge of the sentry, into a court-yard where 500 German troops were drawn up. Whenever an officer spoke to her, the sentry levelled his bayonet and kept the point between her shoulders. The *Kommandant* said, 'You are a woman of intelligence and therefore I should like to tell you what I think of your country.' He kept her standing for full half an hour, while he abused England. That day she had a revolver in her pocket, and she slipped her hand under her apron, grasped the handle, and thought of shooting the brute. But she kept her self-control. She learned afterwards that if it had been known she had a revolver she would have been shot at once.

One night a sergeant told her she was to move her quarters, and sleep in a shed outside the hospital: 'Wounded German officers are coming to the hospital; *Kommandant* will not be responsible for your life. Iron doors would not keep them from murdering you, if they heard that any English person was in the building.'

Then the Germans determined to turn out of Brussels all foreign nurses. They were packed like sardines into a third-class carriage and two armed sentries were posted in it, with orders to shoot down without compunction any one of them who tried to pull up a blind and look out even for a minute. They were told that the journey would last for twenty-four hours, and had rations issued to them for twenty-four hours. The journey lasted forty-eight hours, and they were not allowed to buy coffee or even water on the route. They got so cramped that they took turns to lie on the floor to relieve the strain on the muscles.

The train took them to Copenhagen, where they were kindly received. Thence Miss Gripper went to Russia, and there nursed Russian wounded. The wounds were simply dreadful, but the soldiers were like patient dogs. She asked why is it these wounds are so bad? She was told that the reason was that if soldiers of any other nation had received such wounds they would have died on the field. But the Russians are hardy beyond other nations.

She was told also by one of the nurses in the hospital this incident. One night this nurse thought she heard someone crawling stealthily along the floor of the ward. She took her light and found a Russian soldier who had slipped out of bed and was creeping along the floor. She asked 'What are you going to do?' He explained that there were two German soldiers 'over there'. 'Well, what of that?' she asked. 'I am going to put their eyes out.' 'Oh, you must not do that!' 'Oh yes' was his whispered answer—'That would be a good thing, for then they would not fight us any more.' With some difficulty she persuaded him that such action was strictly forbidden and that he must go back to bed.

I was told this afternoon that Mrs Frank Cloughton, the Lyons Hall shepherd's wife, is the only person in this parish who now 'drops a curtsey'. Done as she does it, it is a very sweet and graceful action.

Wednesday, 19 January. 4.20 p.m. slight shower has begun—wetting because driven before the gale. The cock-pheasant, who finds the Rectory grounds a refuge, has succeeded in eluding all the shooting parties which have been out seeking his life, and just now was calmly walking about and feeding just outside my study window, undisturbed by my presence there writing.

Saturday, 22 January. 6.45 p.m. Major James Caldwell called with a budget of war and other gossip: The question of munitions is a very grave one. The waste at the front is so great, that the supply cannot be kept up. Purchases from America are taking all the money out of the country. Much cartridge-making plant and many factories have been built, but there are no people to work in them. Meanwhile Germany is piling up enormous reserves of cartridges.

Sunday, 23 January. 12.30 p.m. two strapping young fellows, outsiders (i.e. not of Great Leighs) obviously poachers, with two lurchers, came past church gate (as people were coming out) and turned up the field path towards Fuller Street, waiting half-way up the slope of the path till everyone had gone away, probably to begin then their 'sport'.

7.30 p.m. coming out of the Mission Room service I found it so dark that I could not see the step at the railing, into the road, but stumbled down it. Soon afterwards I found myself in the grass by the roadside and had to shuffle with my feet to find the road again. Here a young fellow (Albert Wright by his voice, because I could see neither his face, nor his form) offered me his hand, and brought me to the Rectory gate. Albert Wright thought it would rain in the night because 'the stars looked very sickly', which is a bad sign.

Monday, 24 January. 1 p.m. Miss Eliza Vaughan called. She is on the staff of the VAD hospital, Braintree: Some of the patients are Scots or at least of Scots Regiments. Miss Vaughan told us a hospital story, of a man who was brought in unconscious. When he came to himself he found himself in bandages, head and foot. She explained that he had a vinegar head-swathe because of his fever; a mustard-plaster on his chest because of his lungs; and salt bags on his feet because of frostbite. 'Then, Miss, I think you ought to bring some pepper, and I'll be the complete cruet.'

Wednesday, 26 January. Passed bridge at Church on way to Chelmsford, 9.20 a.m. At the Railway Stables, W. Ketley who was packing vegetables for the fleet, told a long story about his youngest son. He was some time ago invalided from the front (rheumatism); had passed his last examination by the doctors, and had leave to go home prior to going out. His wife was putting on her cap to go to London to see him off. His young boy took up his father's rifle, which went off and went through the soldier's foot. (One toe had to be amputated.) W. Ketley told this in all good faith, without any distant suspicion that it might be interpreted. How did a live cartridge (entirely contrary to orders) happen to be in the rifle? Army doctors say that a great many slight wounds are self-inflicted to escape service.

Sunday, 30 January. 2 p.m. J. Herbert Tritton called: he is serving on the Commission of Appeals in regard of the Treasury's claim from manufacturing firms of half their additional profits earned through the war. His youngest daughter, Olive, goes this week to take charge of the canteen at Erith. At Erith there are very great munition-works. It will be generations before this country recovers from the straits to which it will be reduced by the war. Most burdensome taxes will be imposed; and all people who have money will have it taken from them by the Government exactions. This country, not so long ago, was too rich. The people who had big works were very satisfied with what was being brought in, and made no effort to extend their connections, with the result that Germany stepped in and snapped up everything which had been firmly secured by other nations. After the war the burden of taxation, both in this country and in Germany, will make everything dear; and the chance is that USA, having no such burdens, will secure all the markets of the world.

Monday, 31 January. An odd thing happened at 7.30 p.m. As the Special Constables were on the steps outside the School, just leaving the meeting, there was a succession of dull, but sudden reports, following each other quickly, in the N.W. Twice or thrice, a distant flash was seen faintly. The reports were not continuous enough for thunder; nor sharp enough for cannon. Mr Port, who had heard the sound of the bombs dropped at Chelmsford, said these reports were the same.

   This started a general talk as to recent raids, apparently well-known privately, but which have not been alluded to in the papers. Major Caldwell said that it was absurd to conceal the places where air raids had taken place. The Germans knew all about them. There was not a little village in England that had not an agent in it, making reports to a central German office in London. The London police had for months been searching for this in vain. Thence they were 'coded' 'to the other side'. Major Brown said he agreed entirely with this; and also that the village agents were not Germans but English.

Wednesday, 2 February. 8.45 a.m. morning's post brought me a letter from my daughter, Mildred, 30:1:1916—'. . . Miss Beattie in her duties as censor in Danish at the War Office has discovered two spies. A St Andrews lady travelling to Newcastle was suspicious about a man in her carriage. Wired to York giving the name of the carriage—heard nothing till 6 months later she got a cheque for £100 from the War Office "for information received".'

This morning's paper contained no definite information about the air raid and no allusion to their having been over Essex [on 31 January]. There is a great simmering of discontent and alarm among the villagers. They are convinced that they ought to know just what happened, and fear that a very grave disaster is being concealed.

Friday, 4 February. 9.45 a.m. Morning's post brought a letter from S. J. Willis, formerly driver of Mrs Jas. Jennings (of The Victoria, Great Leighs) carrier's cart—which brought me from Braintree Station and took back the big case with Jesus College, Oxford, buttery-books:

30 January 1916

To Dr. A. Clark,
Dear Sir,
Just a few lines as promised trusting they will reach you am pleased to say that I am well and in the best of spirits we have just had our turn in the trenches and out for a few days rest, the last day and night we were in the shell fire was very heavy, I was with a party carrying bombs up to the bombers in the front line and I must say were favoured with the best of luck as the shells were falling around us some only a few yards away, . . . must now tell you the scenery is very pretty in some parts back from the firing line all hills and dales, you can see for miles around the women and children are all workers on their own farms they thresh the corn out here by horse power it must be very trying for it, as it is standing on a sloping stair case . . . we are back from the line billeted in a barn which is in good repair it was a treat to have a good bath and change of linen will now conclude trusting you Mrs and the Miss Clarks are well with kind regards to all . . .

Saturday, 5 February. 8.45 a.m. morning's post brought a postcard from my *quondam* vacation pupil, Godfrey G. Barker, gone from France to his own regiment in India: 'Have arrived at last after a long sea voyage. Will write you by next mail. I hope you are all well. This is a weird country.'

Tuesday, 8 February. Frank Cloughton is in hospital, with 'a little animal that burrows under the skin'. He was better, but has been taken ill again.

Miss Gee [in Felsted parish] is a great chapel-woman; the chief speaker at the Mother's Meeting in the Mission Room and is a great setter-forth of wonderful 'perfectly-true' stories of the 'conversion', 'temperance', 'gospel', 'spiritual experience' type. This afternoon she had a minutely-told 'perfectly true' story. It was rather vague: thought it was Waterloo Station, but was not sure. A train was going off, taking soldiers to the front. It was in broad daylight. A lady stepped back, as people do under this circumstance. In so doing, she trod on an officer's toe. He (an officer, mind you!) swore softly, and swore *in German*. By sudden inspiration, she dashed to the barrier and told the porter in charge: 'There's a German spy masquerading as an English officer.' So when he presented himself to pass out, he was seized. The lady heard no more about it until three weeks afterwards, and then she had a cheque for £100 from the War Office. I said nothing about this story. I have my doubts whether War Office cheques for £100 fly about exactly in this way although (no doubt) public money is poured forth like ditch-water. And also, the same fable, adapted to the latitude of St Andrews, had been entered by me in these notes on Wedn. 2 Febr. 1916.

This evening, Mr Joseph Smith said that, at Lord Rayleigh's farm, Little Baddow Hall, fifteen women are being trained in farm work.

Wednesday, 9 February. Mrs H. J. Hicks, Supply Stores, frequently sends out a parcel to Ernest Suckling, a prisoner-of-war, and a chum of his in the same prison. Today the parcel is to consist of—two quartern loaves of bread (baked extra long so as to keep), tinned milk, tea, cocoa, cigarettes, tobacco, cigarette-paper, matches, and (whichever will go most conveniently into the parcel) butter or jam.

Wednesday, 16 February. Olive Tritton says that the raiders on 31 Jan. 1916 came within three miles of Woolwich. O. T. and others were serving 350 girls and women-workers in the canteen, when the lights were all turned out. They lit candles, and sat and sang—a few only sobbed and shrieked. They went back to work, but a new alarm was given, and they were sent back to the canteen. That night the sentries had orders to shoot any suspicious person prowling about.

Saturday, 19 February. Lizzie Oddey's report to Mrs Clark of village opinion as to the calling out of the Derby groups: They say that if the married men are taken out before the young ones there will be a civil war in England, but, please mum!, I don't know what that means.

Tuesday, 22 February. Mr George Wright has only yesterday received definite news of the death of his son Herbert ('Hubby') who has been 'missing' since the 'charge' of the Essex Yeomanry. A comrade, who was in the action, was wounded at the same time and says that Herbert Wright died of wounds the day after the action. He, himself, has been so ill, that it is only now that he is able to write.

Wednesday, 23 February. 9 a.m. Morning's post late by reason of snow. Delivered a letter to my man—Charles Henry Ward to appear 6 March [to 'join for service with the Colours' under provision of the 1916 Military Service Act].

Saturday, 26 February. The village talk this morning is of the lads who have been called out. Walter Childs and Hugh Joslin have obtained postponement. Arthur Clark, —— Clark (his brother), William Hales must report themselves next Saturday.

There is a talk that Courtaulds at Braintree would be subject to a penalty of £40 for each of their men who held back, and each of such men subject personally to a penalty of £20.

Sunday, 27 February. I had written to the Recruiting Office, Chelmsford, asking notice of holding of Tribunal to ask exemption or postponement of service of my lad, Charles Henry Ward. I had by this post very courteous letters in answer. C. H. W. is a very useful lad, in this house—where everything has to be done by hand—water pumped from a deep well, drains flushed weekly, as well as the garden tilled and the pony attended to. The place cannot do without a man. On the other hand he has not stamina for service. To take him out in wet would be to send him to hospital with chest trouble, and I do not imagine that recruiting is intended to provide inmates of hospitals.

The Rectory housemaid's two brothers are called out. The mother is an invalid and is in a great way over their going. With the usual *penchant* for the horrible, and the usual proneness to exaggeration, soldiers on leave have made most harrowing descriptions of their horrible experiences, to excite sympathy and to gain notoriety. Hardly one in twenty has been either reticent or at all cheerful at the prospect of going out again. This talk has badly frightened the women-folk.

The Official Bulletin as exhibited at Great Leighs Post Office on Sunday 27 Feb. 1916, with a great show of fulness contrives in its habitual and offensive 'Official' way, to have not a word of assurance that all was well with the *British* forces, although it is scanned in villages by anxious relatives.

Tuesday, 29 February. 3 p.m. Mrs W. Brown, Bishop's Hall, came to say that she had started to go to the Mothers' Meeting in the Mission Room, but the road was a river. She knew I was due to lecture this evening and gave me warning that I need not attempt to get there.

4.30 p.m. I went down to the road to see what it was like. I found a river. It will be a ticklish job, carrying the big school map of Europe for my lecture, and the candle-lantern to keep me out of the Scyllas and Charybdises which hem the road. These streams make a roaring like a big motor-lorry in bad working order.

Now I must tell my 'Odyssey'. I was due this evening at the Mission Room at 7 p.m. to give a lecture on the Homeric story of Odysseus. At 6.45 p.m. when I started, there was a strong wind from N.E., driving a small rain before it, and the night was very dark—but I sallied forth, great school map of Europe rolled up under my left arm, to follow the wanderings over the Mediterranean, lantern in right hand. At the Rectory gate I found Ernest W. Wright coming in to warn me to turn back. I told him I felt bound to be at the Room in case people came from the other end of the parish. I made my way till I came to the floods; the less deep part of these I waded; the deeper parts I escaped by jumping from ancient road-sweepings heap to ditto. So I got as far as the Mission Room. This was in darkness. The reason was not difficult to discover. Poor old Sam Childs, caretaker, coming down the path from his cottage in the field had found himself cut off by a flood. I went on the downhill path as far as the alms houses and found the flood there sufficient to make it certain that no one would come up the road from Church side. So I returned, wading, jumping, thinking of an adaption of Robert Burns' lines—'the last o't, the wars't o't, is only but to' *wade.*

Friday, 3 March. 4.45 p.m. Dr Smallwood called. He says he has just talked with a Berkshire officer. This man told him about the names of the shells—(i) the *pip-squeak* and the *whizz-bang* are two names for the same thing, and describe the explosion of the smallest shell—the 77 millimetre shell; (ii) Little Willie is the next largest; (iii) White Hope is a size larger still; (iv) Jack Johnson is bigger still.[1]

[1] 'Little Willie' was in honour of Crown Prince Wilhelm of Germany, a much hated figure; 'White Hope' and 'Jack Johnson' refer to the proposed 1911 heavyweight match between 'Bombadier Wells', the 'White Hope' and Jack Johnson, the controversial Texas-born world champion. Johnson was the first coloured boxer to hold the title. The match, scheduled for Earls Court, was called off.

Sunday, 5 March. 10.40 a.m. Major Jas. Caldwell told me that the Government, for one reason or other, has concluded that the long projected German attack was about to be launched against Essex or Suffolk. Whereupon it had whirled off the badly trained and imperfectly equipped South Midland Division to Salisbury Plain and had replaced them by a thoroughly trained Division (the Lowland Division). This Division has with it some very powerful field-guns. It is these guns which explain the extremely violent thuds of gun-discharges which I have been noting for some days.

Monday, 6 March. 3.40 p.m. Miss Ethel Wright called about her brother, Herbert George Wright. Her father had received an envelope containing a white folio printed sheet with reference to 1656, Pte. Wright, Herbert G., 1/1 Essex Yeomanry who had not been heard of since 14.5.15 and is now assumed to have died on 14.5.15 or soon after and that his relatives should claim his effects according to the form which would be sent.

Enclosed was a printed slip with lithographed signature: 'The King commands me to assure you of the true sympathy of his majesty and the Queen in your sorrow. Kitchener.'

Miss Ethel Wright said that the singular thing was that the same post which brought the official presumption-of-death certificate brought also a letter from the only friend her brother had made in the Yeomanry. In this letter he said that he was certain that Herbert Wright was a prisoner in Germany. Herbert's fiancée, Ruth Fuller (formerly housemaid here at the Rectory; now in London) had been to see them. Her people live in Felsted—and at Felsted she had seen a letter from a man who said he knew for a certainty of one officer and some men of his unit who were prisoners in Germany and not one of them had been allowed to write home.

The Bench of Bishops seems lost to any sense of manly or true feeling [in issuing a call for a National Mission] and enslaved to the whine and insincerity of cant.[1]

Thursday, 9 March. In Chelmsford visited at the Hospital Mrs Ernest

---

[1] The National Mission of Repentance and Hope was an attempt by the Church to meet those critics who said she was not doing enough in the war effort. Although seventy-five per cent of the Armed Services were Anglican by baptism, many were untouched by the Church's teaching. Churchmen saw it as a failure by the national Church and the Mission was to be an effort of the whole Church to remedy this, as well as to do more in the war effort.

Taylor, of Great Leighs, not yet allowed to sit up. She said it was very cheery to have the bag-pipes pass once every day at least. Went to the Recruiting Tribunal office; waited three-quarters of an hour beyond time; and was refused leave to keep my man, Chas. Henry Ward, till a later date. The tribunal consisted of a dozen or more county people— with military assessors—told off to compel them to refuse exemptions.[1]

Sunday, 12 March. The call of men to the Colours at Terling has, according to gossip in this village, produced great consternation. Several men, in dread of being called out, have gone off their heads— George Frost, a labourer, was taken to (Colchester) Asylum last week. (His wife is forbidden to see him, as her presence excites his violence. There is insanity in his family, a sister of his being in the asylum.) —— Brewer, husband of Lizzie Marshall (formerly cook at Great Leighs Rectory) is left at home with strict doctor's orders that his wife is to keep him out of doors as much as possible and never let him out of her sight.

A number of other men who received summons to attend on Monday, March 6th, have taken no notice and are waiting to see what will next be done.

Saturday, 18 March. Various reports about men called out, in the village and district: 'Jac' Brock of Fairstead is a most valuable work-man, almost the only thatcher and woodman left. His three sons work with him, and he has been most anxious to retain them. But the third son, aet. 20, was taken out this week; and the second son is going soon.

Albert Wright, horseman to Major Wm. Brown, is a starred man, in a privileged occupation. He married a week ago, and is now reported to be glorying over the unmarried labourers that every one of them will have to go before he is called out.

Sunday, 19 March. There is a great out-going of lads from the village and district—end of last week and beginning and end of this week— from Fuller Street, —— Nash, —— Doe; from Great Leighs, Maurice Wright, Arthur Stoddart, Geo. Clark (expects to be sent back, being

---

[1] Mrs Mary Cope remembers that the Rector's appeal against her brother's call-up made the local press. It was asked how his groom-gardener could be strong enough to do all the work he described, but too weak to stand army life. In the event Charlie Ward did have a weak chest and would spend much time in hospitals.

forty-one), Arthur Clark. From Little Leighs, —— Searles. Several of these have been at work at Hoffmann's.

Major Caldwell told me that on Friday afternoon he found Little Waltham in a ferment over a German landing at Harwich. First, old Campen, the farmer, had him off his bike, to tell him 'Germans at Harwich: a telegram to that effect has been received at Grt. Waltham.' Major C's comment, 'What the dickens would they telegraph to Great Waltham for, if there was a landing.' Next the farmer at Wheelers stopped him highly excited: had seen a man who had just come back from Harwich and had seen the Germans there. Major C's comment, 'Why didn't you tell him to shut up for a liar.' The same day there was a wild rumour about the City of a naval action in which five of our ships and more of the enemy had been sunk.

J. Herbert Tritton told me that the War Office had taken nine out of thirty-six men from his farms; only old men were left. He must get eight women at once, for farm work.

Godfrey Hazeltine, on the staff of 1st Indian Division, has written to the Caldwells that army expectation is that war will be over and most troops back in August.

Monday, 20 March. 8 p.m. This is my night of Special Constable patrol: I am not in love with the prospect. I am worn out with a bronchitic cough, and consequent feverishness; and am singularly nervous and inclined to be quarrelsome.

Major Caldwell came to share the patrol. 11.30 p.m. Dark, cloudy, still, damp night: not a creature about, nor a sound to be heard.

Tuesday, 21 March. 8.45 a.m. Morning's post brought a bundle of insufferable trash from 'The Central Committee for National Patriotic Organisations'. I put here part of this rubbish, and preserve elsewhere the rest of the silly leaflets.

Wednesday, 22 March. Maurice Gooday, just called up to Warley on service, was home on leave. He said that the first evening the recruits spent in the huts at Warley, they had a grand time. It was dull and cold. So they sang to keep themselves cheery and danced to keep themselves warm. In the morning there was punishment for noise after 'lights out' had sounded—one on a set-to to scrub floors; another, to clean grates; but they did not mind. The evening's diversion was cheaply paid for by the morning's fatigue work.

Friday, 24 March. 9 a.m. child brought a villager's request for church services. (Father, Charles Joseph Wells, drives agricultural engine for Joseph Smith.) 'Sir Will it be convient for you to Church me and Baptism the Baby to day at 2 o'clock. From Mrs Wells High Road.'

I bought today at A. G. Port's shop two packets of cigarettes (ten in packet; price formerly 3*d.* now 4*d.*). Each packet contained a card with the colours and cap badge of a regiment.

Saturday, 25 March. My daughter, Mildred, arrived from St Andrews. 2.30 p.m. Afternoon post brought yet another foolish bundle of circulars from a person [The National Egg Collection for our Wounded] who possibly does not know at which end a hen deposits an egg, to me whose boyhood was passed amid poultry (hens and ducks), to say nothing of pigs, and who knows a great deal too much about them to try to rear any on this ground, under present circumstances of price of feeding stuffs and supply of labour.

Tuesday, 28 March. 5.30 p.m. went down to the Mission Room to give promised Lantern lecture to schoolchildren. Rain still falling. Partly by wading shallow streams, partly by jumping over narrower but deeper streams, I reach the Mission Room [to] find Mr Thomas Sergeant in trouble with acetelyne supply for the lantern. In spite of the wet and the wind, a good many boys and girls had come from the Church side of the parish. They were making ready to go, when told of the unhappy postponement of the entertainment, when I took courage and said if they would sit down, I would at least tell them a fairy-tale. So I adventured on Glen Queich, the Fairy Knave.[1] After this, I started to come home, but found the wildest storm blowing that I have ever known, not only here, but ever. Spectacles quite blinded, but I could not put up a hand to take them off for fear the basket with my slides would be blown out of my hands. Of all pains I have felt in my life, the unthawing of the fingers when I got home was the worst. I could have stamped; I could hardly keep from crying out, for the insufferable

---

[1] For this Andrew Clark drew on the stories of his childhood in Dollar. Glen Queich (or Glenquey) is a narrow valley leading from Castle Campbell to the north of Dollar. Near the end of the ravine is a small pool known as Maiden's Well and filled with cool spring water. According to one legend the pool contains the spirit of a beautiful maiden, capable of being summoned by a stalwart adventurer on a dark night. Another legend tells of a piper who was invited into a magic castle on the grassy knoll known as Maidens Castle. When he left he discovered he had been there for a hundred years.

tingling. I hope all the children got safe home—one thing was the storm was blowing this way. I hope our ships are safe in harbour. I could wish that Zeppelins had started and were meeting it.

Thursday, 30 March. This morning's post (8.45 a.m.) brought a letter:

26 March 1916

Dear Miss Mildred,

I ask you to excuse me if I have been so long in answering your kind letter . . . I am very sorry to tell you that I am not improving my English . . . I look forwards to return in England and learn again all what I have forgotten.

Have you always refugees near you? Poor people, when shall they go back to their houses! In Orléans we have always our relatives . . . one of their husbands is dead of his wounds last October, another has been buried by a bomb and died, one of the wives is still in the invaded land with three young children and we can't have news of her. Some of our friends are in the 'Verdun district' we are also very anxious about them, but all these sufferings are for our Liberty and for the Victory, and we must support them very happily.

I hope you are not too much improve (impoverished) by that terrible war, it is admirable to see the great effort England is making to help us.

I leave you, dear Miss Mildred, and send you my best love from your affectionate friend

Suz. Goueffon

Mademoiselle Suzanne Goueffon's uncle is a doctor in Orléans (called out at the beginning of war to take charge of a military district); her father is a leading pharmaceutical chemist, her mother a fully qualified dispenser. Several cousins and other relatives have fallen in the field for France.

I hear that my admonition to recruiting committee not to take away at present lads with weak chests is already being justified. Several of those who have been taken to the camp at Tring are already in hospital with chest trouble. 'It was poor recruiting' I said 'just to fill the military hospitals.'

Friday, 31 March. 3.30 p.m. Dr R. P. Smallwood called: He was told this afternoon that the Germans had landed on the East coast yesterday afternoon. He reassured them by suggesting that, if there were such news, it would have been brought at once to the troops. If there is a Zeppelin scare, or a reported invasion, or other alarm, the Cameronians at the Walthams will be called out by the pipers passing along the street.

Saturday, 1 April. On Fr. 31 March 1916, at 9.30 p.m., being very tired and suffering from a bad cold, I finished up this diary as on fol. 63, and wrote headlines for this page and for the next day's entries. Then I went to bed, and by and by went to sleep.

But events were to make my preparations premature. At 11 p.m., just as my wife had come up, there were two tremendous explosions, just to the north which shook the house, and caused her to call out, involuntarily Oh! Oh! The second call woke me, and I got up to find my daughters disturbed by the great bangs, and the dog roused and barking.

At 11.10 p.m. I was dressing-gowned and out. It was a starlit night, slightly foggy. By this time the Zeppelin was roaring like a railway train somewhere near by, apparently just over the Rectory stables. For an appreciable time it continued to roar, but make no progress, like a big engine letting off steam on a railway siding. I tried every way to locate it against the stars, but did not succeed. Then the noise began to be louder and louder as the machine began to move from over-the-stables way to over-the-stable-yard-way. The movements were ridiculously, so far as could be judged from their sound, like those of a crow, flying over a pasture field. I went round to the other (S.) side of house, and listened to the fainter sound as it passed over Great Waltham, and so towards London.

When I was coming round the corner (S.E.) of house, I heard my gate click; and I went towards it and found my neighbour, Major Wm. Brown, coming up the drive. He told me that—about 10—in Chelmsford—it was known that Zeps. were about. He could hear it just north of Bishop's Hall, and listened till it passed south. Then he heard one of my daughters from an upper window chaffing me about being out with a lighted cigarette, when Zeps. were about.

11.50 p.m. several explosions in the south, followed by lights (probably searchlights).

Seeing a light in the maids' room I sent my elder daughter to tell them all danger was over. Ethel Gooday told her that the first explosion had made the window rattle and had made the bed jump.

Just as clock struck 12 midnight, sound was heard of one Zeppelin coming back. When it got this length, it hesitated; hovered about (as if uncertain how to proceed) over N.W. corner of this house, and over the Stokes's cottage opposite the Rectory Gate. It was now distinctly seen—a long, black thing against the stars. About this time, a window was heard to open in the Stokes' cottage, and Miss Stokes voice call out shrilly to her mother (who is rather deaf)—'I can hear the sound, but can't see anything.' Little wonder, since the Zep. was then directly over the cottage.

12.50 a.m. the other Zep. came back this way. About 2 a.m. a great bang as of something bursting was heard in that [Chelmsford] direction, followed by a long sizzle. After 2 a.m. four bangs were heard, in the same direction, but much further away. 2.45 a.m. my children went to bed.

Two of the Great Leighs men called out have been sent back as medically unfit—Albert Clark, having had rheumatic fever; and Maurice (known as 'Mob') Wright, son of Walter Wright, reason not known. My lad, Charles Henry Ward, had his call this morning. He is to present himself at Chelmsford on Su. Apr. 9th.

Village reports as to last night's raid: at Braintree bombs were dropped in High Street, in Martin's yard, and in 'Rifle Hill'. Much glass was broken, the chief damage being to shop of C. Joscelyne, my pet stationer, in High Street. [It was Joscelyne's home, not his shop, that was bombed.] In Martin's yard five people are reported killed; ninety bombs were dropped in all.

7.30 p.m. Major James Caldwell called: the adjutant at Braintree is of opinion that the Zeppelins were hovering over Braintree, not knowing where they were. When the Church clock struck 11 p.m., they realised that they were over a town of some sort, and threw out three bombs on chance.

The Great Leighs Boy Scouts, thanks to the good weather, had a great afternoon over the fields, signalling and scouting. I wish I could get a reasonable collection of the boys' sayings to illustrate the undoubtedly traditional, but altogether contrary-to-accepted-convention use of pronouns, especially. Here is one this afternoon: 'Us will go along this way, and then they will come along after we.'

Sunday, 2 April. Items of news brought back by Rectory housemaid (Ethel M. Gooday) from Bocking: Braintree today was worse than London for crowds. All Braintree had gone to Sudbury (to see the damage there). All Essex had come to Braintree.

11.20 p.m. A Zeppelin passed overhead. After it had passed, the bugles were heard at Little Waltham calling the troops out. When it got to Brentwood (presumably) the guns opened fire; their flashes were distinctly seen; and the rattle of their reports heard.

Monday, 3 April. Notes as to women's work and wages: Ivy Lewin is in her seventeenth year. She had been two years in domestic service in Great Leighs. She received 9s. a month, and of course her food. She tried Lake & Elliot's. In the first of her weeks her wages were 9s.6d. for the week. In the second week, 10s.6d. Of course she had to buy a bicycle, and has to pay for her own food.

Wednesday, 5 April. [The Rector wrote the following letter:]*

5 April, 1916

Dear Mr Redman,

I had been hoping to hear of your Welfare ... We have had the worst weather of any winter of my 23 years here. It has been most depressing being out of Church all these evenings. I hope to get back on the 16th. On Sunday Apr. 9th. I have a set of lantern-slides to show—56 in number—of Assyrian warfare as seen on the monuments, chiefly in the British Museum. They are very good. The lecture which is supposed to go with them is by my neighbour, the Vicar of Terling, a great Assyrian Scholar; but it is very learned, and I must make a lecture more within compass of the village ...

You will be glad to know that my daughter Mildred is continuing a very distinguished course at St Andrews, as a student of Medicine. She has passed all the subjects of the First Professional Examination for the degree of M.B., and has this year gained one of the medals awarded in the Anatomy class.

Mrs Clark's illness is now irremediable. She suffers from time to time intense pain, which can be alleviated only by drugs. She is very weak, and has not been out for many weeks, nor is able to see anyone.

I cannot tell you how much I miss your kind help and sympathy in the Church ...

[P.S.] It has been a grievous time with deaths in the field and in hospital of sons of our old friends, in Scotland and in Oxford especially.

Thursday, 6 April. 8.45 a.m. morning post brought a claim for 'a first installment' of £2.2s.6d. from Great Leighs parish, under the Bench of Bishops' fanciful taxation scheme [diocesan quota]. I pass it on to my church-wardens, my opinion being that arbitrary taxation is to be firmly resisted.

3.30 p.m. Miss Eliza Vaughan called. The civil and military authorities at Braintree played the fool and caused a panic [on 3 April]. They sent round word that people were to go out of their houses, because of

Zeppelins. Thousands of poor people streamed out, with babies in arms, babies in perambulators, children led by the hand or clinging to their mother's skirts. Some went to Rayne; some to the entrenchments in Panfield Wood; some cowered under bushes; some huddled themselves up in ditches. At first the children cried: then, as they regained courage, they all bawled the song, 'Here we are, here we are again.' The din they made in Panfield Wood was heard in Rayne and would have been heard afar off by any Zeppelin.

Next forenoon, after they had returned, all the women in the slum parts of Braintree had carnival. The exposure, by night of Braintree children in damp woods and damp ditches, is likely to cause more deaths from bronchitis and pneumonia than would have resulted from a heavy bomb-dropping.

Friday, 7 April. 4 p.m. Dr R. P. Smallwood called: very tired and with much less in the way of notes than usual: Officers, back from the front say that the label 'reported missing: believed killed' covers a good many cases of men shunning duty from cowardice, or inflicting wounds on themselves in hope of being sent to hospital.

The Cameronians, at Little Waltham, call the Little Waltham Schoolmaster and Special Constable [W. G. Hedgethorn] 'the Hedgehog'. The Oxon. and Bucks. L.I., who preceded them, called him 'the Hedge pig'.

Saturday, 8 April. My lad, Chas. Hy. Ward, went off my service, at 5.30 p.m., being called out for service. I have no one to take his place, and shall have to undertake personally most of the outside work. This an end to studies. Happily, after being in arrears with my war clippings, I have got fairly abreast this evening.

Tuesday, 11 April. My lad, Chas. Hy. Ward, has been 'passed for general service' and assigned to a driver's post in RFA [Royal Field Artillery]. He was to sleep at Warley last night, and go on to Woolwich today.

Saturday, 15 April. I spent all morning moving the great heap of thorns (brambles, dogrose, hawthorne) left by the woodsmen when they removed the great Scotch fir. I have torn my hands badly, but have it all on a great pile in the paddock ready for a bonfire.

My lad (Charles H. Ward) has written home to his mother at

Endway that he has been promoted. Four hundred at Woolwich were paraded to supply 'raiders' for the Royal Horse Artillery. Seven were taken and he is one of the seven. He has been once in the Riding School. The way in which the men swear at each other and at their horses is shocking.

Sunday, 16 April. 6.30 p.m. resumed evening service in Church, after cessation for winter owing to no-light order. Change made at request of parishioners and church-wardens.

Here is a characteristic story of a German-spy told by a Great Leighs woman, confusedly and unintelligibly, but it is impossible to interrupt such narrator and clear up obscurities—by questioning. In Braintree was a cook, who went out as a cook, but dined at the White Hart Hotel. 'She' was dressed as a woman, but had very large feet, and was probably a man dressed as a woman. 'She' disappeared hurriedly. Before 'she' went 'she' prophesied that, after 'she' had gone Zeppelins would come to Braintree, and also go to Scotland. It has all turned out as 'she' said. 'She' was certainly a spy. Anyone with such large feet must have been a spy.

Tuesday, 18 April. 9 a.m. morning post brought a letter-card from my lad [Driver Charles H. Ward]:

Dear Sir hopeing This will find you all quite well as I am not feeling very well at present I have been inoculated this morning they have allowed me 48 hours off I stayed at Warley one night and at the RFA Depot one night the Major picked me and 7 more out and put us in the R H A I have had a rough time and they tell me it will be more rough yet I am in the riding school and they dont half put you through it I think this is all I have to say now kind regards to all

Charlie

8.30 p.m. barometer (edging up) 29.0. But it is a wild night. 9.15 p.m. the moon has risen, but is much in trouble with clouds. Venus has disappeared behind much cloud in the west. Rain still holds off, but wind is high, cold, threatening.

Why do I note these weather conditions in a *War Diary*? Because if they show discomfort to a settled resident in his own room, they show greater hardship to the troops in billets in a great ring round Great Leighs.

Wednesday, 19 April. Afternoon's post (2 p.m.) brought a letter [from Mildred]:

. . . From Cupar, Miss Lyon and myself were entertained by three travelling companions, of the farmer class. The father and son were in top-hats and mourning suits, and clasped tightly their large umbrellas. The daughter was in black also. They said the funeral was a nice, respectable burial, 'wi' no too many there.' The seating accommodation (funeral services, of course, *more Scottico*, in the house) was limited. She could have managed better. 'I'd hae gotten ain o' my neebors to lend me a wheen mair chairs.' As it was, 'I didna ken whaur tae put mysel!' The minister was a soft-hearted, decent sort man. The daughter gave a minute description of the 'chesting' (placing the corpse in the coffin, a great function), as it had been told her by a neighbour. The old man seemed to feel he had not fully done his duty, because, after a pause . . . during which he seemed absorbed in meditation, he said 'What'll she dae wi' the whiskey that's left over?' . . .

Vera Wentworth, a militant suffragette, who was at one time at the Hall, is now working at Woolwich Arsenal. The men were at first violently antagonistical to-wards her and even went so far as to hide her tools. Now, however, they are reconciled and have christened her Blime Bill while the only other woman in the department is known as S'welp me Bob . . .

Friday, 21 April. 11 a.m. Good Friday Service. Although I had not asked them the members of the choir turned out well. There was an exceptional congregation.

Yesterday I had a report that certain excitable people had been greatly distressed by a report that a meeting was to be held in 'the School' in view of 'invasion'. All I had to say was that I had not heard the faintest whisper of it. Today Mr G. S. With, the parish Church-warden and Headmaster of the Council School told me—Major Wm. Brown had asked use of Council School on Thursday for such a meeting, that Major Brown thought the thing was ridiculous—but that he didn't like the responsibility of putting it on the shelf, by himself, that, in his opinion, it was a pity to hold such a meeting—it just upset people, for no purpose.

4 p.m. Dr Smallwood called: a Zeppelin raid is expected tonight, tomorrow night and Sunday night; with this raid, an attempt at invasion is expected, and the moment the approach of the Zeppelins is notified, the military are to be on the *qui-vive*, and everyone who is on leave is to be recalled. One recent attempt at invasion is said to have been turned back by our fleet, but, of course, there is no certainty as to that.

Easter Sunday, 23 April. Late at night, or very early in the morning, the nightingale and the owl, were vying with each other in making a din; 8 a.m. Celebration: 23 + 1; collection 5s.9d.; 11 a.m. very full church, but sky now clouded over and church dull: 23 + 1 communicants. Collection £1.9s.10d. 3.15 p.m. blackbirds feeding on lawn, much singing of birds. Cowslips now fully up, so intimating arrival of brightest time in Great Leighs fields. Barometer (rising) 29.7 $\frac{1}{5}$. As a memorial of this Easter, the last (I hope) of the present war, I preserve two notices [for the music at Evensong] written by the energetic organist, Jas. Caldwell, so often mentioned in this record.

Monday, 24 April. 11 a.m. Easter Vestry. The feeling of the Vestry was against any payment of the new-fangled 'taxation' scheme. We have to provide for replacing of the weathercock and for a new gate at N.W. corner of the churchyard. Mr G. S. With, churchwarden, asked about the use of the Church School for a meeting in connection with the provisions against invasion—and for removal of population from the invaded area. J. Herbert Tritton was scandalised at a meeting with any form of publicity: it would cause unnecessary panic; would set a bad example to other places, and if copied would unsettle the whole Kingdom. Although I differ from Mr Tritton on many points, I have the heartiest admiration for his judgement in public matters. I have never known him speak so forcibly and convincingly as he did on this occasion.

Wednesday, 26 April. A Zeppelin passed over last night about ten; dropped bombs somewhere near London; and returned about midnight.

3 p.m. Dr Smallwood called: when the Zeppelin passed over Little Waltham last night only the 'fire-pickets' were called out; but, the night before last, because of affairs in Dublin, the whole troops were under orders, it being uncertain whether a big force would not be needed in Ireland; even now, the troops were at 'standby', waiting for urgent orders which might come at any moment; military men were more alarmed at the feebleness and fatuity of this government than at any possible development of rebellion in Ireland.[1]

Thursday, 27 April. I hear that on Tuesday night many people in

[1] The Easter Uprising began in Dublin on 24 April, Easter Monday. Fighting continued for four days.

Bocking and Braintree did not go to bed but sat up prepared to flee inland. A report had got about that the Germans had actually landed. The Scots soldiers told them that, unhappily, they had not, so that the Scots would not have the pleasure of making their acquaintance.

7 p.m. in the Council School—the 'Invasion' meeting [seventeen present]. J. Herbert Tritton, as chairman, in a set speech explained that the meeting was called at the request of the authorities who asked that in the case of invasion every parish should be fully organised, even if we had fullest confidence in our army and navy. Taking Great and Little Leighs and dividing them into groups of fifty (as suggested) meant sixteen groups and therefore thirty-two men, and a few over. A Committee was appointed to work out details.

Monday, 1 May. Hedgethorn, the schoolmaster at Little Waltham, is a self-important man and very meddlesome in all ways as a Special Constable. He went to the cooking place behind the Drill Hall at Little Waltham, and told the Cameronians' cook that his things were greasy and that he ought to keep them cleaner. The cook got the cleaver and told Hedgethorn that if he did not get out at once he would split him in two. He hastily retired. Complaint was made to the Colonel and the cook was censured. On Frid. 28 Apr. the cook went to the White Hart and got tipsy. As he toddled back to quarters he recalled and brooded over the insult; took his cleaver and walked about Little Waltham, enquiring for Hedgethorn that he might have his blood. The battalion is sworn to chuck H. into the river, before it leaves.

Thursday, 4 May. My daughter, being at the Post Office this evening, brought a postcard which otherwise I would have had tomorrow morning as to drill of Special Constables [from Major William Brown, requesting Dr Clark's attendance]. I have therefore sent in my resignation. It is useless for me to attend drill, as I do not hear the words of command.

Friday, 5 May. 4.30 p.m. Dr R. P. Smallwood called: said the 5,000 troops who are to be under canvas at Terling are part of the Lowland Brigade. J. H. Tritton told him that the artillery (anti-aircraft guns) had definitely arranged to go under canvas in Lyons Hall park. There were to be twelve big guns, horses for them and 600 men.

Saturday, 6 May. Yesterday morning was the biggest call of men from the parish that has yet been. Eight were called out 'to the war' (as the villagers express it) from Lyons Hall. One of Mr Brown's men from Bishop's Hall. Eldest son of C. Rayner of Lowleys. This morning old Sam Childs told me with malicious glee, that my 'two gardeners' had had their papers and were to go in a fortnight. These are Harry Brown and Charlie Collins, two farm-lads, who, since C. H. Ward went, have been digging my garden. Jimmy Lewin, who brings round the bread for F. Mann, baker, Little Leighs, is called out on Monday. So is Fred Mansfield, of Rochester's farm, formerly in Essex Yeomanry.

Tuesday, 9 May. 2 p.m. barometer 29.4. Afternoon post brought a letter from my former servant:

Dear Sir trusting this will find you all quite well as it leaves me quite well now I am doing room orderly to day we had a draft of about 4 hundred go away from the R H A last week and two of the young men in our room were in it that leaves 16 now they are all nice men . . . there is quite an exciteing time when they are starting the band comes out and the Soldiers all give three cheers we had the Zeplens over here last Tuesday week . . . Sory to hear you will have to part with the pony . . . there are hundreds of recruts comeing into Woolwich now every day our Sargent tells us the war will soon be over but we must not think we are going to get out of the army a[s] soon as it is over but I can't see it gets much forward yet I saw this morning on the Placard the Kiser Kaiser wants peace lets hope he gets it I think this is all I have to say now with kind Regards from Charlie

Wednesday, 10 May. I have used the Scythe today, first time for over forty years and find myself as clumsy and inefficient as I was with it as a boy. Yet women 'on the land' are supposed to learn this at once. I am very pleased with my rough fencing. The cads who follow the East Essex hounds made a shameful hash of the fences of the Rectory paddock by riding through them, everywhere smashing ruthlessly. I do not think they will do so this season.

Thursday, 11 May. Am very tired—heaving wood—cutting grass—sawing wood—mending fence—piling up rubbish on bonfire-heaps. Practically no war news came to me today.

Saturday, 13 May. The water-supply at the Rectory is obtained chiefly by a heavy wheel which draws it from a well seventy feet and forces it into a big cistern under the slates of the kitchen-wing, some thirty feet up. It takes between 200 and 300 revolutions of the wheel, three times a day to keep this cistern supplied. When it is full there is a small escape pipe which throws off a stream of water into the gutter. It is weary, heavy, disheartening work to turn this wheel. There are impudent sparrows which sit along the gutter when I am pumping, crane their necks down to see me better, and screech uncomplimentary remarks, as though to say—'Well, you're a long time about that job.' Then, when the stream comes about them and splashes, they hop off on to the slates just above, with a chatter 'So you have done it, but have been very slow.' Then they perch on the edge of the gutter, waiting for the splashing to cease to have their bath in the gutter. Their procedure is quite comic, but irritating.

Monday, 15 May. 10 a.m. F. R. Lewin left his garden work to give me his company into Braintree. He has had a talk with the soldier son of —— Brown on Gubbions Green. This man had been nine months at the front and had had a week's leave. His report was that the soldiers' belief was that, once the Campaign began, the war would not last long. But a beginning could not be made because of the flooded state of the trenches.

10.20 p.m. Major James Caldwell called for Special Constables patrol. A most brilliant moonlight night. Quite an absurdity to patrol on such a night. Mr Caldwell explained to me, very lucidly, the intentions of the 'Daylight Saving Bill' [to take effect on 21 May and to last until the end of September]. He was of opinion that it would make a very great saving in London in factories, railway stations and street lighting. He advised me to explain to the people, in a sermon, that on Sunday they must put their clocks forward an hour, and keep them so. There would be no confusion if people stuck steadily to the hour on the clock.

Tuesday, 16 May. 11 a.m. Dr R. P. Smallwood called to see my invalids [Mrs Clark and Mary, who was suffering from influenza]: he said it was impossible to tell what was going to happen—reports were so contradictory: (i) a member of Joffre's staff is reported to have said that the big move would take place at the end of May;[1] (ii) a man on Haig's staff is reported to have said that this year the Allies would

[1] Joseph Jacques Césaire Joffre, known as 'Papa Joffre', was French Commander-in-Chief. He would be dismissed after the enormous losses sustained at Verdun and on the Somme later in 1916.

make no big move, but just sit tight and let the Germans beat themselves against the iron bars of their cage.

Saturday, 20 May. 6 p.m. W. H. Dee, Church Clerk, very bitter against the Summer Time Act, on every account. (i) Villagers are at work at present, more or less, from 4 a.m. to 8 p.m. (ii) Mothers will not be able to get children in from play an hour earlier, on the summer nights, and get them to bed; nor get them up an hour earlier and ready for school and Sunday school; (iii) It will prejudicially affect most shops in all the small towns. His boy (Charles) is in a Braintree draper's (Townrow's) shop which opens at 8 a.m. Move 8 a.m. forward to 7 a.m. and open shop at the nominal hour of 8 a.m., will there be any customers come to the shop?

I have added up the cost of the week's work in the garden—casual labour in the stable and in the garden alone—leaving apart all the labour I myself have done every day in garden, ground and house work. It comes out at 4s. more money for the week, than when I had my lad, my own work not thrown in. I have totalled also the part of the work which has consisted in pumping water. The result is for the week, 3,550 turns at the wheel pump and 2,250 strokes at the force pump, a total of 5,800. I put this down to show the futility of the contention of the Chelmsford Military Tribunal that it need not defer calling out my man.

Sunday, 21 May. I did not change the Church clock. I consider that I ought to have had a clear week's notice to let it be known that it would be done. The result justified my action. Only those next the post office and those who go by the daily papers (not many)—arrived at the new time, 10 a.m. (nominally 11 a.m.). The bulk of the congregation arrived at the old time. I said the Church clock would be put forward after Evening Service. I learn that farm-hands, including women on the land, have not arrived at any agreement as to the hour (actually: old or new) at which work will begin tomorrow.

They tell me that 'Ernie' Wright—Major Leslie Tritton's gardener—is called out. He is a married man with several children. Also that his younger brother, Albert Wright, just moved from Bishop's Hall to Lyons Hall work, has been called out.

I am told that great dissatisfaction prevails among women workers as regards rate of pay. Lyons Hall paid only 1s.6d. a day. Long's and

Alsteads were paying 2*s*. or even 2*s*.6*s*. a day. Lyons Hall women demanded more pay. Instead of granting that, Mr Stoddart approached the other farmers to induce them to pay less. This being done, the women, formerly paid at the 2*s*. rate, are going to refuse to work. The 1*s*.6*d*. a day they say, does not compensate for dirt, and discomfort, and wear of clothes and shoes.

1.30 p.m. = 12.30 p.m. (new time) barometer 30.0 $\frac{3}{5}$. 2.30 p.m. (= 1.30 p.m. new time) barometer 30.0 $\frac{2}{5}$.

Major Jas. Caldwell told me that 'Alix' Alefounder's application for exemption was mismanaged by Mr T. Stoddart. Instead of pointing out that A. A. was a hopeless victim of asthma, Mr S. enlarged on the fact that he was the only 'hurdle maker' in the place, but the helpless idiots on the tribunal did not know what a hurdle was, or how necessary for sheep-penning, and they dismissed the application at once.

, When I got back from Church at 8 p.m. (natural time) I put clocks and watches forward to 9 p.m. (official time). This official time will, until further note is made, be that used in this Diary.

Tuesday, 23 May. Richard Arnold, the best practical farmer in the district, has met the 'official time' trouble in a practical way. His men begin, and leave off, at the old hours, only renamed an hour *later* than they used to be. S. Joslin, at Whitehouse, has taken a different line. His men are to begin at the official hour, but are to be paid overtime if they continue after the 'official time' of closing.

Thursday, 25 May. Little Waltham gossip from Miss (Helen) Tancock, eldest daughter of Canon O. W. Tancock, rector. A Broomfield girl became enamoured of a soldier of the first lot quartered there and insisted on marrying him. He has now been for some time at the front, and she has become more enamoured of one of the Scots now at Broomfield. The two search the casualty lists every day to see if shot or shell will oblige by removing the bar to their wooing.

Friday, 26 May. Morning's post (8.45 a.m.) brought another old-wife circular from his Lordship of Chelmsford [concerning the National Mission]; a note from Harry Brown, nephew of Rectory cook (Lizzie Oddey) [stationed at the Tollcross School, Edinburgh]:

Dear Sir,
a card to let you know we are all happy and comfortable in your native

country. it is a very pritty place about Here. It seems a bit strange after been at Leighs I Rather prefer my native village now than been up here so far away from hom. we were in Karkie in less than 6 hrs from the time we left Leighs Good byee to all I remain

Yours Sincerely
Harry Brown

Sunday, 28 May. Various bits of military gossip told me this morning: A week ago Lord French was to inspect the troops in this district. The men were marched off to Mundon beyond Maldon at 6 a.m., having had only the most hurried and insufficient breakfast. At Mundon they were kept standing about, doing nothing, till noon, without (of course) bite or sup. At noon a staff-officer rode up—Why the hell weren't they at Witham, waiting to be inspected *there*? So in full kit and in blazing noon-day heat, they were taken hot foot, to Witham. Two dropped dead on the route, over-exertion. It is an eight mile march.

Wednesday, 31 May. 8.45 a.m.: Last night a party of soldiers bivouaced in Lyons Hall park, in charge of the tents etc. dumped down there. 3.15 p.m.: Charles Collins tells me that the 'camp' in Lyons Hall park is in full swing. Tents are going up.

7.15 p.m. Three fagged-out, foot-weary Tommies passed Rectory gate, *en route* from Lyons Hall to Braintree. Being questioned, one of them told me, in good braid Scots, that they had been at work all day 'preparin'' the camp. Had they been masons' hod men, or house painters' men, a vehicle of some sort would have been provided to take them back after their day's work. As they were only soldiers, of a unit with abundant horses and vehicles, they had to walk the long, bad, dusty road.

Saturday, 3 June. Village report has it that while the camp is here, the public-houses in the district are to open on week-days only Sunday hours.

4.10 p.m.: a company of men marching to camp. The bugler, at the head, played occasionally, and at other times the men sang or whistled. The bugle-notes stirred a cuckoo, in a tree just across the narrow meadow of Bishop's Hall which faces the Rectory gate, to rivalry; and every time the bugle sounded the cuckoo began to answer the challenge by its loudest and clearest calls.

All evening soldiers, in groups of two, three or more have been going back and forward past Rectory gate, probably to and from St Anne's. There is also a great sound of men's voices from the camp, no doubt soldiers larking about. Also a good deal of shouting along the road, an unusual thing in this village.

9.30 p.m. The soldiers, coming back from St Anne's, are very noisy on the road. They have got some musical instrument (concertina or of that sort) and are singing raucously. Today has been a hard day for them, and the muddled camp is not conducive to their comfort.

Sunday, 4 June. I am told that this afternoon and evening, Great Leighs was overrun with girls from Bocking and Braintree who came out to see their soldiers.

Tuesday, 6 June. 9.30 p.m. soldiers passing gate, on way back from St Anne's. They had heard of Lord Kitchener's death.[1] Being Edinburgh lads, they were very pleased to get Monday's *Scotsman*, which I had reserved for them.

Miss Caldwell, about 6 p.m., brought the *Star* as to Lord Kitchener and said that her father had heard in town that the newspaper paragraph had since been officially confirmed by the Admiralty.

Wednesday, 7 June. I had by this morning's post an undated card from Harry Brown:

Dear Sir,
   thanks very much for your kind letter that I Received safely I have found out that their are some lovly places and buildings in Scotland I think I sorry I have not had time to write a letter to you sir yet I hope garden is getting is doing all right I have been noculated again to day. so I do not fell very well. I hope to be home again before long. I Remain yours Sincerely . . .

Dr R. P. Smallwood called—he says that there is a general suspicion that the sinking of the *Hampshire* was due to treachery. Someone high in Cabinet secrets had told the Germans that the ship was ready to sail with some important army officers. Capt. W. S. Roddie called in the evening from Lyons Hall Camp, with the same suspicion. The wife of a cabinet minister, or a cabinet minister, is pointed at.

---

[1] Lord Kitchener went down with HMS *Hampshire* off the Orkneys on the evening of 5 June; he was *en route* to Russia. He was succeeded as Secretary of State for War by Lloyd George who became Prime Minister in the following December.

Mrs F. Mann, the baker's wife, of Little Leighs, has now to go round with the bread-cart herself. She says also that Jim Lewin says he doesn't like the life at all—the men are so rough. A. G. Suckling also says the life is as rough as rough can be.

Thursday, 8 June. The village has already a number of jests about Lyons Hall Camp, though it is only a thousandth part of them will reach my ears. On Sunday night about 11.30 p.m., after the officers were in bed an agitated sergeant came to a captain's tent—'Sorry Sir! but driver ——'s got the kōlick awful bad.' Captain had not thought that his duties would include prescribing for colic. But he took refuge in the national prescription: 'Give him some whisky.' 'We haven't any, Sir.' 'Then give him a big drink of hot water.' 'We haven't any, Sir!' 'Then stir up the fire and heat some.'

A little after another man reported 'awful bad with kōlick.' Before getting to sleep again officer had remembered nursery application of hot salt in a bag for pain in the 'tummy'. So this time he directed the sergeant to heat salt on a shovel over a fire and apply the salt where the pain was. The sergeant proceeded to rouse up two fairly strong heavy men to hold the patient. The officer had forgotten to say that the salt should be enclosed in a flannel bag. When the heated salt was applied, direct from the spade to the bare stomach-skin, first one arm holder was cast forth, and then the other and then the sergeant and his spade violently ejected from the tent, followed by the patient's violently expressed opinion that he'd rather have the kōlick, than the remedy.

Friday, 9 June. There was a report in the village this evening that Lloyd George was dead. 'Alix' Alefounder is sent back, medically unfit. He is subject to asthma and bronchitis, and, as the villagers say, could not walk fast up a hill to save his life. Albert Wright is exempted, driving Mr Tritton's new motor-plough.

Saturday, 10 June. 9 a.m. morning's post brought only circulars from people [a committee supporting conscientious objectors] who wish all the benefits of citizenship without sharing of its burdens.

2.15 p.m. afternoon's post brought a note from my aunt, Miss J. H. Bowie, Oxford, dated 9 June, 1916: '. . . There are a great many men home on leave, and they are all told to notice any peace talk, and report at nearest depot.'

Sunday, 11 June. 9.45 a.m. Soldiers' Service. There were over 300 present and the small church was packed not only nave, but chancel and gallery. 6 p.m. on my way to Church met a great many Tommies, some probably on way to St Anne's, some loitering about (according to Scots proverbial expression 'like knotless threads') this place having nothing to offer them. Two of them had chits of Braintree shop-girls or munition girls hanging on to their arms and showing off in the most offensive fashion.

Wednesday, 14 June. 1 p.m. stopped an army waggon on the way from Braintree to camp, to send by it, several big bundles of bound newspapers and books (e.g. *Robinson Crusoe*—illustrated edition; *Swiss Family Robinson*) for the men in camp. The men were delighted; said reading was the most necessary thing in camp. The soldiers still favour the cheap packets of 'Woodbine' cigarettes. They bring this fact under my notice in an unpleasant sort of way, by tossing their torn wrappers inside my gate—requiring continual picking up to avoid the appearance of a rubbish-heap.

It is odd to hear the sound of the Scots tongue in the various dialects I hear the men use, [they] bring back to me the Scots of my boyhood, after forty years out of Scotland.

Saturday, 17 June. The presence of the camp is shown in the enterprize of Chelmsford tradesmen in getting cottagers to sell for them—Mrs Fred Fuller has table-waters in her window; Mrs Wm. Milton has sweets.

Major James Caldwell called this evening with a budget of military opinions, near and far: Last week, about Thurs. 8 June, an Inspecting Officer (a general) came to inspect the camp. He was none too pleased to find that the Colonel had taken himself off on self-granted leave to town. He turned out all the officers, made them mount, and put them through their paces. They gave a lamentable exhibition of horsemanship, and the general just raged at them, with the most violent language he could command. Thomas Stoddart, land-steward at Lyons Hall, was on the ground at the time, but hastily cleared off. He felt it wrong in him as a Churchwarden, to hear such language used in the parish; and he was ashamed to be present and hear the officers whom he had met rated in such hot terms.

In spite of the protestations by Territorial officers that they are received on equal terms by the Regular officers, Major Caldwell says that the Regulars draw a sharp line between themselves and the TF's and will 'have no truck' with them. Many of the Territorial Forces officers are bounders socially, and terribly ignorant of their regimental duties, and go swanking about in their khaki uniform as though *cucullus facit monachum* [the cowl makes the monk]. When Regular Officers go to a camp where TF officers are, they do not call on them and leave their cards.

Major Caldwell has just met his brother who was in London on a visit from Belfast. He is much in touch with shipping men in Belfast. Belfast shipping people just laugh at the idea that the *Hampshire* struck a mine. For one thing, the channels about the Orkneys are so deep that it would be next to impossible to moor mines. Belfast people have a very different theory. The *Hampshire* was built by Messrs Harland & Wolff of Belfast. When she had been some time at sea, she was brought to Belfast to be thoroughly over-hauled, about three months ago. The refitting-men found electric wires fitted to the magazine, capable of exploding it. Three men were arrested and tried by court-martial. Belfast people believe that their wires were replaced. There are Irishmen who are bitterer against Great Britain than any German and will stop at nothing, even if it involves self-destruction, to damage Great Britain.

Monday, 19 June. I made a ridiculous mistake this morning, owing to my deafness, which made old Sam Childs think I am even madder than I am supposed to be. He asked me if I had heard of Harry Brown and Charlie Collins. I said No. He then, as I supposed, said that they had both been 'sent to Windsor'. I then said, 'Oh, I suppose the King did not feel safe without a trusty body-guard, and so sent for two Great Leighs lads, that he might have two reliable men at least by him.' The old man opened his eyes, in an astonished way, and then laughed in an odd way. I learn afterwards that his news was that both were 'in bed with *inflew-wenza*'.

Friday, 23 June. 9.25 a.m. started to go to Chelmsford. At my hairdresser's I had myself weighed. If the record is correct [15 stone, 6 lbs. 12 ozs.], I have, in the illnesses of the last few months, lost three stone at least in weight. I never used to be less than eighteen and a half stone.

A view of Lyons Hall, home of the Tritton family. In the background is the parish church.

Daisleys Lane

Jesse Wright's willow-merchant's business

The End Way

In the High Street I met two young women, who represented (I assumed) the more swaggering lot of women-workers on the land. They had riding-breeches, like troopers, of a khaki cloth, with brown boots and leggings, and an overall of holland, white, coming down to a little below the knees. Ordinary women's hats. Carrying shortish rattans, such as grooms might have. They looked as if they had gone astray, out of a comic opera.

Saturday, 24 June. 2.15 p.m. afternoon post brought me a letter from my sometime man [at Woolwich]:

Dear Sir hopeing this will find you all quite well Sory I havnt written before . . . the time seems to pop away I suppose you will soon be hay makeing now we had Lord French here about three weeks ago on Church Parade it was rather sudden Death of Lord Kitchener I hear nearly all the Great Leighs boys are up in Scotland it must be very nice I hope it is better than Woolwich I think this is a rotton place none of the chaps like it we went to the Albert Docks and fetched 390 horses they came from South America they were very wild it was a big Liner and nearly all Japs on it. it was very strange to hear them talking I think this is all I have to say now.
yours Sincely   Charlie

Boy Scout notes this afternoon: Lewis Wright says they had a letter from his father on Frid. 23 June. He was then quite well. They must not expect any further letter from him for six weeks. They had been told that they would be able neither to send letters, nor to receive them for that period.

At Lyons Hall Camp men must be in camp at 10.00 p.m. except Saturday when the hour is 10.30; a post of military police is at the gate, to enforce this rule. (But, as has been said in these notes—an indisputable authority—men slip into and out of camp at all hours.)

Sunday, 25 June. This forenoon, when I was at Church, Mrs Barker, wife of Lt. Col. Gerald Edgar Barker called on my invalid wife: In the front line trenches Godfrey Gerald Barker contrived to secure a goat, which became the pet of the battalion and went with it everywhere. G. G. B. was raking his brains to devise some way by which to take this with him to India. Colonel Brassey [1st Life Guards] said 'Most decidedly no! It must go to Knightsbridge barrack, to be the Guards mascot.' The question was how to get it there without its being kept for six weeks in quarantine. The difficulty was solved by giving the goat a strong dose of morphia and putting him in a sack. He did not wake up till he was safe at Knightsbridge barracks. G. G. B. is sending him, from India, a silver collar.

Thursday, 29 June. 1 p.m. My daughter, Mary Alice, brought me some notes of the YMCA canteen at Terling Camp [where she was a voluntary worker]. A note of some prices: at 1*d*.: a cup of tea, cup of coffee, mug of milk, mug of still lemonade, slice of jam sandwich, slice of jam roll, mince pie, small packet of biscuits; at 2*d*.: a bottle of mineral waters—the favourite being lemonade and Stone's ginger beer, mug of Horlick's Malted Milk (specially made for each one who asks for it); buns are in two boxes—one with ½*d*. buns—the other with 1*d*. buns.

3 p.m. I went to pay a promised visit to the Lyons Hall Park Camp: I had put off doing so, because I understood that the camp was far from complete, when these men came here. It was still very far from finished. The sentry at the gate directed our steps toward a blue-stained tent, where he said the brigade officer was to be found. An officer came up and, on my saying that I had come by the Colonel's invitation, led myself and my daughter all over the camp. He showed us a gun; alongside of the gun which the adjutant was explaining to us, was another gun which a man was taking to pieces. I would have liked to have been present and undergone the whole lesson from first to last.

Friday, 30 June. In Braintree, I had short talks with various tradesmen: F. J. Lowden, manager of Messrs Downing & Co., Wine Merchants, told me: Some of the Scots who are now at Lyons Hall were billeted with him when they were in Braintree. They are jubilant at finding a Church in the heart of Essex where they have a service quite to their own mind and a parson who has the prayers and preaches in a black gown, not in the surplice (flag of dread to the Presbyterian mind).

Mr James Bowtell, the chief grocer and provision merchant, stopped me in the street, with funeral face and undertaker's subdued voice, and asked me if I had heard the very bad news. I thought, for the moment, that a telegram had come announcing the loss of a fleet, or the rout of our army. But it was only the 'poisoning' at Terling camp. He had been told that it was due to tinned salmon and was naturally afraid that his piles of this would be unsaleable. He was greatly relieved when I told him that the latest idea was that the trouble came from new lead pipes.

Saturday, 1 July. All this morning the Flanders (as it is supposed) guns have been booming forth, making house quiver at times and shaking window sashes. At 10 a.m. they made almost an uninterrupted roll of sound, like a long roll of distant thunder.

The Post Office people also say that 'it is unofficially reported that a big naval battle is raging in the North Sea.' Heavy concussions of big guns at a distance continue to shake the house.

Notes from the Boy Scouts this afternoon: the airship which passed over last Monday afternoon, passed when the children were in the Council School. Bob Thorogood saw it, and regardless of discipline, dashed from his seat to have a nearer view at the window. The boys next him also ran to the window. Thereupon the children in all other parts of the school 'didn't want to be out of it' and they also ran to the windows. Mr G. S. With sternly ordered them back to their places, and go on with their lessons. But as they showed no sign of obeying, he let them go out to the playground and gaze their fill.

Charles H. Ward got home for first time on week-end leave. He got home last night, and has till Monday.

Sunday, 2 July. 9.35 a.m. the troops swept into church for their service, due at 9.45 a.m. A larger force than ever attended, and filled every part of the Church from chancel to gallery. Quite a considerable number of soldiers came also to the 11 a.m. service, the ordinary parish service.

All the village was talking about 'the good news' of last night, the 'push' of the British troops in Flanders (apparently successfully) begun.[1]

5 p.m. Charles H. Ward called, looking very smart in his RFA uniform, which is a particularly nice shade of khaki. He has till Wednesday. The Sergeant-Major told him that they would be going out next week or week after next to France or to Egypt. As riding-instructors at Woolwich they have a good many 'rough riders'—Australians.

---

[1] Like many others Andrew Clark used 'Flanders' to designate not just the front in Belgium or in French Flanders, but in Belgium and north-west France generally. On this occasion the guns the Rector heard were from the Somme, as English and French troops went 'over the top'. By nightfall the British Army had suffered its greatest losses ever in one day's fighting: 60,000 men killed, wounded, or taken prisoner. Fighting would continue until November. Total Anglo-French casualties would come to 1,200,000. Censorship ensured that the British public did not know the truth.

Official Bulletin as posted at Great Leighs Post Office:

SUMMARY OF SATURDAY'S OFFICIAL WAR NEWS.

British Official. Attack launched 7.30 a.m. north of Somme combined with French. British broken into German forward system on 16 mile front. French attack equally satisfactory. Remainder front successful British raiding parties . . .

Monday, 3 July. Charles Doe and others who have been home for this week end were told that it would be their last visit home before being sent out, but where they are to be sent they do not know.

Heavy cannonade, in the S.E., went all night. They resumed this morning a little after 10 a.m. and kept on, as a continuous rumble, for some time. We take it that these are the guns in Flanders.

Mrs E. Agnes Hammond, the Schoolmistress, says that the men call these four days' leave 'the firing leave'—I suppose because granted just before they are sent to the front.

Tuesday, 11 July. Richard Arnold said that he got exemption for his man Wells so long as he stays in his employ. He used two arguments in his appeal—(i) Wells is the man who looks after his sheep. If he were taken away, he must sell his sheep, and then there would be only one flock left in all this parish (J. H. Tritton's); (ii) he stated that Wells had four young children (ages stated), and if he were taken and killed the country would have a long time to keep them.

Wednesday, 12 July. 10.20 a.m. morning post brought a money-lender's circular [L. Finsberg, 23 Haymarket, London, S.W.]. These devil's imps are always like their father, seeking whom they may devour.

2.30 p.m. I was busy 'spreading out' hay, when rain began with startling suddenness. I made haste to get some of it 'on cock' [heaped, ready for carting], but had made little progress before the grass got too wet to handle.

Friday, 14 July. Village report says the King was to be this morning at Frinton. Was going by train to Colchester. Thence by motor to Brentwood, passing through lines of troops all the way.

The King's 'inspection' of troops in Essex: Notes given me this evening by my sister-in-law (Alice Paterson) and my daughters, hereinafter called 'we'—but expressed in my own way.

At 2.45 p.m. we left Great Leighs Rectory and cycled to 'the Cock' at Boreham. Here, on the road, some seven field cookers were in a row, and the men, seated by the roadside, were receiving their dinner. The dinner consisted of a huge tin of soup, with lumps of beef in it, and new potatoes, scraped and boiled in a dixie by themselves. One of the cooks was pouring the water out but he tipped the dixie too far over and emptied a good many of the potatoes into the gutter. These he promptly picked up; gave them a rub in his hand, and popped them back into the dixie amid yells of derision from the men who were presently to be served with them. For the amusement of the men here, a private, supposed to be a wag acting 'on his own', was walking along the line, bawling 'The troops are requested not to eat their tins. Now then, attend to orders, and don't eat your tins.'

We got to the turning-off to Hatfield Peverel station, at 3.30 p.m., when a Colonel on horse-back called out to a policeman 'make these ladies dismount.' The policeman said 'You must dismount now and get off the road.' He showed us a sadler's yard into which we might put our bicycles. We got our stand, where we could see everything that happened.

At this time also, the officers were wandering along the lines, looking very bored and uneasy. Their nervousness was plain from the flicking of their canes. The men were relieving the long wait by chaffing passers-by and spectators as well as each other. One girl had a bag of sweets and a Tommy called out 'Eh lassie, I'm awful fond o' sweeties', but she shared her bag with her Yeoman and treated him with frigid contempt. Another said to his neighbour 'O, Sandy man! gie the King when he comes a fag, and we'll surely be allowed to smoke.' Another said 'Man, if the King sees your face, he'll have a fit— he'll have a spasm.' To which the answer was 'I'm thinking he's had a spasm already—the time he has been.'

The tedium of waiting was alleviated by the sense, and still more, by the un-sense, of people in the yard (Ward's the sadler's). Here was a man who said he was at 'work on munitions'. The yellowness of his fingers quite bore out his statement. Here was a sergeant present as a mere spectator. Here also was a socialist, unwashed, unshaven, with an exceptionally disreputable bicycle, foul-mouthed and full of venom as the toad 'under the cold stone' in *Macbeth*. He began by telling the bystanders that 'he knew that if he were not a poor man, he would not stand there waiting for twenty minutes to see the King.' Thereafter, he worked off his feelings towards the King and the Almighty Lord God by *strafing* them solidly, but confusedly, for a quarter of an hour. After enduring this the munitions-worker and the soldier got to the end of their patience and told him to shut up and get out. He went off for a little, then came back and got out his disreputable bicycle. He got on to the road, and walked, pushing his bike towards Witham, not at the side of the road like decent citizens, but in the very middle, but (no doubt to his intense disgust) nobody, civilian, police, or military, took the slightest notice of him.

Here also were two absurdities—two young women-members of 'The Women's National Land Service League' who talked in a loud voice, fatuously, to impress the bystanders who were not impressed. They were got up for their part, in tip-top variety-theatre fashion. They were highly scornful of two gaudily-dressed camera-carrying girls. *They* were far more proper-looking in their 'uniform' than these females. Then one said that, if she had not been in uniform she would have come in a black skirt and a purple jersey. She was going out of mourning for her 'dad'. 'Was her dad killed at the front?' the other asked. 'Oh no! but the Zeppelin scare was too much for his poor old nerves and he died.' Now she didn't care to go in to 'colour' again. With poor dear Jack at the front, one never knew what might happen: two London girls, ~~possibly assistant milliners or underlings in variety theatre~~, obviously 'ladies'. (My judgement is reported to be quite wrong.)

Along the road also, two hawkers were doing a roaring trade, with the soldiers, in bananas and apples. All was now ready for the King's procession: 4.26 p.m. A motor-cycle rode past, with a signaller flying the Royal Standard. Immediately the officers shouted orders along the line. The men sprang rigidly to 'attention' and their heels clicked. They were now in a double-line, officers each at his proper station, in front of his company. The hush was now so great that you might have heard the proverbial pin drop. One spectator said that the very birds stopped singing.

A minute after the cycle with the Royal Standard passed, another motor-cycle, ridden by a staff-officer came very slowly along the road from Witham to Chelmsford.

Next came the King's car, a pale green (or grey) car, an open four-seater, driven by a chauffeur in uniform. The King sat, in Field Marshal's uniform, behind the chauffeur, and a staff-officer (said by the soldiers to be Field Marshal French), an elderly man, beside him. The King was leaning forward in his car, leaning his left hand on one knee. He brought his right hand up to the salute immediately he came up to any unit. His eyes seemed to scan steadily every man's face as he passed. Every waggon also seemed to be taken into his view. His car was going slowly and steadily, about eight miles an hour.

(The solemn silence as the King's procession passed was very impressive—not a word spoken—not a note from any band—no cheering. In fact, Reginald Heber's 'majestic silence'.) When the King's car passed the officers just put up their hands in salute and the men stood at attention silently till the officers dropped their hands when the King had passed.

The King looked very ill and sad. Sunken cavities under his eyes and black lines. Directly the King's car [and procession] had passed, there was a movement. The villagers went back into their cottages. The soldiers fell in, to go back to their camp, and the bands began to play them back.

Tuesday, 18 July. All the officers in Lyons Hall Camp have volunteered for France.

Wednesday, 19 July. Charlie Collins is coming home on leave. He is under orders for France, but doesn't want his mother to know till he has started.

Major Bibben Allen, of Black Notley, says that there are a million men, almost fully trained, who will be sent out almost at once. When they have gone, a million others will be required for home defence. This means that (a) all married men between forty-five and fifty will be called up; (b) all 'starred' men will be called up.

TRIP TO OXFORD: 20 July–5 August

Friday, 21 July. 5 a.m. rather gloomy morning. Began my work on Locals Papers (Senior Acts [of the Apostles]) but made very slow progress—feeling ill.

Sunday, 23 July. I did few papers today but was too ill to make much progress. This year the papers have been very stupid. With nothing even accidentally amusing, except one candidate.

Tuesday–Monday, 25 July–31 July. Nothing to report of myself except continued prostration and sickness, and weary effort to do dreary papers.

———

(During my absence at Oxford my younger daughter kept a Great Leighs Diary for me, so as not to interrupt the local items of news:)

Thursday, 20 July. A brigade tea was given yesterday in the Mess tent. Mr and Mrs Tritton were asked as guests. The tea is said to have been very well managed, little tables were dotted about the tent. The cakes were delicious and cherries were provided. The subalterns raced one another in eating cherries stalk first and three of them distinguished themselves by falling backwards off a form in the middle of tea.

Madge Gold's cousin is a half-Spaniard. Some six weeks ago he came back from Berlin. He says that the report that the Berliners are starving is quite false, business of course slack and bread-tickets are issued, but this is only another incidence of their powers of organisation.

Sunday, 23 July. Constance Stoddart, dairy-maid at Lyons Hall, says her brother, Arthur, who is in the Essex regiment was prepared to go to Egypt only to be informed that they would not be required. It is very difficult to elicit exact information from some of these people; they have a curious way of telling one only so much and resent being asked questions. The border line between 'showing interest' and 'being inquisitive about' is very sharply drawn in the Essex mind.

Monday, 24 July. All officers in France now wear privates' uniforms to be less noticeable for snipers and advance with their men. It is not however an advantageous arrangement and when taken prisoner they are of course treated as privates.

Wednesday, 26 July. Two boys connected with these parts have lost their lives in the 'big push'. (a) Victor Carpenter, in the Somersets, son of the housekeeper at Little Leighs Rectory. (b) —— Fitch. The family is a large one consisting of twelve children. They have lost heavily in the war—one son was killed at the front in 1914, a second son went down with his ship, the *Formidable.* Yet a fourth son when home on sick leave was out with a gun, which exploded and badly damaged his right hand.

Friday, 28 July. Capt. Claude Tritton writes from Rouen asking for pictures for the hospital there. The men are too ill to read, but they delight in looking at pictures from old magazines which have nothing to do with the war. If these pictures are cut out of the magazine and pasted some three or four together on brown paper, the men can hold them up to look at them and can pass them from bed to bed.

Saturday, 29 July. On Tuesday last Mrs Tritton gave a tea to the NCOs of the Camp. The soldiers were well entertained by the Lyons Hall maids. Mrs Tritton hopes to ask them again and suggested to the Colonel that the officers' orderlies should be asked as well, but he was of the opinion that they would have to be asked on different days because 'tuppence three-farthings never could abide tuppence half-penny' and the orderlies are all privates.

Tuesday, 1 August. On Sundays in August a special service is held in the afternoon in Lyons Hall gardens, Mr Tritton bringing a preacher down from London for the purpose. The preacher next Sunday is to be a man who was for some time in France with the 3rd Batt. Coldstream Guards as Scripture reader. Since the reader had no food allowed him by the authorities, as he had no official post, Capt. Tritton together with the other officers used to save little bits from their meal to give to the man.

Thursday, 3 August. Plenty of empty houses are to be obtained in Chelmsford, but all are so damaged by the soldiers as to be almost uninhabitable. The house which Mrs Young has taken in Hamlet Road, Moulsham, has a rent of £40 [per year]. In it the soldiers have torn up the boards and joists to make firewood and in compensation the military authorities have given the landlord the wholly inadequate sum of £12.

One of the patients at the Braintree VAD hospital is a man named McCabe, in the Dublin Fusiliers, an Irishman. He is daily expecting his papers of discharge as he is no longer fit for service. When the necessary papers come he will go home for a week or two, stopping for a few days in Dublin to see the damage wrought in the recent revolt, and later will return to Braintree to work in one of the munition factories, 'for' he says, 'if I can't give the Germans hell one way I will another.'

He was in the Regulars before the outbreak of the war and was sent to Gallipoli. He says the landing was so ghastly that he has few recollections of it—except the longing to get back to Ireland and the mad desire to get at the enemy, who were mowing down the men as they tried to gain the shore.

He says that going into the trenches is a hundred times worse than being in them. It means possibly an eight mile walk in single file through narrow trenches bearing such names as 'Piccadilly', 'London Road' and the like; each man is burdened with his kit, his rifle and rations. In muddy weather progress is difficult. He remembers, in particular, 'London Road' when the mud was waist-deep and in order to put one foot in front of another it was necessary to support oneself by resting both hands on the edge of the parapet and slowly lifting first one leg and then the other. By the time the first-line trenches are reached the men are dead-tired.

In reference to the execution of Sir Roger Casement which took place today, McCabe very gravely remarked 'Holy Moses, there's one little Irish boy will be awful' hot tonight!'[1]

Great annoyance was caused in the hospital this afternoon by two old ladies, who came unnoticed and distributed tracts. One man, who had been having very bad nights, they found asleep in a darkened ward; him they shook roughly by the arm and recited texts to him. As most of the men were out at tea the ladies were unable to do all they might have wished and so left three tracts lying on each man's pillow. These tracts were of the most violent type. (They are preserved here as self-supplied evidence of the 'graciousness' of 'Chapel' religion in Essex, and the kindly manners and tactfulness of its exponents.)

[With this, Mildred Clark's entries cease.]

Sunday, 6 August. My daughter, Mildred, has been helping in the VAD hospital at Braintree. She has today several little bits of hospital news and talk: Matthews [a Glasgow patient] is by way of being a wag. One of the 'sisters' is a delightful Australian woman, but very full of 'Advance Australia'. Finding that Matthews was much alone on Sundays she has sat a great deal beside him, having a great deal to say in praise of Australia. So he thought out a counter-attack. She was

[1] Sir Roger Casement had tried to raise an Irish force among British prisoners-of-war in Germany, with German co-operation. He landed in Ireland on Good Friday to tell his fellow rebels that the national uprising was off. He arrived too late to stop the Dublin uprising and was quickly captured.

talking about the effects of the war, and how hard it was that, with her immense population, Germany would have no colonies to send them to. 'Oh' said the Glasgow man, 'I hear that's provided for—at the end of the war we're going to give them as a colonizing port one o' our auld convict stations which we do not now use.' 'Indeed' asked the sister, 'and where may that be.' 'It's just an island that they call Australia.'

Tuesday, 8 August. [Letter from the Rector to William R. Redman.]*

8 August 1916

Dear Mr Redman,
    You must not think too hardly of me for being so negligent in acknowledging your kind remembrances . . .
    I have been, and still am, in great troubles. Mrs Clark is in the grip of a fatal disease, and is now in great weakness, and has to be dazed with drugs day and night to keep away the pain.
    I have myself for some four months been subject to a wasting illness . . . as well as a feeling of weariness which it is difficult to fight against.
    In addition, my one garden-lad has been taken off for military service, and I have to attempt tasks outside the house which are really too much for a man of my age, but must be done.
    I started badly, by cutting myself constantly when I used hook or hatchet, largely owing to my bad sight; but I get on now with fewer scratches and cuts.
    I miss you in everything, but especially because we have in Lyons Hall park . . . a canvas town of about 600 Scots gunners, for whom your influence would have been most helpful . . .
    I trust that, in spite of my faults as a correspondent, you will let me have news from time to time of your welfare and believe me to be always
                    Yours very gratefully,
                    Andrew Clark.

Friday, 11 August. 11 a.m. christening. The father, William Whitelaw, was a butcher in London and is now in RFA in France; the mother (Daisy) is staying with her people in Fuller Street. I asked the name of the child. I made out the first name to be 'Doris'; but as I had never heard the second, and could not make out the mother's indistinct pronunciation, I got the mother to write it down as *supra* [Anquennta]. I enquired further how it was obtained. She said it was a French name which her husband had heard in France, and had written home. I suggested 'Antoinette' but that was rejected with scorn. At last 'Anquenette' was given as a revised spelling, and so entered the Register.

This week the Upminster Chapel women made another raid on the VAD hospital at Braintree. This time they were caught in the act, confronted by Miss Eliza Vaughan and packed off after hearing from her as a Churchwoman and an official of the hospital, her candid opinion of their opinions and their actions.

Saturday, 12 August. Braintree VAD Hospital Notes: There has been sedition among the VAD hospital patients on the question of religion. Last Sunday those who were officially returned as Church of England were appointed to go to church with Miss Leila Vaughan of Braintree, an elderly, staid VAD Nurse; while the Nonconformists were appointed to go to Chapel with Miss Ennersley, another VAD nurse, apparently young and frivolous. Before Service time the C of E men said they were really strict Chapel-men. They had each their story pat. In the end the gay Miss Ennersley conducted a great band to Chapel; and Miss L. Vaughan escorted the one faithful C of E man to Church. Tomorrow, if the nurses in the Hospital get their way, Miss L. Vaughan is to have charge of the party that goes to Chapel!

Corporal Brooks, of the North Somerset Yeomanry, has been a silent, reticent man; but today, possibly in view of getting home he gave his full confidence to one of the hospital staff. His home is a few miles from Cheddar. The farm was worked by the father and his three sons (Corporal Brooks being the youngest). All three sons were in the Yeomanry. When the war broke out Corporal Brooks and his eldest brother went off to join the colours, while the second son promised to help the father with the farm. This second son used to drive the milk to Axbridge station, every day; but people so booed and hooted at him because he was not in khaki that he got sick of it and 'joined'. Now the father is left to work the farm and manage the cows with the help of only three elderly men.

In April 1915 they [the Somerset Yeomanry] were again in Ypres and wandering about the town, looking at it. Corporal Brooks went into the damaged Cathedral and helped himself to two candlesticks— 'a pity to leave them there'. Another man in the regiment went off with two gorgeously embroidered 'priests robes' (copes, probably). When they were coming down the steps (with their loot) a shell dropped on the square tower of the Cathedral and shattered it. Having succeeded so well on their first expedition, they thought that, on the following night, they would slip out for a second 'looting.' They walked into an *estaminet* [café] to wait their chance, but in walked an MP (Military Policeman). He took them to their officer who told them, briefly but forcibly, what he thought of them. After his talk he took them to the Colonel, who made a few more choice remarks. He wound up by saying that, as they were going into the trenches that night, he was unable to punish them then, but he would deal with them when they came out. In those trenches 180 of them were killed, and the Colonel himself wounded. The two unwounded officers felt that it was no part of their duty to punish any troops who survived. So that affair ended.

In France 'looting' is the unpardonable offence. You can get dead-drunk, if you have the wish and the chance; you can do almost any misdeed, and all will be overlooked. But 'looting' is beyond pardon.

Private Turton, who comes from Uxbridge, is in the 18th London. Except at Vimereux (and, to a certain extent, Paris) Turton says that the French people are abominable to English soldiers. The expression heard everywhere is 'English non-bing'. They seem to blame the English for all the damage that has been done to their property.

It is safest not to make asides in English, because even the poorer class may understand. Turton and a friend were in a shop buying tobacco for which they were being charged an exorbitant price. The friend turned to Turton and said 'the damned old swindler'. The shopman, who until then had spoken only French, told the man he was 'a damned fraud like most of the English Tommies'. Whereupon the man plunked the packet of tobacco on the counter and told him he 'could keep it for his precious *poilus*'.

The issues of the English daily papers published in France are totally different from the issues published in England. The French papers are much better, being extremely good and truthful in all their editions. The sum of it is that an English paper's report of a battle is full in the firing-line edition; is slightly censored when it gets to the base; and severely mutilated by the Censor before it appears in England.

When Kitchener's death was first told to the troops in France they did not believe it, but thought it one of the many rumours they got out there. Kitchener and the King had each been killed about four times. The men in the camps and trenches joked over the report and in the trenches they had mock funerals. It was a week or ten days later before the death was officially announced to the troops in France.

Sunday, 13 August. VAD hospital notes: Miss Leila Vaughan marched off to Braintree parish-church today not only without the Church of England man but also without the Chapelites. The men protest that their defection last Sunday was not due to the superior skittishness of Miss Ennersley, but to the intolerable tediousness and dreary length of the parish-church service. Their complaint is well-founded. The old women on the Episcopal bench are devising old-womanish National Missions, and relays of women preachers,[1] but will not move a finger to lighten the Church service of dreary incrustations of a by-gone age, or allow reasonable liberty of substituting reasonable alternatives for intolerably long and weary psalms and lessons for the day. The consequence of this Episcopal stick-in-the-mud policy is that the English people are being driven away from the Anglican Church.

The men from the front never use the word England—only 'Blighty'. Conversations like this occur—Sister: 'When did you come home?' Man: 'Meaning where to, sister?' Sister: 'To England.' Man: 'Oh, to Blighty' and then he continues the date.

Monday, 14 August. I was told this morning the strike of Lyons Hall harvesters began on Saturday, and that none of them would begin work today. [The men wanted an increase of £7 on last year's harvest money to reflect inflation.]

A further instalment of the story of Corporal Brooks: The French soldiers never look clean, because the blue-grey of their uniform shows the mud, although it shows no dust. You never see a French soldier with a clean shirt. They wear a dirty bit of rag round their necks and call it a tie. (To hear our soldiers talk you might imagine they dislike the French more than they do the Germans. Part of the feeling may be due to jealousy.)

Arrangements and humours of the YMCA canteen in Lyons Hall Camp: The canteen is in charge of a YMCA man, by name Price. The Tommies call him 'Roger Casement', or (for short) 'Roger' because of his personal resemblance to the Irish rebel. He is one of those who believe that the prophet's mantle has fallen to them.

The canteen is in a very big tent. At the W. end is a platform. In the middle of the platform is a rostrum or pulpit, and at the north end, a

[1] The Bishop of Chelmsford had come up with a scheme for roving bands of women to tour the diocese to address women's meetings in connection with the National Mission. None came to Great Leighs.

squeaky piano. Last night at 9.30 p.m. Mr Price established himself on the platform and called for his attendant to play for him. When he took his place at the piano, the tent emptied. Only about a dozen remained for the 'service'. As he rose to go, one man said 'Hello, Roger is going to pray' and they all got up and went. Mr Price sent an orderly to shut the shutters of the compartments and so close the canteen. But the shutter of the middle compartment got jammed fast, and as the men still crowded for cake Miss Caldwell went on selling.

Mr Price began his music by singing, in a shaky quivering voice, *Abide With Me*. Mrs Sargeant (a very pleasant, and most capable woman, but with narrow Chapel views) alone accompanied him. Hymn finished, he started to read St Luke XI, the orderly still struggling with the disobliging shutter. At this point a soldier put his hand round from the open middle compartment into the tobacco compartment with 'Please, Miss, two packets of Capstan cigarettes.' The server was then sorting out her pennies and said, 'This bar is closed.' 'But I'm going on trek tomorrow and I want them badly.' the man pleaded. At that moment Mr Price read out 'Ask and it shall be given you.' This was too apposite to be neglected. So the two packets were handed over.

Wednesday, 16 August. Old Sam Childs tells me that the 'Lyon Hall' men had come to agreement and gone back to work. He said he did not know, but, as I rather think, he knew but would not say, how much money they were to have for harvest.

12.10 p.m. Mrs J. Herbert Tritton called. She brought a hand-bill as to a Camp [Fire] concert. She was very eloquent in commendation of a wonderful evangelist they have brought to Lyons Hall Camp. Last night he thrilled the men: tears were running down their cheeks. He is to take service in camp also on Sunday afternoon [the 'Under-the-Cedar-Tree' meeting] and evening and Monday evening. I dare say later I shall hear a soldier's report.

Later: I am told that the man's name is Lane. He was born in Texas and has the American genius for 'religious' fiction. He is said to have been four years in the Coldstreams, and a protégé of the late Capt. Alan G. Tritton. Since leaving the army he has been an evangelist in the employ of YMCA. A cold-headed verdict on him is that he has a very attractive voice and is an 'evangelistic' liar of exceptional daring and ingenuity.

Friday, 18 August. I have mentioned that the Lyons Hall men rejected J. Herbert Tritton's offer of £7 for their 'harvest', since other farms were paying £10 or more. I am told the terms they went back to work on were 5s. a week (over and above the £7) for every week of harvest—representing certainly more than £1 this year.[1]

Monday, 21 August. Harry and Tom Sargeant, sons of Thomas Sargeant, gardener at Lyons Hall, are both in the army, Tom being a cook in the RFC [Royal Flying Corps] and Harry in the infantry. The two brothers had not met for five years. Last week Harry wrote home to his mother from France, saying that he thought Tom had passed him in a motor car but could not be absolutely certain. Yesterday he wrote again to say it was Tom, just back from the trenches; and, curiously enough, they have both been sent to the same base.

The Camp-Fire concert was well managed on the whole, and a great success. Beside the piano was a small shallow platform on which the singers stood. Beside the platform was a plain table, behind which sat a sergeant-major, who rose up before each piece and announced who the singer was and what was the name of the piece.

On one occasion the sergeant-major caused great amusement. He rose up and announced a song by 'Gunner . . . . . . [forgetting the name].' Thereupon the Tommies began to call out the man's name and cheer. The sergeant-major rapped loudly on the table with his walking-cane and called out 'Order! Order!' 'Give Me Your Smile.' The combination was ludicrous. The last words were the title of the song.

Charles Ward was home for the week-end. But he lay so long in bed on Sunday that he had not time to come and see me. He was always a grand hand at a long-lie on Sunday, and I myself or other member of the household had often to go of a Sunday morning to Bishop's Hall for the milk. Since 'Charlie' has left the milk is fetched by Mrs Sarah Digby, of the Almshouses. She charges 3d. a week.

Tuesday, 22 August. The present butler at Lyons Hall is an elderly man with grizzled hair, impoverished by the war. He was butler to the British ambassador in Denmark; he saved money which he invested in

[1] 'Harvest Money' was traditionally paid instead of wages. Therefore the value to the worker depended on the weather: if it were dry and the harvest a quick one, he would soon revert to his weekly wage and have the bulk of the harvest-money left over. If the weather were wet and the harvest prolonged, he could end up with less than he would have got with his normal wages.

an industrial concern in Germany. Before the war he lived comfortably on the proceeds, but all has been lost, and he has had to begin life again. He does not like Great Leighs, after his former experience in great houses in foreign capitals.

Saturday, 26 August. Notes of the Zeppelin raid of Thursd. night 24 Aug. as told in the Cadet camp at Little Waltham today: Outside Ipswich is a heath. When the Ipswich folk heard that Zeppelins were coming, they plunged the town in total darkness. Then some went out on the common and lit a bonfire here and there to look (as seen from a great height) like the flare of big works. They also put up a few acetylene-gas lamps on bushes here and there, to look like lamps at street corners. They lit off a few squibs to attract attention. Then they went back to Ipswich, and waited. Presently a Zeppelin passed right over Ipswich, hovered over the illuminated common, dropped a ton-load of bombs about it. Then, having got rid of their cargo, turned and went back seaward, to report in Germany that it had destroyed a great town.

Tuesday, 29 August. This evening Mrs Selkirk-Wells brought over her gramophone and a great variety of records, for the YMCA tent—the only stipulation being that it should be worked only by some one who understands it. It is a really splendid instrument and the number of records is large. It played from 7 p.m. to 9.30 p.m., a new song almost each time. The songs were much to the men's taste. They included: 'Every Laddie Loves a Lassie'; 'The Pink Lady Waltz'; 'The Chocolate Soldier Waltz'; 'Annie Laurie'; 'O You Beautiful Doll'.

Friday, 1 September. —— Fairhead, of White Notley, was in the Essex Yeomanry, and in the 'charge' of 13th May, 1915 when the regiment suffered so heavily. Not a word had been heard of him since, and he was assumed to have been killed. But this week his mother had a letter from him from Switzerland, where he is severely wounded. Presumably he is one of those desperately wounded men whom the Germans have recently been sending into Switzerland.

Saturday, 2 September. 12.15 p.m. gloomy, wet day. My little songster for some time sang its sweet, gentle song boldly in a small tree, close by which I was standing. But it kept itself quite out of sight. 12.20 p.m.: a great and continuous sound of wheel traffic, coming down Fuller

Street. 12.30 p.m.: continuous rumble of cannon in E. direction.

3.30 p.m. Miss Lucy Tritton came with her great-uncle, the Revd Reginald Fawkes. She said that rigidly righteous people were rather shocked at the 'profanity' of some of the songs at the Camp Concert. Mrs J. Herbert Tritton was shocked at Capt. W. S. Roddie's song, 'Where Have I Met You Before?' This contained allusion to the final destination of the Kaiser. He goes to Heaven's gate but is kept out by S. Peter who tells him that he has made it hot for many people and had better go and try the heat for himself. Mrs Thos. Sargeant was also much shocked by this song. Mrs Sargeant also took great exception to an expression in Miss Bannerman's song—'I've Been to The Pictures'—viz. 'my bloke and I'. Mrs T. S. was strongly of opinion that soldiers' ears should not be wounded by such expressions.

George Avery is a member of the Great Leighs Boy Scouts, and his great ambition is to be bugler of the Troop. He thinks the post lies between himself and Gordon Ward. To increase his chances, he slips up to the Rectory whenever he can, borrows the bugle, retires to 'camp field' (behind Bishop's Hall) and practises by himself. This wet afternoon he was there practising all alone.

Note from Lyons Hall Camp: 'Tommies', even of apparently fair intelligence and education, take no interest in matters (even military matters) outside the narrow round of their company duty, or regimental duty (so far as any comes their way).

Sunday, 3 September. A little after 11 p.m., Sat. 2 Sept. I heard voices in Lyons Hall Camp and whinnying of horses. I knew that the horses were being moved on news having been received of Zeppelins being expected. I went to bed again. The two Rectory maids thought they heard (between 1 a.m. and 1.30 a.m.) a bomb dropped not far off somewhere to north of the Rectory. They saw a very bright flash.

Miss Minnie Taylor said: at the Post Office they were up practically all night, on the telephone, because of the raid. A Zeppelin is reported to have been brought down. A bomb fell in Great Waltham parish.

In the Post Office this morning (circa 9.15 a.m.) 'Con.' Wright, a 'dealer' (buys and re-sells pigs and poultry), was explaining that he had been at Haverhill, Suffolk on Frid. 25 August. There he had seen a bomb dropped by a Zeppelin just there, but date he had neglected to learn. It was a gas-bomb, pear-shaped, about 3 feet high and weighed 156 lb. A War Office expert who saw it said that had it exploded and its contents become gasified, it had enough poisonous gas to have killed man, woman and child throughout Haverhill. The gas was solidified; of a yellow colour; and filled a cylinder as deep as C. W.'s arm.

Monday, 4 September. There was a concert given in YMCA canteen this evening by the howitzer ('D') battery: While Gunner Harris was singing there came in at the back of the canteen a very smartly dressed lady, in a softish blue loose coat and skirt, with ruffles round the sleeves, a blue hat with blue rose at the side and a white veil. She asked one of the lady-servers if she might borrow her umbrella; she bowed pleasantly and smiled to a second lady-server, who returned the bow politely and smiled back, as to an affable stranger. Then the lady asked Mrs Thayre (who was at the coffee-compartment in Mrs Thos. Sargeant's place [and was Mrs Leslie Tritton's cook]) 'How are things getting on?' Mrs Thayre was on the point of answering but suddenly exclaimed 'Why it's Sergeant-Major Young!' He was dressed up to take his part in the next item—a monologue entitled 'the Suffragette'.

This was Mrs Thomas Sargeant's evening to serve at the tea compartment, but she has asked to be excused on concert nights. The expressions used in some of the songs shock her. She thinks it is lowering for the men to hear them.

The cheering reported in Lyons Hall Camp [this morning] seems to have been at the receipt of news that detachments were going to France, as the men have all been longing for. About thirty are to be told off from each battery to go to France. One man, who evidently thinks he will be passed over, grumbled that it was about time they all went if they wanted to get the war ended soon.

Tuesday, 5 September. Mr R. W. Taylor [the new Superintendent of the Lyons Hall YMCA tent] is about nineteen years of age and has been to many military camps, but in none has he heard such terrible swearing and profane language as seems to be habitual among the Scots troops in Essex. Lyons Hall Camp not excepted.

Jests from other YMCA camp canteens. At Thornton Heath there was a Keble man, who helped there during the vacation. He entered 'the competition for the kettle' [war-time tall stories] by a missionary story. A member of the Keble Eight went, as a missionary, to a cannibal island; was promptly seized upon; sentenced to be sacrificed and eaten. Being proud of his Eights blazer, he had taken it with him, and thought he would wear it for the last time as a sacrificial robe. When he was led out to be slain, the cannibal King rushed at him, threw his arms round him, and said 'My dear fellow, why didn't you say you were a Keble man. I was there, not so long since, myself.'

Mrs J. Herbert Tritton has apparently hinted several times that she would like to address the men in the canteen tent, but has been put off on one excuse or another. They don't want 'addresses'. They want a tent where they can have their recreation, and not be bothered by people coming about them. Their verdict on Mrs J. H. T. is that she is 'a dear, good old soul, when she gets it all her own way'.[1]

Sunday, 10 September. 9 a.m. road to Church deep in dust, and roadside dusty: I met James Rogers on his way to dig potatoes for his dinner. He heard from his son, Joseph Rogers, the prisoner in Germany, on Tuesday 29 Aug. He was then at harvest work on a farm, with five other Englishmen, and was very cheerful. James Rogers dated the receipt of the letter as 'a fortnight past next Tuesday'.

Monday, 11 September. Mrs J. Herbert Tritton sent her youngest daughter, Olive, to tell Mr R. W. Taylor, superintendent of the YMCA canteen that he was not conducting the affair properly. He had not, every night, prayers and an address. He said that (i) it was not his place to stand up and preach to men, of whom many were no doubt better men than himself, and all of whom were certainly older, and (ii) while he was in charge he would have no stranger coming in, to address the men.

Mrs Tritton has been very insistent that the men in Camp should sign 'the War Roll' which seems to be a teetotallers' pledge. 'Just to oblige the lady', a number of the men not only put down their own names, but also, 'just to see what would happen', put down, each of them, half a dozen names of their comrades. They were taken aback when Mrs T. asked to tea at Lyons Hall, on Tuesday 5 Sept., all whose names had been put on the list. There was difficulty in inventing excuses, though none of them wanted to go. But, in the long run, everyone invented and sent in, some polite reason of refusal. Undaunted, she has repeated her invitation for tomorrow.

[1] The Trittons felt a certain proprietary interest in the YMCA. They had long supported the movement, both in time and money. In 1880 the first meeting of the YMCA's National Council was held in their London home.

Wednesday, 13 September. 10.45 a.m. 'Tim' Tritton [the squire's grandson], riding Colonel Harris's black horse, and Lucy Tritton, riding the Colonel's brown horse, passed Rectory Gate on way to Great Road. Lucy Tritton said that 1,500 men 'slept' last night under canvas at the west end of Lyons Hall park. Some of the tents were close by the white gate which goes out of the park at the Hole farm, and just under Lucy Tritton's window. Whenever there was a light in her room they called out 'Good night, Mary! Sleep well, Mary!' She could not get to sleep, because they kept talking, joking and laughing all night.

Today, in finishing cutting a field on Moulsham Hall farm, there was a great crowd of villagers with sticks and W. H. Thorogood with a shot-gun. They killed sixteen rabbits and four hares. The rabbits—very good ones—were sold in Great Leighs for 9*d.* each. In old days this was the harvest workers' perquisite. No rabbits were shot, but they were clubbed and each labourer got each rabbit he clubbed. The only shots heard today were those of farm-men after rabbits in the harvest fields.

Miss Eliza Vaughan called this afternoon with a budget of news: Zeppelin raid of 2 Sept./Su. 3 Sept: There is high ground on the side of Finchingfield which lies toward Sampford called Hankins Hill. An old woman there says 'If I am not speaking the truth, may this be the last word I may speak—but they passed so low that I could hear the old mocks a-talking. They were a-singing.' 'mocks' (? mucks) is an Essex word for things or people you don't like.

Saturday, 16 September. A little after noon Mrs J. Herbert Tritton called: She said she is very disappointed that in the YMCA canteen they do not have prayers when they close at 9.30 p.m. every night. She herself would have undertaken the duty, but her husband will not hear of it. On Sunday she is having Mr Hayes [YMCA secretary] to tea, and some of the officers to tea and supper, and is going to broach the subject. She is very gratified that twenty-two men put down their names to the War Roll. She has twice asked them to tea. Sergeant Hunter, a dear man, has been so very kind in going round with the invitations, but it is so hard on the poor fellows that on each occasion they have been unexpectedly called off on military duty and so unable to come.

She has had erected of her own, at the end of the YMCA tent, a tent, called 'The Quiet Tent', to which the men can withdraw to say their prayers. She hopes to have a Bible class there once a week. She goes there often to chat with the men, but generally, when she gets there, a nice boy comes in with a polite message that just at present the men in camp are much occupied with duty and cannot come in.

Friday, 22 September. Thomas Sargeant, gardener at Lyons Hall, had an official message this morning that his second youngest son, Harry Sargeant, had been killed in France, on Mond. 4 Sept.

Passing Lyons Hall Camp this morning my elder daughter saw a very sick horse in the lines. It had had a bed of chaff made for it, and was lying with its head on a pillow.

Sunday, 24 September. 1.15 a.m. a curious noise, very distinct, and apparently almost outside my bedroom window. It was a harsh, metallic-sounding *churr-churr*, like the sharpening of a scythe, or the rasping of a file on metal, repeated about three times in quick succession. It was repeated after a few seconds, and again repeated after a few other seconds. I had heard it once before in the earlier part of the night. I took it to be the noise made by some bird.

W. Herbert Dee, Church Clerk, told me that T. Lewin told him he had seen what he thought was a Zeppelin pass over just before 11 p.m. Then three or four times afterwards, there were explosions. He thinks that close on twenty bombs were dropped. Several ('a lot of them' Mr Dee said) Zeppelins passed, returning N.-wards.

Everybody who heard it said it had been hit and would soon come down. Just after 1 a.m. in the S.E. they saw a handful of fire, high up in the sky, burst out. This quickly spread, and they saw a Zeppelin, end downwards, slowly falling. The light was so bright that you could have seen to pick up a needle from the road. This was the Zepp. which came down between Billericay and Brentwood. 'It was a lovely sight to see it.' A second Zepp. seemed to be in a blaze in the N.E. This was the one which came down at Wivenhoe. [It was actually at Peldon, about two miles from Mersea.]

The brother of Moore, the Lynderswood housemaid, is in the Lancashire Fusiliers and has got the DCM [Distinguished Conduct Medal]. On the strength of this, Moore carries her head very high and has snubbed Mrs B. senior [the colonel's mother] three times today.

Notes of the Zeppelin raid from Major Wm. Brown: In that field when the [second] Zeppelin came down is a little boarded cottage. The people there were terrified. They were still more alarmed when the crew (twenty of them) came to the cottage and in perfect English told them to quit it at once, because they were going to set fire to the Zepp. and if the flames from it burnt the cottage while its inhabitants were in it they feared they might be hanged. There was among them a lady, quite a young girl. When the inmates had left the cottage, one of the crew went forward to the Zeppelin and set fire to it. An explosion followed which blew off the man's leg and killed him.

Special Constables then came up and a few soldiers immediately after them. The burning of the Zeppelin at Peldon did the Germans no good. There was very little wood in the fabric—only the skin was burnt. The ribs are intact and the engines are quite whole.

Monday, 25 September. I went to Braintree this morning. The 'pneumonia' patient [at the VAD hospital] is still alive, but in a very critical condition. The history of his case is this: he had pleurisy in France; on his way to this country he contracted also pneumonia; by careless treatment at Clacton-on-Sea and on his journey thence to VAD hospital, Braintree, pyo-pneumo-thorax ('pus' and air in the pleural cavities) supervened. By 'tapping' Dr H. G. K. Young removed twelve pints of fluid. Since then he has inserted a tube to withdraw the suppuration ('pus'). Dr Young had an idea this was a case where *sphagnum moss* dressings would be of use. My daughter, Mildred, at once wrote to St Andrews for two lb. of the prepared moss to be sent.

The officers in Lyons Hall Camp have now to do physical exercise. The Tritton children at the Hole farm say it is great fun to watch them. They are particularly taken by Lieut. (acting adjutant) H. E. Butler doing leap-frogging over another officer.

On Su. 24 Sept. Mrs Hannan, wife of Lieut. Hannan of 'D' Battery, drove over to Billericay, taking with her as her groom, Driver A. Bell. She did very splendidly in the way of picking up souvenirs, viz. fragments of the wrecked Zeppelin. But Driver A. Bell of 'A' battery outdid her. Being in khaki, he strolled up to the cordon of soldiers who were stationed to keep off the public. Presently, when sentries were changed, he did sentry-go, as if he were one of them, stooping down as occasion served, to stick some fragment in his pocket. When his pockets failed from fulness, he slipped other fragments under the collar of his tunic. In this way he amassed quite a number of pieces of aluminium and of bits of the burnt cord of the netting of the Zeppelin gas-bag.

On Monday evening, he was quite the biggest man in camp, selling a bit of aluminium and a piece of charred string at 1s. the pair, to his mates and to the Canteen-ladies. He made about £1 on the sales, and heartily wished his tunic-pockets had been larger.

Driver A. Bell reported that one of the men from Billericay Camp who found the compass of the Zeppelin, refused an offer of £5 for it from a Londoner.

Wednesday, 27 September. A note was handed in this morning from Mr T. Sargeant:

26 September, 1916

Dear Sir,

We beg to return our Sincere Thanks for your kind note of Sympathy in the loss of our dear Boy We feel we are among the many who are sharing the same sorry. But we are thankfull for the Knowledge that He was prepared for the Call.

Thanking you for all your Kindness . . .

Miss Eliza Vaughan called about 3.30 p.m. She had, as usual, a little budget of news: The National Mission: She had gone to a 'National Mission' Service at Braintree Church. The 'Bishop's Messenger' was the Rt. Revd the Lord Bishop of Sodor and Man. He frowned, he smiled, he wept, he wrung his hands, he waved his hands; he thumped the pulpit; he whispered, he roared; and, all through he babbled, for over forty minutes. For the most part he said, with greatest emphasis, things that had no meaning. One part is worth recording:

The world is full of joy. Insects buzz, because they are full of joy. Beasts call out, because they are full of joy. Oh my friends, have any of you had the privilege, the very great privilege, of a long illness? I was once so weak that I had to be fed with a spoon. Have any of you ever known the privilege, the very great privilege, of being fed with a spoon? One day I said to my wife 'I think, my dear, I could now hold the spoon myself.' 'No, dear' she answered, 'not today, certainly; perhaps tomorrow.' When the morrow came, I said 'I think today I could hold the spoon.' 'No, dear' she answered 'today we will hold the spoon together.' Oh the joy, the joy, the JOY of being able to hold the spoon. You will never know the joy I had that day when I was able to hold the spoon.

His Lordship gave the congregation a joyful moment. He had, as he was anxious to show the people, a gold watch, which he laid on the side of the pulpit. In one of his hand-wavings he sent this spinning, smash into the aisle. When the smash came he said—'Oh my brethren, dearly beloved, don't think of my watch. There are things more important than my watch. There is the mission. *There is the Mission.*'

Another joyful moment for the weary congregation was when the Vicar of Braintree, after the forty minutes, went to the altar to say the concluding prayers, but had to wait while old lawn sleeves picked up the shattered watch.[1]

Braintree VAD hospital: The pneumonia-case has small chance of recovery. His name is Roberts. His father and mother have been twice to see him. The father works on a railway in Wales. They are Welsh Methodists. Happily there is among the Braintree ministers one not merely of their own sect, but who is able to talk to the lad, and pray with him, in Welsh.

Sunday, 1 October. This morning the clocks were set back an hour to bring them to the national time. No one connected with country-work that I have spoken to on the subject during the past months has had anything but condemnation for the artificial time.

Monday, 2 October. George Wiseman (nicknamed 'Wiby') was in Great Leighs yesterday, visiting Mrs Ward (widow) who brought him up. He is much distressed at the cursing and swearing which goes on in the army. Edward Bearman is also home on leave. He has got his two stripes as corporal. Sergeant Harry Taylor (Great Leighs Post Office) has written to Connie Stoddart that he has just seen her brother, Arthur, go off to France in a batch of 300. They were all very happy.

Tuesday, 3 October. The *sphagnum moss* has arrived at Braintree VAD hospital in record-time. Dr H. G. K. Young is using it in several cases and finds it just what he wants. The pneumonia-patient is still in life, but that is all that can be said of him. The moss is in oblong cakes, sterilized and prepared.

Miss Eliza Vaughan's (the suffragette, of Rayne) great ambition has been to see a Zeppelin. Hearing that Zeppelins were expected on Su. night (1 Oct.) she went out, with a bag of peppermint bulls-eyes, at 9.30 p.m. and sat on the bridge at Rayne in the midst of all the roughs

---

[1] 'Old Lawn Sleeves' was the Rt Revd James Denton Thompson, Bishop of Sodor and Man from 1912 to 1924.

of the place. Just before midnight, when her mouth was sore with sucking peppermints, and she was very bored with the conversation of the yokels, she managed to see the Zeppelin.

Wednesday 4 October. I preserve a letter of Dr H. G. K. Young, the surgeon of the VAD hospital, Braintree, as to sphagnum moss [to Mildred Clark]:

1 October, 1916

Thanks so much for writing to the Sphagnum Moss people. They sent me a supply yesterday. I am finding it particularly useful as an absorbent and deodorant dressing in a couple of cases in the V.A.D. Thank you also for your note. We have had some busy times lately at the Hospital—As I am writing I hear the sinister dinning of a Zeppelin which apparently is passing more or less over the house—a loathesome noise . . .

Thursday, 5 October. As I passed (old) Cole Hill cottages James Rogers was packing the second load of his belongings in a two-horse wagon. As I came back Mrs Rogers was perched in straw in the middle of the waggon and they were preparing to move off. I am sorry they are leaving the parish. They were nice people to have in a parish.

Monday, 9 October. Braintree VAD hospital: —— Roberts, the pneumonia patient, died on 4 Oct. His brother came and took the body for burial at their home in North Wales.

Dr R. P. Smallwood called 12.30 p.m. Sir Richard Pennyfeather has given up Little Waltham Hall. The new tenant is to be Mrs Noel Vickers ('Linda'). Sir R. P. has taken a house in Chelmsford.

This afternoon's post brought an advertisement [for 'The Man Who Dined With the Kaiser' who will lecture on his thrilling experiences at the 'Empire' Theatre, Chelmsford, for Wounded British Horses. Tickets: 5s., 3s., 2s., and 1s.].

Tuesday, 10 October. Edith Caldwell called: Secretary of Entertainment Committee and one of the lady-helpers in YMCA canteen in Lyons Hall Camp. They had no concert in camp last evening but the men made such a noise and began to sing such filthy 'comic' songs that the YMCA Superintendent had to order them to leave off.

Most of the best of the Scots Tommies have gone to France. Most of the Scots NCOs and nearly all officers are left. Most of the newcomers are 'Derbyites' and from East London. They are described as being 'awful swine'.

Wednesday, 11 October. Major Jas. Caldwell is in hope of being taken on in army service. A former member of his firm has been wounded and Mr Caldwell thinks that, if he is invalided, he may quite well take his place, as he knows as much about the business as Mr Caldwell himself. Mr Caldwell's family, however, say that, after his accident, no doctor will ever pass him for foreign service.

Friday, 13 October. The steam-engine of the threshing machine is hard at work at Rectory barn driving chaff-cutter, chopping up oat-straw for chaff. Richard Arnold, tenant of the Glebe farm, feeds bullocks in the barn and yard during the winter.

Popular reports in Chelmsford today (Florence Hicks) that this winter (a) the soldiers are to be all billeted in towns, not in villages; (b) that the soldiers are all to go to meals in a tent and no rations are to be taken round to the houses. Last winter it was found that the rations issued fed the billeting-people as well as the soldiers.

Monday, 16 October. Report in Braintree is that the inmates of the Halstead Union Workhouse are all to be transferred for the winter to Braintree Union so that Halstead Union may be wholly given up for quarters of soldiers (from Lyons Hall Camp). The present lot of men in Lyons Hall Camp do not seem favourites in the district.

Tuesday, 17 October. 11.45 a.m. Miss Tritton of Lyons Hall called. She says Lyons Hall Camp is to be broken up very early next week.

Thursday, 19 October. 10.15 a.m. this morning's post brought me a letter from my former groom-gardener [now in France]:

12 October 1916

Dear Sir trusting this will find you all quite well as it leaves me the same it has been a long time since I wrote last. it is much better weather this week but rather cold. it makes one think of school days here to see the windmills on the go. how is the pony and lad [?] getting on I haven't heard from home yet it seems a long time to get a letter I am sory I cant say much hopeing to see you all soon yours Sincerely Charlie

Saturday, 21 October. 'Bill' Duke has been called up and left this morning. He was called up before and then rejected, as unfit for service, because of bad feet. He managed the electric light apparatus at Lyons Hall, and since the household was reduced owing to the war, has cleaned boots and done other housework. He has been, since he came here, a most faithful member of the choir.

8 p.m. Major James Caldwell called: he is furious with 'Bill' Duke. He ought to have told the officers at the recruiting station that he was a skilled electrician. In that case he would have been put into the Royal Engineers, given work he is well capable of, and had 5s. to 6s. more weekly pay than he will have in the RGA [Royal Garrison Artillery] to which he has been attached and in which he will be of no manner of use.

Monday, 23 October. A note was handed in from Mrs Henry Wells, Endway, as to her neighbour, Mrs John Ketley. This is the case of a girl of a consumptive family marrying, unadvisedly:

Sir Mrs J. Ketley is ordered away to Halstead Sanatorium for a six weeks' treatment, her husband was wondering if you thought Mr Tritton would send her there as she is to weak to go by trap sorry to trouble you but would you let Ketley know if he ought to go to see them or could you arrange for him Mrs Ketley is to go on Wednesday next 25th inst. her sister is with her and has to take charge of the four little children . . .

My answer to the note was that I had no doubt that J. H. Tritton would send his chauffeur (Harry Ward) and car, but that as Miss Tritton (Eliz. M.) was at Lyons Hall, the husband ought to go there this evening and see her.

Saturday, 28 October. 10.10 a.m. Lyons Hall Camp actually on the move. Traction-engine drawing lorry with heavy wooden camp-fittings.

10.45 a.m. Dr R. P. Smallwood called.[1]

Monday, 30 October. Signum filii hominis ['And then shall appear the

---

[1] Dr Smallwood's visit was to see Mrs Clark, who died that evening. She was sixty-five. Although Andrew Clark was deeply hurt, his grief did not make him interrupt his War Diary or cause him to violate his rule against inserting personal matter unrelated to the war. He ordered that Mildred not be told of her mother's death until she had finished sitting her exams in St Andrews. Her daughter remembers that Mildred would never forgive her sister for agreeing. Mrs Clark was buried on Tuesday 31 October and the service was taken by the Rector himself, another example of his amazing self-control.

sign of the Son of man in heaven . . .'] (S. Matt. 24.30). This saying is deeply impressed in the minds of rustics. Yesterday evening, the man in Driver's shop (the chief Chelmsford news agent and stationer) said this forenoon the setting sun and clouds produced for a little the appearance of a large opal cross in the sky. This was seen by many people. This morning country customers who came to the shop commented on it, and said that 'the end of the world was coming'.

Recent casualties have been heavily felt in Chelmsford and district. Messrs. J. G. Bond Ltd, said this forenoon that the mourning orders during the last three months had been overwhelming. They cannot get in materials fast enough to meet the demand.

Friday, 3 November. Lyons Hall Camp is now represented, as to its personnel, by one very sick horse; one man to look after the horse; one officer, to look after the man; and one soldier-servant, to look after the officer. Miss Tritton says that Lyons Hall park will be used as a site for a summer camp as long as the war lasts.

Saturday, 4 November. 6.30 p.m. Major James Caldwell called. Very great military changes are impending. The whole of what is called 'the second line' will presently be sent out to France. Men who have enlisted only 'for Home Defence' will take it badly when they have to go abroad, but abroad they will go. Even such elderly men as the Territorials 6 Essex who at present do sentry-go at Chelmsford station, will be sent out. These older men will be stationed on the lines of communication and in dockyards and set younger men free to be sent to the front. All men up to fifty-one will be called up to drill for home defence.

Monday, 6 November. The Rayners have heard nothing as to their son, Charlie Rayner, being missing, and are hurt at the report which had run through the village.

Thursday, 9 November. 10.15 a.m. morning's post brought: a letter from my former groom-gardener; also an advertisement slip from a North Essex weekly asking me to insert my advertisement of my pony and trap for sale, which I am parting with after my wife's death.

31 October 1916

Dear Sir I was glad to Receive your letter so sory to hear that Mrs Clark was so ill and that you had been so sadly I am sure these are very trying times for

Every one it was very good of you to tell me all the news I was surprised to hear the garden had done so badly as I thought every thing looked so nice when I was down in the Summer but the insects and jays were a nusance to me every year. I was glad to hear the pony had been so good the dogs work so hard out hear one will see a big wooden wheel attached to the wall of every cottage a dog works it for water and making the butter and when walking along the road one will meet a little trap or barrow with three dogs pulling it and a man sitting in it and goods which he has to sell.[1] we dont know Sunday week-day out here we simply go on with work just the same I think this is all I have to say now . . .

Friday, 10 November. Mention has been made in a previous volume of Jack Childs who was sent home on completion of his army service. His father, old Sam Childs, says 'my son Jack told me that the war would not be over for a twelvemonth yet. So many young Germans were coming forward every year. They were still fighting at the very same place where he was before he came back a year ago.'

Saturday, 11 November. The report in the village is that Frank Cloughton also is 'missing' (son of Fred Cloughton, shepherd on Lyons Hall estate). 'Billy' Brock's mother has not heard from 'Billy' for a month and fears that he also is 'missing'.

Another of her sons—'Jack' Brock is at Felixstowe with the Essex Regiment. He has written that 120 of the battalion were ordered to the front. When they were on the station-platform waiting for the train, a sergeant-major (or an officer, report not clear which) shot himself. The village verdict is that this was a more than usually foolish suicide, as the man had a chance of shooting Germans.

The farmers in Great Leighs have had papers from the military authorities, with forms to fill in particulars as to their young men on the farms. Intimation is given that if they fail to do so, the authorities will fill them up for themselves. Richard Arnold says he will just let them do so.

I sold this morning my pony, harness, trap etc. to Mr F. Fuller, Cole Farm [for two guineas], less than half their real value. But there are many sales of ponies and traps at present on account of the extreme cost of horse-food.

8.15 p.m. Major James Caldwell called: Talk in the City is that there

---

[1] Andrew Clark had noted in his *Great Leighs Collection* (vol. xviii) that similar dog-carts had been used in Great Leighs in the 1840s.

is to be a big movement presently, a further surprize for the Germans. There is a general feeling of expectancy. Every man in the land—unmarried—and up to age of thirty—will now be called out.

[Letter from the Rector to William R. Redman.]*

11 November 1916

Dear Mr Redman,

Accept my sincere thanks for your most kind, thoughtful and helpful message.

My wife suffered latterly very great pain and discomfort and weakness, but her patience and cheerfulness throughout were a great help to us.

The last few years have been years of partings with me, and have left me a very lonely man, lingering behind my old friends. I often think of Henry Vaughan's lines—[in *Friends Departed*]

> They are all gone into the world of light!
> And I alone sit ling'ring here,
> I see them walking in an air of glory,
> Whose light doth trample on my days
> Ever yours very gratefully,
> A. Clark.

Monday, 13 November. Charlie Cook, who worked for Major William Brown at Bishop's Hall, has been killed. He was slightly wounded and sent back in to the trenches with his hand bound up. This time he was wounded 'from top to toe', and died either as he was being taken to hospital or just after he was admitted.

The authorities are asking the Essex roadmen to go to France to do road-work. Their work will consist in following up the troops as they advance, making good the roads. They were at William Herbert Dee, the Church Clerk, on Wedn. (8 Nov.). The terms they offered him were food, billeting, uniform as an ordinary soldier, 3s. pay a day, and separation-allowance which will amount to 25s. a week for his wife and children. He consulted Major Wm. Brown who used to be superintendent of road-work for the County Council. Major Brown rather advised him to accept. It was not compulsory yet, but he had little doubt that before long it would be and then the terms would be less favourable.

The official intimation that Charles Rayner was 'missing' stated that he was 'missing' on 7th September, but mentioned no place. 7th September was the date of the last letter they had from him. The probability was that he was killed, but there is a bare possibility that he may be wounded and a prisoner. The Rayners had a story that a woman had an ordinary field postcard from her relative at the front; and, on that day year, had a postcard from him, a prisoner in Germany, saying he had not been allowed to write before.

Wednesday, 15 November. Frank Cloughton has been heard from this week. —— Hales, son of Widow —— Hales, opposite Post Office has not been heard of for some time.

Thursday, 16 November. Mrs Harry Ward had today a letter from her son, Charles H. Ward. He is in hospital, but she does not understand whether he is there because sick or wounded.

Saturday, 18 November. Major James Caldwell called: He heard from his nephew, Sidney Caldwell, with the RFA in France. He has been in several 'pushes' but this 'push' puts them all in the shade. They have been going at it night and day, 'hammer and tongs', for five continuous weeks. He wonders whether he will ever recover his normal hearing.

Major Caldwell had a very amusing journey from Liverpool Street Station to Chelmsford this week. There were three people in the compartment: Major Caldwell himself; a New Zealander, of most formidable physique—6ft. 2in. high, broad proportionally, and thewed like a Hercules; the most utter contrast in the scale of humanity, a thin, anaemic, shred of a man. Just as the train was starting, a porter ran up escorting a late arrival—a soldier on leave from France bundled himself in, and banged the door. The soldier wiped his brow, after his run and sat down. Presently he began to grumble to the anaemic. Everything out there was wrong. Nothing was done for the soldier's comfort and so on. Major Caldwell thought that the New Zealander was asleep: his eyes at least were closed. But he suddenly sprang up, crossed over to the soldier, shook his fist in his face, and threatened to chuck him out at the window. Here was he, who had chucked up his job, and come 12,000 miles to fight for England, and there was a cad who had been compelled to fight—an Englishman *compelled* to fight for England—and was grumbling at it. Major Caldwell said the vocabulary of abuse which was showered on the 'grouser' overpassed not only everything he had heard but even his imagination of such things. The 'grouser' collapsed; the anaemic was in abject terror lest his sympathetic chorus to the grouser's grumbling should bring a shift of the storm on him.

Charles H. Ward, Royal Horse
Artillery

Leonard Port in his Church Lads'
Brigade uniform

Soldiers of the 5th Essex Regiment

Reg Ketley, Essex Yeomanry   Ernest Wright, Essex Yeomanry

The 5th Essex Territorial camp, 1911. Harry Taylor is second from the left.

Tuesday, 21 November. Charlie Ward is, his mother thinks, suffering from eczema to which he has always been subject. He has not been in the firing-line but has been helping to build stables. He writes home that it is worth being ill to have the comfort of sleeping in a bed again. He was always a great hand for bed and was often late for his work here by delay in getting up.

Wednesday, 22 November. Morning's post (10.15 a.m.) brought various letters, including one from the hon. secr. of the Royal Historical Society suggesting that I should become a Fellow of it. I declined the proposal—ostensibly, uncertain health; partly also because I am reducing all subscriptions and do not care to pay £2.2s. a year.

Saturday, 25 November. Charlie Ward has written home that he is better and out. It is very cold. Harry Milton has fever, in France. 'Billy' Brock has not been heard from for a considerable time, but there has been no notice from the War Office that he is missing; so his people suppose that he is somewhere in the fighting line where he can't write.

Mrs Jack Ketley died this morning at 1.30 a.m.: Emily Ketley: aet 40.

7 p.m. Major James Caldwell called. He was very depressed about both the war and about commerce—rather an unusual thing for him. He says the most extraordinary thing about the war is the prodigious use of high explosives by Germany. He hears from officers on leave that the official bulletins suppress vital facts, if they are unfavourable. Thus they announce 600 German prisoners at a particular position but say nothing of 20,000 British casualties in taking it. Nearly all the newspapers concur in this policy of hushing up losses. The *Daily Mail* is an exception.

His nephew, Sidney Caldwell, in the Artillery, writes from France, that the mud at the front is so bad that wheels cannot be used and ammunition for the guns and other supplies, has to be drawn forward in sledges. Officers from the front told Major Caldwell that the official statements of the 'pushes' in France are dishonest. They mention the 'taking' of a position. A little later they speak of the 'retaking' of the same position. They are silent as to the very heavy British casualties incurred when the Germans recovered it, and the heavy losses in 'retaking' it.

Officers and NCO's back from the front who have conversed with very frank and intelligent German prisoners say that the stuff in our newspapers about scarcity of food in Germany is all 'bunkum'.

Tuesday, 28 November. William Jiggins, an old man, somewhat deficient intellect came to me some days ago in distress about his application for an Old Age Pension. He had been assured he would require a certificate of age from Mr A. S. Duffield's (Solicitor, Chelmsford), for which the fee would be 4s.7d.—a large sum to a helpless old fellow who is now earning nothing. I wrote to the Registrar General's Office and received (first post today) a satisfactory reply. No certificate is needed on making application.

Wednesday, 29 November. 10.15 a.m. morning's post brought a letter from my sister-in-law [Miss Alice Paterson]. She is manageress of the Tayside Laundry, Newport.

20 November 1916

My dear Andrew,
... How are your 'war' notes getting on and have you had any good contributions to them lately? Some of the lads who come home from the front seem to have developed their imaginations marvellously in France, judging by the tales they tell. The latest fiction here is that Kitchener is a prisoner in Germany but if that was a fact don't you think the Germans would be proud to blazon it abroad?
Two of my workers have gone to make munitions at Gretna Green, and about a fortnight ago they, along with 200 others, were poisoned, some so badly that they nearly died but fortunately all recovered. All the flour in that set of huts was found to have been poisoned and the cook has disappeared! She was an Englishwoman but they *suppose* she must have been bribed by the Germans. There is no doubt about the poisoned flour ...

Friday, 1 December. 5 p.m. Dr Smallwood called. He said that the German aeroplane which 'raided' London on Tuesd. 28 November dropped a bomb just behind 4, Lowndes Sq., S.W., the London residence of J. Herbert Tritton.

Saturday, 2 December. A village-woman's opinion of whole-meal bread [to be introduced on 1 January 1917 under the Flour and Bread Order of 29 November]—'That will be the black stuff the Germans eat. Fancy bringing English people to eat that stuff. It ain't fit for pigs.'

Wednesday, 6 December. The Rayner twins have received papers calling them up. They will be eighteen before Christmas. It is very hard on their father because they work the farm with him. Nothing has been heard further about their elder brother, Charles Rayner.

2.15 p.m. afternoon's post brought a letter from Miss Elizabeth M. Tritton:

5 December, 1916

I suppose you heard that the aeroplane over London last week visited 14 Lowndes Square, and dropped a bomb in the kitchen there (which is built out behind). The bomb chose a china cupboard as its destination. The cook was considerably surprised but not hurt. All sorts of people rang up No. 4, saying they heard Lowndes Square was entirely demolished and was it true and how did my parents feel under the circumstances. I hear (but not from home) that the aeroplane was an English one, caught by the Germans—and that was why it got to London with no opposition.

Major James Caldwell told me on Sat. evening that the 'German' aeroplane, when it dropped a bomb at the back of Lowndes Square, was really aiming for Buckingham Palace.

Sunday, 10 December. I preserve the official bulletin for today. It is insolent in its brevity: 'Summary of Saturday's Official War News. There is nothing of importance to report on any front.'

Monday, 11 December. Dr Smallwood called this morning. He said the Scottish troops at Braintree were under orders to leave for Ireland. The whole of the Lowland Division is to go from Essex. Its place is to be taken by Colonials, including Canadians.

He was very pessimistic about the war. 'The war is really over and we have lost. The Germans have command of the North Sea. I met last week an officer from a submarine and he said "Last year we chased the Germans, now we have to turn round and they chase us."'

Mrs Drummond (daughter of the Revd John Green, sometime rector of Little Leighs) is going to present Little Leighs with a 'war-shrine', to be set up in the churchyard there and to have on it the names of all Little Leighs men who have fallen in the war.

Monday, 18 December. My younger daughter, Mildred, returned from University Hall, St Andrews for the University vacation, on Sat. 16 Dec. 1916. From her I had a number of notes:

Passports. In order to go anywhere in the neighbourhood of

Inverness or Dingwall or Cromarty, it is now necessary to have a passport. This precaution is supposed to prevent news leaking out about movements of our ships. It is more or less futile, because from the gossip of seamen's wives, mothers and sisters, the arrival of ships is known all over each district.

A report current in Scotland gives out that, in the battle of Loos, the Warwickshire regiment, both officers and men, got so out of hand and so undisciplined that the Scots Guards turned their machine-guns on them.

Thursday, 21 December. Thos. Stoddart, my Churchwarden, called yesterday afternoon to say goodbye. He was leaving Great Leighs, for good and all, today. He was on his way to the Almshouses with 30s. from the Ann Jenkins benefaction for each of the two inmates. The benefaction says 'gift of coal at Christmas' but such gift would be too large for use. So I have advised the Churchwardens to give some part of it for under-clothing.

Yesterday, 20 Dec. 1916, F. Mann of Little Leighs (our baker on M., W., and F.) brought what he said was the first 'war bread'. I myself can perceive very little difference between it and our former bread.

On Friday I sent a Postal Order to a well-known firm of London tobacconists, asking for a packet of cigarettes to be sent out to my sometime groom-gardener.

Saturday, 23 December. Frank Cloughton is home on leave till today week. He has not had leave since he went to France eighteen months ago. He is shoeing-smith and often has to go out into the fields to shoe the horses: 'often and often' he has 'to walk over the dead'. Frank Cloughton says 'Although they have to put up with a great deal in France, the food served out to them is excellent, and they get plenty to eat.'

Sunday, 24 December. No 'Official Bulletin' was sent to Great Leighs today.

Monday, 25 December. 10 a.m. Cold dreary day. Snow is rushing into water. Naturally there was the smallest Christmas morning congregation I have ever had here. Twelve communicants—seven men, five women.

Morning's post brought an undated letter from Chilton Polden, Somerset [Miss L. P. Adams to Mildred Clark]:

. . . So many of our lads have been killed, and very often the parents die of broken hearts. In one family of farmers we liked very much, the sons have been killed. The mother died a week after, and the father twelve hours after her, leaving some daughters all alone . . .

Thursday, 28 December. Mrs J. H. Tritton sent this Xmas, to every Great Leighs man on military service a wallet with note-paper and envelopes.

On Boxing Day, Braintree people gave a party to the men in the VAD hospital there. They had a 'sit-down' supper and afterwards played games and had competitions. One very shy patient was told that after supper he would have to sing a solo. At this, the boy was so frightened that, to avoid it, he went to bed. He had to be pulled out of bed, after being told it was a hoax, to join in the games.

Friday, 29 December. Sergt. Harry Taylor was called on to embark at Devonport on Sat. 23 Dec. but the ship did not sail till Th. 28 Dec. H. T.'s destination is Bombay. The ship is going round by the Cape. Charlie Ward is out of hospital.

Saturday, 30 December. 10.45 a.m. morning's post (unusually late) brought a letter from Mademoiselle Yvonne Dubrulle of Orléans, a friend of my younger daughter and also a card in which the boy, Robert Dubrulle [her brother] tries to show his English and tries to express his enthusiasm for approaching service. He is a very delicate lad, extremely thin and fragile looking:

26 December, 1916

Dear Miss Clark,

I had promised myself, this year, to write to you the first upon the occasion of new year's day, but I have been yet surprised by your letter to my sister . . . The year 1917 will be, I hope, the one of my incorporation in the army. I shall pass the medical examination in three weeks and will be soon, I hope, a »poilu«. I am very glad when I think that I shall go perhaps in Germany where I should be happy to destroy all that I shall can in order to punish those Boches of their crimes. If I am a soldier I shall pass the examination to be an officer. I am in the first form at the lycée . . . I think one day to go to England and then I shall not fail to go to Chelmsford . . .

173

The 2/7 Royal Scots are under orders for Dublin, to leave Chelmsford about 4 Jan. 1917. Someone, probably 'pulling their leg', has assured them that in Dublin etiquette demands that officers should kiss each other whenever *God Save the King* is sung. They are also told that because of the unfriendliness of the *canaille* of Dublin they must, in the evening, go out only in mufti.

7 p.m. Major Caldwell called: his lease of 'Long's' is up in Nov. 1917. He has been five years there. His landlord is not likely to grant him an extension of his lease.

Sunday, 31 December. No 'Official Bulletin' was sent out to Great Leighs Post Office today. Intimation given that such bulletins will not be issued, unless there is news of importance. It is 'something to tell' that a government office has developed some sense of shame at its fatuity. As pointed out often in these notes, the 'Official Bulletins' have been silly and contemptible and insulting to the nation in their ineptitude.

1917

Tuesday, 2 January. This morning, as a lady was cycling with great effort up the muddy cemetery hill [in Braintree] one of the soldiers called out 'I suppose, Miss, you would call this *the Big Push*.'

Major Caldwell says there is a big push in preparation on the Somme directly the weather improves. An Act of Parliament will be made shortly compelling all boys of fourteen to join a cadet-corps.

Wounded men from France say that their most wretched time is waiting for transport at Boulogne. They came to Boulogne, expecting to be on their way to 'Blighty' in a few hours, and are often kept there for three or even four days.

Thursday, 4 January. Some of the soldiers from Braintree went off to Ireland yesterday afternoon. Others are under order to go today. They do not know to what town they are going but entirely dislike the idea. It is hateful to be shot at in the streets, and forbidden to defend themselves—which is the Government's way in Ireland.

Sunday, 7 January. Notes from Mrs Leslie Tritton: Her elder daughter, Lucy, a nurse in the military hospital at Colchester, is paid at the rate of £20 a year, but spends it all in extras for the patients' teas. Her brother-in-law, Claude Tritton, Capt. ASC at Rouen, has had influenza and laryngitis and is being invalided home.

Monday, 8 January. 4 p.m. Thomas Sargeant, head-gardener at Lyons Hall, called to have his claim for his son's (Harry Sargeant's) effects attested. They have had nothing as yet, and have not even been told where he was killed. He has three surviving sons (Thomas and Archie—both in France—and Cyril, not yet of military age, working in Lyons Hall gardens).

Tuesday, 9 January. Afternoon's post brought a letter from my younger daughter:

6 January, 1917

My dear Father,

I travelled up . . . with a Belgian girl of about five or six and twenty . . . Her home is in the part of Belgium occupied by the British . . . and six miles behind the first line of trenches. All round about her are the large guns, and the whole village is occupied by soldiers . . . Enemy shells pass frequently over the village and on one Sunday it was actually bombarded . . . At one farm the father was not well and was sitting in front of the fire. Mass was being held at ten o'clock in a barn, as the Church had been commandeered but the young daughter of about twenty was too frightened to go out. At eleven she was coming in from the back kitchen, as the same time as her mother entered from the bedroom. A shell fell through the roof into the kitchen. When the noise was over the girl found herself lying on the floor; and, as she felt no pain, concluded that she had been knocked over by some of the furniture. When, however, she tried to rise, she found that her right leg had been blown off from just below the hip. The stretcher-party arrived immediately . . . The following day the girl died in hospital, and four weeks later her father died. He had not been seriously injured, but he could never for one minute forget her piteous pleading that the doctors should kill her rather than let her live like that.

Mademoiselle described also the first gas attack. It was totally unexpected and the men were quite unprepared for it. About 4 a.m. when her father rose he remarked on the suffocating atmosphere and on opening the front-door noticed that the grass in front of the door was blackened. A gunnery sergeant said that the attack had started at 3 a.m. About six o'clock all the buildings were filled with gassed men, and the fresh arrivals were laid on the village green, where it was ghastly to see them withering and struggling for breath. The few available doctors and some of the gunnery-officers went round, giving emetics and every man who cd. stand on his feet was used to give artificial respiration to the bad cases. The number of deaths were appalling and frightfully pathetic was the courage of the men, of those who had been gassed and of those who were taking their places in the trenches . . .

The men returning from the trenches are simply a ghastly spectacle with mud and slime and water, and are always so grateful for a glass of milk, and still more so if the farmer asks them in for a game of cards. They cannot speak one another's language but card games are much the same, and Tommy captivates everyone's heart by his grin of sheer delight . . .

Of spy stories she had plenty: To get to the trenches it is necessary to go up a slight brae. Frequently when a regiment wd. be on this open ground a shell wd. fall amongst them—the range was always correct. The Tommies got fed [up] with this and so one night carried out an investigation on their own account . . . Concealed in a wood within sight of this brae was a hole in which was a German lady with a field telephone connecting her with a German firing station . . . The Tommies' one regret is that these spies are taken away in cars to be shot at some distant town. They themselves wd. love to form the firing party . . .

These stories were told Mad^{lle} by a Scotch sergeant and when repeated to me, always finished 'Says I, No'—says she, 'Yes.' It was rather difficult always to follow the story as she knew—or acknowledged—no other pronoun than 'she' . . .

When the Germans began to carry off the Belgian boys to work in Germany, a lady living near Brussels encouraged her two sons to attempt to escape. One, a boy of 16 came into the British lines one tempestuous night. Of the other, a boy of $14\frac{1}{2}$, not a word has been heard and they fear he has either been captured or electrocuted on the wires lying along the frontier.

Thursday, 11 January. Harry Taylor is to be Sergeant-Major during the voyage to Bombay, with charge of various things for 1,500 men. His duties involve a great amount of clerical work. He has a cabin to himself and has his meals with the officers. He is a good man, equal to any duties put on him, and deserves all promotion.

Monday, 15 January. James Humpfreys was called up recently for military service. He is a carpenter and house-painter, and has a bicycle-shop in the High Road. He appealed for exemption on the grounds (a) that he has had twenty-six teeth drawn; that his gums are not suitable for false teeth; and that he can eat only one meal a day. This plea has caused great hilarity in the village. (b) that he has lost six men through the war. The villagers say that this is a lie.

Tuesday, 16 January. One indirect result of the war has been an enormous increase in cigarette smoking, both among ladies and lads. This began before the war but the example of officers and men, who are continually smoking cigarettes, has given it a great impulse. You never meet now a farm lad in the road, especially on a Sunday, who is not smoking a cigarette. Like Amy in Tennyson's 'Locksley Hall' I make no pretence to be myself 'exempt'. Since my man (Chas. Hy. Ward) was called up I have had to do all the out-door work. In these months I have smoked in each week more cigarettes than I used to do in any whole year before the war.

Saturday, 20 January. This is a time when a country parson would need to be made of silver pieces. I preserve the latest arrival of these appeals. This is a large family of young children, nice little things. The mother [Mrs Harry Lewin] has the reputation of being 'an awful liar'.

Dr Sir

Could you Please help me to a little coals as the weather is so very cold and baby is not well and I have only my husband's wages to do upon for 6 children and our 2 selves to live out of one mans wages and so expencive are things I can scarcely get enough to eat and cant get anything for boots or clothes and nearly all are without boots if you can spare me just a trifle I shall be extremely thankful I would not ask you Sir if I did not need it badly . . .

Sunday, 21 January. 1 p.m. instead of going to the Rectory, I went across to Lyons Hall and lunched with the Leslie Trittons who are at present there. Major Tritton said when the real history of the war comes to be written, it will stagger belief when it is found to what extent all the allies have been dependent on this country for munitions. Russia's part in the war has so far been extremely disappointing. The men of the 'C' class who are now being drafted into the army are not worth having. They go into hospital at once and are only a waste of the country's money. Major Tritton has had some ten of them in his own command, and they have been all 'crocks', only fit to be sent away at once. The outstanding features of the war are (i) that it is essentially a young man's war—men of twenty to twenty-five do not get hopelessly knocked up with rheumatism in the way older men do; (ii) that the rifle is of comparatively little value, bombs having come so conspicuously to the front; (iii) the marvellous physical improvement in the men taken from sedentary occupations into military training. It is not at all certain that this year, 1917, will see the end of the war.

Received by today's post from my younger daughter:

14 January 1917

My dear Father,

More gossip! . . . The English-speaking soldiers are in trouble again at Inverness. An old woman went from the country to visit her daughter who is in service in the town. She arrived all right and spent a very pleasant day but at night, when she was just boarding her train she was arrested and marched between two soldiers with fixed bayonets to the staff-office, where an interpreter intervening, it was explained to the over-zealous Tommies that what the woman was talking was Gaelic and not German . . .

The wealthiest people of the period are the dockers at Invergordon many of whom are earning £8 a week and never less than £4. As much as £30 will be going into one house. They hire motor cars on Sundays and go for long excursions over the country with their wives resplendent in furs and jewels . . .

Saturday, 27 January. Major James Caldwell called: He met this week an officer of what was formerly a passenger steamer [the St Denys] but since the Government took it it has been fitted out as a hospital transport, to fetch wounded from Boulogne. During the big battles on the Somme, it used to fetch 300 or 400 wounded every journey. The wounded were for the time well-kept and well-fed, but they were atrociously treated by the RAMC attendants, who have been the biggest lot of thieves and blackguards to be found anywhere. The RAMC men stole the watches, knicknacks, and money of the wounded. They were brutishly unkind to the wounded men. The Captain of the *St Denys* heard some whisper of the thefts and swore that if he could fetch a theft home to any RAMC man that he would have him triced up on deck and flogged in a way that he would never forget, nor would the others. The wounded men were afraid to complain, lest the RAMC lot would make it hot for them in hospital. But the medical officers have complained and in the present shortage of men, all the RAMC men have been taken off the *St Denys* and plumped into the firing line and their place is to be taken by women.

8 p.m. William Childs, youngest son of old Sam Childs, came to have his banns published. Eliza Annie Riley, the young woman, came from town with him, possibly to keep him sober. The village report is that he is always tipsy when he comes to Great Leighs, and always maudlin when he is tipsy, crying like a baby.

Thursday, 1 February. My sometime groom-gardener (Chas. H. Ward) is again in hospital—rheumatism in the knees. It was in the week before Christmas that he last came out of hospital. I told the tribunal when he was called up that he had not the stamina for campaigning, but they would not listen to me.

Sunday, 4 February. Reggie Ketley, after various moves from regiment to regiment, is now in the 9th Essex. He writes from France that the weather is 'very sharp'. He and his mates sleep in a loft. They take off their boots at night to find them hard frozen in the morning. Their bread also gets frozen. He is well. There are several Great Leighs lads near him, and he has seen some of them.

Monday, 5 February. Morning's first post brought only a circular as to War Shrines. Widow Ward, Daisley's Lane, had a letter from her nurse-child, George Wiseman. They have a week in the trenches and a week out. They were promised long leave at Christmas, but have heard nothing more of it. A son has been born to him since he went to France.

The prolonged frost has given Essex opportunities for skating, not had for over twenty years. At Braintree the Mill Field has been flooded and there has been, night after night, skating by moonlight. Yesterday evening the lake at Gosfield was quite a sight, being so crowded with skaters in the moonlight.

Tuesday, 6 February. 10 a.m. Morning's first post brought a letter from my sometime groom-gardener, undated:

Dear Sir, I now take the Pleasure in writing to thank you very much for the Parcel [cigarettes] you sent out to me which I received quite safe it is very kind of you I am sure. it has been a long way round I received it on the 30 of January I had left the hospital before it arrived I have been in hospital again since I have been at the Base. with Rhumatism but am better now the weather is rather Cold out here and a little snow I hope you are feeling better yourself . . .

Wednesday, 7 February. 7.30 p.m. Major Caldwell called, very cheerful and chatty. I have remembered only a few patches of his most interesting but discursive talk: The 'coal famine' in London is no fiction but a real fact. Mr Caldwell's firm in London today had to abandon fires in all but one room. The explanation is that the people who have been managing the railways for the government have sent so much rolling stock over to France that there is not enough to supply the ordinary needs at home. Liverpool is just as badly off.

Major Caldwell still keeps up patrolling as Special Constable though it is a farce. His supposed companion of the round ('Alix' Alefounder), being asthmatic, cannot come out in this weather. So he tottles round by himself.

The Times and the *Daily Mail* are trying to raise a scare about U-boats. In their list of ships sunk they include ships sunk as far back as November 1916, leaving people to conclude that *all* ships in their list have been sunk since the present German declaration about submarine war.[1]

[1] On 1 February 1917, Germany declared unrestricted submarine warfare.

Monday, 12 February. 10 a.m. brought a letter from my younger daughter:

9 February 1917

Many thanks for 'Country Life' and the book [a volume of this Diary] wh. I have sent on to the Bodleian . . . I learn that the R-13, the largest submarine in the world, has just met with a disaster. She was built in the Fairfield Works on the Clyde and seems to have been unfortunate throughout. Twice on trial-trips she was obliged to return, owing to some fault in the engines. Then, when she was reported to be thoroughly trustworthy she went into the Gareloch for her last trial trip, taking with her 84 men, some of them experts from the Fairfield Works. Twice she dived successfully, but the third time she remained under. For two nights and a day the men remained down there; then, in desperation a man was shot up through a torpedo 'hole'. He, banging against the keel of a boat, was killed instantly. A few hours later the Commander was shot up in the same way and managed to get picked up by a boat. Oxygen and liquid food were pumped down to the men in the submerged submarine and with great difficulty it was raised to within 10 feet of the surface. Only half the men were rescued alive.

Letters from Glasgow have been since censored and I got my information from a visitor . . . to St Andrews.

Thursday, 15 February. Fred Fuller's son had been out ever since the battle of the Somme. On Monday 5th Febr. he was taken very ill. On Sat. 10 Febr. he was at the Military Hospital at Colchester.

He told his father that out in the trenches the mud is so terrible that he had seen horses absolutely sink out of sight. He is inclined to think that several people who have not been traced (e.g. Colonel Deacon, Herbert ('Hubby') G. Wright), and have long been reported missing may have disappeared in this way. Billy Brock's parents had a letter on Su. 28 Jan. in which he was officially reported missing. Harry J. Brown (nephew of Lizzie Oddey, Rectory cook) has written that he is now working with the big guns and that the big battle is to be on 27 Febr.[1]

My elder daughter returned today from a London visit, first to Mrs Leslie Tritton at 13, Rutland Gate, S.W. and then to Mrs Arthur Tritton at 12, Southwick Crescent, W. and brought a good many war notes: Nearly every house in Park Lane is given up to hospital

[1] On 25 February German troops began a strategic withdrawal from the Noyon Bulge to their highly fortified Hindenburg Line; at its deepest point the withdrawal was over thirty-one miles. They left behind a devastated 'scorched earth' with booby-trapped wreckage and poisoned wells.

purposes. On Sat. 10 Feb. a War Department wagon was sent round to sell coal to the poor at 1s.8d. per cwt (the government price). Coal has been so scarce that even the War Office was short of it. Yesterday my daughter met the wife of a Major Watson who seems to be a typical pessimist. She says her husband says (a) that just as many British soldiers are surrendering to the Germans as German soldiers to us; (b) that the war will end in a draw.

Friday, 16 February. 8 a.m. Fog still thick. I cannot see the Rectory barn across the paddock, nor Bishop's Hall buildings. Song of small birds and chattering of sparrows continuing.

5.15 p.m. Dr Smallwood called: In some of the cottages very little food is taken except bread. Cottagers are terribly alarmed as to what will happen if they are put on fixed weight of bread. One family of seven uses thirty two-lb. loaves a week. Under the official scale this household would be allowed only twenty-eight lb., four lb. per head, per week.

The Bishop of Chelmsford has given great amusement to the medical [men] of the district. One day this week Dr Storr had a telegram: 'Come at once to Bishopscourt. Chauffeur overcome with fumes from the motor car.' He could not credit this. You would need, to be so overcome, to have been breathing very close to the exhaust-pipe for some time in a room.

When he arrived he found the man lying on the ground, the Bishop and the Chaplain beside him, exhorting him to move his hand or open his eyes. Storr felt his pulse, and found it regular and strong. His colour was quite good. He concluded that it was simply hysteria: ordered the man to open his eyes, and take his hand (Storr's) and be pulled up. Then he led him to the cottage where the man was received by his wife with floods of tears. She and the children then sat round the room 'howling'.

It turned out that the chauffeur had been away, on probation from the Royal Naval Air Service. Meanwhile the Chaplain had been driving the motor car, and had got it all out of order. The chaplain and the chauffeur had then tried to tinker it, to get it to go again, and Dr Storr thinks the chauffeur had actually gone into hysteria over the job.

The frost here had frozen the ground hard to a depth of some eight inches. In France it is frozen three feet deep.

A great house in the district, where 'economy' has always been preached in respect of servants' food—to the verge of meanness—has now made the happy discovery that true patriotism requires still further reductions. The cook at once gave notice to leave; she was not 'going to be put on one oat a day'.

Saturday, 17 February. Harry Hull has written home from France to Great Leighs that recently he washed his head, but the cold was so sharp that the hair froze before he could get it dried.

On my way back from Church I saw Mrs Charles Collins, from the cottage in the field, making her purchases from Mr H. J. Hicks' bread cart. She waited till I came up, to show me a large cake (2s. at least, as I judged; and apparently a currant cake) which she had bought to send out to her son, Charlie. She had had a letter on Monday, from Salonika, saying he would be glad of a parcel with food in any shape. He was well when he wrote, living in a dug-out. It was very cold. They had had much snow, followed by wet.

7.30 p.m. Major Caldwell called, very cheery and chatty on a great range of topics: The number of ships sunk by U-boats since the beginning of this campaign looks large; but it is made up chiefly of trawlers and other small craft, and the tonnage is insignificant. As regards the War Loans, he said that a financier in London had told him that this country had raised, by way of Loan, £2,000,000,000 (two billion £). As regards war bread: the new bread is more appetising than the former white bread; people are eating more of it; and are astonished to find their weekly baker's bill larger than formerly. After next week, all flour is to have 2 per cent. of barley in it.

Sunday, 18 February. Mrs James Humpfreys on the High Road, is indignant that her husband (carpenter and house-painter) has to go to military service in about a week. She would not have grudged him to munitions work, but thinks it unjust that unmarried men should be left at munition work while skilled workmen, married, are sent straight into the army.

Monday, 19 February. The case of James Humpfreys is not yet finally decided. He has started a new plea for exemption, viz. that he repairs bicycles for sixty-four people who live in Great and Little Leighs, and bicycle into munitions work in Braintree and Chelmsford, and that there is no one else to do this work. He went into Chelmsford on Thursday but the Tribunal refused to hear him. Mrs Humpfreys says that Captain Smith, the Military Assessor 'has his knife into' Humpfreys, for what reason they cannot guess. M. E. Hughes-Hughes of Leez Priory, Churchwarden of Little Leighs, and the Rev Jas. Bowen, Rector, are trying to get him exemption. (Mrs Humpfreys plays the harmonium in Little Leighs church.) Humpfreys this morning had a letter asking him to call on a lawyer in Chelmsford. Mrs Humpfreys thinks this may be some one in whose hands Mr Hughes-Hughes has put the case.

Harry Taylor's wife says that she knows, from a private code arranged between her and him, that his letter was written from Sierra Leone.

Saturday, 24 February. 2.20 p.m. afternoon's post brought me: a circular from the Food Controller [urging all ministers of religion to encourage a voluntary cut-back in food consumption to avoid rationing. Suggested limits were four pounds of bread, two and a half pounds of meat and three-quarters of a pound of sugar per head per week].

7 p.m. Major James Caldwell called: Agricultural labourers assure Mr Caldwell that few of the young men who have been taken off the land will come back to work on the land again. They are certain, they say, that their sons will not.

Sunday, 25 February. 9.30 a.m. cold, dank, cheerless day. Road very rotten, wet, with pools of water and tracts of mud. The only cheerful note of the day is the song of small birds. I did not venture to go home between services but stayed (12.30 p.m. to 3.30 p.m.) in the Vestry.

W. H. Dee, Church Clerk, told me that he had a letter this morning from Reggie Ketley. He writes that the mud in France is awful. Even on the roads it is over the men's boots, though they keep sweeping it off like water. He had got his parcel. It was delivered to him just as he was sitting down to tea, and was very welcome.

Thursday, 1 March. 2.10 p.m. J. Herbert Tritton called, very cheerful and looking very well. He said he had been very tired with the War Loan business, but had had a week's rest. They are not coming to Lyons Hall for Easter but are giving the house to Mrs Claude Tritton and her two boys (Ronald and John) and Mrs Arthur Tritton and her four children. He does not think the submarine campaign will amount to much. The danger is that neutral countries might take fright and hold back from sending their ships to this country with goods. If all stories are true (but he does not believe them) which are confidently told-about in London, there will soon be not many submarines left. Claude Tritton, ASC, is well since his return to France, and has been promoted Major. He is very worried about supply of labour for the land. He wants at least seven women to work full time and has applied to the government. He thinks he might put four into 'Valentines' with a matron. He did not think there was, as yet at least, any real shortage of food-stuffs in the Country.

Friday, 2 March. Verses by James D. McLaren—son of Mrs Christopher Willis (by her first husband)—Goodman's farm, now serving on a submarine. These verses were brought to the Rectory today by J. D. McLaren's sister, Lily McLaren. They were sent home by 'Jimmy' as his own composition, and are artless enough to be so. His handwriting is good. At the time, he was a stoker on board HMS *Roberts*. Recently he has been transferred to one of the new submarines.

A FIRST WATCH REVERIE

You have heard of the terrible warfare
'Twixt right and the heartless Hun,
As here, in the second September
Our battling is not yet done.
'Tis night in the Royal Navy
Some taking a well earned sleep,
While out on the ocean yonder,
Some still plough the angry deep.

. . . . .

The bugler sounds off 'Action!'
The boys shake things up for a spell—
A flash, a report, an explosion
And the Turk gets a taste of ——L.
Fourteen inch are the pop guns
With which we do the bizz.
And, I bet, on the spot we land 'em
Things just about go 'gee whizz.'
It's a credit to all the sailors
And to the gunnery officers too
But there's a branch I'd like to mention—
They're a black and motley crew.

It's the stokers at whom I'm hinting—
They don't get a chance, you see
To distinguish themselves in gunnery
Or to get a grand V.C.

. . . . .

The British navy is theirs to-day.
I think you'll agree with me,
The brave sweating British stoker
Gives England her run of the sea.
I thought this last night—I may as well tell—
While I was on the 'first' (= first watch)
I trust you will take the meaning well
Though the rhyming be of the worst.

With apologies

(= I suppose, Leading Stoker)   J. D. McLaren Ldg. Str.

Sept. 25, '15

Saturday, 10 March. Men of the Colonial forces in France are very keen to have a girl-correspondent in this country. Pte. Humphries, of New Zealand, was recently in hospital with Charles H. Ward. C. H. W. showed him the photo. of Ethel M. Gooday. He at once wrote to her home address at Bocking asking her to correspond with him. A reply went off to Pte. Humphries today. Charlie Ward is probably glad to have Ethel Gooday corresponding with someone else. Although he flirted with her and writes her occasionally from France, his real flame is Ruth Fuller, formerly housemaid at this Rectory. C. W.'s mother says that if he comes back, he and R. F. 'may make a match of it'.[1]

Sunday, 18 March. 11 a.m. Minnie Taylor of the Post Office brought to the choir report that Chelmsford PO had just sent to Great Leighs very good news from France—taking of fifteen villages near Bapaume (this would be the Official Bulletin). In the afternoon I overheard W. H. Dee explaining that within the last few days the wind had dried the ground very fast and hard and enabled our men to take forward their guns quickly.

Thursday, 22 March. 10 a.m. morning's post brought (a) the inevit-

[1] Charlie's sister remembered in 1984 that his real flame *was* Ethel May Gooday. Ruth Fuller only really took up with Charlie when her boy-friend, Herbert Wright, was reported killed.

able circular [for the Church of England Temperance Society] from the Bishop of Chelmsford, a great teetotaller; (b) a letter from Canon O. W. Tancock at instance of a foolish set of Chelmsford busybodies [urging the establishment of local Committees for War Savings]. Canon Tancock enjoys 'fussing' over 'business' as thoroughly as I despise and loathe it.

Sunday, 25 March. There was a Zeppelin scare at Braintree last night. About 7 p.m. a police sergeant came into the shop of —— Townrow, clothier (where Charlie Dee, son of W. H. Dee, serves) and told him the blinds must be drawn down and the windows darkened. There was also a scare of invasion. A Felsted boy came into the shop, and said it was reported that the Fleet was in action. All the soldiers were packed off.

Major Caldwell found Chelmsford in a stir. All the troops there had been called out, with their kits, bedding and blankets, and the transport wagons were standing ready with their lamps lit. The Special Constables were also called out. The Volunteers were also warned to hold themselves in readiness.

There was a report in the village last night that someone had had a letter from France in which it was said that we were on the eve of a very big battle because there was an unusual push getting our largest guns well to the front.[1]

7.15 p.m. James Caldwell called. He brought me the leaflet as to the parade at Chelmsford today which had been arranged for the glorification of sponsors from London 'of the Neville Chamberlain crowd'. Business men say the 'National Service' is 'all bunkum'—you send in your name and you hear no more about it.[2]

Major Caldwell says there were endless reports in Chelmsford today, but no one had any definite ideas. One rumour was that Germans had landed in Yorkshire. Another was that Germans had attacked Harwich.

Wednesday, 28 March. 9.50 a.m. morning's post brought a letter

---

[1] On 9 April British troops launched an attack at Arras to gain Vimy Ridge. Despite 84,000 casualties it would prove only a limited success.

[2] In March 1917 the Ministry of National Service was established under Neville Chamberlain to 'rationalize' civilian employment. It attempted to create a type of national employment bureau, which would match the skills of volunteers with the needs of industry and agriculture. It failed.

from my daughter, at her uncle's, the Revd Canon G. W. Paterson, the Parsonage, Cupar, Fife:

25 March 1917

. . . The second housemaid at the Crawford's house near Aberfoyle was coming from Edinburgh over the Forth Bridge to I don't know where. In her compartment were two men who took a very great interest in the bridge and began to ask her detailed questions about it. When they went to look out of the window she pulled the communication cord and pointed them out to the guard who arrived and took them into custody. One of the men was very anxious to get his stick which the guard fetched, finding it to be a hollow tube, closed at one end by a knob and filled with maps of the district. The girl has been rewarded by the War Office . . .

Thursday, 29 March. A Sergeant of the RFA who was at Lyons Hall Camp yesterday said they expected to be all in camp there on 10th April.

The gunners in Lyons Hall Camp used to buy eggs from Mrs John Cousins, Gatehouse farm, get her to boil them hard for them, and take them away. One night a party of these soldiers stole all the eggs about the place including the addled nest egg. Next day, some turned up wanting to buy eggs, as meek as meek might be. She said she had none that day and she thought they knew the reason. She added—'I wonder which of you had the rotten egg. I hope he liked it.' She could see, by their faces, that they all knew who had had it.

Saturday, 31 March. 7 p.m. Major James Caldwell said the 'tanks' were now little used and had not been of the service they were expected to be. They are too slow in their advance, and have to be left behind. The Dean of Bocking's nephew (a Commander RN) has told him that the Navy is very worried about German submarines. We destroy a great many, but the Germans put them into the water twice as fast as we destroy them.

Wednesday, 4 April. Mrs Griffets had a letter yesterday from her elder son in France. He is well but they do not know how to keep warm. Till recently they had ten sleeping in the tent, and were able to keep each other's feet warm. Now four of these have left and the other six miss them sorely.

Friday, 6 April. 11 a.m. Service in Church (Good Friday). Larger congregation and fuller choir than I looked for on such a day. Charles Robert Tritton, manager of Pall Mall branch of Barclay & Co.'s Bank, second son of J. Herbert Tritton, was at Lyons Hall today. He says private reports from people who have recently come from Germany represent the distress there as very great.

Sunday, 8 April. (Official time: 1 hour in advance of true time began this morning.) 8 a.m. Early Celebration—twenty-three present—including nine of the Girl Guides from 'Valentines'.

Tuesday, 10 April. 1 p.m. F. J. Cooper, Inland Revenue Officer, Felsted, called. He said that the soldiers met on leave all say that when the war is over they will seek some very quiet occupation, such as minding pigs.

Wednesday, 11 April. John Gooday, Bocking, father of Ethel M. Gooday, Rectory housemaid, says that this wintry weather would go on 'till old-March was out'. The tradition of the change of the twelve days in the reckoning of the year still lingers.[1]

Men back from the front say that the French infantry show great dash in attacking, but are deficient in steady resistance. When the Germans reach them in a bayonet charge, the French turn and run.

Wednesday, 18 April. 4.30 p.m. Dr Smallwood called. He said: Percy Holt, Essex Yeomanry, badly disfigured in face by wounds in the 'charge' of that regiment, went out to France again as soon as he was able. When the general saw him, he asked who that man was. He then said 'I won't have him here.' So P. H. was sent back to England. Since then he has been at Aldershot, on the permanent staff. Yesterday morning, according to Major H. L. M. Tritton, nothing official had come through about Essex people recently wounded.

Saturday, 21 April. I was weighed in Chelmsford yesterday—11 stone 10 lb. My loss of weight from 18 st. 9 lb., in a year, is not assuring.

The report that Essex men had been badly cut up was well founded but referred to the Essex Yeomanry in the great battle in France. The Essex Yeomanry were sent forward to take and hold a position, which proved to have been insufficiently shaken by our artillery. They got

[1] The change in the calendar referred to by John Gooday occurred 165 years before, in 1752. In that year Great Britain dropped the Julian calendar for the Gregorian: 2 September 1752 was followed by 14 September 1752.

much the worse of the encounter. 'Ted' Smith, of Terling, had part of his face shot away. His recovery is doubtful.

7.30 p.m. Major James Caldwell called. He said: nothing is being imported now except food-stuffs and materials for making munitions (especially explosives). Every ton of shipping therefore, which is reported in the week's official return, as sunk, represents so much food gone to the bottom; altho' the ships lost are only a fraction of the arrivals, the food-stuffs lost in them represent a very grave diminution of the food supply.

Sunday, 22 April. —— Clark, lives at Chatham Green, used to work on the Warren Farm, Little Leighs, is at home on leave. Had been 'gassed', and is still 'very short of breath'. Thinks gassing worse than a wound.

W. H. Dee says that for some days he has had severe pains in the front of the body in the region of the midriff. He says many people in the district have had like pains. Some Braintree people have consulted their doctors, who say they are caused by the latest form of war-bread. I myself have had like distressing pains, off and on for some days, but attribute them to one of my severe chills.

W. H. Dee also said that there had been a letter from his half-brother, Reggie Ketley. In this R. K. said that Easter Monday had been a great day's sport—something like following partridges from field to field at home and watching them run. The Germans had that day really run. The quarters his battalion are now in are fifteen miles further forward than they last were.

The Brocks have heard from the War Office that nothing has been heard of Billy Brock since he was officially reported missing, some time ago. He is, therefore, now to be presumed dead.

Wednesday, 25 April. There is great pressure put on men in this district to go munition-working. George Stokes, blacksmith, has to go this week. H. W. Thorogood, landlord of 'the Dog and Partridge', has also had to go. James Humpfreys has obtained exemption from military service on condition of munition-working.

Wednesday, 2 May. The main body of gunners from Halstead (and Earls Colne) [355th Brigade, Royal Field Artillery] began to arrive in Lyons Hall Camp today. The road is very dusty and torn-up, and the successive batches of them moved in clouds of dust as they passed the Rectory gate.

4.30 p.m. F. J. Cooper called. He came back from London on Monday, Apr. 30, having spent some days there with his brother, Capt. William Cooper, who had been home (from Arras) on ten days' leave. He had been out since 1915. He gave, F. J. C. said, a most hopeful account of the Western Campaign. The Germans had more men in front of the British line than they had ever had, but they were beaten, and their men were not of the same quality as before. The prisoners now included a large proportion of quite old men, and of young lads. It is impossible for any troops to endure our artillery. Our shells just tear the German trenches to pieces, and, when they pass into our hands, they are found to be quite knocked to bits. This efficiency of our gunnery makes our own progress slow, because, before we can go forward beyond a captured position, the holes made by our shells have to be filled up and practicable roads made through the havoc. Vimy ridge is a most important gain. Cambrai and Lens must both soon pass into our hands. Great things are presently expected from the French. For some time they have been only 'demonstrating', preparatory to another 'big push'.

Saturday, 5 May. 7.15 p.m. Major Caldwell called: It is great folly which is spoken by young officers just back from the front, who say the war will be over in June or July. July next year would be nearer the mark. Our progress now on the Western front can only be by yards.

Monday, 7 May. Major James Caldwell called at 6.30 p.m. He said that in military circles it was not thought improbable that Germany might yet attempt an invasion. That was why so many troops were being kept in this district.

Wednesday, 9 May. Report is that two or three soldiers ran away from Lyons Hall Camp one day last week, but were caught at Romford.

Saturday, 12 May. 4.15 a.m. (= 3.15 a.m. by the sun) nightingales singing lustily. Cuckoo has begun to call. When the nightingales ceased the cuckoo became very vociferous. Soon after, other birds burst into a volume of song. Cushat soon after that began crooning in trees by the moat and kept on.

Reggie Ketley's people had a letter from him this morning. He is in

Northern General Hospital at Lincoln [Leeds]. His hand was X-rayed on Thursday (10 May). Three fragments of shrapnel were discovered in it. At least two other Great Leighs lads are in hospital: (a) a son (wounded in the arm) of——Carter, tenant of Rochester's farm; (b) a son of —— Goddard. Father works on Lyons Hall farm. Ernest Wright is in hospital in France—ill, not wounded.

8.45 p.m. Major James Caldwell called: This week opinion in London was more cheerful. It was now thought that we were engaged in the hardest struggle we would have in France, and were doing well. The German army was making its utmost effort there, to keep us fully employed to enable their submarines to do their best to make us willing to treat for peace by causing shortage of supplies.

Sunday, 13 May. The officers in Lyons Hall Camp are said to be, almost without exception, 'rankers', i.e. formerly privates, who have received commissions.

As regards the brother of the Rectory housemaid (Ethel M. Gooday): Jack Gooday writes that he 'has consented to have his toes off'. The doctor said he was unfit for military service because of them.

Wednesday, 16 May. The son of J. Hicks, restaurant-keeper, Chelmsford, was in London one day last week. At the restaurant where he had lunch, he noticed that people ate just as much as they ever did. He himself, just to see what would happen, asked for a second piece of bread. The waiter said 'Well, Sir, you are not supposed to have it', but immediately brought it.

The women-clerks in Barclay & Co.'s bank, Chelmsford, are now all dressed in green over-alls.

Monday, 21 May. [Letter from the Rector to William R. Redman.]*

21 May, 1917

Dear Mr Redman,
It was most kind of you to write, and I was very glad to have your letters. There are not any Leighs lads, so far as I have been able to learn, in any London hospital . . . The parish is very empty. The young men being on military service, and the young women at munition work.

Lyons Hall Camp is again occupied by two batteries of RFA . . . They are very quiet, and we hear as well as see little of them. They have Service in Church on Sundays at 8.30 a.m. . . .

I cannot give a good account of my own health. I have gone steadily down hill for quite a year. I have lost 8 stone weight, and am now lighter and thinner than when I went up to Oxford, a lad of 19, in 1874. My heart is very weak and has caused a beginning of dropsy and an enlargement of the liver, which make walking very difficult and painful.

I keep on trying to make the grounds less of a wilderness . . . Mary is at home and helps me with the grounds. Mildred is getting on with her medical course; has passed the Second Professional Examinations; is now transferred from St Andrews to the Dundee Medical School, and has begun clinical work in the hospital there. They have, in addition to the ordinary cases of a large town, about 200 wounded. I am always glad to hear from you . . .

The policeman (Chas. Cole) says it is sickening the way in which girls from Braintree run after the soldiers in Lyons Hall Camp. 'Alix' Alefounder has had his 'papers' again and is again to present himself for medical examination.

7.15 p.m. Major James Caldwell called. He had just met his brother who had been in Edinburgh last week. This brother said that Edinburgh was a most sorrowful sight. You may go about London, Manchester, and other large towns in England without seeing much of the severely wounded, but in Edinburgh every other soldier you met had lost an arm or a leg. It was, he said, 'the old story': the Scottish regiments, being thoroughly to be trusted, had been 'planked down' in the very forefront of every action and had suffered out of all proportion in comparison with other regiments which, being unreliable, were kept back. He had seen different parties of American sailors in London, obviously liberty men from the American fleet, having a look-round.[1]

Friday, 25 May. 10 a.m. morning's post brought this letter:

(To the Vicar of Great Leighs . . . 'Banns of Marriage' urgent): Dear Sir, Will you please Publish the 'Banns of Marriage' between Wy [?] Cummings bachlor of Great Leighs (soldier) and Winnifred Mary Ellis spinster of this Parish St Peters Bocking . . .

2.30 p.m. a soldier arrived with a note:

Dr Sir would you Kindly inform me if you have had the order to publish the Banns for the wedding between Miss Ellis & Mr Cummings if so would you kindly inform me and Cancel the same I am Sir yours Obedient Mr Cummings.

This is the first instance I have had of this in all my clerical experience.

[1] The United States had declared war on Germany on 6 April.

Saturday, 26 May. From Col. Ralph Egerton, Chatham Hall, Great Waltham: Since the Revolution the Russian soldier will obey nobody. They say they won't have officers. It is, with them, 'Jack's as good as his master.' They will do nothing for anybody. Some people think this may be a lure to deceive the Germans.[1]

This week, staying with Mrs Vickers, at Waltham Manor, Great Waltham, have been a niece of hers and her husband. The husband, John Laing, was a banker in India but came back to this country at the beginning of this year. John Laing says that nowadays, when boats pass through the Suez Canal, Australian soldiers line up on each bank. When the boat is coming from Australia these men make a very thin line—some yards between each man—and shout their name as the boat passes, each in the hope of being recognised by some friend on board. Nearly always there is some recognition and exchange of friendly greetings. In the boat in which he came by, passengers had water-tight tins of cigarettes. These they threw as far as they could into the water, and the soldiers swam in and picked them up.

Sunday, 27 May. I found on the Vestry table a small open basket with 15s. in it, chiefly in pennies, and a scrap of paper intimating that it was a collection taken this morning at the soldiers' service (8.30 a.m.). Those here last summer never gave a penny.

Monday, 28 May. This afternoon, a note from Mrs Brown, from whom we have our milk, intimating increase in price of milk [to 2½d. a pint].

Friday, 1 June. 10.10 a.m. morning's post brought a letter from my younger daughter:

30 May 1917

In case you have not heard the latest rumour I am writing to enlighten you. Lady Jellicoe has been arrested as a spy and is now in the Tower! ... Being one of the last people to leave the boat on which Lord Kitchener sailed for Russia, his death is said to be traceable to her actions as a spy ... In the YWCA canteen the men say that Sir John has also been arrested! I assure you that we are very excited about it ... Many thanks for the cheque.

Saturday, 2 June. The men in Lyons Hall Camp are anxious to have

[1] The Russian Revolution began with strikes and mutinies in the second week of March and culminated in the Tsar's abdication on 15 March.

mending done for them. Mrs Brown of Bishop's Hall, head of the Mothers' Meeting, thinks some of its members would do this. Village women are shy of undertaking work for soldiers because those here last year went off, many of them, without paying for the washing and mending done for them.

7.55 p.m. Major James Caldwell called. He said: 'Alix' Alefounder went to Warley on Th. 31st May. He received no papers, which means that he is considered unfit for service.

Monday, 4 June. 10 a.m. morning's post brought a letter from my younger daughter (dated 2 June): '. . . We have now court-martialled and shot Sir John Jellicoe for losing the Battle of Jutland and Lady Jellicoe was shot at day-break on Thursday! So now we have settled down to await more thrilling rumours.'

Louis P. Wright, Essex Yeomanry, came home today on leave, looking very well. He has been in France continuously almost two years. He was entrusted with a great many letters (including a letter and a gold watch from her son to Mrs Morley, Gubbions Hall) from comrades to post in England. At Boulogne, every letter was torn up, the Censor not even reading them. He was allowed to bring on the gold watch.

Thursday, 7 June. Mrs 'Alix' Alefounder is doing farm-work today, and was working in a field with Mrs Everett, wife of a farm-hand at Long's. Mrs A. A. helps in the canteen. She greatly angered Mrs E. today by telling her that 'only ladies' helped in the canteen. She wears gloves when at out-of-door work, so as not to have brown hands when serving in the canteen.

Friday, 8 June. 10.5 a.m. morning's post brought two postcards from my younger daughter: (Post Stamp 9.15 a.m., and 3.15 p.m. 6 Ju. 17):

Do you know of any Leighs boy or anyone in the neighbourhood who is in the 9th Essex Regt. in France and could give any information about Pte. Jack Leng of that regiment. He was wounded about five weeks ago and since then his parents (Leng of the 'Advertiser') have lost all trace of him. The depot at Warley can give no information and poor Mrs Leng has quite given up hope. She is afraid he must be missing . . .

Jack Leng was this morning reported killed on the 3rd of May.   M. C.

Saturday, 9 June. Today two Girton girls arrived at 'Valentines'. They are to work on Lyons Hall land for six or seven weeks.

Reggie Ketley came home on Thursday on leave. He says that, at Easter, everything was ready for the advance [at Arras]. Our troops had ploughed forward through four miles of mud, knee-deep; the guns and ammunition had been brought right to the front; and the railways laid. Then came a severe snow-storm and other bad weather, making further progress impossible, giving the Germans a longer time to strengthen their front. He was in the trench when the rush was at last made. Our men waited till 3 a.m. when the moon went down, and then over the trench and raced to the German trench, throwing bombs in. The Germans ran off for all they were worth, most of them getting away by their communication-trench. Immediately we had attacked, German flare lights went up, and their guns opened a heavy fire on the trench we had taken and the trench we had come from. He himself was out of the trench when he was wounded by the bursting of a shrapnel shell. Had the German explosive been as powerful as our own, he would have been blown to pieces.

7 p.m. Major Caldwell called: Yesterday he had a talk with an officer who was on leave after being in France for almost two years continuously. The officer was extremely sorry that it was the Bavarians who had been holding the Messines ridge, and who had had 'such a dressing' from us.[1] The Bavarians were not only stout fighters, but they fought without malice. The Prussians were very different. When the Prussian guards were opposed to us, they were malicious and brutal. Our men would have rejoiced had it been Prussians.

Wednesday, 13 June. This forenoon (10.45 a.m. as I remember) we heard an unusual drumming noise in the E. and S. E. It went on for a considerable time. My daughter heard it about 11.15 a.m. I thought it was drums in Terling Camp, or a regiment on a route-march on the road beyond that. My daughter thought it was an aeroplane, but out of order. It now appears as if it had been a squadron of German aeroplanes. 6.15 p.m. —— Thrugood, the Terling carrier, on his way back from Braintree market, told me there had been a German air raid on London; that they had 'upset' Liverpool Street Station and appeared to have done a lot of damage. (I made a pencil note of the

---

[1] The British attack on the Messines Ridge two days before was an attempt against the Ypres salient. There were nineteen mines and 500 tons of explosives used.

noise as I was mending the fence of the Rectory paddock, but did not enter it when I came into the house, as I could not definitely account for it. This shows that I must not destroy even my hasty notes of things.)

Mr C. W. Rayner had a letter from the War Office asking him to send the last letters received from his son, Charlie, 'missing' in France. When they returned them they said they had, after minutest enquiry, been unable to find any trace of him.

At the YMCA canteen in Lyons Hall Camp Mr Buchanan, the superintendent said that in London there is a new rule that no person in khaki can get any food or drink after 8 p.m. He himself, as a YMCA official, wears a khaki uniform. He was in London on Sat. and though starving, could get nothing, not even a cup of tea, though people in civilian clothes were being served with dinner.

8.30 p.m. Edith Caldwell came. She brought me a hastily written note from her father in which he had jotted down only what he himself had seen; she was very excited and poured out her information, disjointedly. Her father was in his office at the time of the raid. It was in the very centre of the damage, being within five minutes walk of Liverpool Street Station. It was itself untouched, though buildings all about it were destroyed or badly injured.

He wanted to get out to see the aircraft, but this was impossible because shrapnel was flying about everywhere. The street-fronts of several of these buildings were crashing down. The women all went mad, shrieking and yelling.

Thursday, 14 June. It appears that Major James Caldwell had a narrow escape in the air raid yesterday. He does a large business with Japan, and was on his way to the Yokohama bank when the raid began. A friend stopped him on the street and spoke to him. Otherwise he would have been in the Yokohama bank just when it was demolished.

Saturday, 16 June. 7.45 p.m. Major Jas. Caldwell called. He said: This air raid was skilfully planned and will serve well its purpose to divert attention in Germany from the unpleasantness in other quarters. The German government is like a rat in a trap, the harder it is pressed, the more fiercely it will bite. The Germans have for more than a generation been fully persuaded that they are invincible. It will take most complete defeat to get that fixed idea out of their minds. It is their deep-rooted conviction of invincibility which has made it so easy for their Government to hoodwink the German people. His elder daughter, Edith Caldwell, is charged with finding artistes for a concert every Monday night in Lyons Hall Camp. She finds much greater difficulty this year than last. People are very reluctant to promise to come and send excuses for withdrawing their promises very frequently. These withdrawals put her to her wits' end. The novelty of singing in camp has worn off.

Thursday, 21 June. 10 a.m. brought another government circular [from the Ministry of Food urging people to reduce consumption of bread and to wear the approved purple ribbon as a token]. Waste of paper; useless expenditure of clerks' time and of postman's time as though everyone had not heard the whole story over and over again or had any trust in a government office, especially in one which has so discredited itself.

Mr F. Chapping of Mr Jas. Bowtell's grocery-business, Braintree, came at 1.30 p.m. He said that applicants for sugar will receive only a third of what they asked to preserve their own fruits.

Saturday, 23 June. The Tritton family all came for the summer, yesterday. Hay-making (meadow hay) is in full swing everywhere. Pea-picking has begun. The Council School had to close on Th. and Fr. because so many children were absent.

6 p.m. a meeting at Mrs Brown's, Bishop's Hall, to set afoot a local branch of the National War Savings Committee.[1]

Monday, 25 June. 9 p.m. my daughter, Mary Alice, returned from London. She said that Marjorie Tritton said that a large contingent of Australians left Victoria Station this morning to join the Australian forces who are now N. of Ypres. There is a strong report in the Australian canteen that there will presently be a 'big push' in that quarter.[2] The commander of the Zeppelin brought down in Suffolk was killed. It is the second in command who is in Colchester Military

[1] Mary Alice Clark attended the meeting to represent the Girls Club. The scheme encouraged people to buy, with 6d. stamps, War Savings Certificates with a nominal value of 20s. which actually cost 15s.6d.

[2] The Third Battle of Ypres would begin with an infantry assault on 31 July. The battle would see the first use by the Germans of mustard gas.

hospital. He is in the ward in which Lucy Tritton is a nurse. He seems a very nice fellow, quite young. Lucy Tritton asked him if he had ever seen Colchester. He said he had seen it from his aeroplane. She asked him why they came over here in the way they do. He said, 'Well, you know, you English forced the war upon us.' L. T. then thought she had better change the topic.

Monday, 2 July. 7.30 p.m. Edward Hardingham, of Southwold, called and stayed till 10 p.m. He was very good company. He has three sons—'Jack', formerly Curate at Southwold, is now chaplain to the mine-sweepers at Havre. He had a great deal to say about incidents in the war from conversation with his son: When at the front and visiting one of the hospitals, he was taken to a German, just brought in, desperately wounded. The Revd J. H. knows hardly any German, and is utterly unable to speak it or understand it. All he could do was to repeat to the man the first verse—all he knew of it—of Luther's hymn, 'Ein Feste Burg ist Unser Gott.' The man's face lit up. When the Revd J. H. had finished the verse the man repeated it, and died just when he had finished the last line.

The French peasantry in the theatre of war are the meanest people the Revd J. H. has ever met. They will not give a glass of water to a British soldier, after a long march on a hot day, unless they are paid for it. Our men's common talk is that they hope that our next war will be with these people. The French soldiers are all right with our men. On one occasion the folk of a village knew that Australian troops would arrive that evening after a long, hot march. They, therefore, boarded up the well, to prevent the men drawing water without payment. When the Australians arrived and found the well boarded up, they made no parley. In a few minutes, the boards had been torn up and thrown in every direction, and bucket after bucket of water was hauled up. No payment. The Belgian peasantry are even worse than the French.

The Australian troops are splendid fellows, but very independent. They will not take any order which they think unreasonable, from any officer, whatever his rank. At mess one evening, the Revd J. H. heard a General tell good humouredly, how he had been discomfited by the Australians that afternoon. He had come upon a party of Australians lying about anyhow on that hot afternoon. They were some sleeping, some smoking after a march. Altho' they were not in his command, he thought he would like to inspect them. So he gave the order to fall in. Not a man stirred. He repeated the command in a louder voice, but all that happened was that a few faces were turned toward him and looked him up and down, and a few smokers took the pipes out of their mouths and blew a long puff of smoke from their lips. He was nettled, and called out testily, 'Men, I said *fall in.*' One voice answered him 'Fall in yourself, and be damned.' He saw he had gone too far and rode to his own quarters, taking in the ridiculous part he had played; and told the story against himself, with great glee that evening.

At Havre the Revd J. H. was expected to go about the boats and speak to the men, but no provision was made for any service for them. He started a service and has generally forty of a congregation. As the crew of a mine-sweeper is seven or eight this means that everyone comes except those who are on duty looking after the boats.

Saturday, 7 July. An air raid of exceptional magnitude is in progress: 9.50 a.m. firing of heavy guns (presumably anti-aircraft) continuous in greater volume than I have heard them before. 9.55 a.m. a fleet of aeroplanes passed, flying slowly from N. to S., well E. of Rectory, high up. They looked like a flight of starlings. Ethel M. Gooday, Rectory house-maid, who has keen eyesight, counted nineteen and says another followed. Major Wm. Brown of Bishop's Hall, with his glasses, saw twenty-one. 10.30 a.m. raiding-aircraft must have reached London. There is an incessant roll of explosions in S. (no doubt bombs and anti-aircraft guns). 10.50 a.m. the raiders seem on their way back; 10.55 a.m. the firing has come northwards and is now in E. where it is decidedly heavy. 11 a.m. solitary airplane passed E. of Rectory flying (high) N. to S. 11.20 a.m. air raid over: firing quite ceased.

Major Jas. Caldwell told me this evening that he thinks the raiders struck London somewhere about Epping. They made for the dome of St Paul's which always guides them to the very centre of the City. That was the course they took before. Later in the day he bicycled to Little Waltham with some letters to post, but came up in the road with the Little Waltham postman who told him that a message had come through from the General Post Office that bombs, causing great damage, had been dropped in the General Post Office building in St Martin's le Grand and on St Bartholomew's hospital behind it. A Jewish synagogue there had been destroyed, as also some places on the

Captain Alan George Tritton, Coldstream Guards

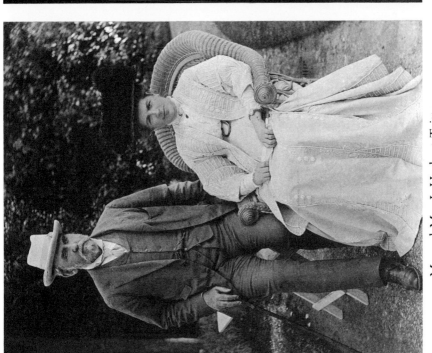

Mr and Mrs J. Herbert Tritton

The village post office on the Great Road. The Taylor family, who kept the post office, were also the village wheelwrights

One of the Official War News bulletins posted at Great Leighs Post Office. As few villagers took newspapers, the bulletins, although heavily censored, were still the main source of news

Sunday's Official War News.   31st March '18

Nothing serious on my line has stacked today. A few prisoners and machine guns have been secured by us in local fighting. South of Somme a hostile attack developed in considerable force midday south of Perone Amiens road. Fighting continuing and between villages of Luce and Avre where possession of tactical features was progressing. On 30th inst. in spite of driving rain our pilots continued to take part in the battle south of Somme dropping bombs and using machine guns on enemy. Heavy fighting took place between our two flying machines and enemys. Twelve hostile aeroplanes brought down and three driven down. One hostile balloon destroyed and another two German aeroplanes shot down by anti-aircraft guns. Five of our machines missing.

French Official.

Only local enemy attacks today.

North of Moreuil enemy succeeded in entering Hangarden Plantaire. Between Moreuil and Assigny we retaken Aubercourt and Le Monchel and made an advance near Orvillers on Oise front. An enemy battalion after crossing river near Chauny was entirely destroyed or captured.

Embankment. It is feared that the slaughter is even greater than on the last raid. Many children are reported to have been killed.

Sunday, 8 July. No bulletin came to Great Leighs Post Office when my daughter was there. Just before Miss Minnie Taylor started to come to Church, an official message was telephoned and she wrote a copy of it and brought it to Church for me:

OFFICIAL WAR NEWS

Casualties air raid Metropolitan area and Isle of Thanet. Killed 37, Injured 131. a. a. a. 1 machine brought down by R. F. C. off mouth of Thames. The raiding Squadron was chased by Royal Naval Machines and two enemy machines were brought down 40 miles out at sea . . . In the course of their operations, however, 4 enemy machines were destroyed and 3 driven down. The Russian offensive continues. 1000 prisoners captured.

Monday, 9 July. Fred Fuller, Cole Farm, says that peas this year are not a good crop. 1s.6d. a peck was the price the other day in Braintree.

My daughter, Mildred Clark, returned home today, after the term at the Medical School, Dundee. She said there have been a great many aircraft accidents reported as happening 'on the east coast of Scotland'. As a matter of fact, most of these happened at Montrose. One morning quite early, the major in command of the air-station there wanted to go up, and asked the air-mechanic then in charge to come up with him as pilot. The man refused, and persisted in his refusal. The major had the machine examined, found that several screws not seen unless looked for had been loosened, and had the man at once arrested. Some half-dozen other mechanics there have, it is said, also been arrested.

She was in London on Sat. at the time of the air raid, and saw the raiders. They came at 10.30 a.m. The bombing was all over at 11.45 a.m. They ran out to the end of Gower Street to watch them going off. People were pouring out of the houses to watch the raid.

Tuesday, 10 July. A 'hero' in Chelmsford: It was reported in Chelmsford that a Chelmsford man in the RFC had distinguished himself during the aircraft attack on London and that he was coming home on short leave on Sunday evening. When his train was about due, his friends crowded to the arrival-platform stairs. When they had cheered themselves hoarse, they asked him to tell them about his great feat. He said, angrily, only 'I didn't do a damned thing.'

Wednesday, 11 July. 8 a.m. Herrick's line 'Sweet day, so cool, so calm, so bright' might well be quoted as to this morning.

From my younger daughter: The dispensary in Dundee hospital is much plagued with malingerers and with people shamming to get exemption from military service. Recently a man came to Dr Milne to get an exemption certificate. His right side was fairly right, he said, and he could do a certain amount of work; but his left side was paralysed and he had no feeling in it. Dr Milne blindfolded him and put him through an elaborate succession of pinches, in different places, and at irregular times. Whenever he pinched the left side, the man said 'I don't feel that.' Mr Milne then removed the veil from the eyes and said—'If you had no feeling in your left side, how could you say "I don't feel that" when I pinched you. No certificate from me.'

Olive Tritton says that the sounds in the East which we have heard for two days, and which I have been doubtful whether to set down as cannon-firing or bomb-practice [at Chelmsford] have been the bombardment of our line at Nieuport by German cannon of the heaviest kind, and that the news this afternoon was that the Germans had scored a success there, forcing back our line and inflicting heavy loss.

Thursday, 12 July. It is said by Col. Findlay [the officer in command of Lyons Hall Camp] that a good many lads in Camp are not quite of military age, who contrived to get over to France, but have been sent back when their real age was discovered.

From my daughter, Mildred: Mr Anderson is a young surgeon, recently in Dundee on furlough. He said that one of the embarkation officers at Boulogne was sent home on leave to be fitted with an artificial arm. He came to France, and very soon after, by some chance, broke the artificial arm. He was sent back to England to have another fitted, and was at home for six weeks. Some other embarkation officers at Boulogne, also with artificial limbs, thought it might be a royal road to long leave to break an artificial limb, but found that a very hard thing to do. At least one of them managed to do it, and was sent to England to have another; but he was allowed only three weeks leave. Now the officers think they had better drop for the present their desire to break their artificial limb. The leave now allowed does not seem long enough to justify them.

Saturday, 14 July. 7.30 p.m. Major James Caldwell called. He says: Much indignation is felt at the front at the misleading information given in our newspapers as to the doings of our colonial troops. The Australians, in particular, have done nothing like what they are credited with in the papers: (a) by sheer disregard of orders, and want of discipline, the Colonials have repeatedly got into hopeless dangers and our regiments have been badly cut up in getting these blockheads out of the messes they had got themselves into; (b) owing to their much larger pay the Colonials selfishly buy up for themselves all odd supplies and leave our men to do without. Canadian Tommies e.g. have about 6s. a day against our men's 1s.2d. They call their officers Tom, Jim, Bill and so on, and show the utmost disrespect to officers of our army.

Thursday, 19 July. 6.50 p.m. M. E. Hughes-Hughes, esq., Leez Priory, called to get my signature to accept service on Committee of War Savings Association [which duty the Rector had reluctantly accepted that morning]. M. E. H. H. said he thought the scheme might be of some service. They had eighteen names of contributors and he thought they saw their way to thirty. But on his own showing, this list would be an artificial one. He is going to put on it his younger daughter and his surviving son, aet. 2. He is also going to impress his two outdoor men.

Friday, 20 July. Major Jas. Caldwell told me on Sat. 14 July that people back from the front report most unfavourably of some of our officers. There are, of course, a multitude of officers who behave well to their men and inspire perfect confidence and who therefore are followed by the men under all circumstances. But there are officers, and these not a few, who are conceited cads, and behave so badly to the men that the men detest them. It is no uncommon thing to hear a growl in billets—'So and so is a brute. Wait till I get him in front of me in action, and I will put a bullet into him.' Of course, the man has no intention of doing so but the remark shows the bitterness of his feelings.

This forenoon, when my daughter, Mildred, passed the gate of Lyons Hall Camp on her way to help in the YMCA canteen, the sentry asked her if she would do him the great service to post a letter for him at the pillar-box in the canteen. He was very anxious to have it posted, but could not leave his place and he did not want to entrust it to any soldier lest he should read the address.

Monday, 23 July. A sergeant, an Irishman, back wounded from the front, had been made orderly at a convalescent military home at Strathpeffer. He was given a week's leave, and went to Ireland. But he came back after two days. He could not stick it any longer, he said; he was subjected to so much insult and abuse. Even the men he had been at school with insulted him, and soldiers in Ireland are under strictest orders to take it all 'lying down', not to retaliate.

Wednesday, 25 July. Miss Elizb. M. Tritton was ill today. Her canteen duty was taken by her mother's lady's-maid, Miss Truelove. On her way back, Miss T. passed between the horse-lines, carrying, outspread, a very bright green parasol. One of the horses was being led by an unusually small man. The horse took fright at the parasol; backed a bit; and then ran round and round, dragging the man, at a run, with it. All innocent of the fact that she was the cause of the commotion, Miss T. stood stock still in the middle of the path and watched the performance. The horse finally had to be taken round by another way. The gunners who saw the affair laughed consumedly. Some of them had to sit down on the poles of the limbers to recover themselves, after the exhaustion of their laughing.

Thursday, 26 July. The Lyons Hall family have again arranged for a meeting in their grounds (or barn, if wet) each Sunday afternoon in August, with Moody and Sankey hymns, extemporary prayers and evangelistic address. The gunners in camp are taking great offence at being put under pressure to attend these meetings. The Sergeants in camp have been asked to tea at Lyons Hall, after which they are to be pressed to canvass in camp for attendance. They are making game of it. The Regimental Sergeant Major is said to be going about camp, trying to borrow a big Bible because he understands that no soldier can go to tea at Lyons Hall without such equipment.

Saturday, 28 July. Optimist military experiences of Gerald Cruickshank, capt. in Manchester Regiment. In his opinion the men who go back to France after recovery from wounds or after having been home on leave, are altogether inferior to those who go out to France for the first time. They have not got the hot blood and are far more canny.

In G. C.'s opinion the victory may be either this year, or, with the help of the Americans, early next year. Holding as we do the sea, Vimy ridge and the Chemin des Dames we can 'shell to the devil' the German troops on the lower ground. He thinks the French are absolutely played out, and that the victory will have to be gained by us and the Americans. The French have not the stamina to stand a long campaign. They have also very little inventfulness, although they made good aeronauts at the beginning of the war.

Whatever North Russia may do, he does not think South Russia and Rumania will give up the war. He understands from Staff Officers in the Intelligence Department that S. Russia and Rumania are preparing a big offensive. If this is successful they will force peace on Turkey, Bulgaria and Austria. The Turks will not be forced out of Europe this war.

Friday, 3 August. ———Humphries, the New Zealander, who is mentioned in a previous volume of these notes as corresponding with Ethel M. Gooday has been killed in France.

The 'government cheese', officially supplied to Mr H. J. Hicks, Supply Stores, Great Leighs, to be sold in the village at 1s. 4d. a lb. is New Zealand cheese, badly made and rank-tasted. Mr Hicks has also on sale Canadian cheese at 1s. 8d. a lb., also badly made, rank-tasted and over-salted. Mrs Hicks says she has sold hardly any margarine these last weeks. The village-women made much money pea-picking and at present will buy nothing but butter at 2s. a lb.

Friday, 10 August. On Su. morning 5 Aug. Mr C. W. Rayner received official intimation that his son, Charlie Rayner, long 'missing', was now considered killed—missing since Oct. 1916.

Saturday, 11 August. The discontent about food in Lyons Hall Camp came to breaking-out point on Thursd. The men of 'A' battery said they were not getting enough to eat for dinner. They would not eat anything of what was served, but sat for the regulation three-quarters of an hour, drumming on the table and making 'a horrid noise'. When time was up, the sergeant-major took them to the lines and ordered them to clean harness. This they refused to do; sat down and did nothing. Major Cockayne had been at lunch at Mrs Leslie Tritton's, the Hole farm. He was fetched and said the men were to blame for insubordination, but that their complaint was well-founded. He took them to the mess-tent; saw that they had a proper dinner; and promised that, in future, things would be better.

Morning's post also brought me an official letter from F. J. Cooper asking information about length of service with me, date of leaving, and wages and allowances of Charles H. Ward, taken from my service for army duty. His father, Harry Ward, a most steady and trusted workman on Fulbourne's farm, is now wholly incapacitated for work, and, in fact, is slowly dying of a painful, malignant internal growth. The mother had made a claim for 'Separation Allowance', now being 'dependent' on her son. It is a most deserving, as well as a necessitous case.

Sunday, 12 August. 6.45 p.m. I found Major Caldwell and W. H. Dee in the churchyard, watching the Eastern horizon and listening intently. Warning had recently come to Lyons Hall Camp that an air raid was in progress. Major C. and Mr Dee supposed it was on the Essex coast, but they detected no sight or sound of it.

Tuesday, 14 August. If open imbecility could win a war we are on the sure road to victory. To justify their high salaries, the unspeakable fools who are government officials [the Tobacco Control Committee as instructed by the Royal Commission on Paper] have 'thought' out a new device for beating the Germans: the prohibition of pictures in packets of cigarettes [to take effect on 1 September]. One would have thought that many of these (Raemaker's cartoons, e.g.) were silly enough to have appealed strongly to these feeble minded officials, as 'work' like their own. [The Rector then included thirty-two specimens received with Godfrey Phillips & Sons' B. D. V. cigarettes.]

Thursday, 16 August. 6 a.m. the cannonade in S. E. distance (presumably in Flanders) is of a continuance and violence beyond anything of recent days. The air is full of the rumble of it and the house quivers.

As regards Southend air raid [of 12 August] many people from Braintree—munition workers—were there for the Bank-Holiday week when the works were closed. Several people from Great Leighs were there; among them, Eva Willis and a friend. They had taken their seats in the train, ready to return here, when the raid began. They immediately ran to shelter, leaving their belongings in the compartment. When they came back they found their luggage still there, but their hand-bags had been opened and every penny taken out of their purses. One small child which was on the platform had its head and arm taken right off. An old couple were walking, arm in arm, along the platform. The man was knocked down and killed on the spot. The woman was uninjured.

Friday, 17 August. Mr T. Sargeant, gardener, Lyons Hall, sent me a detailed note of the rainfall of this year as registered by him here and a most kindly note:

17 August 1917

Dear Sir

. . . I beg to thank you for your kind letter which was most interesting to me. And I feel sure the record you are keeping will be much valued in days to come. I will keep you informed each month with the rainfall to the End of the year . . .

Saturday, 18 August. Notes from my younger daughter: Mrs Fortescue was in a bus on her way from Oxford Street to Ealing. There came into the bus a Tommy with a frightful black-eye. Somebody asked how he got it. He answered, in a pronounced Yorkshire accent, that he had been fighting with an American soldier who had been bragging about coming over here to carry through what we had been unable to do ourselves. Someone in the bus suggested 'You seem to have got the worst of it.' 'Na. Ah didn't: because he cannot see out of either of his eyes.'

Opinions differ about the physique and bearing of the Americans. The streets through which they passed were crowded and on the whole, they had a very good reception. When the film showing the march-past was exhibited at the Coliseum on Fr., only about two people showed any enthusiasm until it came to the scene outside Buckingham palace where Queen Alexandra was seen putting up her umbrella. Then there were cheers, and shrieks and yells from the whole house.

Friday, 24 August. Most of the men from Lyons Hall Camp who were at Salisbury plain for gunnery-practice returned to Lyons Hall Camp this morning.

On Wedn. 22 Aug. Mrs J. Herbert Tritton invited all the soldiers who were left in Camp to tea from 4.30 p.m. to 7.30 p.m. On Wedn. she provided bread and butter, potted-meats, tomatoes and cake. All the men but one loved the tomatoes. He asked if he might have jam instead and had a pot of jam set before him, which he took care to finish all by himself. Tea was served under the big cedar tree in front of the house. Mrs J. H. T.'s brother-in-law (the Revd Reginald Fawkes) and her daughters, Violet and Olive, waited. The Lyons Hall maid-servants sat at the tables and acted as hostesses. Some of the men said that this was the first 'home tea', even since they came back from France. Mrs J. H. T. found that by 'home tea' they meant tea where a table-cloth was provided. After tea they went and strolled in the kitchen-garden. Then they came back to Lyons Hall lawn and played child's games, such as blind man's bluff, in which two of J. H. T.'s grandsons, 'Ronnie' (Ronald) and John (sons of Major Claude Tritton) and the two little house-boys took part.

Thursday, 30 August. On Wedn. evening (29 Aug.) a man, who seemed to be hiding at the lane-side edge of a field in Long's Lane, stood up and shouted something across the fence to a woman who was passing. She thought it might be in English but was too frightened to understand a word. She just noticed that he was a dark-haired man. She ran and told her husband. The husband concluded that the man must be one of the escaped German prisoners, and went and told the policeman. Then the policeman and he had a hunt for the man, unsuccessfully.

Sunday, 2 September. 10.30 a.m. As I went out to Church I disturbed a small, bluish-plumaged dove (a young cushat, as I think) which was feeding in a laurel clump at the corner of the drive nearest Rectory. It showed little fear and only flew up to a branch of the nearest fir-tree, where it perched and looked down on me. When I came back at 1.15 p.m. it was feeding at the foot of the yew trees and did not even take the trouble to fly off—just looked up as I passed and began feeding again.

Monday, 3 September. Miss 'Tina' Preeston called this afternoon: Miss Preeston says that German prisoners were at work on farms at Dunmow, and that it was reported that one had made off but been recaptured. Possibly this was the man in Long's Lane.

Wednesday, 5 September. Braintree VAD hospital notes: difficulty is now found in getting a sufficient number of ladies to act as VAD helpers. There is no love lost between Miss Leila Vaughan (nicknamed 'the Beautiful') and the 'Sister' (who came from Australia). The other day Miss L. V. pointed her out to a lady visitor and said, loud enough to be heard, 'That is the Australian sister.' The lady stared at her somewhat rudely; walked off a few steps; and turned round and stared again. 'Gracious me!' said the Sister to a by-stander, 'does the woman expect me to hop like a kangaroo?'

The sister today played a practical joke on one of the men, James Spearman by name. She had over-heard him telling Miss Parmeter that a year ago he was doing farm-work and had no expectation of being in hospital here this year. The sister had got a pictorial postcard, representing a man milking a cow and a lady asking him 'Why are you not at the front?'—With his answer 'Because the milk doesn't come out there.' She got a visitor to address it to him, so that he might have it tomorrow, and none of the VAD nurses might guess who had sent it.

Thursday, 6 September. 3.30 p.m. commingled sounds of peace and war. Pleasant whirr of reaping-machines in the barley fields. Very loud explosions, in E., in regular succession, only a few seconds between each. Probably bomb practice at Witham. Some of the explosions are extremely violent, and with them a second smaller thud accompanies the first big one.

Friday, 7 September. J. Herbert Tritton called this afternoon. What profit comes from the high price of grain disappears in the increase of wages. 25s. a week is now the regular wage, fixed by law as a minimum. For 'harvest' he used to pay £7.5s.; this year it has been £10.15s. to each harvester. He counts that his wages bill will be half as much again what it used to be.

Notes of this evening's entertainment in YMCA tent: Miss Playfair has been working for some time at the Munition Workers Canteen at Woolwich. She is a very pretty girl and took immensely with the men in the concert. When she sang 'I've got my eye on you' she wagged her finger at the Chairman (Major Cockayne). When the song was over Major C. went over to ask her to sing an encore and the men all burst out with 'I've got my eye on you.'

Saturday, 8 September. I have at last the correct story of the incident which gave rise to the 'escaped prisoner' story. Mrs Ward and her little daughter Lydia, were walking along the road at the end of Long's Lane. They heard a man coming along the road behind them humming to himself. It was then getting dusk. Mrs Ward was expecting her husband and called out 'Is that you, dad?' The man went on humming and made no answer. The second time she spoke he was alongside of her: he just glowered at her, and walked past without speaking. She told Mrs Everett about this. Mrs E. said it would be old Mr Hardingham. They found out that Mr Hardingham had not been near the place that night. So Mrs Ward and Mrs Everett are convinced that the man must have been 'a spy'.

7.15 p.m. Major Jas. Caldwell called. He does not think much will now be attempted in Flanders till next year. Probably small advances will be made in the hope of getting possession of Lens. It is thought that, after that, we will wait till the large American forces now in training are ready to take the field. The war will certainly go on through this winter.

Monday, 10 September. Morning's post today (10 a.m.) brought the official form for a sugar-ration card.

Village rumour has again touched its high-water mark. Yesterday evening Lizzie Oddey, the Rectory cook, was told in the village, apparently in all good faith and not as a hoax (at least by her immediate informant) that 'the Kaiser's dining-room had been smashed by bombs by the Austrians who are fighting on our side.'

Driver Deacon was at Loos. He says that soldiers who were there are not supposed to tell what happened: we advanced 2,000 yds. and were then driven back 3,000 yds.; our casualties were three times as many as was allowed to appear in the newspapers. The Germans have taught us nearly everything in this war, especially artillery-firing. They come on like a football scrimmage, one man shoving another man in front of him so as to expose the man in front to being shot and saving himself.

Friday, 14 September. From Annie Rayner, daughter of C. W. Rayner, Lowley's farm: her brother, Fred Rayner, had to go on military service on Sept. 30th, but he is suffering from eczema. The mother hopes that the eczema will continue and keep him at home for some time yet. His twin brother, George, was to go when they got a 'substitute'. He is an admirable worker; they do not think they can get a substitute who will work so well and so they are not trying to get one.

Tuesday, 18 September. 5 p.m. the first of the farms called for the customary harvest gift. It is the custom here, some time after end of harvest, for the men of a farm to go one evening to a public-house and have beer and for this they ask a gift from the Rector. When I came here, it was always asked for as 'a largesse'. Now the old word is being forgotten. The man, —— Parish, who came now for Bishop's Hall, asked for 'a harvest thanksgiving'.

Notes from Dr R. P. Smallwood: Many of the country people have absolute faith in the predictions of 'Old Moore's' *Almanac*. Several have told Dr Smallwood how relieved they are to know that the war will be over in 1918; 'Old Moore says so.' He also says that in April 'the foe will be pressing at the gates' so they are quite sure that in that month the Germans will try an invasion of this country.

Thursday, 20 September. Within the last fortnight three deserters have come back to Camp and given themselves up. Four months ago they went off, and have since been working for some people, and 'jolly well enjoying themselves'. When they had got on their beam ends and had no more money left they came back here. The ring-leader got 112 days CB; the second, fifty-six days; and the third, twenty-eight days.

Saturday, 22 September. 7.15 p.m. Major Caldwell called: In London opinion is that there will be a renewal of air raids when moonlight nights return, i.e. about Sept. 26 to Oct. 3. The Dean of Bocking is searching for a curate. He says that, until he began making enquiries about applicants, he had no idea there were so many men of bad character among the clergy of the Church of England.

Grace Wright, daughter of Jesse Samuel Wright, often earns two pounds 10s. a week at munitions work, and (says her cousin, Lily Wright) spends it all.

Monday, 24 September. 8.10 p.m. a very beautiful evening. Starlit sky: Rectory housemaid came to tell me that a raid was on. Being in my study, with the shutters closed because of the lights, I could hear nothing. Outside there was the loud humming of an aeroplane on its way to London. A stream of bright lights was going up in Chelmsford direction, like the bulbs of electric lights, of a sort I have never seen before. Going out to the gate from the road into Weir pasture, I found Major Wm. Brown seated on the stile there, watching. He said similar lights had, before that, gone up also in the E. He supposed they were star-shells.[1] 8.15 p.m. cannon began to fire. 8.20 p.m. there was a multiple crash as of several big bombs exploding. 8.30 p.m. I came into the house and watched from my bedroom window. 8.45 p.m. the

---

[1] Star-shells were exploding shells designed to bring down enemy aeroplanes.

cannonade was no longer heard. I went out again and met Mr Brown. He said he did not think the raider (or raiders) was coming back this way. 9.30 p.m. I went out again. Everything was now quiet.

My daughters were helping at YMCA canteen this evening: About 8.5 p.m. the raiders were heard very distinctly coming. The aeroplane, at 8.10 p.m., was heard quite near, but apparently flying very high; as it passed one of the men said 'There must be hundreds up there.' Then, after listening for a bit, 'More than thirty.' After a longer pause, 'At least more than one.'

Some five Tommies came to the canteen to cheer up the lady canteen-helpers. Their comfort was 'You had much better stay here because if you go home you will probably just walk into it.' The following are some scraps of their disjointed talk among themselves:
(a) 'Eh, Charlie, if they come over here, you will be blown to bits.'
(b) 'A good one for Blighty, old man.'
(c) 'Hope they don't drop one on the camp.'
(d) 'Lord, my feet are cold.'
(e) 'Ah! God help the women and children in London' to which the others all said 'yes'.

Mrs Joyce, Chatham Green, who washes up for the canteen, was in a frantic state of nerves. So they gave her a chair in a corrugated iron hut and there she wept solidly for half-an-hour. Her daughter was with her, saying 'Oh, Ma, you must not take on so.' Then the daughter came out of the hut to the lady canteen helpers and begged them to say nothing to ma about it, because she is frightened. Then she herself, two minutes later, went back to 'ma' and called out in her ear—'Don't come out, Ma! They are passing overhead. They are coming right over here.' All tried to comfort Mrs Joyce, but in vain, until a Scotsman thought it might comfort her if they sang Harry Lauder's songs to her. So, for an hour, two of them sat in the hut, singing comic songs. Then the old girl either felt much better or felt that the air raid was a lesser evil than the singing, because she came out of the hut and began to look about to see if there were any signs of 'the Zeppelins'.

Wednesday, 26 September. Charles H. Ward today called. He has ten days leave. He was looking well, but, if possible, more boyish-like than ever.

Sunday, 30 September. Miss Templeton [in charge of the laboratory at

Courtauld's] is here on a visit to my younger daughter. She told us: that the average wage [for women workers there] is 30s. a week. Mrs Lever, who seems to be a head-person in Crittall's factory some time ago, interviewed, in London, 100 women who had applied for posts in the munitions factory at Braintree and engaged them for work there. Of the hundred who came down only six now remain. One girl left at the end of six weeks, and when asked why she was leaving said 'You see I have now done my bit.'

Monday, 1 October. Air raid of Sunday evening, 30 Sept. 1917. From Mrs Dee: She and the people on the High Road find that a sure way to keep children from being nervous during a raid is to take them out of doors to look at the star-shells. They get so excited about these that they don't think of the aeroplanes. John Ketley, Endway (works at Hoffmann's) has found out another way of quieting his little mother-less boy, Jack Ketley. He has made him a wooden sword, and the child parades the road, declaring, as he flourishes his sword, 'If any German comes here I will cut off his head.'

12.30 p.m. Charles H. Ward called to say goodbye. He goes back to France early tomorrow morning.

Air raid warning received in Lyons Hall Camp at 7.10 p.m. 'All-clear' notice received at 11 p.m. In the course of the evening Great Leighs people, who live in the High Road, stood in groups on the road, listening to the cannonade and watching the ceaseless ascent of star-shells (which was really a wonderful sight). Policeman Charles Cole was sent along to ask them to go indoors. Fragments of shrapnel (from the guns at Writtle or Willingale) were falling and some might conceivably come as far as Great Leighs. They were not, however, to be denied the grand fireworks and pooh-poohed him.

Tuesday, 2 October. Gertie Witney, daughter of George Witney, Chadwix farm, is aet. 18 or 19. The other day she went about telling everybody that her cousin, an assistant in a Post Office near London, had been killed by a bomb. This impression on her mind came solely from a jocular postcard sent by the cousin—'I can only sleep from 11 p.m. to 7 a.m., and can only eat at meal-times, and I was killed last week by a bomb.'

Thursday, 4 October. The Church School and the Council School here have had a printed circular issued by the Board of Education at the request of the Minister of Munitions and the Food Controller. The substance of it is that much grain is being used in processes needed for the war. After experiments, it has been found that horse-chesnuts can be used in these processes. One ton of horse-chesnuts can save half a ton of grain. Schoolchildren in this parish have taken much interest in this matter. Mrs Dee's two youngest boys had taken all the clothes out of their drawers and laid them on chairs so as to have the drawers clear for storing chesnuts. G. S. With, Headmaster of the Council School, had read out the circular to the children in school. Mrs Dee's youngest boy had taken it up as meaning that for every lb. of chesnuts he brought in he would get half a lb. of food to take home.

Wednesday, 10 October. Fred Fuller, Cole farm, says that last year when the Camp broke up and went to Halstead, he found outside Cole farm, a soldier-lad, shivering with fright, riding one horse and leading a second. He was utterly unable to manage them, and had had to let them feed by the roadside as they came along, and so had got quite behind all the rest of the column. He told F. F. that he had never been on horseback before, and that those who sent him out knew that perfectly well. F. F. asked him who had harnessed the horses for him. He said 'One of the men in camp.' The bridles had been put on, but the bits not put in the horses' mouths. F. F. bridled them properly, and sent the lad along over Gubbions Green. Presently two officers came and made to go by St Anne's. But F. F. told them they had better go by the woods—otherwise they ran the risk of losing a soldier and two horses.

Thursday, 11 October. Miss Annette Tritton called at 10.30 a.m. to have her application for a passport and photograph attested. She goes to Rouen to take charge of YMCA and YWCA huts there.

The men moved out of Lyons Hall Camp about 9.45 a.m. this morning.

Saturday, 13 October. Major James Caldwell called, 7.45 p.m. He said: —— Joyce, of Bocking, who was a corporal in the Church Lads' Brigade, has been home on leave after being wounded. He was to join up tonight. He was through the Somme battles. He says the Germans, when they got taken prisoners, simply chuckled. It was very difficult to make the prisoners wake up so as to understand what they were wanted to do. They were dazed with the constant noise. Our poison-gas is worse than the Germans'. They came over not in ones or twos, but in droves. The Germans have quite a lot of artful dodges with a view to saving their men and giving them a rest. Joyce, on one occasion, was eight days in one of our trenches opposite a German trench, some parts of which were only thirty-six yards away. Now and again Very-lights were fired off from the Germans' trench, but it was so strangely quiet that a Lieut. and some of our men went over and entered it. They found in the whole German trench only one German soldier who put his hands up at once and called out cheerfully 'Kamerad'. When they brought this man back to our trench he explained that he had been left in the trench, all by himself with rations for eight days, with orders to go up and down the trench and fire off lights from different parts of it to give the impression that it was occupied. Meanwhile the others were further back resting.

The battles of the Somme, Joyce says, were the worst and fiercest. These battles really decided the war. The Germans had their best men there and their best appliances. But they are still 'awful beggars to fight'. The noise is so constant and the racket so appalling that the ears cease to take it in. In the firing-line you almost think you are in a perfect silence until you try to speak to the man next you and cannot make your voice heard.

Tuesday, 16 October. Claude Tritton, Major, ASC, Rouen, says that his duties now include providing and sending regularly to the trenches food for canaries. Canaries are now kept in all the trenches. They are most sensitive to the gas from gas-shells and gas-sprays. They faint at the faintest suspicion of gas and give the men time to get on their masks.

J. Herbert Tritton says that white mice are kept on all our submarines. These are very sensitive to deficiency in oxygen and their uneasiness gives the first warning that the air wants renewing.

Mr Leng [the officer in charge of clearing up Lyons Hall Camp] says that there is a confident opinion that we will take Ostend before long, and that the war will be over early next spring.

4 p.m. high cold wet west wind. So ill that I had now to go to bed. 10 p.m. heavy rain.

Thursday, 18 October. Report in village is that Great Leighs people could not buy tea in Braintree yesterday. Mr A. G. Port, shopman, Great Leighs, says he has no tea and no butter for sale, and only 11 lb.

of very fat bacon. Farmers refuse to sell oats and he can let me have no oats for my ducks. He brought however half a bushel of barley, 5s.6d.; fourteen lb. of bran, cost 2s.

Friday, 19 October. Village gossip has it that Chas. H. Ward is engaged to Ruth Fuller, formerly housemaid here.[1] Also that the wife of Sergeant Lewis supposed herself (when she married Lewis) to be the widow of a soldier who was killed early in the war. The first husband has turned up again.

Saturday, 20 October. 11.15 a.m. M. E. Hughes-Hughes called. An army paper has been issued suggesting that parents of soldiers (who have been killed) should apply for an allowance to make up for the weekly sum formerly received from their sons. Herbert George Wright's father is now aet. 77; the mother is blind; Ethel Wright, daughter, has had to leave domestic service to look after her parents. M. E. H. H. came to ask if I could verify the statements on the application form.

Arthur Stoddart was wounded on 20 Sept. It will be six weeks yet before he can be brought to England. His sister's (Connie Stoddart's) fiancé is in Belgium. They have to sleep there in dug-outs. On some mornings the Post Corporal had to swim from the dug-out to get the letters.

Air raid of Friday evening 19 Oct. 1917: Fred Fuller says that several people were killed outside Swan & Edgar's. When there is an air raid London police go about the streets with a placard 'Take Shelter' hung round their necks. When the raid is over, they go out with another placard 'All Clear'.

Thursday, 25 October. 10.15 a.m. Mr Chas. Wm. Rayner called to have attested his application to the War Office for the effects of his son (supposed killed in action).

---

[1] On his last leave, Charlie had got his mother to give him £2 from his savings (which came to £20) in order to buy a fire-screen for his recently married sister. However, when he arrived at Liverpool Street Station from Great Leighs, Ruth Fuller, a waitress at the Commercial Hotel in the Waterloo Road, met him. She 'wheedled' the money for an engagement ring. Charlie's sister remembered that Ruth would have been 'far too expensive for my brother': she 'dressed to equal the Trittons' and even had her own calling cards printed. She eventually married an older man with some money.

Wednesday, 31 October. One of the soldiers working for Mrs Flack at Fitzandrews farm, Great Waltham, is surnamed —— James. He says he is the best shot in his regiment, and for that reason, gets extra pay. He was at Mons. He and four others were buried for three days. When they were dug out, three were dead. He has had an injury between the neck and the shoulder-blade which makes one shoulder higher than the other. He is suffering from shell-shock. When there is an air raid he trembles all over—not that he is frightened—but that he can't control his nerves.

Eggs in Great Waltham are selling for 3*d.* each.

Saturday, 3 November. Today's post brought a letter from my former man-servant, very typical of a village lad's letter:

Dear Sir

I now take the Pleasure in writing a few lines to you trusting you are getting on alright and keeping well I was so glad to see you all I am afraid you have been working very hard since I left . . . I expect you are having some cold weather at home now it is very cold out here one or two mornings of white Frost it is getting quite winter now it will be a blessing when we can all get back for good the time soon flys past it cant last for ever I must now close as I cant find any more to say to night

Yours Obediently
Charlie Ward

W. Herbert Dee has heard from his brother (Reggie Ketley) who has been in the front fighting line in France. He does not know how his regiment got through it, with big shells and gas shells bursting all about. It was also 'bad travelling'. During the advance he himself was up to the neck in mud and water. Rumour has it that his battalion, now some miles behind the front line, has been brought back for two or three months' rest.

There is a great demand from the front for Engineers. Major Holman, RE [Royal Engineers], at 'Brooklands', Broomfield [the house next to Major Caldwell's new home] is under orders to send off at once a large batch of RE men. The ground where we have recently advanced is in a dreadful state. The Germans do not bury their dead, but just stick them into the mud. The conditions are sufficient to brew a pestilence.

Monday, 12 November. There is a report in the village that at

Chelmsford on Sat. (10 Nov.) a soldier, ordered out to France again, threw himself over the stone bridge into the river. A comrade who was with him jumped in after him to pull him out. Both are now in hospital in Chelmsford.

4 p.m. F. J. Cooper called: He had a letter from France the other day from his brother, Capt. Wm. Cooper, to this effect—You think you know what mud is but you don't. Here, for the first three feet down it is like warm treacle. What it is like underneath, that no one knows. Explorers have never returned.

Thursday, 15 November. The Taylors at the Post Office are officially asked to collect razors to be sent to the army. The general public are not asked but the PO people are to canvass quietly. C. Cole, the policeman, has given them one which he took from a man who tried to cut his throat with it.

Friday, 16 November. At 11 a.m. outside 'the Maypole' shop in Chelmsford, a notice was stuck up—'We are sold out of Tea, Butter, and Margarine.' The 'International' was selling margarine by half-pound only to each applicant. So was 'Lipton's', charging 6d. the half-pound. 'Debnam's' was selling more liberally in quantity but charging 1s.3d. or 1s.4d. a lb.

Sunday, 18 November. Mrs Cobb, at the grocer's shop, Little Waltham, thinks that a good many of the girls who have gone to munition-work are longing to get back to domestic service. Munition-work is much harder than they reckoned for. They have everything to provide for themselves and the apparently high wages are soon spent.

Tuesday, 27 November. Mr G. S. With, master of the Council School, says the children of his school have collected six bushels of horse-chesnuts.

Connie Stoddart has had a wire that her brother, Arthur T. Stoddart, is rather better. Ernest Wright is very ill in France— bronchitis and pneumonia—too ill to write home.

Thursday, 29 November. Yesterday morning's post brought a letter of enquiry [from Crittalls of Braintree regarding suitability for munitions work] as to Ethel May Gooday, Rectory housemaid till 13 Oct. 1917. I neglected to enter it yesterday.

Friday, 30 November. Arthur Stoddart has had to have his leg amputated. He is reported to be in a very weak state. His father and mother will stay in France, near the hospital where he is, till he is out of danger.

Saturday, 1 December. Notes given me by my elder daughter, Mary Alice, on Friday 23rd Nov. on her return from a visit to Mrs Leslie Tritton at 13, Rutland Gate, S.W. 7—but not written out till this evening. I have been very busy in the grounds: My daughter visited the Australian canteen in Horseferry Road, Westminster. It is run entirely by the Commonwealth of Australia and is not in any way under the War Office here. The King and Queen went to see this canteen the other day. The King was struck by the Boy-Scout, who acts as door porter; and pointing to his 'shorts' asked him when he was going into trousers. The boy is only fourteen years old, but is a very big fellow. The King was very much taken with the 'double-decker' beds. These are four-poster iron bedsteads, but with the posts carried up so as to carry a second bed. The War Office objects to these. Mrs Samuel, the leader of the canteen, told one of the War Office lords that the King approved of them. He answered, curtly, 'The King has nothing to do with it.' In the Australian canteen all the meat used comes from Australia. It is open day and night, never closed. During an air raid in London, anti-aircraft guns mounted on trolleys, are run along to street corners and fired from there.

Tuesday, 4 December. My daughter (Mary Alice) went to Rayne this afternoon and saw Connie Stoddart. She said Arthur Stoddart had haemorrhaged three times from his shattered thigh (right leg). The third time was when the doctor was dressing the wound. The surgeon then said that there was no hope for it, the leg must be amputated. A. S. pleaded to have the leg spared, but the surgeon said that that could not be done, the leg must come off at once. Mr and Mrs Stoddart got the wire from the War Office on Wedn. night, bidding them come at once. Connie Stoddart bicycled into Braintree to get their papers signed at the Police Station. When they got to London they had to get their permits to cross to France. They left Rayne Station on Thursday morning and reached Boulogne that same night. They were motored about sixty miles to Treport. They had quarters provided for them in a YMCA building, where they were most kindly treated. Directly they arrived the YMCA secretary took them to the hospital and fetched the

Sister to see them. She went in to the ward, and told Arthur 'I think your father and mother have come to see you.' Then Mr and Mrs S. went in. They found Arthur terribly weak and as white as wax. He said to his mother 'Don't excite me, mother. Don't excite me.' Then he whispered to his father that he had had his leg taken off. 'Ought they to tell his mother or not?' he asked. Mrs Stoddart wanted to know what the whispering was about. When she was told, she said 'Never mind, so long as your life is spared'. For several days he had nothing but champagne and port. Now he is allowed anything he can take. For a few days before it was taken off, and in his worse agony he kept calling for his mother. The ward in which Arthur Stoddart is has forty beds, all for helpless cases—eyes, legs or arms. Before Mr and Mrs Stoddart had left, Arthur was quite able to talk to them, though weak.

On Sat. 1 Dec. PC Cole here told Fred R. Lewin that he had a warrant out for the arrest of a man in khaki with his arm in a sling who has been going about collecting (as he said) for wounded soldiers.

Tuesday, 11 December. 9.45 a.m. Morning's post brought yet another silly bundle of official papers [from The League of National Safety to encourage a voluntary association of 'patriotic citizens pledged to economise in food and checking of all forms of waste'].

Afternoon's post brought Harry Ward, Endway, word that his son Charles Henry Ward, RHA, had been killed on 16 Nov. The letter was from his major:

30 November 1917

Dear Madam,

I much regret that I have been unable to write before to you to express my deepest condolences with you on the death of your son. All the officers, NCO's and men join me in deepest sympathy with you in your great loss. He was a most excellent soldier and much liked by all ranks in the battery, who miss him very much.

His death was entirely accidental and absolutely instantaneous. He stepped on to the step of a truck while it was moving out of the station and the step came away, throwing him under the train. We had to leave him at the station with his sergeant as the battery was en route for Italy.

The French doctor of the village made all arrangements for the funeral and the whole population turned out to mark their respects and they gave your boy a very fine funeral and covered the coffin with flowers. A cross was erected to his memory by the battery. He was buried in the village cemetery at Seurre, Cote d'Or, France on the 17th Novr 1917, the day after his death on the 16th. Owing to the move of the battery we have been unable to send letters off till the present moment.

Again let me express my own personal sorrow in the loss of your very fine son who gave his life for his country no less than if he had died in battle . . .

Yours truly,

R. F. Adam

Charlie Ward was twenty-five last April. His last letter (received at his home S. 17 Nov., the day, as it proved, of his funeral) was written on M., 12 Nov.

Wednesday, 12 December. 9.30 a.m. morning's post brought a letter from Eliz. Gillies, daughter of a farmer in a lonely part of Inverness-shire. She and her brothers speak Gaelic and have very little English. Miss Gladys Cruickshank, then of Somerville College, Oxford, and my two daughters lodged there in the summer of 1915:

10 December 1917

To My Dearest Miss M[ary]. Clark,

I am sitting a long last to rite few lines to let you know the way I am getting along . . . my Dearest Boy was Called up fore the army Johnie Stephen he was only two month training when he was sent to france . . . I am sorry to tell you that he was gassed last month on the 24 he is now in England in Essex Hospital so I am getting enough of this world but their is nothing like this horrid war I hope to God it will soon be over . . . Dear Miss Clark if you are near the Place where Johnie is I would like if you could go to see him and you would tell me rite how he is getting alonge I am sure he would be glad to see you and so far away from home ... I am your loving friend   Eliza A. Gillies

The lad who drives the butcher's (C. Wroot, Little Waltham) cart says that he is assured that —— Fitch, who used to work on Lyons Hall farm, has had six sons killed in this war.

Friday, 14 December. [Letter from the Rector to Falconer Madan.]*

14 December, 1917

My dear Madan,

Thanks for your p. c. I have been continuously ill for many weeks, at times, rather critically. Once or twice I really did not expect to live till Xmas. During the last few weeks I have picked up somewhat and this week the doctor pronounces me out of present danger. So I think I may fulfill the old saying of there's being 'life in the old dog yet' . . .

Times here are rather miserable. We have great difficulty in getting coal, owing to railway deficiencies and shortage of carting. We cannot get lamp oil. Evenings have to be managed in feeble candlelight. I go to bed very early and my daughter concludes the evening by reading with her bicycle lamp ('carbide', she tells me).

Church has been very miserable. The Church Wardens were unable to get coal or coke or lamp oil, so all day the Church has been very cold and damp; and in the afternoons, very gloomy, the service concluding in darkness . . . The roads were dreadful . . .

I have not been able to do either reading or writing for a great many weeks, more from mental lassitude than from anything else. But I have, in a way, kept on my War Diary, and have several volumes to send to Bodley, when I get some of the cross-references filled in.

I have two big boxes of documents, and records, one manorial of early date, the other archidiaconal of Elizabethan and Stuart times, waiting better days. My Jesus College notes have also surceased for the present . . .

7.45 p.m. Major James Caldwell called: He had much to say about the Cambrai battle, gathered from his partner, —— Davies and other officers, wounded, back from the front.[1] The following are the chief items I remember:- (a) the Cambrai 'victory' was really a failure. While the joy-bells were ringing in London, men out there were almost in tears. It was a 'most unholy muddle'.

It is a frequent practice of the Germans to get information by dressing up a man in the uniform of a British soldier and sending the man into our trenches. They have plenty of men who speak English perfectly. They often get information in this way. To prevent this the Argyll and Sutherlands adopted pass-words which were great puzzles to the Welshmen. [Davies's Welsh Brigade was alongside the Argyll and Sutherland Highlanders.] On one occasion the word was 'Balla-chulish'. Mr Davies practised this word himself and set four of his men to practise it. He then sent the man of the four who seemed to have best mastery of it along the trench. The A. and S. were in a very bad temper, because a shell had smashed in part of the trench and they were cleaning up. When the Welshman came along, making a stumble of the pass-word, they were on the point of bayoneting him, when he yelled out 'I'm not German; I'm Welsh.' When he got back to his own

---

[1] The Cambrai battle, an offensive against the Hindenburg Line, had begun on 20 November and continued until 7 December. It saw the first really effective use of tanks by British forces. The attack did have an initial success but a lack of reserves and fresh tanks meant that the captured ground was lost.

part of the trench, he believed he had had the escape of his life and vowed he would never again venture near the A. and S. Mr Davies was very anxious to know what Ballachulish meant. He thought it was a Gaelic swear-word and was astonished to hear that it was only the name of a place.

Saturday, 15 December. Reggie Ketley says they are generally up to their knees in mud; often almost to the waist. Yesterday in Chelmsford there was no tea and no sugar and very little margarine. Today Mrs A. G. Port at the village shop here had no jam and no marmalade.

Sunday, 16 December. Charlie Cloughton, Welsh Guards, has been killed. Son of old Walter Cloughton.

Monday, 17 December. There was a burglar in this house early. How he got in, I do not know. I seem to have disturbed him by my early rising. He had lit one of the candles in the brass candlesticks in the study; opened the shutters of one of the study windows; threw up the sash and went out that way. I have missed nothing, except possibly half-a-crown from the study. He seems also to have been in the store-room.

Thursday, 20 December. 10.10 a.m. morning's post brought a letter [from the assistant matron, Military Hospital, Colchester to Miss Mary Alice Clark, dated 18 December] about 'Johnnie' Stephen: 'A.B. John Stevens is making very good progress—he has recovered his voice and his eyes no longer require treatment—he is also up now and walking about.'

I bought in Chelmsford today the official forms of Intercessory Service for 6 Jan. 1918. The price in this form was 1s.9d. for fifty. I do not think highly of it as a liturgical performance.

In Chelmsford today butter was 2s.6d. a lb.; lard was 1s.6d. a lb.; Wiltshire sausages, 1s.8d. a lb.

Friday, 21 December. The burglar at the Rectory is believed to have been a stranger who was in the village, ostensibly buying rabbit skins. He went into Mr A. G. Port's shop, and when Mrs Port was out for the moment, pocketed some packets of soup. He was observed and Mr Port's son, Leonard, ran after him, made him turn out his pockets, and recovered the packets.

7.45 p.m. Major James Caldwell called: From a City friend in the Russian trade he was told that it was known that the fighting in the streets of Petrograd had been very severe. The Bolsheviks were really in the minority. Lenin and Trotsky were mere adventurers, but had, each on their own account, been remitting to banks in Berlin large sums of plundered money. The Bolsheviks are the extreme anarchists who wish to seize small property and divide it among themselves. Still, the better class of Russians hoped that things would settle down before long and come out right.

Friday, 28 December. 7.30 p.m. Major Jas. Caldwell called: Information is being steadily withheld as to the grievous losses in the Cambrai disaster. The aerodrome at Chelmsford is making progress. German prisoners are to be employed to work in its construction and will be quartered in Chelmsford Union Workhouse. Munition-workers have received notice that half the present output will be sufficient. The ostensible reason is that we do not now supply Russia. The real reason is that the younger men may be 'released' and so no longer able to claim exemption.

Monday, 31 December. The paste used in this volume and in several preceding volumes, and likely to be used in the volumes for 1918 is bad, being made from G. R. (Government Regulation) flour. It is deficient in adhesive quality and I fear the pasted-in slips may soon get detached. [They did not.] 12 p.m. rain.

1918

Tuesday, 1 January. 3 p.m. afternoon post brought a letter from my daughter, Mildred, which enclosed one from an Orléans girl [Mlle Suzanne Goueffon]:

22 December 1917

Dear Miss Mildred,

I send you my best wishes for Christmas and New Year. May 1918 be the year of Victory is always our greatest wish!... I am always looking forwards to meet you; I remember with great pleasure the good lessons I took with you. Since that time I didn't improve my English.

Weather must be very cold in England. Here we had snow and now all is frozen, −10° [centigrade] we had last night in the country; our poor soldiers must be very bad in their trenches.

Orléans is always a military town, Canadians, Americans, Russians are mixed with our soldiers ... Our refugees from the north are now with us; they had horribly suffered with the Germans and are very pleased to be far from those horrible people ...

Friday, 11 January. 7.45 p.m. Major Jas. Caldwell called: There is great scarcity of timber. You cannot get even a plank of wood to make a garden frame without an official licence. Major Caldwell has been told by West-End army men that the Government apprehends great disquiet after the war. Munition work will stop, and wages will fall and there will be a bad time of unrest. The government are therefore encouraging the enrolment of as many Special Constables and Volunteers as possible, to have a large force of partly trained men to preserve order.

Sunday, 20 January. Major James Caldwell told me: about 1,000 men are to be taken from Hoffmann's, Chelmsford, for military service and all night-shifts there are to be stopped.

Friday, 25 January. 10 a.m. morning's post brought an application-form for cards for butter or margarine. The Food Controller is accused of making an artificial famine of butter and eggs by prohibiting imports from Ireland.

Alfred Skeggs, a London life assurance agent, says that the anti-aircraft barrage round London is being moved back, because the loss of life from our own shells has been terrible. Mr Skeggs says that opinion in London is that the war will not be ended by military effort, but by financial and economic stress.

Veronica Burt is a friend of Mrs John Foucar (née Lydia Hughes-Hughes of Leez Priory). Her husband, Capt. Burt, had his thigh smashed and was taken prisoner at the same time that Lydia's brother, William Hughes-Hughes, was killed. Capt. Burt died after amputation. The German doctor wrote an exceedingly kind letter to his wife.

Harry Hull (on leave from France) says that they are preparing for a big battle, and that the soldiers say that the war will be over in March.

Saturday, 26 January. F. R. Lewin says the agitation among the food queues in Braintree yesterday amounted almost to a riot, and the police were at their wit's end. Similar turbulence is looked for at Chelmsford today.

Saturday, 2 February. Robert Armstrong, a private in the Australian Expeditionary Force, is engaged to Louise Flack, Fitzandrews farm, Great Waltham. Today he was at Fitzandrews and I jot down here some notes of his talk, as reported to me: On 4 Oct. 1917, when they took Passchendaele ridge, his battalion went into action 800 strong, but only 110 came out. The Australians are so infuriated at the favourite trick of the Germans in shamming to be wounded, and when the Australians have gone on, jumping up and shooting them from behind, that they now bayonet the German wounded as they pass on. He himself has not the heart to do this but he carefully disarms them. The Germans are very much given to shooting our stretcher-bearers. There is terrible waste of ammunition at the front. This is largely the fault of the authorities. These insist on the men starting with more ammunition than they can comfortably carry, and the men take the first opportunity to throw part of their burden away. Bombs cost 3s.5d. each. He has seen whole boxes of unused bombs sunk in the mud. He has no doubt that after the war, when farming is begun, ploughs will strike on some of these and plough-team and man be blown to pieces. On 4 Oct. 1917 at Passchendaele a German Colonel was amongst the prisoners taken. One of the Australian officers, Bennet by name, questioned him. Two men came up ready to bayonet the German. But Bennet said 'Spare this man; I am getting valuable information from him.' When these men turned to go away the German whipped out a revolver, saying 'my love for my country is greater than death, and I would not give information.' The angry soldiers at once bayoneted him.

Sunday, 3 February. Harry Milton has been discharged from the army. He had been wounded in the head. His aunt (Mrs Fred Fuller) with whom he has been staying here for a bit, says he is 'very queer'.

Mrs Griffet's son (Cole Hill Cottages) says there is terrible thieving in the camps in France. Soldiers help themselves to whatever they have a mind to. He himself has had his oilskin stolen. He and his mate put a padlock on their hut, but the thieves not only forced it off, but took padlock and key away with them.

Monday, 4 February. His people had the greatest difficulty yesterday in sending off Harry Hull to France after his leave. Finally they put him and his young lady into John Dean's (St Anne's Castle) trap and sent him off to Chelmsford station. His brother (Albert), 'Bubb' Digby, and Frank Hurrell cycled with the trap to make sure of him. In his train at Chelmsford they found two men of his battalion, and saw him safe off with them.

Monday, 11 February. 4 p.m. Madge Gold called. She was on her way home to Chatham Hall, Great Waltham, having got a week off duty at Braintree VAD hospital. She said: On the Intercession Sunday (6 Jan.) she was in London with her two nieces. They wanted to go to the Westminster Abbey 11.15 a.m. service. They got to the Abbey at 10.30 a.m. only to find crowds being turned away, every seat being already full. They went to St Margaret's, Westminster, and stood in a queue which was being slowly admitted. When there were only about twenty people in front of them, the doors were shut. They then went a little further down the Embankment but found the Church there also turning people away. They finally got into the R.C. Westminster Cathedral. Every Church in London was packed.

Thursday, 14 February. 9.40 a.m. morning's post brought ration cards (a) butter and margarine; (b) butcher's meat for each of the three members of this household. One of the ducks today laid an egg—the first I have seen. I have had the four ducks since September 1917.

Tuesday, 26 February. Sidney Willis has got his discharge and is back to work for Mrs Jennings, at 'the Victoria'. He had an attack of paralysis, is getting slowly better, but has still great difficulty in walking. He can drive the pony-trap all right.

Friday, 1 March. 7.45 p.m. Major Jas. Caldwell called: He had a talk with a brigadier on leave from France, who said that he expected there would be nothing of great moment on the Western front at present. He thought the Germans would not take the offensive because they knew they could effect nothing without terrible sacrifice and the German authorities were afraid of the feeling in Germany which would result from further heavy losses. We would certainly not take the offensive until the USA had great forces in readiness. He thought we were in for another year of war.

Monday, 4 March. Kynoch's munition-works at Stanford-le-hope is to be closed. Eight hundred girl-workers are being sent away. The reason given is that there is now a sufficient supply of the things they have been making there.

The German prisoners are hard at work on the aerodrome at Chelmsford. They have quarters in the Union Workhouse and are marched back there from their work about 4.30 p.m. each day. They are said to be very happy, laughing and joking with each other as they pass along the streets. Several Chelmsford girls have been taken before the magistrates for giving them stamps and chocolate.

Friday, 8 March. Air raid of Thursday night, 7 March 1918: 11.15 p.m. extremely heavy gun-firing in S. Cannon going off singly, in rapid succession, concussions severer than any I have known on these occasions. They rattled the window-sashes and, as I sat watching, beside the open window, I could feel the house tremble.

Notice posted outside Dance's, tobacconist, Braintree to the effect that, owing to paper restrictions, picture-cards inside packets of cigarettes will not be used after present stock is used up.

Dr R. P. Smallwood called at 4.45 p.m. He said the raid was at Paddington and that several houses had been destroyed. He says also that, now that raiders have come on a moonless night, they may come at any time.

Saturday, 9 March. J. Herbert Tritton thought that air raids were over with the moon and took Mrs Tritton (an invalid) on Wedn. 6 Mch. back to their town-house just in time for Thursday night's raid.

Friday, 15 March. The moon again serving, a renewal of air raids on London is expected. J. Herbert Tritton is therefore bringing his household back from 4, Lowndes Square to Lyons Hall.

7.30 p.m. Major James Caldwell called: This afternoon there were over 100 American airmen on a platform at Liverpool Street Station and he was told that as many again had marched off to get some grub. They were likely-looking, well-set-up chaps and if the rest of the American troops are at all like them, they will help us materially. Altogether they gave a most favourable impression.

The expectation in London is that we are going again to get 'a big dose' of air raids. The Dean of Bocking told Major C. last evening that a general in the air-service told him that they were looking forward to a big air-battle over London. It is not improbable that the war will be decided in the air. It will be wonderful if Germany has the materials to match the output of aircraft of Great Britain, France and USA.[1]

Tuesday, 19 March. 2 p.m. afternoon's post brought a letter from my daughter, Mildred—16:iii:1918: 'I enclose a letter from Miss Thistlethwaite written from "Ravenscroft", Strathpeffer on Wednesday':

At Perth my porter talked very seriously to me. 'Are you quite sure you want to go to Strathpeffer? You know all the north of Scotland from Invergordon round the coast to Kyle of Lochalsh now belongs to America, and they are queer people etc. etc.'

However I assured him I was determined to risk it. On my arrival here I was at once introduced to two American sailors—such delightful boys and as we drove through the village we passed dozens of them . . . They have comandeered the Highland hotel for surgical cases . . . The Ben Nevis for medical cases. They said to the manageress 'How long to get this place in order and

---

[1] By the end of the war, the Royal Flying Corps, which became the Royal Air Force on 1 April 1918, had about 2,600 aircraft. The French had about 3,850 and the Americans about 740 planes behind the front. Total Allied air forces would number over 8,000 planes against the Central Powers' 3,400.

clean it?' 'A month.' 'Oh, I guess you're wrong' says the Yankee 'we did one of the largest hotels in London in three days!' They are gems. On Monday they comandeered three large houses and to-day every stick of furniture has been removed and locked up in the hotel cellars . . . Also the houses have been refurnished by those energetic sailors and everything is ready. Wish they'd take our house, only we are out of the village . . . Never has the village been so hustled, but the American navy has so far won everyone's heart . . .

Sunday, 24 March. ('Palm' Sunday) 2 a.m. natural time became 3 a.m. artificial time which will henceforth be used in these notes. On Lyons Hall farms they are still keeping the old time and will do so for a fortnight longer. Some farmers (e.g. Richard Arnold) kept by the old time all last year, and will do so this year also.

Recognizing the general anxiety as to the Western front,[1] the War Office had a bulletin—the first for a very long time. [The last was issued on 2 December 1917.]

SUMMARY OF SATURDAY'S OFFICIAL WAR NEWS
24th. March 12.49 $\frac{A}{M}$

The Battle is continuing with the greatest intensity on the whole front south of the Scarpe River. South and West of St Quentin our Troops have taken up their new positions and are heavily engaged with the enemy . . . On the northern portion of the Battle Front the enemy's attacks have been pressed with the utmost determination and regardless of losses. Our Troops have maintained their positions on the greater part of this Front after a fierce and prolonged struggle.

Great gallantry has been shown by the Troops engaged in the fighting in this area and to the South of it . . . The enemy's attacks continue with great violence.

Saturday, 30 March. J. Herbert Tritton had this morning definite word from the War authorities that there would be no camp in Lyons Hall park this year.

Tuesday, 2 April. 10.30 a.m. Mrs Wm. Brown, Bishop's Hall, called to have her sugar-application signed. She said everybody was agreed that

---

[1] On 21 March, three days before this bulletin, the Germans had launched their big offensive with the Second Battle of the Somme. Although they met with initial success, British troops stood their ground and by 5 April the move had petered out: Amiens and its railway network remained in Allied hands. British losses would stand at 160,000 including 90,000 prisoners-of-war.

the form is silly. It asks you to state how many lbs. of fruit you are going to make into jam in June and July and how many in autumn, as if anyone could, at this time of year, forecast what fruit there is likely to be. If you don't apply before Apr. 4, you will be allowed no sugar.

Several Great Leighs lads are being called up this week. E.g. 'Bub' (Albert) Digby, son of old Chas. Digby, Gubbions Green; Albert Hull, High Road, appears before the Medical Board on M. 8 Apr.

Kenneth Sadgrove, Lieut. South Lancs Regt., son of the Revd Thomas Sadgrove, Rector of Fairstead, is 'missing'. This seems to have happened before the recent big battle (happened on 22nd March).

Wednesday, 3 April. Miss Olive Tritton, of the Chelmsford branch of the Women Land-workers' association asks a special service for Women Land-workers. She says the Chelmsford branch has been officially informed that 30,000 soldiers, promised for land-work, will not now be set free for it. It is said that many girls from Essex country villages, who had gone to London for munition work or domestic-service, have tired of it, or been scared by the air raids, and have gone home.

I received today a copy of the Official Bulletin posted up at Great Leighs Post Office on Monday 1st April 1918. The country villages are very concerned about the present fighting.

Friday, 5 April. 7.30 p.m. Major Jas. Caldwell called: the 10th Essex has been almost wiped out and many lads from this district are 'missing'.

Thursday, 11 April. Widow Hales is very anxious about her son, William, in France. Nothing has been heard from him for five weeks. Other people in the district have had letters and field-postcards, meanwhile, from their boys at the front. Widow Jonathan Ketley had (on Tues. 9 Apr.) a letter from her son Reggie Ketley written on 5th April. He was quite well when he wrote. A great many of 'the boys' had been killed. 'Ernie' (Ernest) Digby, Gubbions Green, is reported by the War Office as missing. His nephew is in the same battalion, and has written that, when he got back from a charge, Ernie's chum told him that he had seen Ernie, wounded, carried off as a prisoner.

Friday, 12 April. Morning's post brought a letter from Fairstead Rectory [from Mrs Thomas Sadgrove to Mary Alice Clark]:

11 April, 1918

My dear Mary,

Thank you for your kind letter of sympathy for us in our awful suspense about my darling Kenneth, it is almost more than I can bear . . . We had a letter from the Chaplain on Sunday morning, he said he spoke to Kenneth on the 21st as he was going into battle and he seemed as cheery as usual. The Colonel also wrote and told us that there was some hope that he might be a prisoner of war and not a casualty but I did not think the Chaplain's letter held out much hope . . . I pray all day long that my boy may be safe somewhere and I am sure you will remember him too . . .

Saturday, 13 April. Albert Digby was cleared A-1. Albert Hull was passed for 'home defence only' because of some defect in the legs.

As regards 'registering' for bacon, H. J. Hicks, Supply Stores, Great Leighs, says that, even if we do not (at present prices) use bacon, we ought to register to provide for household meat-supply. We can take out our bacon-allowance in corned beef.

Sunday, 14 April. Mrs Jonathan Ketley this morning had a long letter, written M., 8 Apr. from her son, Reggie, in France. He wrote it in an old barn, where they were resting for a little. The barn was within reach of shell-fire, and they had all their things packed, ready to bolt if shells began to fall there. They had had nothing off for three weeks. Latterly they had had 'wonderful wet weather' and he would be glad to get dry again. His special 'pal' had been killed, quite a young fellow. He was very sorry for the French villagers. They had had to flee, leaving everything. Their cows, calves, pigs were wandering about. Our soldiers milk the cows whenever they can. There are plenty of potatoes and carrots to be had for the digging them up.

Thursday, 18 April. At Rayne—on one side of the street, nineteen men have been killed in action in the course of the war.

Friday, 19 April. 7 p.m. Major Jas. Caldwell called. He said: This week he met a young officer back from France with a slight wound who told him that he thought the Germans had got as far as they would; the defences our troops have fallen back on are enormously strong, and not the least likely to be shaken. The German losses have been really terrible. Many of our men grew sick at seeing them mowed down. The first lot were pushed on by a second; and when the first lot were cut down, a third wave pushed on the second lot.

135.

Mrs. Chas. Collins, cottage in Cole Hill field had a letter yesterday from her son Charlie Collins. He was still at Salonica when he wrote & was well.

Widow Jonathan Ketley had a long letter last week from her son Reggie Ketley (pl. 55, v91). He said they had been drawn back, for a rest, from Noyon to "a place with six letters in its name, the first letter A" (Amiens, I suppose). Just before being brought back, they had retaken a village. The Germans in it waited till they got within 3 yards of them, firing their rifles at them all the time. Our men do not mind rifle-fire: it is the big guns that do the damage.

6.45 p.m. Still rifle-shooting at Witham batts; so also 7.45 p.m.

Primroses & cowslips ("paigles" folk call them here) are out in great profusion.

8 p.m. evening rather brighter, but N. wind still rough & bitter. There is much cloud-drift still, N. to S., but some spaces of blue sky. The cloud-drift is in 3 layers — upper, sun-whitened; middle, darkish cloud-fields, slow-moving; lowest layer, dark, very ragged spin-drift, driven along at a great pace.
Read somewhat dried Andrew Clark: 28 April 1918.

A page of the Diary for 28 April 1918, showing how Andrew Clark signed and dated each day's entries

HARRY LAUDER'S STORY.

THIS Story was told by Harry Lauder to the Montreal Canadian Club, as it was told to him by his Son, Capt. Lauder, who gave his life for his Country :

THE Germans had captured Six Men of the Black Watch.

THEY stripped them naked, made them stand at Attention through the Cold Night, and at Dawn said, "You Swine! Get Back to your Trenches."

THEN, as the Helpless, Frozen and Naked Men stumbled over No Man's Land, they were Mown Down by Machine Guns.

THIS IS "KULTUR"

One of the official war posters preserved in the Diary by Andrew Clark

---

CHELMSFORD RURAL FOOD CONTROL COMMITTEE

IMPORTANT NOTICE

TO

Applicants for Supplementary Rations for Heavy Workers.

Mr. F. G. MARRIAGE

ON BEHALF OF THE COMMITTEE WILL ATTEND AT

The Great Leighs Council School

on ~~day and~~ *Thursday* evening# next, the and *25* April, 1918, between *7* and *8* p.m., to distribute the Supplementary Meat Cards granted by the Committee.

All Applicants residing in the Parish of GREAT LEIGHS must then attend (personally or by Agent) to receive their Cards, and

Must bring their Meat Cards with them

for production and marking.

Unless the Meat Card is produced, the Supplementary Card cannot be handed out.

ARTHUR S. DUFFIELD,

Executive Officer.

96, High Street, Chelmsford,
15th April, 1918.

DUTTON, PRINTER, CHELMSFORD.

A ration notice posted in Great Leighs in April 1918

Saturday, 20 April. The [call-up] papers received by Dr R. P. Small-wood prove not to have been intended for him, but for another doctor. Col. W. N. Tufnell does not like the new parson at Ford End, and now goes to Church at Pleshey. He is not supposed to use petrol to motor to Church; so he wears knickerbockers that he may be supposed to be inspecting steam-ploughs.

Monday, 22 April. Old Chas. Digby has just heard officially from the War Office that his son Ernest Digby is 'wounded and missing'.

11.30 a.m. day still cold, but now cheerful. Sun shines out brightly and is warmer. A big sulphur-coloured butterfly was fluttering about over the road at the old oak in Cole Mead. 'Star of Bethlehem' and the sessile, glittering-petalled buttercup are out in great profusion. The red-flowered dead-nettle is in extraordinary strong growth this year.

Tuesday, 23 April. F. R. Lewin says that on Sat. 20 Apr. he saw in Braintree Arthur Stoddart. A. S. has so grown in height and width that he cannot wear any of his civilian clothes. He has not got his artificial leg yet, but expects it in about three months, and he will then get his discharge. He is being paid at present £2 a week. After his discharge he will be paid 27s.6d. a week and will be taught a trade. [Stoddart's mother later said the figure was 23s.]

F. R. Lewin says that there is a great comb out at Hoffmann's, Chelmsford. All able-bodied men up to twenty-five have been taken away, and a lot also of twenty-six, twenty-seven, twenty-eight.

Sunday, 28 April. Widow Hales had official notice from the War Office this morning that her son is 'missing'. The Taylors at the Post Office had a letter this week from Sergt. Harry Taylor. He was still in Mesopotamia, but expected soon to be removed.

[Letter from the Rector to Falconer Madan.]*

28 April, 1918

My dear Madan,

I have had another long, bad time but am pulling through. The doctor now opines that I am going to astonish him by getting quite well again.

I am still very disinclined for reading or writing, but am able to be out for long spells sawing or chopping wood or, if the weather permits, in the garden and grounds.

The weeds this year are again 'disthresful.' I keep burning barrow load after barrow load, but have to quote Macbeth 'still they come.'

I have now by me the intervening 'Diary' vols. of 1917, and hope to send them this week . . .

Tuesday, 30 April. 9.45 a.m. morning's post brought a letter from the wife of the Revd Thos. Sadgrove:

29 April, 1918

My dear Mary,

I am thankful to be able to tell you that we heard from Kenneth yesterday. He is a prisoner of war in Germany. The card just says 'Sound in mind and limb' . . . We are too thankful for words and were it not that I have a violent influenza cold I should rush up to Town and have a real good time . . . I feel it would relieve my feelings to go and buy hats and frocks!

Friday, 3 May. 4 p.m. F. J. Cooper called. He said: The German prisoners-of-war who are doing farm-work in the Dunmow district have become very slack and unruly. Farmers say that if they are set to work at hoeing, they do as much damage as they can. These men have become much worse since the beginning of the present German offensive.

Reggie Ketley is reported very seriously wounded in the chest; Harry Hurrell, son of Walter Hurrell (engine-man at Bishop's Hall) is also wounded in right arm.

Saturday, 4 May. Harry Hurrell is at Cardiff. The bullet went right through his right arm and flattened out in a pocket-book (given him, when he was called up, by Miss Elizb. M. Tritton) in pocket of tunic. It is said in the village that no leave to go out to visit the wounded is now given—it is supposed because of the enormous number of casualties.[1]

Sunday, 5 May. Charles Thorogood, son of W. H. Thorogood, 'Dog and Partridge', Great Road, has not been heard of for some time.

9.15 p.m. wet, dripping, thick fog close in.

Saturday, 11 May. 7.45 p.m. Major James Caldwell called: Colonel Buckle [in command of the anti-aircraft defences north of London] says that formerly the German air-raiders all came up the Blackwater and on to the Great Road leading S. to London. That is why they always passed over this district. Now they have a course marked out for them before they start and are directed by wireless.

[1] By 1 May Allied casualties were at least 350,000 men after six weeks of the German offensive.

Major Caldwell also said that Col. Buckle had been in London today and had seen the march-past of the American troops at Buckingham Palace. He thought them likely-looking men, well-set-up and they went with a good swing; that the Aeroplane Week at Chelmsford, up to this afternoon, had realized £42,000; and that some of the large works (Hoffmann's, Crompton's Arc Works) had each promised £2,000 for tomorrow.

M. E. Hughes-Hughes took out 500 £1 war-bonds this week to help Chelmsford Aeroplane Week. [The final total was £86,800.]

Wednesday, 15 May. 9.40 a.m. morning's post brought a letter from my daughter [Mildred]:

10 May 1918

Wounded came in to Dundee in batches of 50 . . . One of my patients . . . comes from Taine in Rosshire. He is a dear chubby boy . . . He wears a medallion of the Virgin tied round his neck with a red, white and blue ribbon. I asked if he were a catholic but he told me he wears it in memory of a favourite officer. This officer was sent out on patrol-duty one night with a lance-corporal and five men. Before starting—I don't know for what reason—he gave each of them a similar medallion. That night he was killed by a sniper—and the same bullet wh. went through him blinded the lance-corporal in both eyes.

The irrepressible gaiety of these boys is wonderful. Each day they have a new comic song to sing while their dressings are being done and the great joke is to look while a huge probe is being thrust through a penetrating wound, remarking 'It almost looks as if I had been wounded' or 'You'd think to look at that I had been in the Army.' . . .

Thursday, 16 May. Jack Taylor, a younger son of Geo. D. Taylor, carpenter of Lyons Hall farm, went soldiering yesterday. Albert (nicknamed 'Bob') Lewin goes on Sat. C. W. Rayner's twin sons, Geo. and Fred are called up for next week—the tribunal would not listen to his appeal. He says it is impossible for him to do the work of the farm with help only of his daughter, Annie. He must sell all his stock. Ernest Wright, son of Con. Wright, is also called up next week.

Widow Jonathan Ketley had a letter this morning from her son Reggie. He is getting on splendidly. He is allowed up for a short time, but cannot sit up long because of the wound in his neck and back.

Friday, 17 May. Herbert Simons, who farms Little Leighs Hall, is now in years and enfeebled by paralytic strokes. He has a boy, —— Digby, who is very serviceable on the farm. Digby is just of military age and H. S. dare not let him go out with the cart on the road, lest he be picked up: he keeps him at work in the yards.

Monday, 20 May. 9.30 a.m. morning's post brought a letter from my daughter [Mildred]:

17 May 1918

There was such a scene in the soldiers' ward this morning. About twenty are going to a convalescent home, or to their own homes, and were in very gay spirits. A Black Watch man at one end of the ward related how on one occasion the order, according to him, was given 'The Black Watch are to stand fast. Let the Manchesters retire.' A poor Manchester man at the other end of the ward sat up in bed waving his arms and legs; having been badly gassed, he is almost voiceless, but his expression spoke volumes. 'Doctor, doctor' he gasped, 'go and tell him what I think of him.' And I went!

We are so cheered in hospital to-day; we've got a case of botulism—the first in the district . . . We were discussing it in the common-room . . . when a fourth-year medical came in. We told her what we were discussing: 'Oh' said she, 'that's the new Revolution in Russia, isn't it?'

The Sadgroves have staying with them for Whitsuntide, Mr and Mrs Grant, Londoners, elderly people, terribly nervous about air raids. They have a heavy table with mattresses on it drawn up against the empty fire-place in their dining room. When an air-raid warning is given Mrs G. creeps under to the fire-place and sits there with a tea-cosy on her head; Mr G. crouches under the table.

Friday, 24 May. John Hurrell, who works for Major Wm. Brown is expected to be called up on Tuesd. May 28th. (He got further exemption.) Geo. Ketley, High Road, works in Lyons Hall farm, was pronounced unfit by the Medical Board today. He had a kidney extirpated some years ago. Lake & Elliot, Braintree, on account of activity in munition-work have got ten of their lads exempted. One of them is 'Bub' Digby, Gubbions Green.

Saturday, 25 May. 8 p.m. Major Jas. Caldwell called: Various explanations have been given as to the delay of the expected German offensive—(a) the Germans intended making their big push on the Italian front, but, finding that the front towards the British could not be left, have had to shift their masses to it. (b) an officer said to the

Dean of Bocking that the Germans had been delayed by inability to mass their men and guns caused by our incessant harassing of their communications (roads, railways) both by our gunfire and by bombs from aircraft.

The anti-air raid arrangements on this side of London are now complete. Col. Buckle is very confident that no raider will now pass the barrage on this side London. The possibility is that, being turned back, they may get rid of their bombs by dropping them about Essex.

An officer from the front told the Dean of Bocking that a big forward movement on the Western front was impending, but would not be before the middle of June. The Yankees are moving up fast to the front.

Col. Buckle says that at the Horse Guards there is a general and strong belief that the Germans will make another great assault on our front. The puzzle is to know where it is going to be made. With all our air-scouting that has not been discovered. But active preparations are being made everywhere.[1]

Old Chas. Digby has now been told officially that his son, Ernest, is wounded and a prisoner-of-war.

Monday, 27 May. 9.10 a.m. morning's post [from Mildred Clark]:

24 May 1918

Rather bad news has come to us from Inverness this week. We have known for some time that feeling between our sailors and the U.S.A. men was very bitter. Yesterday when Miss Thistlethwaite . . . had . . . just had a letter from a sister in Inverness, saying even as she wrote a train-load of American sailors had come in yelling and vowing to murder every [British] sailor they met, and heaven knew where it would all end since there had already been a very bad fight in which at least one of our naval men had been killed . . . The Dundee bakers have been on strike this week from Monday to Thursday. They demand a weekly increase of 17s. . . . some . . . are earning over £3 a week . . .

Thursday, 30 May. At the working-party at Col. W. N. Tufnell's at 'Langleys', Great Waltham, today, it was said that, in a party of German prisoners, going from Boston to be exchanged, one man had a bag of dog-biscuits which he was taking to show in Germany as the

[1] The next German offensive would actually begin two days later, on 27 May, in the Third Battle of the Aisne. By the first week of June, German troops would be within fifty-six miles of Paris. The German plan was to score a decisive victory before American troops had reached their full strength.

food which the English give their German prisoners. He was allowed to take it.

Mrs Trow, wife of the Bursar of Felsted School, says that the farmers complain bitterly of the German prisoners who have been sent to work. The guards are no good—mostly old men, who spend almost the whole day in sleep. They think the guards ought to be English soldiers who have come back from German prisons. Mrs Trow says the flirtation of girls with the prisoners is scandalous.

Friday, 31 May. Ernest Wright, Con. Wright's boy, went off yesterday. It is not known into what battalion he will be sent.

Major Caldwell says there is great dissatisfaction in London as to the conduct of the war. It was known, before the German advance began, for two or three days, from German prisoners, just where it would take place, but our generals made no use of the information. It is also said that, at this rate, there is no reason why the war should not go on for ten years longer.

Sunday, 2 June. Major Jas. Caldwell says that last night Chelmsford was full of reports of successes in France, said to be intimated in telegrams received, e.g. (i) the Germans have been driven back on a fifteen mile front; (ii) 25,000 Germans (Crown Prince in their midst) were surrounded and most surrendered.

F. R. Lewin, says that the surgeons are still trying to save the leg of his son, Bob Lewin. They have had another operation to try to stop the bleeding.

Monday, 3 June. There was, I am told, no beer yesterday in St Anne's Castle, or Dog and Partridge, or in Fairstead (at the Square and Compasses). At the Dog and Gun, there was only a little which the retailer doled out only in half-pints, all to be consumed on the premises.

Wednesday, 5 June. 2.5 p.m. afternoon's post brought a letter from my daughter [Mildred]:

3 June 1918

They have at last, after three years, found the cause of the numerous accidents at the flying school at Montrose. Popular report has, you know, shot half the mechanics as spies. Now, however, they have come to the conclusion that the currents of air in that region are such that you can never be certain when you go up what the current will be like when you land. The school is, therefore, to be for seniors in future . . .

Thursday, 6 June. M. E. Hughes-Hughes called this evening. He said: When the local War Savings Association was first suggested to him by Canon O. W. Tancock he threw cold water on it, not believing that people in Great and Little Leighs would have any savings to invest. He has been greatly surprized by the number of members who have joined, and at the amount they have paid in. All his indoor servants, and almost all his outdoor men are regular contributors. He sits solemnly in his office every Monday morning and they bring him their books and their money.

Saturday, 8 June. Arthur Stoddart has heard from some soldier-friends that all infantry leave from France is stopped. This looks like some large move presently.

Tuesday, 11 June. Today, for their annual meeting, the Mothers' Meeting go to Pleshey, in a two-horse waggonette hired from Fred Fuller. They prefer going to Maldon, but have not done so, because of the difficulty of getting permit to go anywhere near the coast.

Sunday, 16 June. On Wedn. 12 June Reggie Ketley's sister Bessie and his niece Aggie Ketley went to Winchester to see him. He was wounded just before 5 a.m. He had just got over the trench and was stooping as he ran forward when a big shell broke over them. A fragment struck him on the back just at the bottom of the shoulder blade on the left side, passed through his body (making a big hole where it went in) and out through the hollow below the throat just above the collar-bone. The surgeons are surprised that the shock did not displace his heart. He had a very long way to go to find a dresser to bandage him up and thought, all the time, he was 'done in for'. Others who were wounded by the same shell were able to stop and run back; he had to walk slowly and erect. When he got to the dressing station he fainted right away. He lay for eight days at the clearing-station before he could be removed to the base-hospital, but received every attention all the time. The shoulder-wound is pretty well healed. The stitches are still in the wound in his neck. His hand, which was also wounded, is not yet healed.

Tuesday, 25 June. Maurice Clive Gooday, brother of Ethel M. Gooday, formerly Rectory housemaid, has been wounded in the head in France. This morning Fred Fuller had a letter written from the trenches in France. Maurice had been in the trenches for some time. He was quite well when he wrote, but most of his chums had 'gone west'.

Wednesday, 26 June. 'To swing the lead' is soldiers' slang and seems to mean 'to make a fuss'. E.g. in Dundee hospital a wounded soldier made an outcry as the surgeon was probing the wounds. 'Don't mind him, doctor,' said the soldier in the next cot, 'he's only swinging the lead.'

Sunday, 30 June. Violet Tritton says that influenza is raging in London. Of the girl-employées of a very large London firm, 2,000 were down at the same time.

Notes from Fairstead Rectory (the Revd Thomas Sadgrove): Prisoners-of-war in Germany have only acorn-coffee, a small piece of black bread and potatoes. The Sadgroves pay £4.2s.0d. a month to the Central Prisoners of War Committee which makes up six parcels a month and 26 lb. of bread or biscuit. Kenneth S. does not allow his parents to pay for this, but has made an order on the Army bankers, Cox & Co., to send them for it £5 every month. In addition the Sadgroves have six permits which allow them to send, through the post, extra parcels.

Col. Wm. Neville Tufnell, D.L., JP, Langleys, Great Waltham, was held up by a Special Constable (one of the men on his own estate) when going in his car to Church at Pleshey on Su. 23 June. He is to be summoned for breach of the Regulation which forbids use of motors for Church-going.

Friday, 5 July. 4 p.m. G. S. With called. He said that the Great and Little Leighs War Savings members had paid in £461.5s.6d. last month, but of this £387 was part of M. E. Hughes-Hughes' subscription to the Chelmsford aeroplane week. Since it started on 21 July 1917 the local association had paid in £691.5s.0d.

The village has it 'on best authority' that there will be no more air raids. 'The Kayzer says he don't want no more air raids.' 'But we are to go on bombing them just the same: they were so cruel to our women and children.'

Mrs Richard Arnold sent me this morning two halves of country cheese of her own making.

Saturday, 6 July. 4.30 p.m. Miss O'Reilly, 2, The Grove, London Road, Braintree called. A Bocking woman told Miss O'Reilly that while she was walking with her brother (who is a soldier discharged after being wounded), who was wearing his silver badge, they met some German prisoners who laughed and jeered at him. The prisoners, with their guard, were marching up Bocking street. A party of German prisoners, with their guard, met some of our wounded from Braintree VAD hospital and hissed at them.

7.30 p.m. Major Jas. Caldwell called: The Great Leighs Special Constables have still a nominal existence, but are now very few in number and do nothing. Lewis Walter Campen, the principal farmer in Little Waltham, says he pays 3s. a bag for peas picked this year. He concludes that most families which picked peas for him this year made £1 a day. An officer from France says that neither side is at all anxious to take the offensive; half of our men are out of it with the flu', and half of the Germans are out of it for the same reason.

Tuesday, 9 July. Annette Tritton has been awarded the Belgian Order of St Elizabeth for her work, some time ago, among the Belgian refugees at Earls Court. She is the more delighted, because there is a large camp of Belgian refugees at Rouen, which she often visits, and Belgians are very pleased to see anyone who wears the ribbon of that order. She is giving up her YWCA work among the WAAC [Women's Army Auxiliary Corps] at Rouen in August, being wishful to undertake work among Slav people.

Wednesday, 10 July. Mrs Louis Wright had a field-card this week from her husband. He is in hospital in France. Their son, Louis Wright, is to be before the Tribunal on M. 15 July. His employers (Lake & Elliot) are trying to get him exempted, but they have little hope of doing so.

Ernest Digby, son of old Chas. Digby, wounded and taken prisoner on 21st March, has written home. He is in a prisoners' camp at Lemberg, and is getting better.

3.30 p.m. Miss Madge Gold, acting as a nurse in Braintree VAD hospital, called. At the hospital they had a little concert last night. One of the gassed patients, Murphy by name, a splendid violinist, played his violin at it. Two large sacks of peas had been sent into the hospital in the afternoon, and, during the concert, the whole of the audience busily shelled peas.

A little while ago *Na pooh* was the great expression among the soldiers—it was *Na pooh* for everything. Recently 'swinging the lead' has taken its place, as also a 'cushy Blighty' as a popular slang-term for a slight wound.

Thursday, 11 July. The soldier patients who were sent to sleep in the Workhouse are tonight to have beds on the floor of the VAD hospital. They complained that, the last two nights, they have had no sleep, because the lunatic woman raved all night.

Saturday, 13 July. Since the war began, tramps have almost disappeared from the roads. One passed the Rectory gate at 7 a.m. looking very ill and footsore. He said he was seventy-six, and was on his way from Chelmsford to Braintree, looking for temporary employment. He was, by his voice and way of speaking, a man of some education. He preached to me most fluently on Providence and other topics. He said the latest news in Chelmsford last night was that there had been a great battle in which we had taken 30,000 prisoners and much booty. The Germans had massacred, with every circumstance of brutality, many prisoners, including interned women and children. He had heard some gentlemen discussing this, who declared that all German prisoners ought, in retaliation, to be shot. This 'glorious victory' is a good example of Chelmsford lies and the manner in which they are spread abroad.

Monday, 15 July. Much work in the district is being done by women-labourers. WAAC girls were driving heavy motor lorries about Chelmsford. Practically every baker's cart and nearly all other tradesmen's delivery vans are now driven by women.

Wednesday, 17 July. 8 p.m. vivid flash of lightning. As in Byron's line 'Streams, like the thunder-cloud against the wind' the W. thunder-clouds are now streaming eastwards.

The RGA men at Brooklands have told Dr Smallwood, that the concussions we hear about 11 p.m. are not from bomb-dropping on this coast, but in Flanders. They are also heard here distinctly between 11 a.m. and noon—the low tide before midnight and before noon rendering them very distinct.

Saturday, 20 July. Afternoon's post brought a circular as to forms of Prayer for use on the 4th August ['being the day appointed for Intercession on behalf of the Nation and Empire and our Allies in this time of War']. J. Herbert Tritton is supplying copies of the special service so I need not send my order.

Monday, 22 July. On Sat. night, the moon being full, the lunatic woman in Braintree Workhouse was again very noisy. The men from the VAD hospital who were sent there had no sleep. The men who go to the Workhouse for the night say they would rather have the noise of bomb-dropping than her outcry.

Wednesday, 24 July. 9.50 a.m. morning's post brought a charitable appeal [for the National Egg Collection for the Wounded, stating that nearly 40,000,000 eggs had been collected so far].

9.30 a.m. large brake and large waggonette, crowded with women and children drove down hill past Rectory gate. No doubt a Sunday-school Treat (from Great Leighs, from the High Road side, chapel people—farmers' wives and their friends) and going to Maldon.

Saturday, 27 July. 11.15 a.m. Mrs Harry Ward, mother of my late gardener, Charles Henry Ward, called. She had Charlie's things a week ago,—very few—his fountain-pen, his purse with three farthings in it, a ring given him by his sister's husband, and a few letters from home. This morning she had a notice that she had been granted a pension of 4s. a week. She is aged fifty-five years. Her husband is dying of an incurable internal trouble.

Tuesday, 30 July. Dr Smallwood went today before the Medical Board at Chelmsford. It was a Special Board. He was kept there an hour and a half, and was placed in Grade II.

Col. Gerald Edgar Barker is of opinion that the Germans will make a desperate attempt on London with a great fleet of 'Gothas', dropping poison gas bombs.

Friday, 2 August. On 4 Aug. at 3 p.m. there is to be a 'combined service' in Langleys Park, Great Waltham (Colonel W. N. Tufnell's) in which Church people, Nonconformists and Salvation Army are to take part.

Saturday, 3 August. In the unoccupied—'Homeleigh'—Cottage (next to Thomas Sargeant's) are a party of ten girl-guides, under a 'captain'. They are Belgians from Earls Court. They stay here till Sat. 10 Aug., when they are to be replaced by another party, also to stay for a week. There were shrieks of delight in Lyons Hall farm-yard yesterday afternoon when they were filling their mattresses with straw. The cause was the black pigs. They had never seen a black pig before. All the pigs in Belgium are white.

Sunday, 4 August. The villagers have got a singular idea of Lloyd George's much advertised and stagey pronouncement tomorrow. At 9.30 p.m. on M. 5 Aug. L.-G. is to announce the conclusion of peace, all public-houses are to be closed at 9 p.m. to prevent people getting too festive.[1]

Monday, 5 August. For the first time since he lived at Lyons Hall, J. Herbert Tritton is having no evangelistic services there on Sunday afternoons in August. This year difficulties of conveyance forbid bringing evangelists from outside and J. H. T. does not feel equal this year to taking the services himself.

Tuesday, 6 August. Violet Tritton has a friend who was nursing at Cairo. The Trittons sent lavender out to her. The British Tommies loved it beyond everything—'the scent was so homely.' She has now been transferred to a hospital at Jerusalem and the Trittons are sending lavender to her there.

Thursday, 8 August. In Braintree yesterday (market-day) there was no beer to be had; no port-wine; and very little whiskey.

I had today from Mrs Ellen Monk, coal-merchant, Little Waltham, a ton of kitchen coal ('cobbles'). The price is now £2.10s. a ton. Mrs Monk also sent me a copy of the Fuel Regulations which I preserve. [This limited the amount of coal one could buy according to the number of rooms in one's house.]

The ordinary weekly wage of farm-labourers is now 30s. When I came to Great Leighs it was 12s. and it was thought a great thing when

[1] The fifth of August was Bank Holiday Monday. The Prime Minister's 'Message to the British Empire' was an attempt to revive flagging spirits. The message was read out in cinemas, theatres and public places. It urged people to 'Hold Fast! because our prospects of victory have never been so bright as they are to-day . . .'

it was advanced to 14s. 'Harvest' used to be £5 and then advanced to £7 and £8. This year J. H. Tritton and other farmers are paying £15 as harvest-money. Given a dry harvest, this represents £3.15s. a week.

Saturday, 10 August. 9.30 a.m. morning's post brought a Tea Registration notice from our tea-merchants [asking the Rector to send his new Ration Book to them as his normal supplier].

Sunday, 11 August.

SUMMARY OF OFFICIAL WAR NEWS

Press Bureau   11.0 p.m.   10th Aug. '18

British Attack launched yesterday by the right of the French first Army South of Montdidier was developed by our allies this morning with complete success. Montdidier fell to the French before midday together with many prisoners and quantity of material . . . South of Lihons British Troops have overcome Enemy's resistance and made substantial progress . . . Number of prisoners increasing. No further news to hand.[1]

Monday, 12 August. I am told the 'Combined Service' at Little Waltham was a failure. It was decided that the Rectory lawn was too wet to hold it there, and it was removed to the Congregational chapel. Many of the people, including the officers of the Cadets camp, would not go there. The Congregational minister (the Revd John Neville) who conducted the service had nothing to say except 'This is a terrible war, my brethren. This is a terrible war—a terrible war.'

Thursday, 15 August. J. Herbert Tritton was in Town today. He found people very pleased with the war news. He was told that the Duke of Connaught had said that if people only knew the whole truth they would be still better pleased.

Saturday, 17 August. Notes from my younger daughter: On Su. 11 Aug. Mildred saw a great crowd collected round a temporary war-shrine in Hyde Park near the Marble Arch, but was unable to get near it. It seemed to be a white pillar, draped with red, white and blue at the base. Lying at the foot of it were a great many flowers, probably

---

[1] On 8 August the German army had suffered its 'black day' when discipline broke for the first time. On 14 August the Kaiser and his generals agreed to look for a favourable opportunity to seek an end to the war. The tide had definitely turned against them.

wreaths.[1] All the big motor lorries and all the officers' cars in London are now driven by women.

Widow Hales has been officially informed that her son, Wm. Hy. Hales, Essex Regiment, is counted 'killed'. She had not heard from him since 28th March. He was baptized at Great Leighs 30 Nov. 1884.

Sunday, 18 August. Lizzie Oddey went for the drive in the brake [belonging to Fred Fuller]. She found people in Chelmsford in a state of great agitation, talking about a murder by a German prisoner-of-war at the end of last week. Eight prisoners were at work, cutting the border of a field so that the reaping machine might get to work. The farm-foreman in charge had occasion to reprimand one of them. The German seized his bill-hook and 'slashed off the foreman's head'. The soldier on guard fired his rifle—a party came up and marched the eight Germans off. ('Jimmy' Hurrell—works at Bishop's Hall—told Miss Stokes about it today.)

Monday, 19 August. I preserve an obituary notice [*Essex Weekly News*, 16 August 1918] of Sir Richard Pennyfeather. He was mentioned in these notes in connection with the swearing-in of the first Great Leighs Special Constables. [He died on 14 August, aged seventy-four.]

Friday, 23 August. Notes as to Brooklands, Broomfield: Quite recently one of the WAAC drivers was driving Col. Cuthbert Buckle at a furious pace and ran the car into a ditch. The Col. had to get out and go for men to haul the car out. The WAAC's apology for the accident consisted in saying 'What a silly place to put a ditch!'

Saturday, 24 August. 4.30 p.m. Ethel M. Gooday called. She said: The German prisoners-of-war who are working at Rayne are a very civil lot. They raise their hat to you if they meet you walking in the lanes. Her brother, Jack Gooday, was home recently for a fortnight's leave. He came home quite unexpectedly in the middle of the night, and had to stand in the street calling for some time before he could make them hear. He says he prefers France to Bocking any day—Bocking is too

---

[1] The 'floral shrine' had been dedicated by the Bishop of London on 4 August, which was called 'Remembrance Day.' One bunch of flowers was from Queen Alexandra with a card reading 'In grateful memory to our brave and splendid soldiers who gave their lives for King and Country. God bless them all. Alexandra.'

slow. He has, E. M. G. says, no fear and has no idea of danger of any sort.

Sunday, 25 August. Harvest got on splendidly last week. Most farmers have their wheat thatched 'close up' (i.e. the stacks thatched as soon as they are finished). Oats are not being thatched yet, for fear of their heating.

Tuesday, 27 August. 9.30 a.m. Sounds of distant guns. Many aeroplanes, all going S. this morning—whether to France, or not, I do not know. There has been a group of four, and another of three; the rest were single. Two German prisoners are working on the farm just below this house. I saw them with the harvest waggon last night.

Bulletin put up in Post Office: Su. 25 Aug. 1918: 'Despite considerable hostile reinforcements we have progressed on the whole front. Numbers of prisoners and quantities of material have been captured . . .'

Wednesday, 28 August. 9.50 a.m. this morning's post brought a letter [from Miss Gladys Cruickshank to Mildred Clark]:

26 August 1918

This week I have twice visited a prisoner—a Manchester man—just returned from Germany. He had been there since 1914. After 2 years had to have his leg off. When one sees the way German prisoners are treated over here, it makes one sick. He had a sense of humour that was quite extraordinary. I think it is to a lively sense of humour that many of our prisoners keep going. When the British Tommy possesses it he is quite irrepressible. And how the Hun hates it—it's quite beyond his ken . . .

Thursday, 29 August. A girl was driving a baker's van in a lane at Leaden Roding. She was stopped by a group of German prisoners, who demanded bread, and threatened her if she refused to give it. They took six loaves, but paid for them. She was summoned before the magistrate at Dunmow, for supplying bread to German prisoners. The magistrate dismissed the case, adding that it is a pity that prisoners are allowed on Essex lanes without a guard.

Mrs Matthew, (Chignall?) has four German prisoners doing work on her farm. They are brought in a lorry at 8 a.m. These prisoners have a meal at Chelmsford Workhouse before they start in the morning, and bring another meal with them. She does not think that this is enough, because they work till 7 or 8 p.m. She is annoyed because the authorities forbid her giving them more food, but quietly ignores the prohibition. These men are excellent workers.

Saturday, 31 August. 7.40 p.m. Major Caldwell called: The Germans are supposed to be building a new type of aircraft to raid London, capable of flying at a height of 20,000 feet. Col. Cuthbert Buckle is very worried about what may come of this. One might as well use pop-guns against them at that height. Very great developments are likely soon on the Flanders front. We are accumulating great forces there which have not yet been put in movement. There are also battalions which have been brought from Palestine.

Thursday, 5 September. Percy Holt, Essex Yeomanry, mentioned some long time ago as wounded in the face and disfigured, is going to Wandsworth General Hospital for an operation on his nose.

Saturday, 7 September. 7.25 p.m. Major Caldwell said: The general opinion is that, when our advance has been carried to a pre-determined point, our troops will be concentrated northwards, so that the American army-corps can come into line S. of them. But nobody knows what the plans really are. 250,000 American troops arrived last month.

Wednesday, 11 September. Chelmsford notes today: At Early Bunn's (late Bush) shop, a toothbrush which used to be 4d. is now 10½d., and one which used to be 10½d. is now 2s. Freeman Hardy & Willis's boot shop have got only a quarter of their usual supply. Many of these shoes are 'war-time' and not the old leather sort.

Sidney Willis, wounded in the leg and discharged a long time ago, is back to work for Mrs Jennings, at her coal and carrier's business. It seems as though he would never recover the full use of his leg; he is still very uncertain on his feet, and often falls. The nerve has probably been injured.

Thursday, 12 September. A munition-girl came into Aldiss' shop, the draper's, Braintree, to buy a hat. She was shown one at 12s.11d. That, she said, was not nearly good enough for her. Aldiss said he had no better but could trim up one for her. She said she would call in and see it in the evening. He took the flower out; put another flower in; and priced it at 18s.11d. She was entirely pleased with it.

A nephew of Miss Truelove (Mrs Tritton's maid) spent last night at Lyons Hall. He is twenty-one years old. Before the war he was a clerk in an accountant's office. He enlisted at the age of eighteen. This spring he was offered a commission and was sent for training to Pembroke College, Cambridge. There he has had the time of his life. Apart from their military duties, the cadets had been privileged to attend lectures given by some of the best Cambridge professors on subjects of general interest. They have also had real sports, such as town-bred lads like himself had never before enjoyed. He feels that, after the war, he ought to be able to get a much better post than he previously had, because he is now better educated and is more 'widely informed' than he was three years ago.

Monday, 16 September. Mrs Jennings who supplies a good many of the villagers with coal, says that the coal forms are no end of worry. The villagers have made a horrid mess of the forms. They did not fill in the number of the rooms, or filled them in wrong, putting 10 for 2 or 3. Her man (Sidney Willis) says he didn't know there were so many palaces in Great Leighs.

The card [of a rag and bone man] was left here on Sat. forenoon, 14 Sept. by W. Jones, who said he would call back for it, but as he stole apples on his way out, he did not come back.

Wednesday, 18 September. My daughters, Mary Alice and Mildred, went today to London for the day. There were not many soldiers about the streets in London but a great number of officers. Also a considerable number of American sailors. They are almost invariably chewing something—gum or what?

Thursday, 19 September. In Braintree today I noticed this war-placard outside F. A. Dancer's, fruiterer's: 'National Salvage Council: We are asked to collect fruit-stones and hard shells urgently needed in the manufacture of anti-gas masks. Save them and bring them here, however few. You may save a soldier's life.'

Friday, 20 September. The request for 'largesse' by the harvesters has begun. A man from Chadwick's farm came at 5.30 p.m. asking for it. He said they had had a 'pretty middling' harvest, by which he meant (I suppose) 'rather good'.

Sunday, 22 September. W. H. Dee was for a week's visit to his wife's sister's at Billingborough, Lincolnshire. In the train with him to Dunmow was a young soldier just back from the front. He said the weather in France has been very rough and had greatly hampered our advance. It had rained day and night. Germans were surrendering in hundreds—as fast as they could. The troops out there thought, that if things go on as they are now going, the war will be over by Christmas. The Americans had been wonderful in the way they had been making railways. W. H. Dee's half-brother, Reggie Ketley, had his finger off a fortnight ago.

Today was Harvest Festival—good congregations, but almost entirely of women—collection for Chelmsford Hospital—morning £1.19s.4½d.; evening, £1.11s.6d. Major Jas. Caldwell says that there is a feeling that 'there is another big move on' in France, because 'they are sending out men wholesale.'

Monday, 23 September. 10.25 a.m. a small motor-plough came uphill past the Rectory. It was driven by a woman in trousers, wearing a small close-fitting cap. It stuck at the end of the Terling road, again at the entrance into Weir pasture, and again, for a long time, at Mrs Stoke's cottage. Old Mrs Stokes came out and asked 'Is that a man or a woman?' Being told it was a woman, she commented 'It isn't decent to come out dressed like that. One never knows what women will do nowadays. I'm sorry I came out and saw her.'

Wednesday, 25 September. Yesterday evening Col. Buckle was escorting Edith Caldwell and Mildred Clark from Broomfield toward Little Waltham, and was bicycling rather to the right so as to give them room to keep well away from the ditch. A soldier came bicycling from behind, escorting the girl who lives with Tina Rust. The man shouted ''Ere! 'Ow much of the road do you want?' After he passed, Col. Buckle said 'That was Mills, my servant. I shall tell him in the morning that his Colonel wants a good deal of the road when he is bicycling after dinner.' Mills is a man who thinks much of himself and will not enjoy a joke at his expense.

Thursday, 26 September. I have been lifting my late potatoes, and find a great many bored by grub. Henry Wells says that the same has happened to his crop and that other people in the parish are making the same complaint.

Sunday, 29 September. Col. Buckle says that he and his officers paid, on principle, the [£10] fine for the WAAC who was convicted of careless driving. She was a Miss Gordon-Bennett, and could probably have bought up every one of the officers; but with that he did not concern himself.

Thursday, 3 October. News was received this morning that 'Ernie' Wright has been killed. He leaves six quite young children, and a wife who is not always quite in her right mind.

Mrs Louis Wright, High Road, has not heard from France from her husband for a long time. She supposes that, being in the cavalry, he is moved about fast from place to place. Their son, Louis Wright, has been in hospital with severe bronchitis but is now better and expects to be home soon on draft-leave. His mother can't think what good a lad with so weak a chest will be in France in the winter.

Friday, 4 October. 1.20 p.m. afternoon's post brought me a note from the Subrector of Lincoln College: 'My dear Clark, Can you come and preach the Latin Sermon on Jan. 19, 1919? It falls to me to nominate the preacher in consequence of the vacancy in the Rectorship. Do come, if possible. Yours sincerely, E. C. Marchant.'

Notes from Lyons Hall: A letter was received from Major Claude Tritton, ASC from Dieppe this morning. When he wrote they had just had official notice of the surrender of Bulgaria and everyone out there thought it too good news to be true.[1]

I learnt this forenoon how easy it is for a child to be badly burnt. I was lifting potatoes. A sudden, violent gust of wind blew part of my burning cigarette-end on to my cotton neckerchief and set it on fire. I had to act quick in saving my neck and burnt my wrist in doing so.

Saturday, 5 October. 7.30 p.m. Major Jas. Caldwell called: The average life of an airman who goes to France is reckoned to be fourteen days. Some are killed the first day they are up; others may escape for four or five months. These last get quite nerve-shaken, and are brought home to posts as instructors. When they have been home for some time they go out again.

My daughter, Mildred, started yesterday morning to go back to her

---

[1] On this day Germany and Austria–Hungary asked President Wilson for an armistice on the basis of his 'fourteen points'. On 5 October, British troops broke through the Hindenburg Line.

medical studies at Dundee. My elder daughter, Mary Alice, spent the day with her in London.

Sunday, 6 October. News came today that Chas. Digby, junr. had been killed; was married; has three quite little children; worked for Herbert Simons, of Little Leighs Hall. He had been a soldier and had served his time before the war. His younger brother, Ernest Digby, was wounded and is a prisoner-of-war.

Wednesday, 9 October. Mrs Cruickshank [daughter of the Chelmsford restaurant keeper, J. Hicks] says that at Salonika the men have to do their own washing and darning. Her husband blesses his mother that she taught him darning. One day when he was sitting by the roadside darning, an old tramp-woman, with a sack she had probably stolen from somewhere, came up; spread it out, pointed to a hole in it, and motioned that she wanted to darn it. On his lending her a darning needle from his haversack she sat down beside him and darned her sack.

Thursday, 10 October. Fred Mansfield (several times mentioned in these volumes) was killed on 29 Sept. When he was dying on the battlefield, he took out his pocket-book and asked his mate to send it to his twin-sister, Tessie Mansfield, now of Little Leighs. He was unmarried.

9.30 a.m. morning's post brought a letter from my younger daughter:

9 October 1918

. . . The Americans at Strathpeffer now find that only three houses are open to them. The inhabitants wanted to give a big fete to welcome them, but when they approached the commanding officer they were told that the Unit had come over to work, not for amusement, so after that snub they have wisely left them to work.

The Countess of Cromartie has not been very judicious in her entertainments. She invited a few doctors and some orderlies—who are medical students—to dinner, received them all together in the drawing-room and thereafter sent the orderlies down to dinner in the servants-hall. On another occasion, when she met two of the 'boys' in the grounds she offered to show them over the castle. On their round of inspection they met the housekeeper to whom the countess said something and the boys didn't hear what. 'Won't you stay and have some tea with me?' she asked. They accepted, she rang a bell, a servant came and the two medical students found themselves having tea in the kitchen . . .

Unfortunately most of the unit, both men and women, have taken to drinking heavily. The chef is reported to be rarely sober. It is such a tragedy . . .

Friday, 11 October. Louis Wright, son of Louis Wright, High Road, Great Leighs, is at home on final leave.

Saturday, 12 October. 7.30 p.m. Major Jas. Caldwell called. He said our losses in killed and wounded, in the recent fighting, are said to have been tremendous. They are sending very young, untrained soldiers at once into the fighting line—the need for men being so great. Dr Smallwood said that three-quarters of the boarders at Chelmsford Grammar School, and half the day boys, have gone down with influenza. The attack in nearly all instances, came quite suddenly.

Tuesday, 15 October. 4 p.m. there was brought to me a begging note from the person often known as 'that woman at the Castle' because living in a cottage next the public-house of that name. I preserve it as a characteristic Essex note and a testimony (among many) of the badness of war-time foot-wear: 'Please sir will you [be] so kind as to give me a trifle as to get my little girl a pair of boots as I brought (bought) them all soom (some) about 2 month ago and are all gone to pice (pieces) . . .'[1]

Wednesday, 16 October. Reggie Ward, son of Harry Ward, Lyons Hall chauffeur, has died of influenza and pneumonia, at Salonika.

Friday, 18 October. Today I finished picking my apples. Of the large older trees only one had a crop. They are very sweet, good-sized apples. The wasps have shown their appreciation by eating a big hole in the riper side of many of the largest and best of them.

On 29th. Sept., George Rayner was one of a party of lads who were taken out by an officer. They made prisoners of three Germans, and Geo. R. and a lad named Twinn were told off to take these prisoners to the base, while the officer and the others went on. It was a very foggy day. The two lads lost their way; found themselves in the German lines and were at once made prisoners. Two hours afterwards, they were set

---

[1] The Rector's policy when asked for a 'trifle' was to send 2s. Such requests came from 'that woman' about every three to four months.

free by our tanks coming along and taking the German post (sixty prisoners). The first person Geo. Rayner met, after his release, was his twin-brother Fred. Later in the day our men had to fall back, and, during the retreat, the lad, Twinn, was killed by Geo. Rayner's side.

Saturday, 19 October. Crittall's Manufacturing Company, Braintree paid off forty of their girls, having no more work for them. The girls were told that, if they could get good places, they should at once take them. The war will soon be over now, and, what employment the Coy. could give would, of course, go to the men-workers, formerly in the Coy's. service, who had gone on military service. The girls were advised to take great care of their money. Hard times were coming, even harder than at present, and people would no longer be getting high wages.

Notes from the Revd Thomas Sadgrove, Fairstead Rectory: Kenneth S., eldest son, is prisoner-of-war in Germany. He was at first at Rastatt camp (in Baden). That is a 'sorting-camp'. There he, like other officers, had to do his own washing. Then he was moved to a camp for officer-prisoners at Pforzheim (in Baden), where he is still. Mrs Sadgrove doesn't know whether at Pforzheim he has to do his own share of the cooking. In his last letter he said he was in sad disgrace because one morning he had burnt the porridge which was for breakfast. Formerly they had only the back-yard for exercise, but lately things have much improved and a football-ground has been added; a temporary chapel, with an altar fitted up, (a beautiful little thing). They have lately had a piano and a gramophone. Kenneth Sadgrove will be twenty-six on 28 Nov. 1918. He began by reading up for his degree, but has given that up.

Audrey Sadgrove, the youngest daughter, is in the War Office, at a salary of £150, which in Febr. 1919 is to be raised to £170. She is promised the OBE then, but the talk is that the order will be done away with because it has been given so indiscriminately. At present she has had a break-down and had to go away.

Tuesday, 22 October. 9.45 a.m. morning's post brought a letter from my younger daughter:

18 October 1918

We are in for another influenza epidemic here. Cases have come pouring into the Out-Patient department to-day . . . We had great excitement the other day—3,500 Yorkshire men stayed in the town all night awaiting transports to take them to Russia ... The men said they were going to the port of Archangel ... The Americans have a curious habit of eating jam with everything—meat, puddings and cheese—a dish is put in front of each guest to help him or herself. They usually prefer to drink tea or coffee, and to have cigarettes *before* the pudding. They are slow, untidy eaters because it is almost a universal custom to cut up all the meat first of all, then laying aside the knife, to start to eat ...

Annette Tritton is going back to the Belgian refugee settlement at Earls Court which accommodates 2,000. She was there when it was a clearing-station. She would like to be there when it is the clearing-station for them on their way back to Belgium.

Harold Weller, RFA, was in Lyons Hall Camp in 1916. He became engaged to Dorothy Hammond, daughter of the Mistress of Great Leighs Church School. H. W. told the Hammonds that when British soldiers enter a French village they are often told 'we would rather the Germans were here than you.' The German big guns are much better than any guns of ours. The German soldiers, in all military movements, are far better than our men.

Friday, 25 October. Mr Thos. Wells is today hanging curtains in Church to darken the windows as required by the police.

Mrs Mann, the baker, said this afternoon that yesterday, both in Lake & Elliot's and in Crittalls works, Braintree, the girls were dropping down, one after another, with influenza. They could be laughing and talking one minute, and the very next collapse.

Influenza is quite an epidemic this week in Great and Little Leighs.

Saturday, 26 October. A notice is put up in Great Leighs Post Office, forbidding the sending of Christmas puddings to men at the front by parcel-post. It says that arrangements have been made for supplying Christmas puddings to the troops. Louis Wright is still home on leave. In his khaki he looks very diminutive.

Tuesday, 29 October. J. Herbert Tritton has working for him on Lyons Hall farm a man named Wilkins, now in a Labour battalion, formerly in the Coldstream Guards. He was with J. H. T.'s son, Capt. Alan Tritton, in the South African campaign. He was also in the Mons campaign. He says that there is a strong feeling in the army against

King George, solely because of his German ancestry. The soldiers cannot forget that.

Friday, 1 November. I preserve a clipping from yesterday's *Daily Telegraph* as to a new verse to *God Save the King*. It is natural, in view of the great part they have taken in the war, that the Britains across the seas should seek for fuller recognition. But, if this is the best of the efforts to express it, what like must the worse effusions have been?

[The competition for an 'Empire Verse' was sponsored by the Royal Colonial Institute. Some 400 competitors sent in verses. The judges chose the following:

> Wide o'er the linking seas,
> Polar and tropic breeze
>   Our song shall bring.
> Brothers of each domain,
> Bound but by Freedom's chain,
> Shout as your sires, again—
>   'God Save the King!']

Sunday, 3 November. Reggie Ketley came home yesterday evening. He looks very well. He will not go out to France again, but is reserved for home defence. He says that a tremendous lot of our casualties are due to our own shells falling short. This was what happened to himself.

Tuesday, 5 November. 8.15 p.m. Miss Eliza Vaughan called: They are all getting very tired of the hospital, and sincerely wish that the war may be over and the hospital closed before Xmas. Crittalls have told their work people that when the war ends, it will end suddenly, and the firm will not know what to do. There will be no work for the people, but Crittalls, when they send them away, will give each a fortnight's wages.

—— Clark had been out for seventeen months. When he was here just now he had a fortnight's leave. He says that the talk among our soldiers is 'After having seen what the Germans have done, we will not, if we have our own way, take prisoners. We will tuck all the Germans cosily up with a shovel.'

Mrs Richardson lives in Fortune Watts cottage in Council School lane. Her husband is a prisoner-of-war. He will be glad to get home, since he has no boots and his clothes are in rags. He is working on a farm where the people are extremely kind to him, but they cannot help him, being just as badly off themselves as he is.

Wednesday, 6 November. 10.30 a.m. for a wonder, a man is doing something to the road between Bishop's Hall and Rectory gate—but only to the extent of raking dirt from the side-channels into the deep ruts in the middle of the road. He seems a half-witted fellow, and relieves his job by laying down his rake and holding a chat with every passer-by who will stop and converse with him.

Friday, 8 November. Braintree was agitated yesterday by a rumour that the war was over. Fresh cases of influenza still occur. Though some attacks have been severe, there has been no death in this parish from it, directly or indirectly. Chelmsford today (market-day) was full of rumour that Germany had laid down arms.

Saturday, 9 November. 7.30 p.m. Major Jas. Caldwell called. For the Memorial Service here tomorrow evening he hopes to have the bugler of the Chelmsford Cadets to sound 'The Last Post'. At the Board of Inland Waters Navigation Major Caldwell this week met Col. (Capt.?) Ince, a most capable officer. Ince told him that the newspaper reports were giving a very false impression as to the opposition our troops were overcoming. Far from surrendering readily, the Germans were fighting desperately. Their machine-gunners fought as long as a man of them was left.

Sunday, 10 November. A short bulletin was shown at Great Leighs Post Office today:

SUMMARY OF SATURDAY'S OFFICIAL WAR NEWS

Press Bureau.   November 9th 1918.   10.30 P M

British. On our right, Fourth and Third Armies are advancing along Sambre towards Belgian frontier meeting with little organised resistance. In centre First Army progressed rapidly astride Mons-Conde Canal . . .

The German Chancellor announces that 'the KAISER and his SON decided to renounce the THRONE'

No other news of importance to hand.

Ernest Digby, wounded, prisoner-of-war in Germany, died there in May. His father (old Charles Digby) did not receive notice of his death till yesterday.

6.30 p.m. Memorial Service for Great Leighs men who have died in the war. Full choir. Good congregation. Service lasted exactly one hour. Collection for St Dunstan's blinded soldiers, 15s.1½d.

Monday, 11 November. 3.30 a.m.: dark morning. Sky all clouded over. White fog. No rain as yet. 9 a.m: Sky gloomy with cloud-drift S.W. to N.E. F. Fuller, Cole farm, has offered Mrs Arnold 7½d. for every egg she can let him have. I do not know at what figure he re-sells them, but he has to drive them into Braintree or Chelmsford and make his profit.

News of the signing of the armistice by Germany (at 5 a.m. this morning: hostilities to cease at 11 a.m.) reached Chelmsford soon after 11 a.m. The works there immediately went on holiday. 'Jim' Carpenter, who works at Crompton's Arc Works, Chelmsford, when he came back said that the workers were so excited that it would have been no use carrying on. The news reached Braintree about same time. The High School (Upper forms only at school: lower forms discontinued till Wednesday, 13 Nov. [because of the influenza epidemic]) was given a holiday. Leonard Port, when he came back from School, said that Braintree was wild with excitement. The news was passed on to Great Leighs Post Office from Chelmsford; spread rapidly and the cottagers were very excited. Major Wm. Brown gave his men a holiday. Mrs E. A. Hammond sent across from the Church School to ask a half-holiday. The school flag was hoisted. (The Council School is closed because of influenza.)

Mr Sam. Woodirvin, Great Waltham, who was at Great Leighs PO said he might now hope to have back undamaged his son who had been at the front in France for four years. J. L. Palmer, Wakerings, sent one of his men ('Alix' Alefounder, one of the ringers) to W. H. Dee, Church clerk, to ask if the Church bells might be rung. The five ringers arranged to ring for half an hour at 5 p.m. When W. H. Dee came to the Rectory for the belfry key at 4.30 p.m. he said that the hooters had begun at Braintree and all about a little after 11 a.m. and went on for about an hour.

At Felsted the School was given a half-holiday today and is to have one tomorrow. The schoolboys paraded the village with their band and a very large flag, cheering. In Felsted village, by 1 p.m., nearly every house had hung out a flag. Little Waltham was gay with flags. Dr R. P. Smallwood had three or four flags (apparently those of the allies) set up in a 'stack' in his front garden. Fred Skinner, (next door to the Bell inn: formerly cellarer to King Edward VII), had a very large flag draped down the front of his house; a smaller flag on each side of it; and a string of small flags hung across the road to one of the shops opposite. Several cottages had hung out the Royal Standard.

2 p.m. Very dreary afternoon: Whole sky is gloomy with unbroken sodden cloud pall. Wet fog two fields off and quite thick in distance. Air bitingly raw. Everything sopping wet.

Ernest Wright expects to be sent to Malta. The prevalent idea among the people is that younger soldiers will be sent to our garrisons abroad, to allow of the discharge of the older men.

Young Louis Wright, aet. 19, died in hospital at Sheerness today of double-pneumonia. His mother was told yesterday that on Sat. at 9 p.m. he was dangerously ill. Being herself ill and her daughter ill, with influenza, she was unable to go. His uncle, Ernest Wilsher Wright went (at 10.30 a.m.) this morning, but arrived at Sheerness only at 4 p.m., too late. Louis was the only son. They are bringing the body home for burial.

There was a considerable display of flags along the Great Road today. Jesse S. Wright had an enormous Union Jack at his gate, near Deers Bridge. Mrs Jennings, at 'the Victoria' (coffee-house), Mr A. G. Port, shopkeeper; Mrs Humpfreys, bicycle shop; Mrs H. Hicks, Supply Stores—all had flags out. St Anne's (public house) contented itself with a written notice in one of its windows 'Armistice signed. Hostilities cease today.'

9 p.m. Clouded sky. Subdued moonlight. Air damp.

Tuesday, 12 November. 10.30 a.m. bright day: Sky bright with only a few white, scattered, cloud-fleeces sailing very slowly N.W. to S.E. Petrol-vans and furniture-removal vans passing along Great Road today have flags on them. The villagers have it that, when peace is declared, all public-houses are to be closed for a fortnight to keep rejoicings within limits.

6 p.m: Chelmsford Cathedral bells ringing and heard here. I am told that they rung all day yesterday, but I did not notice them here.

Chelmsford people had not resumed work today. The streets were so crowded that people could hardly move along them. A gun taken at Cambrai was being placed in front of the Shire Hall, for 'Feed the Guns' week. This evening Chelmsford Station was all lighted up as before the war. Chelmsford sends up a searchlight every night. Last night it made a special effort and sent up an enormous one.

Wednesday, 13 November. 10.45 a.m. low rumble of cannon-firing in S. or S.E. distance. It went on for some time after 11 a.m. There was some again at 2 p.m. and for a little afterwards. 2.15 p.m. some little rifle-shooting at Boreham butts. Because of the armistice, Braintree town-band was parading the streets this afternoon (market-day). Braintree had flags hung from side to side of the street in Bank Street and High Street.

Louis Wright's body was expected at Chelmsford today. It was to be brought from the station to Great Leighs by a gun-carriage from the camp at Great Baddow. (Word came to Great Leighs this afternoon that it would not be brought to Great Leighs till 8.30 a.m. tomorrow.)

G. S. With says that on Monday evening, 11 Nov. the German prisoners-of-war, who are at work in Hyde Wood, on their way back through Great Leighs to Braintree Station were singing 'It's a long, long way to Tipperary' in very good English, and obviously in very good spirits.

Some of the girls at Hoffmann's works, Chelmsford, were told on Tuesd. 12 Nov. that their wages would be reduced from £2.5s. a week to 25s. a week.

Thursday, 14 November. 9.40 a.m. morning's post brought a letter from my younger daughter:

11 November 1918

Dear Father,
The first intimation we had here of the signing came from the boats in the river. At 9.30 every one let off sirens and hooters . . . A band of the Royal Scots Guards stationed here has been going about the town nearly all morning followed by a large crowd of mill-girls and school-children. As often as not the band is playing the 'Cambells are coming' while the crowd sings 'Tipperary' or 'A Broken Doll' or both.

The crowd in the streets is tremendous—(at midday) people are wandering aimlessly in groups, many wearing flags or patriotic ribbons—groups of boys with accordians and tin-whistles are making a noise—sailors are going down the street arm-in-arm in long rows. Flags are flying from the public-buildings, the shops and most of the windows—the church bells are ringing.

The effect on the patients was most amusing. Dr Mackie Whyte is medical officer at the docks so all the influenza and pneumonia sailors are sent up to us. This morning they were sitting up in bed singing, chaffing the doctors, and even out of their beds dancing on the floor. One who is frightfully ill is so disappointed that we won't let him out to-night because he had always promised himself to get drunk—gloriously drunk—the day war ended.

In the women's wards there's only one remark: 'Ma man will be home soon noo.'

Thistley [Miss Thistlethwaite] has learnt from some street-urchins part of a new and original song apparently about the Kaiser:

> '. . . his heavenly crown
> But the Lord said "No
> You go down below"
> So he's all dressed up and no-where to go.'

She saw a very fat and cheerful old woman standing at the street-corner waving a minute Union Jack. Said the old lady 'This seems to be my duty to-day. I allus does my duty.' . . .

Midnight. The bells have been ringing at intervals all day. At 6.15 p.m. the ships again let off their syrens and also rockets.

At 9 o'clock most of the students arrayed in gowns or fancy dress assembled at the College and proceeded to march with torches through the town singing 'Varsity songs. We then went to Airlie Place, which is the Harley Street of Dundee, and serenaded Prof. McEwan (who came out and told us that this was the proudest day of his life), Prof. Kynock, Dr Mackie Whyte and Mr Price. Then we went to the college garden, hanged an effigy of the Kaiser and set fire to it. Finally we went to the Union and danced for about two hours. It was a great night . . .

H. Gordon M. Vickers [of Waltham House, Great Waltham] was killed on the morning of the last day's (?31 Oct.) fighting in Mesopotamia.

Friday, 15 November. 9.50 a.m. morning's post brought a letter from my younger daughter:

13 November 1918

What a ticket I looked on Monday night. I had on a woolly, over which were two jerseys, over which was my kimono over which was a skirt. I blackened my face, and put on a red and yellow bandana to say nothing of beads and a nose-ring: one gaiter and one green stocking. Oh but it was great fun!

There was such a pretty sight here yesterday at two o'clock. It was a bright, frosty afternoon and a large air-ship—the C8—flew round and round over the town at such a low altitude that one could see the men leaning over the cradle—or whatever you call it—waving a flag . . .

Morning's post brought also a form of Thanksgiving for the Armistice [to be used on 17 November, 'Being the Sunday after the cessation of hostilities between the Allied Powers and the German Empire']. In my own opinion it would have been more reverent to have waited till the conclusion of peace.

The loss of the *Audacious* was noted in this Diary at the time [2 November 1914]. The newspapers were not allowed to mention it till yesterday.

On Wedn. 13 Nov. the Braintree Town band went through all the works there—Courtaulds, Crittalls, Lake & Elliot's. The managers tried to keep them out.

The authorities are giving young Louis Wright a military funeral—gun-car and firing-party from Baddow. Louis Wright, his father, got back to Great Leighs this evening. (This was a false report.)

7.30 p.m. Major Jas. Blyth Caldwell called: Major Caldwell thinks the Appeal which Germany is making to the Allies, to supply it with food is 'all bunkum'. Germany, certainly, has not nearly used up its harvest yet. The military authorities are not at all confident of the situation. On Mon. (11 Nov.) afternoon Col. Buckle at Brooklands had a notice that he might now 'ease off' his war time routine. On Tuesd. (12 Nov.) morning he had fresh orders, to carry on everything as if the war were still in progress.

Major Caldwell does not think that peace will be concluded before Aug. 1919. He knows of two officers, in different brigades, who asked their brigadier-general when they might hope to be released from military service, because they were anxious to resume their civilian employment. In each case the general said 'Don't begin to think of that. It will be months yet before you are free.'

Saturday, 16 November. When meat was so scarce in Chelmsford in the spring, Fred Jas. Underwood, butcher, sent a leg of mutton across the street to Dr Newton's, Fairfield House. The boy was mobbed on his way across the street; people whipped out knives and cut slices for themselves off the joint.

Sunday, 17 November. Louis Wright, the father, did not arrive last night. He has not been heard from for about three weeks. Mrs Louis Wright is very anxious about him. The rumour in this district is that there were heavy casualties (yet unpublished) in the last days of the fighting, and, in particular, that the Dragoons in which he is now serving (but he is in the 9th Lancers) have been 'badly cut up'. Telegrams to him about his son's funeral have brought no answer.

Louis Wright was a short lad, but his coffin was 6 ft. 2 in. Geo. Taylor, the undertaker in Great Leighs (who had charge of the funeral) says that at hospitals and other places where there have been many deaths they do not measure for coffins. They stock the coffins in two sizes—one size for men, one for women and fill up any vacant space with cotton wool.

The party of soldiers was half-an-hour late at the Wrights' house. The military party seemed to be 'RF' (Royal Fusiliers), and consisted of six bearers; a firing party of fourteen; a bugler; and the sergeant in charge. The firing party stood in two ranks. They fired three volleys in the air. I had never seen a firing-party before, and did not think it at all a solemn proceeding. There was too much hoarse shouting of orders by the sergeant. Just as the firing-party moved off, the bearers stepped forward and picked up the spent cartridges, before falling into the line of march. I thought this very undignified, but Major Caldwell says it is always done—the spent cartridges being taken back to be re-filled.

After the volleys had been fired, the bugler, who stood beside the sergeant just behind the firing-party, sounded 'the last post'. Order was then given to fix bayonets; shoulder rifles; to march off two-abreast. The bearers (who carried no rifles) fell in behind the others.

The funeral was to have been at 3 p.m. but the cortege did not reach the Church-gate till 3.45 p.m. There was a very large crowd of young people waiting all the time at the gate. It was a very dull, cloudy afternoon, with a very cold N.E. wind.

Major James Caldwell came to the Rectory between the funeral and evening service. He said: On his way from Chelmsford to Broomfield [on 11 November] he met the brake which was driving back to their quarters the German prisoners-of-war who are working for Jas. Nichs. Christy. The men looked very dejected. The boy who was driving was 'very cocky' and was whistling the *Marseillaise*.

Albert Green, engaged to Lizzie Oddey, Rectory cook, was one of the firing-party at Prince Henry of Battenberg's burial. L. O. expresses it 'My Albert fired the Last Post over Prince Henry of Battenberg's grave.'

Today's post brought circulars as to the approaching Election of Members of Parliament. Politicians are greatly exercised as to the unknown issues of 'the leap in the dark' taken by the enlarged franchise.[1]

Tuesday, 19 November. Louis Wright has not been heard from, or of. The Revd Jas. Bowen, rector of Little Leighs, has written to his Colonel to enquire.

Theophilus Fuller (aet. 77), Gubbions Green, has died after a very short illness. Great Leighs villagers have a strong belief that attention from a robin is a sign of death. They are now saying that, before T. F. took ill, a robin followed him about in his garden for two days. A robin also came in at the window where his daughter, Rosanna, aet. 40, was lying ill with pleurisy. She died this forenoon. A robin, hopping about near a villager, is more feared than ever.

Saturday, 23 November. 10 a.m. Funeral of Thos. Henry Searles, aet. 5, near Moulsham Hall. For the first time in my experience not one relative came. The father and step-mother are both ill with influenza. The only persons present were the undertaker (Geo. Taylor) and his assistant (R. F. Hammond) and the Church Clerk (W. H. Dee).

Monday, 25 November. Louis Wright's delay to get home was due to the telegram taking three days to reach him. When he got it his regiment was just entering Brussels. He started at once. He had a German bayonet, which he had carried about for some weeks to bring home as a souvenir to his son, Louis. When he heard of his son's death, he threw the bayonet away, as he did not wish anyone else to have it.

[Letter from the Rector to Falconer Madan.]*

25 November 1918

I was very pleased to have your letter.

There are several volumes of the 1917 Diary and several of the 1918 Diary. I have not counted how many—on my cupboard shelves, waiting to be sent. Every now and again I reproach myself for not having packed them up and sent them off. But it is so easy to excuse myself. The work of the garden and the grounds has kept me busy all year . . . In addition the Coal Controller has assigned me a coal allowance insufficient even to keep the kitchen fire going.

[1] The 1918 Representation of the People Act altered the electoral system in several ways: all men over the age of twenty-one could now vote; men serving in HM Forces could now vote; all women over the age of thirty who were also occupiers (or whose husbands were) could vote; all voting was to occur on the same day; all constituencies were made more or less uniform, with, normally, only one MP; women were now able to sit in the Commons.

So to have a fire at all, I have to spend some hours before daylight and some after nightfall sawing wood by candlelight in the wood house . . .

I have been for me very well, on the whole, for some time back. I seem to have got over my complicated ailments, and to be very sound again, though weary for a change and for some chance of reading or writing.

This parish is absolutely empty of young men. Farmers who vowed they never would have women land-workers have been compelled to employ them. They do not think much of their work, but they cannot get on without it . . .

Not many of the lads who went out from this district are left to come back. The Flanders campaign was very deadly this year to our lads, and Palestine and Salonika have also taken victims on the field or in hospital.

I have kept up my Diary steadily, but been able to complete nothing else . . .

Thursday, 28 November. I see that there is to be a woman candidate [for the Combined Scottish Universities' constituency]. I shall vote for her, whoever she is and whatever her political party. I think the women-graduates of St Andrews University ought to have their representation.[1]

Friday, 29 November. Joseph Rogers, mentioned formerly in these notes as a prisoner-of-war in Germany got home on M. or Tu. this week. George Wiseman (mentioned before in these notes) came to Clara Ward's at 7.30 p.m. this evening. Widow Hales has heard that her son, William, prisoner-of-war, has arrived in France and is there in hospital. Mrs Wm. Suckling is without news of her son, Ernest, prisoner-of-war since Mons.

Sunday, 1 December. It is said that the troops in Mesopotamia are to be sent to restore order in the S. of Russia [and] that as soon as our prisoners-of-war came to Chelmsford they came to blows with the German prisoners there. Their experience of prison-life has exasperated our men at what they consider the pampering of German prisoners here.

6.30 p.m. very dark evening. Fog quite thick. Notwithstanding the darkness and the terrible mud there were eighteen people in church, and a fair choir in the gallery.

[1] The Rector had two votes: one as a resident of Great Leighs and one as a University graduate. This second vote could either be used towards the two MPs for Oxford or for the three MPs for the Combined Scottish Universities. Andrew Clark chose to use it toward the three Scottish MPs.

Wednesday, 4 December. On Monday evening, 2 Dec., Major Wm. Brown, Sergeant of the Special Constables, called them to a meeting and dismissed them for the time being.

Friday, 6 December. The workers at Hoffmann's are said to be all going to vote for the 'labour' candidate.

7.30 p.m. Major Jas. Caldwell called: Cubitt's works in London have been employing a great many women in the making of gas-masks. As these are no longer needed, this work has come to an end, and the women have been paid off. This week Major Caldwell saw a procession of about 1,000 of them, with a big flag, and singing, marching to Downing Street, to interview the Prime Minister and demand continuance of employment and high wages. The women who have been discharged from various Government offices are receiving temporarily weekly pay. A friend this week saw a crowd of them outside a pay-office, waiting for their pay. They were very showily dressed (fur coats; jewellery), and looked for all the world like flash barmaids.

Sunday, 8 December. Barometer 6.30 a.m.: $29.5\frac{2}{5}$, nice morning. Major Jas. Caldwell says that there is great uneasiness among the German prisoners here at the prospect of being soon sent back to Germany. They do not want to go. They want to stay in this country.

Tuesday, 10 December. Harry J. Brown, Lizzie Oddey's nephew, writes that they were just going into action when the order came to cease firing. They could not believe it. Now, with the silence following on the ceasing of cannon-firing and bursting shells, they hardly know where they are. Harry A. Brewer, cottage, near St Anne's Castle, has been constantly in action ever since he went out, but never told his wife until after the armistice.

Thursday, 12 December. 11.15 a.m. morning's post—delayed I suppose by distributing election cards—brought a letter from my daughter [Mildred]:

8 December 1918

I have found out the whole of the rhyme about the Kaiser:

> When the war is ended, the Kaiser said
> I want to go to Heaven with a crown upon my head.
> But the Lord said 'No, you go down below.'
> And he's all dressed up and nowhere to go.

J. W. Hayes, Superintendent of the YMCA, Chelmsford, said today: A soldier who has just come back from Russia says that country is in a dreadful state. He asked a woman to do some washing for him, offering her two (? shillings) but she refused to do it for the money, but she cheerfully did it for two spoonfuls of sugar. He also asked a man to go an errand for him, offering him one (? shilling)—the man refused, but did it for a packet of Woodbines.

Robert Jiggins, grandson of old Wm. Jiggins, was here on leave having been wounded in the leg. He did not go back when his leave was up. A party came on M. 10 Dec. and took him away.

Friday, 13 December. 10.15 a.m. morning's post brought a slip intimating discontinuance of rationing for tea.

I got today two war-posters, long stuck up at Great Leighs Post Office. There was a third poster, which had the word 'damn' on it. This was torn down and carried off, presumably by someone who objected to the swear-word, and wanted to put it out of the sight of passing schoolchildren.

Saturday, 14 December. F. Fuller had a letter from his son, recently. When he wrote he was at Valenciennes, but expected soon to go into billets at Mons. He is very anxious to get back into his employment in London. His firm has been paying part of his wages all the time he has been on service and he thinks they have a strong claim for his discharge. He has been suffering from boils.

[Today was polling day for the General Election at the Council School, from 8 a.m. to 8 p.m.]

Sunday, 15 December. W. H. Dee says that when he was in Chelmsford yesterday afternoon there were no posters about, and practically no signs of an election. When he voted at Great Leighs, later in the afternoon, Mrs Geo. Witney was the only voter at the polling-place. Later (he was told) i.e. between 6 p.m. and 7 p.m., polling was brisker and the door of the Council School had to be closed, and voters taken in in batches.

G. S. With, Council Schoolmaster, who acted as Returning Officer here, says he thinks about 7/12ths of the voters in Great and Little Leighs polled.[1]

---

[1] Election results would be delayed until after Christmas because of the time required to count ballot papers from men in the armed forces.

Mrs Suckling has not yet heard anything from, or about, her son, Ernest.

Monday, 16 December. 1 p.m. Miss Eliza Vaughan called. There are twenty-six cases in Braintree VAD hospital and the hospital is being pressed to take more. The cases are now sickness, not wounds. The VAD staff is anxious for the hospital to be closed, so that they can go back to their ordinary duties.

Tuesday, 17 December. In Braintree this forenoon many soldiers were sauntering about the streets—of all corps—Royal Flying Corps, RFA, RE, Buffs, etc.—also one naval man—No doubt men on Christmas leave. In the shops in Braintree were hand bills to the effect that Jan. 12–19, 1919, would be 'Gratitude Week' there—i.e. collecting for King George's fund for disabled soldiers and sailors.

J. H. Tritton had recently working on one of his farms a soldier who was in the Coldstreams and with Capt. Alan George Tritton. This soldier has now got his discharge, and is to be permanently at work on Lyons Hall farm. One of J. H. T.'s Daisley's Lane cottages is being fitted up for him and his family.

Wednesday, 18 December. 10 a.m. morning's post brought a letter from Miss Eliza Gillies [in Inverness-shire] as to J. Stephens, AB:

16 December 1918

My dear Miss [Mary] Clark,

how so nice and kind of you to rite to me asking so kindly about dear Johnie and all of us . . . about my dear Johnie he came back from france the second time he is in England Back thank God he is in Hospital since nearly two months he got the flue so badly and had the Plursey the second time in his right side he had his share of this horrid war I am very glad it is over now . . . I hope that I will heare from you soon dear Miss Clark any word about getting married at all such a nice looking Lady like you I hope you will not be like me an old maid but the first love will never be new again My Brothers are sending their best love to you none of them got married yet their was a lot of the young Boys from this Country was killed in this war Poor Chaps . . . I wish that you would send me your Phot. I would be very Pleased to have it. I must come to a Close . . .

11 a.m. Mrs Selina Cloughton called to have her pension-paper signed (in respect of her son Charlie Cloughton, mentioned in these notes as killed). She said 'They ain't done mangling yet on Lord

Rayleigh's farms (Fairstead and Terling)—So many of the men have had influenza; and the horses have been bad.' Mangling = mangilding = lifting the mangolds and putting them in clamps.

12 noon Eliz. L. M. Tritton called: (i) her brother, Claude Tritton, Major, ASC was decorated (OBE) yesterday. He goes back to France, to Dieppe, tomorrow. (ii) As regards the widow and children of Ernest Wright, Daisley's Lane: her father and brother (Major H. Leslie M. Tritton) are paying what is needed over the allowance as a child of a deceased soldier to bring up the eldest girl, Beatrice, at Halstead Industrial School. The Trittons are sending the eldest boy, Ronald, to a training-school from which he will pass to the *Arethusa* training-ship. Mrs Wright and the four younger children are going to Higham Green just outside Bury St Edmunds in a cottage next to Mrs W's father and mother. The cottages and the estate there belong to Major Robin Barclay, secretary of the YMCA, a great friend of Major H. L. M. Tritton.

Thursday, 19 December. Major Jas. Caldwell says that women who have been engaged in fuse-work in munition works, are now as good as skilled workmen, and will go on being employed on such jobs as bending brass for chandeliers, twisting wire for electric lamps, and the like. There will be no work for the unskilled.

Saturday, 21 December. 7.45 p.m. Major Jas. Caldwell called: He said he met Arthur Suckling, organist of Broomfield, who is now home. He was looking very well. The 'Volunteer' system is a complete wreck. Most of the men in it joined to escape being called up. Now that men are not needed for the army they want to break off 'Volunteer' service altogether. The authorities have called in their rifles and other equipment, leaving their uniforms only. Thousands of troops are being sent every week to the Murman coast.

Sunday, 22 December. Reggie Ketley came home on Wedn. 18 Dec., having at last got his discharge. Edward Bearman ('Teddie') and Cyril Sargeant (RAF) were in Church—home on Christmas leave. I have been told that soldiers took no interest in the election, and tore up their voting papers right and left.

Tuesday, 24 December. The Lloyd George party is using every effort to get men in the Army and Navy to record their votes. I preserve, in this connection, two advertisements.

9 p.m. a party of Carol singers came to this house for 'St Dunstans'.

Wednesday, 25 December. 9 a.m. a right 'seasonable' winter's day. River full and water frostily clear. Hard road quite a treat to walk on. Mr C. W. Rayner had a letter yesterday from France from his twin-sons, Fred and George. Both are well: sorry not to be home for Christmas: had had their parcels: the mince-pies were good: they had never realised how good their mother's mince-pies are.

Monday, 30 December. Harry Ward, father of Charlie Ward (often mentioned in these notes) died at 2 a.m. this morning, after a long and painful illness. Mrs Hurrell had a wire from France yesterday that her son, Harry Hurrell, was very ill there.

I depart from my practice of excluding, as far as possible, newspaper clippings from this Diary, unless they bear directly on matters or persons mentioned in it, to insert a number of clippings from today's *Daily Telegraph* as to the results of the General Election. These are a natural appendix to this War-Diary, since the question present to the mind of voters was which party could be trusted not to cave in to Germany in determining the conditions of peace. Voters were determined to have nothing to do with those members of the late Parliament who favoured Germany. Incidentally also the possibility of women MPs and the boasting of the Labour Party as to what it would do if it secured the large number of members it hoped for, occur in these clippings. They need no further comment, explaining themselves.[1]

---

[1] The election results for the 706 MPs in the House of Commons were: Coalition Unionists, 333; Coalition Liberals, 135; Independent Unionists, 51; Independent Liberals, 28; Sinn Fein, 72; Labour, 62; Irish Nationalists, 8; others, 17.

1919

Wednesday, 1 January. Peace not having been signed yet, I shall go on noting, in Diary form, what few things I now hear concerning the war as it affects Great Leighs or immediate neighbourhood.

Thursday, 2 January. 10 a.m. morning's post brought a letter to my daughter, Mary Alice, from Laure Beckers, daughter of a doctor in Antwerp, dated 19th December 1918: 'We breathe again now, delivered from those horrible brutes of Germans. They were beasts, you know, and deserve their crushing down.'

Capt. Kenneth Sadgrove is home from his prison in Germany.

Braintree VAD hospital is soon to be closed. The patients are being discharged, on convalescence. The military hospitals are, now, able to take in all the cases that come to them.

Saturday, 4 January. 7.30 p.m. Major Jas. Caldwell called: Major C. thinks there will be no rapid progress with demobilisation. The authorities are weeding out the inefficient as fast as they can and sending them away. But efficient men will be kept under arms, until there is better prospect of the ferment in Europe settling down.

Sunday, 5 January. Lucy Jane, wife of J. Herbert Tritton, died at 4 Lowndes Sq., SW1, yesterday, aet. 68—blocked vein in the brain.

Monday, 6 January. 4.45 p.m. F. Mann, baker, Little Leighs, called. He brought a letter from 'Jimmy' his man—James Herbert Lewin, asking me to write a letter to the CO commanding his battalion, appealing for his discharge. He would come under the provisions of 'contract' (for renewed employment) with his pre-war employer.

Wednesday, 8 January. Mrs Suckling, High Road, has not yet heard from her son, Ernest, and has asked me to write to the War Office to make enquiries. The last she heard from him was a postcard dated 24/8/1918.

12 noon: funeral of Mrs Tritton. The Revd Reginald Fawkes, brother-in-law, officiated. The Revd George Twentyman, a friend of the Bishop's Domestic Chaplain (Edwd. Geo. Augustus Gardener, who is ill) came to represent the Bishop of Chelmsford and read the lesson. Mrs Montgomery Boyle, Mrs Tritton's sister, played the organ.

Friday, 10 January. 10.40 a.m. morning's post brought an interesting letter forwarded to me by my younger daughter from Mademoiselle Goueffon:

20 December, 1918

My dear Miss Mildred,

Excuse me to have been so long in answering your last letter but we have been so busy with the influenza epidemic than I could do nothing except preparations for my father; this epidemic was terrible especially in Tours and Lyon, terrible also for our poor soldiers; I know by 'Papers' that England did much suffer of it . . .

In September I was called in a French hospital near home for three young English soldiers . . . sent in a French hospital without knowing a word of French, I was very pleased to be useful to them, happily all three were saved and went back England after a month . . .

You gave me interesting information about English life during the war; In France women were also employed in factories; for the cars, but for the land we employed prisoners and convalescents; now everyone has to retake his place, unhappily there is much change everywhere soldiers killed, refugees with no more home..........but all these sufferings have been so useful than we must not cry; Germany has been defeated!..........We shall never forget that England helped us for this great work and suffered side by side with France during these four years! . . .

Saturday, 11 January. Mrs Suckling had a letter today from her son, Ernest. He is in Holland, and is waiting for a boat to bring him across.

The hounds met this forenoon at St Anne's Castle. They went to Lynderswood and to Chopping's Wood, and are said to have had a very fine day.

7.30 p.m. Major Jas. Caldwell called: He said the rush of young officers to get their discharge is fast ebbing.—It was largely due to the belief that good posts would be open immediately after the armistice and would go to the first comers. But there are no such posts. London merchants will not venture on business until it is clear what this new Government is going to do.

Monday, 13 January. 12 noon—thick, wet, dripping fog. It has never lifted all day. Morning's post did not arrive till 12.30 p.m. [Letter from Mildred Clark.]

9 January 1919

Miss Thistlethwaite came back from Strathpeffer yesterday with quite a lot of stories: An officer in the Air Force told Miss Thistlethwaite that . . . during the British Retreat he saw one very amusing scene. A few British Tommies were standing in a group watching an aeroplane descend. It proved to be an enemy one; the pilot of which, jumping out, levelled his pistol at the group of *sweinhund* British. Nobody in the group turned a hair but just as the man was preparing to fire, an empty bully-beef tin hit him full in the face and knocked him backwards! The Tommies with a laugh turned on their heels without bothering to make him prisoner.

The Australian Staff is . . . quite the best owing to the fact that if anything displeases the men, they raid the head-quarters and throw boots and furniture at the Staff and go away back to their billets again . . .

The Australians were not very friendly towards the Portuguese who were in the village in neighbouring billets. On one occasion they procured some empty Mill's bombs—rushed into all the *estaminets* in the village where the Portuguese were drinking and amusing themselves, placed a bomb in the centre of the room and rushed out again locking the *estaminet* door. The subsequent noise was deplorable; the Portuguese rushed round the rooms, shrieking and even attacking one another with knives until they discovered that the bombs would never explode.

Shortly after this appeared General Birdwood's famous order that it had come to his ears that the Australian Expeditionary Force was accustomed to speaking of the Portuguese troops as 'those damned Dagos'; in future they will be known as 'our gallant allies.' 'By Order'![1]

Reggie George Ketley called this afternoon to have his pension-paper attested. He has been offered, through the Labour Exchange, a job in Chelmsford, but doesn't think he can cycle backward and forward. The wound in his neck and chest has left a shortness of breath.

Tuesday, 14 January. Ernest Suckling is home today—said to be a mere skeleton.

Wednesday, 15 January. Ernest Suckling came home between 11 and

[1] The Australians perhaps had heard that in April, 1918, during the Battle of Lys, a Portuguese division collapsed in the face of the German advance and left a hole in the Allied front.

12 on Sunday night. His father does not believe he is so ill as he gives out and is inclined to scoff at him for saying that he has, in his opinion, less than two years to live and for making so much of his leanness.

Friday, 17 January. From Mrs F. Mann, wife of the baker, Little Leighs: Her husband has seen Ernest Suckling. He is in a terribly nervous state, and cannot realise that he is free. He is on the jump the whole time, constantly looking round expecting people behind him. He never received one of his parcels, but was made to write cards saying 'thank you' for them. Amongst the things he had to eat were frogs and young clover. On Xmas day their dinner was Swede-turnips and black bread, and that they thought a tremendous treat. When they were called in the morning, the guard brought round dogs; and if the men did not get up at once, these dogs were set on them. The first thing taken from them when they were taken prisoners was their jack-knives. On one occasion he saw German soldiers pinning our wounded to the ground with their knives and gouging out their eyes. At last a German officer came along and said there had been enough of that cruelty. They wore awful old clothes. He was very surprized, when he came to England, to find German prisoners smoking. Our men would have been shot if they did so.

Saturday, 18 January. 8.15 a.m. left Great Leighs Rectory [for Oxford to give the Latin Sermon on the following day].

Sunday, 19 January. 7 p.m. dined in Jesus College. At 11.30 a.m. today Dr Heinrich Krebs, Librarian of the Taylor Institute, called on me. He has been resident in England for fifty years, but was not naturalised. Now he is ordered to return to Germany before 31 March. I very cheerfully added my name to a memorial asking exemption from the Repatriation orders for him.[1]

Tuesday, 21 January. Harry J. Brown has got his discharge. The Rayner twins (Fred and Geo.) have had 'all their papers passed', and hope very soon to come back to their work on their father's farm.

Mr F. Fuller's son is home on leave. He was latterly in a largish town near Mons. He has seen many horrid sights. Once he saw two

---

[1] The repatriation order was rescinded. Ironically, Dr Krebs retired in 1920 and appears to have returned to Germany, where he died in the same year. The Taylorian Institute is a University centre for the study of modern languages.

ammunition waggons coming along, each pulled by six horses. A German shell burst on them, and there was nothing left, but mangled fragments of officers, men, and horses. He thinks this sort of thing accounts for many of those reported 'missing' and untraced.

Saturday, 25 January. Notes from Mrs Sadgrove, Fairstead Rectory: Kenneth Sadgrove went into action on 21 March 1918; and, in the late afternoon of 22 March was slightly wounded and taken prisoner. The Germans marched them three days and three nights, without giving them any food, except that at one place they gave them soup made of Swede turnips, but they were then so ill with fasting so long that the soup made every one of them sick. At one town they came to, there was a water-fountain. The guard, knowing that they were parched with thirst, said they might fall out and drink. They surrounded the fountain, but, before they could drink, other guards drove them off and allowed none of them to drink. At one town through which they were passing some French girls came with bread and 'smokes' for the prisoners. The guard tried to drive them off, but the girls just jeered at them and gave the prisoners what they had brought. While on this march, K. S. fell asleep while marching, and stumbled; and he was then beaten on the head with a lamp.

Rastatt was the first camp they were taken to. Here K. S. had his slight wound dressed for the first time. At Rastatt K. S. was taken before a general, who seemed a decent sort, and clicked his heels together when he acknowledged K. S.'s salute. K. S. asked this general where he was to be sent to, and the general said 'Oh, you will see beautiful places. You will go down our beautiful Rhine. You will probably go to Cologne. You will have a fine time of it.' But, during his interview, the German soldier who was standing behind K. S. stole part of the contents of a small pack which K. S. had on his back; amongst other things, his razor and his soap. For three weeks K. S. had no soap, and had to grow a beard.

At Rastatt the prisoners-of-war were kept in cages, British in one cage, Russians in another, Portuguese in another. At Rastatt plague broke out among the Russians, but it did not spread to the other cages, as they feared it would. Before the food-parcels began to arrive, the majority of the men could not walk across the room without fainting. Many died at Rastatt. One Scots officer who was at Rastatt was a big burly fellow of over fourteen stone, but in about six weeks he went down to eleven stone, when he went to Pforzheim with Kenneth Sadgrove. At Pforzheim, when this officer began to get his parcels, he at once 'began to fill up again: you could see him visibly growing.' These parcels were sent out through the Prisoners-of-War association. Among other things, they contained flour, lard, dripping, butter, dates. Before the parcels arrived, the officers were so hungry that they marked where the potato-peelings were thrown to feed the animals and used to slip out at dusk, bring the peelings in, boil them, and eat them.

At Pforzheim the place in which the officers was imprisoned was a Board School. In each room there was a kind of ventilator, attached to which were listening wires so that the guard on duty could hear what the prisoners were saying, and if they were discussing any plans of escape. At Pforzheim were 300 officers. The only furniture was hard wooden chairs (or benches), plank-beds, and two blankets. If an officer wished a deck-chair, or other 'luxury', he was allowed to buy it, but was charged an extortionate price. At Pforzheim Kenneth Sadgrove was in a room with twelve others. He had, once in six days, to cook.

There was an Irishman among the officers, and the only things he could, or would, cook, when his turn came, were stew and boiled rice. From the Germans they bought tinned fish which had gone bad (the tins were all rusty inside)—this they cooked and ate. When K. S. came home he suffered terribly from boils, caused by the bad food, and especially the tinned meat. At Pforzheim once in three days, long rolls of bread were given to the prisoners, but, when it had been cut into the portions for each prisoner, each portion was no bigger than the roll you get for lunch at a London restaurant. This portion had to last three days.

The Irishman mentioned above was a firm believer in 'the little folks', (i.e. the fairies). He used to save most carefully the crumbs of his precious bread, and put them out, at nightfall, for 'the little folks'. When the crumbs had gone in the morning, he was satisfied that the little folks had had them. When the armistice came, he declared that the little folks had done them the service of bringing it about.

Three of the officers died at Pforzheim. At Pforzheim the prisoners had a football ground, and asphalt courts where they played tennis. The imprisoned officers had a journal printed for them in the town, to which they themselves contributed the articles. They called it 'Our Outlook'. One number only appeared.

The little children at Pforzheim were starved. The officers used to adopt one each and give them biscuits, etc., out of their parcels. Kenneth Sadgrove had, for his share of this charity, a boy of six who used to come to him every morning. The night before they left, they had this boy to dinner. He ate, and ate, and ate, till they thought he would be ill. When he went away they stuffed his pockets with biscuits that they would be leaving. He was wearing paper trousers and the pockets burst; so he had to shuffle off holding in the contents of his burst pockets. A crowd of children was waiting in the street to rob him. K. S. had to walk home with him, to see him safely at his mother's.

When the armistice was declared the people of Pforzheim came in front of the prison-quarters and shouted 'come out'. After the armistice, there was a good deal of rioting in Pforzheim. The Irishman mentioned above did not think they managed it well: 'In Ireland they would have had banners and a band.'

Tuesday, 28 January. What used to be Taylor's Restaurant and Confectioner's shop, The Square, Braintree, is now the Labour Unemployment Bureau. As the villagers express it—'those people (= ex-munition-workers) who get 25s. a week for doing nothing, go there for it.'

Wednesday, 29 January. Ernest Suckling told Mrs H. J. Hicks that, although he would not like to be again in Germany as a prisoner, he would very much like to be back there with his regiment. They are offering a bonus to induce men to join up for four years, and he thinks he will do so. He would not care to be about Great Leighs again. Mrs Hicks says it is all nonsense about Ernest Suckling's being so very ill.

Thursday, 30 January. 4.30 p.m. Kenneth Sadgrove called: When rum was served out in the trenches, an officer stood with a dixey and a large spoon. The men passed him in a single file, and as each man passed he had a spoonful of rum put into his mouth. One man objected to using the same spoon as the others, and brought his own—it was an enormously big one.

Latterly at Pforzheim, the officer-prisoners were not allowed to speak to each other before 10 a.m. This was because they had had violent altercations between each other.

Sunday, 2 February. Major Jas. Caldwell told me today: On Friday 31 Jan. there was a mutiny of RAF and ASC men at Fulham. The mutineers were very insolent, and very defiant even after a strong force of marines had arrived there. But when the marines were ordered to load up their rifles and their machine-guns, the mutineers 'skedad-dled'. The ASC men are, in many cases, bad lots. They were largely recruited from men who could do some clerical work, but were out of jobs because they had, for some grave fault or other, been sacked by their employers. The trouble with the RAF is that it has no officers of experience and authority. The whole force, officers and men, is a new, 'scratch' lot.

One day last week he was at Woolwich arsenal; came out at No. 4 gate, and came along the street towards the main entrance. He saw on the street a well-dressed Jew carrying (as he thought) a hand-bag. When the men began to come out of the Arsenal, the Jew put what he was carrying on the ground. It proved to be a small, portable platform, on which he stood, and preached sedition to the men who gathered round him. He told them he would go on from where he had left off the day before, and then explained how far they might go in defying authority.

Tuesday, 4 February. Ernest Suckling has had a fight, in Braintree, with a German prisoner-of-war and got the best of it.

'Dot' (= Harry) Hull, Great Road, home on leave, goes into Braintree or Chelmsford almost every day; gets drunk on each occasion; and has to be led home by his girl, who 'jaws' him all the way.

Thursday, 6 February. Mrs E. A. Hammond says her daughter Dorothy's fiancé, Harold Weller, is with the RFA in Belgium. His last letter said that there had been an émeute there over the demobilisation. Several NCO's had in consequence been reduced to the ranks and one had been sentenced to six months' imprisonment. He said he did not venture to say more about it—because of the censor.

Monday, 10 February. 11 a.m. Annie Rayner, daughter of C. W. Rayner, called with a request that I should write to the CO of his sons' battalion, asking for the release, to come back to the work of his farms of his twin-sons. They are both anxious not to go to the Rhine, but to be released to begin again their work on the farms.

4.15 p.m. Dr R. P. Smallwood called. He said Braintree VAD hospital was closed on Fr. 9 Febr., the last patients leaving that day.

Wednesday, 12 February. From Mrs Lister, on a visit at Waltham House. A friend of hers, a flying man, was seen to fall with his machine within the enemy lines. Two or three days later an enemy aeroplane flew over our lines, and dropped a paper, saying that he had been killed. There were several other occasions in which notice of a death was given in the same way.

Sunday, 16 February. As regards the Rayner twins, Mr C. W. Rayner, their father, had a letter this morning from Fred. Mr Rayner does not know where Fred is now. George Rayner walked in at Lowleys yesterday afternoon, quite unexpected. He is looking extremely well, and has filled up to a big fellow since he was called up. He was in Church this morning in civilian dress, having got his discharge. The reason why he was not demobilised earlier was that the duty of putting the names down for demobilisation was left to an old corporal. This corporal had a spite at Fred Rayner who had been promoted sergeant over his head, and he put out his spite on George Rayner. When George Rayner found this out, he had a row with the corporal. As a result George's name was in three days put down because the corporal knew that if the matter were brought to headquarters there would be trouble. George Rayner brought with him a German sword, an ash tray made out of a German dixey, a silver German watch, two tins of bully beef, about thirty sticks of chocolate, and two French paper-knives.

Wednesday, 19 February. The army refuses to 'demobilise' Geo. Wiseman ('Wibey' = mentioned in earlier volumes). He himself is sick of it, and his former employers, the Prudential Insurance Company, have written asking for his return. But his captain says he is his chief clerk, and cannot be spared. He has three lads to train as telephonists but they know that inefficiency is the way out of the army and pretend that they cannot learn. They make as though they did not know how to turn the handle yet.

Mrs F. Mann, Little Leighs, finished up her rounds with the baker's cart this week. 'Jimmy' Lewin resumes his old job next week.

Tuesday, 25 February. As regards the sons of G. F. Bawden, Cole Hill (new) Cottages: Clifford Bawden the youngest son, was kept at Dover for four years. His colonel put him up and up as a warrant-officer, and would not let him apply for a commission, because he knew he would lose him. He was told to report for the Western front. After being told this, he was sent to the Tower, where he was told that he was to go on a secret mission with some other warrant-officers, men, and officers. Where their destination was to be, they were not to know till they had embarked. When they were on board, they were informed that they were going to the Kola peninsula (opposite Archangel). Clifford Bawden says that it is dark three parts of the day, but they are very busy. But his letters are so severely censored that he is not allowed to say anything about his work.

Saturday, 1 March. Harry Hurrell and Charlie Thorogood have both 'signed on' again. They have both got three months' leave, that being one of the bribes to induce young men to remain in the army.

The Belgian refugees (the Doehaerdt family), who have been at Great Waltham, go back to Belgium on Monday 17 March. M. Emile Doehaerdt, the father, who has gone to see their house in Brussels, writes that there is not a window left in it. He says nothing about the furniture, or the other goods, so they are in hopes that these are intact.

Thursday, 6 March. Dorothy Hammond's fiancé (Harold Waller) cannot get his discharge although his only duties now are connected with waiting at the officers' mess. The colonel is still so incensed at the 'mutiny' about demobilisation (see entry for 6 February) that he absolutely refuses to consider any application for discharge.

Saturday, 8 March. Albert Smith, son of Robert Smith, Goodman's Lane, has re-joined the army. Jack Taylor, son of Geo. D. Taylor, carpenter, has also rejoined. Charlie Collins is already grumbling at the dulness of farm-work. He says 'it is like being taken from among a thousand men and put into a coal-hole'.

Sunday, 9 March. I have been greatly annoyed for several weeks by inroads of a score or so of pigs of Major Wm. Brown which he suffered to wander about. They have torn up the Rectory paddock and the Rectory orchard in a shameful way. Richard Arnold, Fulbourne's and Glebe farms, says that when he had Goodman's farm, and Wm. Brown had the next farm to him (the Hole farm), he suffered much from the trespass of W. B.'s beasts. He once told W. B. that 'he had not a straight bone in his body.' This seems to be an Essex expression implying dishonest conduct.

Saturday, 15 March. —— Hawkins, the Coldstreamer who has been working on Lyons Hall farm, goes up to London today to take part in the march through London of the Guards. His wife refuses to come so he is leaving Great Leighs. Lyons Hall is now well supplied with farm-hands, so many of the young men who had been called up having come back.

Friday, 21 March. A new sign-post has been put up at the end of Fuller Street. The former one had the 'hands' torn off it by reveller-soldiers returning at night from Braintree to Terling Camp.

4.15 p.m. Dr R. P. Smallwood called. He said the Doehaerdt family go back to Belgium on 1 Apr.

Saturday, 22 March. F. R. Lewin says that, after her husband had not been heard of for three years, the War Office told a woman in one of the Rodings [villages near Great Leighs] that he was 'missing: presumed killed'. She married again. The first husband has recently turned up. He had been put to work down a mine, and was not allowed to send out any message, and received none. He was often starved. He became so weak that he could not stand. Then he was put into hospital. Essex villagers are now conjecturing that some British 'missing' are still prisoners in German mines.

Tuesday, 25 March. Mr and Mrs George Wright, cottage behind Malting's, are still in hope that their son Herbert ('Hubby') Wright, 'missing' since the 'charge' of the Essex Yeomanry and never heard of, may yet turn up as a returned prisoner.

Saturday, 5 April. My daughter, Mary Alice, this afternoon met her aunt (May, widow of Thos. Arnold Paterson, Liverpool) at Chelmsford. She was on her way to London. Her daughter, Dorice Paterson has been mentioned as at the British Legation at Copenhagen. Dorice Paterson is now at the Peace Conference at Paris as a short-hand typist. The Hotel Majestique has been taken over for their accommodation. They have chaperons. Unless a girl is over twenty-five she is not allowed to go out with a man at all. If any girl is out after

10 p.m. she has to give an account of why, and where she has been. When Disraeli went to a peace conference at the Hague, a grant of £25 was made, to each member of his staff, to obtain uniform. Ever since, that has been made a precedent. When Dorice P. went to the Peace Conference she had her grant of £25 for dress. She went to Paris on Mond. 24 March.

All prisoners-of-war, except those who were in the very south of Germany, pass through Denmark on their way to England. When it was known that these prisoners were to pass through, a Danish committee was formed and the Danes were able to send gifts for the men. The gifts so flowed in that the Red Cross premises where Mrs P. was working would not contain them. When the prisoners got to Copenhagen, they were treated right royally by the Danes, especially the British Tommies. When any kilties came, they could not move along the street for people hanging on to them. A kilted officer was sent from England to help in the repatriation work. He went one day into a tobacconist's shop, and so great was the crowd that had followed his petticoat that he could not get out of the shop.

Many of the men had no desire to be repatriated. Several of them took off their uniform and settled down in Denmark. Out of one camp thirteen men sent to ask that they might not be repatriated. Even from Germany there have been demands from men that they should not be repatriated. 60,000 Frenchmen have asked that they may not be repatriated. The French officials are in great dismay at this, because they have published bitter reports as to the ill-treatment of their men, and they do not know how to tell the public.

Mrs P. thinks there may be a good many British prisoners still detained at work in German mines.

Sunday, 13 April. Reggie Ketley has begun to work again on Moulsham Hall farm. But he is not yet able to work regularly, still suffering very much from the effects of being gassed.

Sunday, 27 April. 4.50 p.m. a man with discharged soldier's papers, giving the name of Pte. Francis Harrington Halstead, came begging. He said he used to come round here with the threshing machine; had been four and a half years at the front; and hoped tomorrow to get a job at Courtauld's factory. I thought him a fraud and a rogue, but a very fair-spoken one.

Monday, 28 April. Rapid thawing. Roads inches deep in slush. Branches of trees down everywhere. Telegraph and telephone wires mostly down. Big oak down in Fuller Street, lying across the road. 'Oh to be in England now that April's here'—Robert Browning wrote in Italy.

Wednesday, 30 April. 10 a.m. morning's post brought a letter from my daughter [Mildred]:

28 April 1919

The sergeant-major at the Stannergate aerodrome was at the retreat from Mons, a sergeant in the Argyll and Sutherlands . . . B. company . . . was told to hold a position until a certain hour and then to rejoin the rest of the battalion. The stated hour came and passed and not one man appeared. At night patrols were sent out to scout and found B. Company in the place it had been told to defend—riddled with machine-gun and rifle bullets, with not one man alive and not one round of unspent ammunition. And each of the survivors as he rifled the cartridges of his dead comrades must have asked himself: 'Why the Hell should I stay here to be killed?'—but he stayed.

6 p.m. meeting of committee of Great and Little Leighs War Savings Association. The number of members, once 126, is now 112. Since the association began on 21 July 1917, to 31 March 1919, £895.18s. have been raised; up to 26 April 1919 by 6d. stamps 427 War Bonds had been bought; 659 had been bought by single payments (including 500 bought at once by M. E. Hughes-Hughes).

Thursday, 1 May. Nettie Tritton, Lyons Hall, says that most of the Belgian refugees have now gone back to Belgium. They are not to the mind of the Belgians who have remained in Belgium throughout the war. The little children cannot speak French, and the older children have got into English ways which are not approved of by the Belgians.

Sunday, 4 May. Harry Taylor was in his old place in the choir this morning.

Tuesday, 13 May. 2 a.m. most brilliant moonlight. 4 a.m. sleep impossible, by the din of nightingales just outside my window. 10.15 a.m. left Great Leighs Rectory to attend clerical meeting. It was a lovely day. F. Fuller drove me. He said it was mostly women who were at work (chiefly weeding beans) in the fields. They had no training for field-work, but the men, who had been brought up to it, were content to be idle and to go into Braintree and draw unemployment pay. Agricultural labourers were being paid £2 and over a week, and worked too short hours and too slowly to be worth it, but they were continually grumbling. 10.45 a.m. in a large bean field three German prisoners-of-war were weeding. Although they had taken off their coats, they looked very hot.

Monday, 26 May. 11.30 a.m. Harry Taylor called. He says he finds a very great difference in the conditions of work here since he went out. His father's (aet. 84 this next July) wheelwright's business is now practically *nil.* He himself leaves tomorrow for Coggeshall where he has got work in a carpenter's work-shop. He brought with him a great variety of picture-cards and snapshots.

Friday, 30 May. On Saturday, by Government order, farm-hands in this district had 6s.6d. added to their weekly wage. Mr C. W. Rayner says that his men now receive £2.0s.6d. weekly, and free cottages. When I came here in 1894 an ordinary farm-hand's wage was 12s. or 14s. a week; horseman's, 16s. Fred Rayner is still at Canterbury: has no hope yet of his discharge: has now nothing to do and is very wearied.

Thursday, 5 June. 1.30 p.m. afternoon's post brought 'anti-Bolshevist' circular [from the National Security Union to Combat Bolshevism, 5 St James's Place, London].

Friday, 6 June. 9.45 a.m. morning's post brought more 'Anti-Bolshevist' circulars [from The Reconstruction Society, 58 and 60, Victoria Street, London, SW1. The circulars referred to 'the wave of Bolshevism passing over the country.']

Saturday, 7 June. Mrs Stuart Trotter, Broomfield Lodge, gave shelter to a Belgian woman and her little girl, during the war. A short time ago the woman committed suicide. Quite recently, the woman's sister, who had been resident in Brussels all through the war, came to Broomfield and took her little niece back with her to Brussels. She told Mrs Trotter that they had had a terrible time, as regards food and clothes, in Brussels since 1915. They could not get potatoes: so the women sewed long narrow pockets to their under-skirts, slipped out into the fields, and brought back what potatoes they could find. But when the Germans found out this, they set sentries with sticks, to tap on the women's skirts when they came back and made them give up what potatoes they were carrying. They had to cut up their bed-sheets to make underclothing and their blankets to make clothes. The Germans commandeered all their mattresses. They did not take away the hair, but the wool, allowing, to those who were willing to pick the wool out, four marks per mattress.

Monday, 9 June. Tract-distributing has begun again, having ceased during the war and the paper-scarcity. Three were handed in at 11.15 a.m. today, by a young fellow who was riding, bare-headed, on a bicycle.

Friday, 13 June. On Friday night, 13 June 1919, my younger daughter, Mildred, travelled from Dundee to St Pancras. At Galashiels two Australian soldiers came into the compartment, one of whom, Ovid Vatekin, was very talkative, aet. about 20; his companion, 'Bert' ——, aet. about 27, was more silent: Many of the marriages of Australian soldiers have proved absolute failures. Still more, women have not taken the trouble to write to the Australian Record Office to find out about the men they were marrying. Letters are frequently coming to the police asking them to trace this, or that, man. One letter came addressed to 'Mr Jack Sharman' from 'A devoted wife in England'— but Mr J. S. is the Harrod's of Sydney, and is a man of irreproachable morals who has never left Australia.

Sunday, 22 June. Telephone message received at Lyons Hall this morning said that the Germans had sunk all their vessels of war in Scapa Flow, but would sign the peace-treaty.

Friday, 27 June. Notes from J. Herbert Tritton: Yesterday J. H. T. saw a long procession of Jews (men and women) from the E. end, in Hyde Park. They were diminutive people, none (J. H. T. thought) over five feet high. They were carrying black banners—on which were 'We protest against the massacre of Jews in Poland', and similar inscriptions. J. H. T.'s comment was 'very futile: but what can they do.'

The restrictions on excursions by road in this district have now been altogether removed. On Th. 26 June the Mothers' Meeting went on excursion to Southend, by motor-bus. The bus holds thirty-four: thirty-five went. They had a nice, but cold, day.

7.45 p.m. Major Jas. Caldwell called: Harold Hardingham [another son of his friend Edward Hardingham of Southwold], a bank-cashier before the war, is back from Salonika where he has been in the Army Accountants' department. At Salonika the climate is bad. The town is a beastly place, dirty beyond description. The mortality in hospital was frightful, and more than half of it was due to the gross neglect of the RAMC. Many of the nurses were abominable, just like women off the streets. They left their work, and flaunted about as mistresses of the officers. H. H. has visited the hospital, where men were dying by tens for want of nursing. The 'sisters' being away gallivanting about with officers in motor cars. It was the same all over Macedonia. When they came from Salonika they had a journey of seven days in a train of cattle-trucks, absolutely without sanitary conditions. H. H. was offered a commission, but declined it, thinking it more honourable to be in the paymaster's office than to be associated with the officers. H. H. thinks that, now the troops are coming back from Macedonia, the scandals there are bound to come out.

The men from about here who have been in actual fighting are mostly shy of talking about it, E. g. —— Stubbins, who served in the 12th Lancers; and —— Goodfellow, an Edinburgh man, who is now at Little Waltham.

Saturday, 28 June. 7.30 p.m. dull evening: Evening paper (the *Star*) intimated signing of Peace Treaty: 'Versailles, Saturday. The German Plenipotentiaries signed the Peace Treaty at 3.12 p.m. this afternoon. — Reuter.'

Sunday, 29 June. Major Caldwell says that the RAF men at 'Brooklands' went crazy last night. At midnight they had out a big portable searchlight and ran it along the road, flashing it towards Chelmsford, frightening all the horses in the place. They disturbed the people by their shouting. They kept on till 2 a.m., when they went to the Colonel's house and cheered till he came out and sent them off to quarters.

8.30 p.m. high, westerly wind: much cloud-drift W. to E., but no present promise of much-needed rain. (Rain held off till Monday night, when it fell softly for a good while. Tuesd. 1st. July was also showery.)

Andrew Clark: 29 June 1919.

This Diary in its present form is discontinued. Such notes and papers as come in afterwards are to be remitted into an Appendix Volume— Vol. V of this year's series. [In the event there were two additional volumes for 1919.]

Tuesday, 1 July. John Clark goes back to France. He is one of the guards at a camp of German prisoners at Tourville. The prisoners are all very decent fellows: there is not a bad one in the camp. They wait hand and foot on their British guards. They have shown not the least wish to escape. On some occasions when the door of the camp was negligently left open, the prisoners themselves shut it.

Thursday, 3 July. The Government is in an indecent hurry over the Church Services on occasion of signing of peace-treaty. Why the Service should not have been put down for Su. 13 July, when forms might have been available for use of congregation is not explained. [The national Day of Thanksgiving was scheduled for 6 July.]

Sunday, 6 July. Mr C. W. Rayner has applied again for the discharge of his son, Corporal Fred Rayner, who is at Canterbury, doing nothing. The answer from the War Office was that no discharge would be granted except to men who had three wound-stripes, or to men who were thirty-seven years of age.

[Great Leighs did not hold its Thanksgiving Service today.]

Sunday, 13 July. At morning service I used the third form of the official Thanksgiving Service, with expedient omissions. With omissions the Service lasted one and a quarter hours.

Sunday, 20 July. W. H. Dee says that the sports yesterday afternoon [during the Peace Celebrations] went off very nicely. The children's tea was very good, but there were, he thinks, no 'souvenirs' given. The evening at the Council School was most enjoyable. At night he saw fireworks going somewhere in S.E.; also a big bonfire at Great Waltham. Later at night the sky was lit up, by (as he supposes) the searchlights of the Fleet off Southend.

Monday, 21 July. Nice bright day. Several children are absent from the Church School; they say they are entitled to a holiday because of Peace day!

Thursday, 21 August. Col. W. N. Tufnell says that German prisoners, housed in Chelmsford Workhouse, are still at work cleaning the river Chelmer. Yesterday, when they arrived in Great Waltham, they had their brake arrayed with Union Jacks and a great placard 'We want to go home.'

[From September, the regular daily entries begun in August 1914 gave way to occasional notes which continued until December 1919.]

Friday, 5 September. 7.30 p.m. Major Jas. Caldwell called: There is great unrest among the employées at Marconi's, Chelmsford. The men feel that the days of high wages are fast slipping away and vaguely think that by agitation they may be able to prolong them. There is much unrest also among the employées at Hoffmann's Chelmsford, for the same reason. At Crompton's Arc Works (electrical appliances) there has been a short strike recently. At Bocking Deanery last night Major Caldwell met the Dean's nephew, the Revd George Selby-Lowndes, of Lowestoft. The Revd G. S.-L. told him that, though Lowestoft is not a manufacturing town, it is astonishing what violent under-currents of discontent are running among the working-classes.

The Discharged Soldiers & Sailors Society has become a mere agency of 'Bolsheviks'.

The working-class people are now extremely averse to military training in any form. They do all they can to prevent their sons from joining the 'cadets' (Church Lads' Brigade). They feel that, if the revolutionary rising which is expected takes place, it would have a poor chance against even lads under discipline and with rifles.

Wednesday, 10 September. Notice handed in at 4.40 p.m. [regarding a meeting of the Great Leighs Parish Council on 11 September to consider the question of a 'Parish War Memorial' and asking the Rector's attendance]. (The meeting decided to have a public meeting on 23rd Septr.)

Monday, 15 September. Afternoon's post brought a letter from my younger daughter:

13 September 1919

Does war news still interest you even though the diary is finished?

To-day Colonel Montford came to see me on his way back from Russia. He was a subaltern in the Rifle Brigade in France and went out to Murmansk about a year ago—since December he has been on the Dvina south of Archangel ... Colonel Montford hates the Russians—they are, he says, thoroughly unreliable and so proud that they will never take advice ... They tell, he says, the most inartistic lies and know that you don't believe them. The Russian peasant likes first drink and then cigarettes—and nothing else. After an engagement they came to the officer and demanded drink. Often when drink was given out the officers would take it all and would be gloriously drunk and that of course gave the Bolos [Bolsheviks] in the regiment opportunity to push their propaganda. It is impossible in any regiment to root out the Bolos, no man can really be trusted. We have again and again given the Russians an opportunity to fight for themselves but they are incapable of doing it ...

For a bottle of rum or whiskey you could get anything. Furs are now more expensive but many men made their fortune by pinching whiskey from the stores and exchanging it for fox-furs ... I wish I could tell you more but I have no time.

Saturday, 27 September. Neither morning nor afternoon post came today because of the railway strike.[1]

Monday, 29 September. Mrs (Col. Gerald E.) Barker called this forenoon. Her son, Godfrey Gerald Barker, Lieut. 21st Lancers, has gone into Braintree to offer to drive a train during the strike. He learnt locomotive work when in India with his regiment.

Wednesday, 1 October. This Diary, even in its latest casual form, is now practically ended.

Thursday, 9 October. [Letter from the Rector to H. H. E. Craster.]*

9 October 1919

My dear Craster,
... Several interesting notes from men and officers from Archangel and Salonika came to me after I had closed the Diary. I have put them ... into two Appendix vols. These I will send with the others. I hope the vol. just finished will be the last, absolutely.

I have been, for a good while back, extremely well. Busy gardening, but I have at last got an old man to work for me, and hope to be less a slave to the ground than I have been for 5 years.

[1] This particular railway strike began on 26 September and ended on 5 October.

Saturday, 1 November. The War Memorial Committee met at the Church and agreed to Mr J. H. Tritton's suggestion of a Memorial Tablet in the churchyard wall (facing the road), a little to the north of the Church Tower. I agreed to have one of the thick pollard elms removed to make space for it. (The cutting down of this was very troublesome, because of the tombstones beside it. It was got down without any damage to any of them, but cost me £2.10s.)

Thursday, 18 December. Yesterday some of the villagers were much exercised about the expected 'end of the world'. Mrs Baldwin, 'Dog and Gun' public-house, did not send her three children to school, but sent a message that she wanted them to be with her when the end of the world came.

EPILOGUE
by James Munson

ANDREW CLARK'S short entry on Mrs Baldwin's fears about the end of the world was the last he made in the Diary. Five days later the Bodleian Library recorded the deposit of the ninety-second and final volume. True to his word, it was the 'last, absolutely'. In some ways he was reluctant to stop: for over five years he had daily, often hourly, made entries. The Diary had become a focus of family life: Mary had contributed notes and letters, had meticulously sewn in the hundreds of pamphlets and leaflets and had provided the red tape with which each volume was tied. Mildred had read over many volumes before sending them on to the Bodleian and sent her own superb letters to be added as well.

In some ways Andrew Clark was happy to be rid of the Diary for now he could return to his scholarly pursuits. In January 1920 he wrote to his Oxford friend, Falconer Madan, that Mildred had completed her medical training and was now an MD. She returned to Great Leighs to nurse her sister who was seriously ill. The Rector finally found 'an old man to do some of my out-of-door work regularly'. This meant he could tackle those 'manorial and archidiaconal' records at last.

The coal shortages that had plagued the Rectory passed, and village life reverted to the old patterns. The Rector carried on coaching village lads and was delighted when young Leonard Port won a place at the London School of Economics. Evensong went back to its old place and the black-out curtains were taken down; it was thought they would never be used again.

In December 1920, the villagers gathered in front of the flint and mortar boundary wall, built in 1715, that separated the churchyard from the Boreham Road. They had come to dedicate the Memorial Tablet that 'old Squire Tritton' had given. The guest of honour was Major-General Sir George Scott Moncrieff, whose niece was a friend of the Misses Tritton. There was a short service; the Rector gave an address and Sir George unveiled the tablet, which read:

> This tablet was placed here by the parishioners of Great Leighs, in honored memory of fellow parishioners who gave their lives for our country in the Great War 1914–1919. They whom this tablet commemorates were numbered among those who at the call of King and Country left all that was dear to them, endured hardness, faced danger and finally passed out of the sight of men by the path of duty and self-sacrifice, giving up their own lives that others might live in freedom. Let those who come after see to it that their names be not forgotten.

Charles Cloughton	Frederick Mansfield
Ernest George Cloughton	Charles Jonathan Rayner
Charles Cook	Harry Sargeant
Charles Joseph Digby	Alan George Tritton
Ernest Digby	Alfred Reginald Ward
William Duke	Charles Henry Ward
Archie Fitch	Ernest Wright
Arthur Fitch	Herbert George Wright
Dick Fitch	Louis Walter Wright
George Bennett Fitch	

It bears all the hallmarks of Andrew Clark's writing: a deep and restrained patriotism, dignified language and an emphasis on the village and its continuing life.

After nursing her sister back to health, Mildred found work in London, but she was not content and in the summer of 1921 she decided to emigrate to South Africa to join a practice in Durban. Andrew Clark never recovered from this loss. Four days after sailing Mildred met an English-born priest returning to Australia to take up a curacy in Queensland. Six days later they were engaged. Jim Carpenter, who as a munitions worker had wanted another Boy Scout to do his 'dirty work', remembers after sixty years how Andrew Clark stormed up to his father. He had just got the news and was furious: 'Mildred's got engaged to a blasted parson—as if she couldn't do better than that!' They were married in Adelaide when the ship docked in September.

The Rector's health now steadily began to go downhill. In October 1921 he wrote to Leonard Port that 'I am still very far from well. I dread this coming winter . . . If I survive till after Easter, I shall see how things will be with me then.' He decided to resign his living in the summer of 1922, but he did not survive beyond Easter. Leonard Port's wife remembers that during these final months Andrew Clark used frequently to break down during services, especially when giving the Blessing. He became extremely absent-minded. After Mildred's departure he was 'a broken man'.

On Christmas Day 1921, he celebrated the early morning Eucharist. He did not take another service until Ash Wednesday, 1 March 1922, when he made a last feeble entry in the Register of Services: 'Ashes'. He died on 24 March, which his old friend William Redman would have reminded him was the Feast Day of St Gabriel the Archangel. In his study were some thirty exercise books filled with transcriptions and notes and on his floor were documents awaiting an examination that never came. He died in harness, not only as a priest but as a scholar. He was buried in the same grave as his wife. Mrs Port remembers the villagers' reaction to his death: 'I think everybody loved him; he was a very lovable man.'

J. Herbert Tritton, who had retired from Barclays in 1919, died in September 1923. The uneasy partnership between low-church squire and high-church parson was a thing of the past. The new squire was the eldest son, Major Leslie Tritton. J. Herbert Tritton's four daughters never married. They took a house in Finchingfield and turned one corner of their sitting-room into a virtual shrine to their brother Alan, killed by a sniper's bullet in 1914. The 'Tin Tabernacle' vanished together with the old cedar tree, under which the Trittons had held their August evangelistic services. Family tradition is that Major Leslie Tritton had the Mission Room pulled down when his daughter Lucy 'turned Catholic'. She wanted to convert it to a Roman Catholic chapel.

Farming continued to dominate village life and mechanization made steady inroads. In his last letter to William Redman, back in 1920, Andrew Clark wrote that Richard Arnold had retired from farming. His successor had introduced a motor-plough, 'a new thing for a small Great Leighs farm'. But there were still places for farm-workers and Reg Ketley stayed on at Moulsham Hall farm, where he eventually became foreman. In 1958 he was awarded the Royal Agricultural Society's medal 'For Loyal Service' after fifty-two years on the land. Arthur Stoddart, whom Reg Ketley remembers as being 'above us working ones', found a position at Barclays Bank in

Dunmow and eventually became manager. Miss Eliza Vaughan, 'the suffragette of Rayne' not only got the vote but, in time, local fame as an authority on Essex life and history. She would always be grateful for the help Andrew Clark had given her. Charlie Ward's mother moved to Little Waltham, where she took a cottage opposite Wroots the butcher. Sergeant Harry Taylor eventually settled in nearby Kelvedon and worked first as a carpenter and then at Hoffmann's. Before his death he asked to be buried in Great Leighs and now rests some fifteen feet away from his friend and mentor, Andrew Clark.

After her father's death, Mary Alice decided to join her sister in Queensland. She arrived only to find Mildred, now Dr Mildred Oberlin-Harris, packing to move to Durban. Mildred had not been able to stand the isolation and lack of opportunities in Queensland. In Durban her outstanding abilities earned her a high reputation, especially as a diagnostician. But she and her husband always missed Britain and in 1946 they returned. She died in 1954 and is buried in Broughton, Huntingdonshire, where her husband was Vicar. Mary Alice Clark returned in the same year and died in 1957.

Mildred Clark had two children who survived childhood: David, now a civil servant in England, and Alison, like her mother a doctor, in Tasmania. In 1941 she followed her mother and grandfather to St Andrews and in the vacations she was a Land Worker in Great Leighs, where she met many villagers who remembered the grandfather she had never known.

In Great Leighs today the old Church School is now a private home. The old Council School stands derelict. Its windows, to which the boys had rushed to see the Zeppelin despite Mr With's remonstrations, are boarded up and grass grows in the yard. But there is a new Council School, set in the midst of a new estate. The village has grown and the A131, unlike the Great Road of Andrew Clark's day, throbs with traffic. The Rectory, which Andrew Clark denounced as being too large, was sold in 1970 and a new one built in the field adjacent to the paddock where Charlie Ward used to look after the pony. St Anne's Castle and the Dog and Partridge remain but Mrs Jennings's Victoria Coffee House is now a private residence. The dreadful roads are now paved but the lanes are just as narrow and the parish just as scattered. The Wrights carry on their trade in willow-wood although thankfully order-books are no longer swelled by the need for artificial legs and arms so much as by demands for cricket bats. Since 1958 the village has been the permanent site of the annual Essex Show.

Farms still dominate this far-flung village—Long's, Chadwicks, Bishop's Hall, Wakerings, Goodman's, Fulbournes and Moulsham Hall. Lyons Hall is once again the home of the Trittons. For over forty years the vast house suffered decline. During the Second World War it housed Italian prisoners-of-war, one of whom carved a beautiful wooden Madonna that now hangs in the Church. The present lord of the manor, named after his father's uncle killed by the sniper in France, has restored the house and pulled down as many of his great-grandfather's Victorian additions as was structurally possible. The house is once again a home.

Across the road from Lyons Hall the parish church of St Mary the Virgin still looks out over the fields and lanes that Andrew Clark knew. The church is beautifully cared for. On special occasions William Redman's silk altar frontal, made from Mrs Clark's wedding dress of 1886, is brought out, a silent reminder of those far-off days. In the chancel is a plaque dedicated by the parishioners of Great Leighs in 1923 to the memory of Andrew Clark, for twenty-eight years their parish priest. At the dedication ceremony the new Rector, the Revd A. E. Negus, who had been a pupil of Andrew Clark's at Oxford, paid his former tutor a warm tribute:

Andrew Clark was great, and the world, unfortunately, will never know the extent of his learning and the pains that he took to make the past speak to us . . . He was good at heart, and no trouble was too much for him to take on behalf of those who sought him out and desired his help, whether from his pocket or from the great storehouse of his mind.

The tablet, which only recorded his academic degrees and his time at Great Leighs was, Negus went on, a 'simple record'. Even so, it would remind people 'of a fast-disappearing type of clergyman, learned and scholarly, yet content to live quietly in a country parish, diffusing a kindly and neighbourly influence, and making the world a sweeter place to live in'. Sixty-two years later the parishioners of Great Leighs, led by their Rector, the Revd John Bryant, again gathered in the chancel after the BBC broadcasts had brought Andrew Clark's name before the public. They were there to dedicate a second plaque to go under the old one. This was also a 'simple record' and added only one additional fact concerning Andrew Clark: 'Compiler of the Diaries of

Great Leighs life August 1914 – June 1919'. I suspect Andrew Clark would have desired no grander tribute.

In 1985 the village also decided to renew the lettering on the War Memorial. Each year on Remembrance Sunday the people of Great Leighs gather round it to remember before God those men who died 'that others might live in freedom'. That memorial commemorates those who did not come home. In his War Diary, Andrew Clark, whom Reg Ketley remembers as being 'one of ourselves', commemorated the home to which they never returned and the stories, humour, tragedies, rumours, hopes and fears of the men and women who lived through the Great War.

INDEX